Flight Sim 98

Tricks of the Trade

Werner Leinhos

Full Throttle
Abacus

DATA BECKER

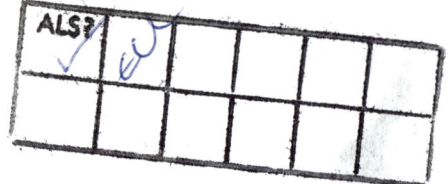

Contents

Chapter 3
Putting Multiplayer To The Test 71

Chapter 5
Adventure Programming 123

Chapter 6
Building Your Own Aircraft 173

Chapter 7
The FS Cockpit 247

Chapter 8
Creating Scenery 275

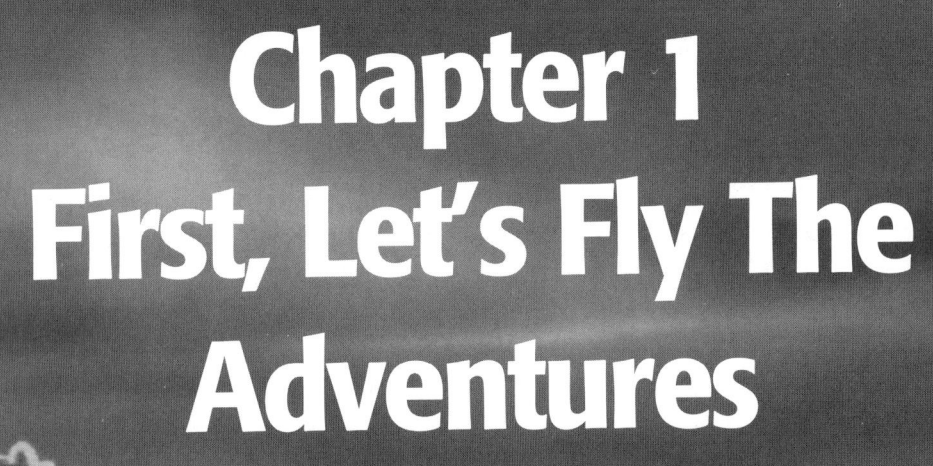

Chapter 1
First, Let's Fly The Adventures

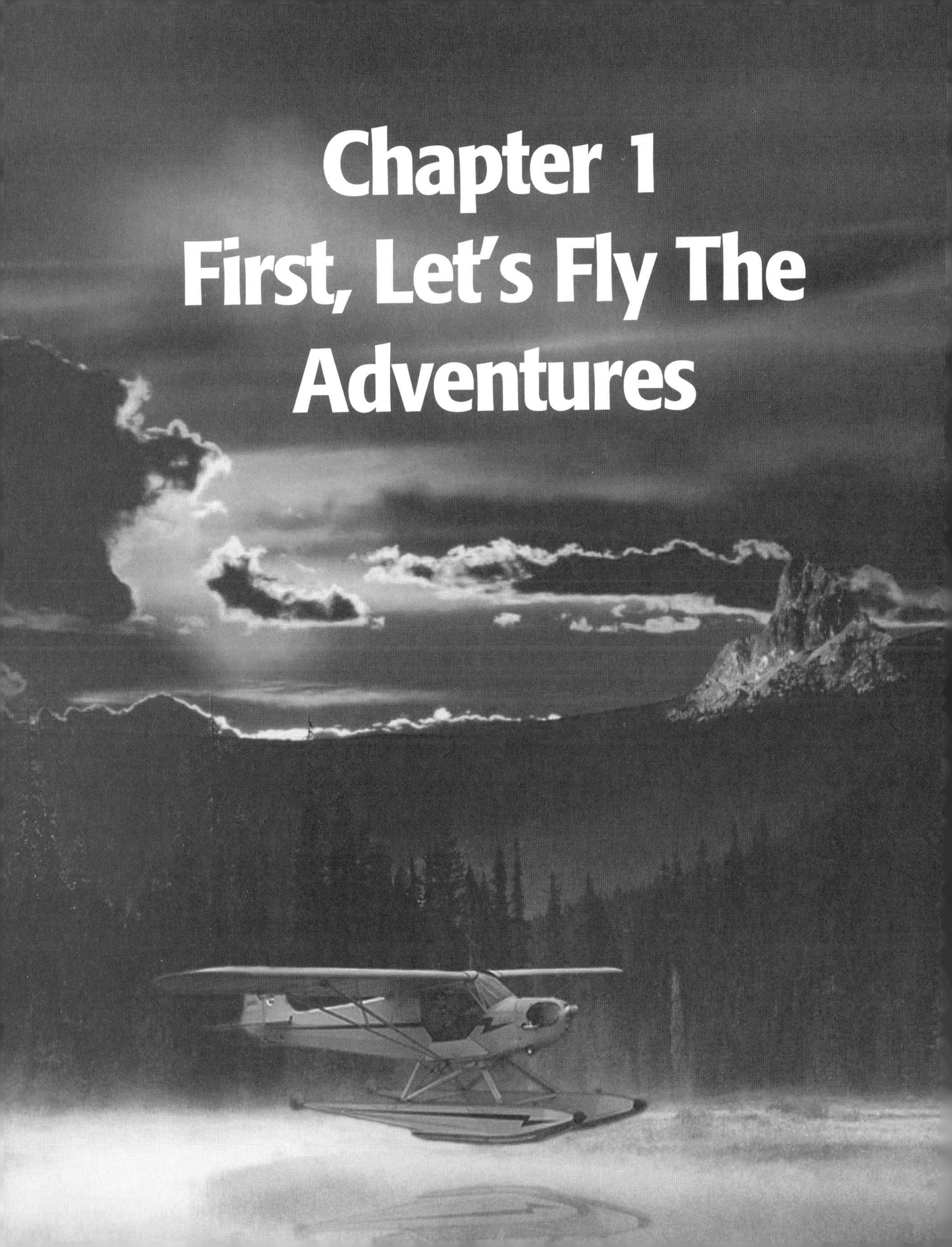

Chapter 1 gets right into simulation operation and assumes mastery of the airplane. This is where you'll find detailed descriptions of some of the most interesting tours from the "adventure flights." Even experienced simmers can have problems starting an adventure because limited information is available about these default situations. So we will provide complete flight preparation for you here.

Adventure Flights With The Cessna

The cozy Cessna 182 S or the 182 RG are best for your first adventure flights. We say "cozy" because this airplane is very good-natured in flight practice and not too fast. However, flight planning and other tasks are the same or similar to flying the big planes. Therefore, you can consider this to be basic training for flying the big jets.

Shopping trip in London

This flight adventure tests both your sense of direction and navigational knowledge in the congested skies above Europe. The fully tanked Cessna 182 RG is at Le Havre Octeville on runway 05. It's set for a visual flight (VFR) over the English Channel to the downtown airport London City. Therefore, make certain the CROCTLCY.ADV and CROCT05.STN files are in the Adv folder so they're available in Flight Simulator.

Also, make certain to disable Apollo's Europe 2 scenery (also called BAO) if you have it installed and use the default FS scenery instead. Otherwise, the CROCT05.STN situation file will put the Cessna on a slightly displaced airport.

To load this adventure, click **Flights | Adventures...** and select "London Shopping Trip: Cessna Skylane RG" from the list. You may read a description of this adventure on the rightside of the window.

Checks before the flight

While the trip from France to England only takes about an hour, crossing the channel gives it an entirely different character than a flight over land. Extra precautions are required for flights over water. For example, you'll need to include life preservers, a life boat and other lifesaving resources. You'll also need to carefully plan your fuel reserves. Although carrying extra fuel isn't a bad idea (in the event you get lost), don't exaggerate the possibility either. This is because it takes fuel to carry fuel and the extra weight can cause a performance decrease of the airplane. Obviously this is something to avoid.

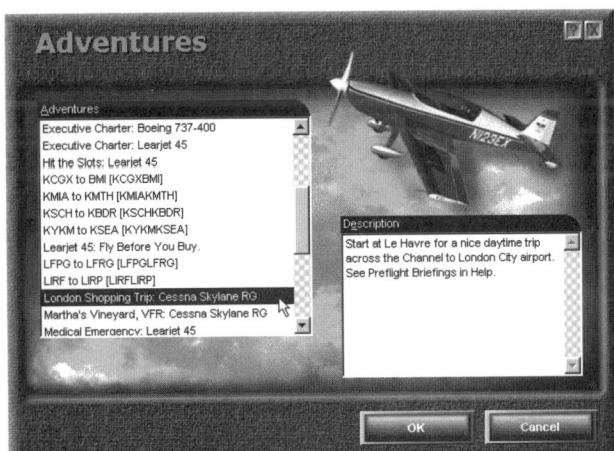

Click OK when you're ready to continue. Because Le Havre's airport is so close to the Atlantic coast, it's frequently blanketed in sudden fog. However, today a dry east wind weather situation provides almost unlimited sight. The airport itself is calm at ground level with normal air pressure of 29.91 inches of mercury. The adventure will be announced as a VFR flight and requested as such by the pilot over the radio. However, without VOR or NDB navigational aids, this adventure could quickly end in tragedy since water offers no visible landmarks you can use to get your bearings.

Make certain you're familiar with basic flight maneuvers before you start. These maneuvers include starts, climbing flights, turns, descending flights and landings. Most importantly, you need to understand the basics of radio navigation.

ATC clearance

You'll find information about the airports, VORs or NDBs along the route in the **World | Airports/Facility Directory...** menu. Once you open this menu, click Europe on the map.

Scroll down to until you see the relevant information for Le Havre.

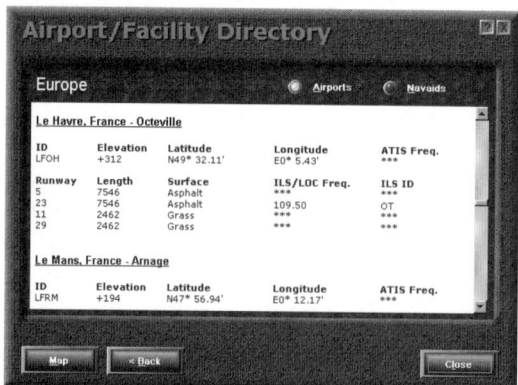

Here is the clearance from air traffic control for this flight:

> *Cessna 2001 Zulu, cleared to London City airport, after departure Radial 350 Deauville to intersection DRAKE, on Radial 196 Seaford to Seaford, then 003-Radial Seaford to Mayfield and on 001-Radial Mayfield to London City. Maintain Flight Level 60 and squawk 1333.*

The ATC clearance to London City Airport contains a completely official flight path because it uses the published standard departure 055 Departure from Le Havre. Also, the channel crossing takes place below flight level 100 on Airway A34, which is reserved only for flights in a southerly direction.

The flight plan for the route from Le Havre to London City:

Wpt ID	Freq	Hdg	Dist	ETE	ATE
Le Havre	132.1				
LHO	346	048°	5	3'	
(DVL	110.2)				
ETRAT	D23	350°	5	3'	
SIDid	D49	350°	26	11'	
DRAKE			8	3'	
SFD	117.0	016°	31	13'	
MAY	117.9	003°	15	7'	
(BIG	115.1)				
LCY	322	000°	30	13'	
London City					
Total			120	53'	

Notice the waypoints in parenthesis. You won't directly overfly these waypoints; you only require them to determine radials of the intersections or for determining position. The determined times ETE (Estimated Time Enroute) refer to the true air speed TAS 140 kts without accounting for the wind.

Regarding the wind and the weather: In the adventure a global weather zone with a 4/8 layer of clouds between 7,500 and 10,000 feet is reported, above 3,000 to 6,500 feet an easterly wind is blowing 090° at 15 kts. At the most northerly direction of flight, a correction angle of about 5° to 7° into the wind is advised. You might even attempt an angle about 10°. The speed above ground will hardly be influenced by the lateral wind.

After the start from runway 05, climb to flight level 60 (or 6,000 feet) on runway heading 048°. At the outer marker signal (from the ILS of landing runway 28), turn to the radial R350 from Deauville (110.2 DVL). This is the approximate position where you'll have reached the French Channel coast. The route segment over water begins with the ETRAT intersection (N49° 41.0' E000° 09.8') that marks this transition at 23 DME DVL.

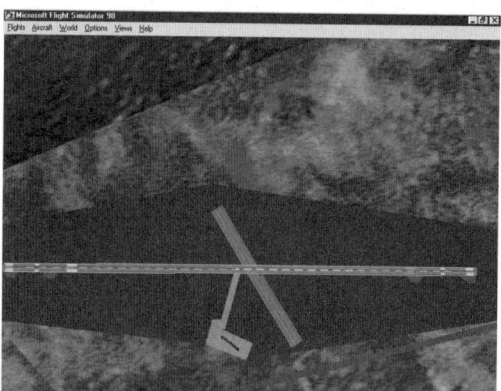

The radial 350 from Deauville VOR then continues over intersection SIDid (a very interesting place: You fly across the prime meridian here. You may watch this with the position indicator ((Shift) + (Z)) to the cleared intersection DRAKE.

Three airways, R25, A34 and A56 come together over DRAKE and

Be careful about deviating from the course

Although you can can continue flying if you deviate far from the flight route assigned by the air traffic control, you won't receive updated instructions. (Also in this example, the Federal Aviation Agency may want to have a word with with you if this was real life flying.)

are defined in southern English airspace. The last airway mentioned, A56 on radial 196 from Seaford VOR (117.0 SFD), is the next route segment that was cleared by ATC for the flight. The flight continues from Seaford to the Mayfield VOR (117.9 MAY) on the R003 SFD or R183 MAY.

On the 001° radial from Mayfield, the flight path leads precisely in the direction of London City. The correct direction should also be indicated by the airport NDB at London City on ADF frequency 322 and the ID LCY. After the Mayfield VOR, the approach controller from London will request a descent to 1,500 feet, which runs into landing runway 28 of London City Airport at circling altitude downwind. In the upwind leg of a left circling approach, the landing configuration (let down landing gear and flaps) is set and the landing is prepared on runway 28.

Orlando adventure

The second adventure flight is a vacation trip from Charlotte, North Carolina to Orlando, Florida in the Cessna. For this flight adventure you'll need the CRCLTORl.ADV and CRCLT23.STN files in the FS98\Adv folder. To load this adventure, click **Flights | Adventures...** and select "Orlando Adventure: Cessna Skylane RG" in the list.

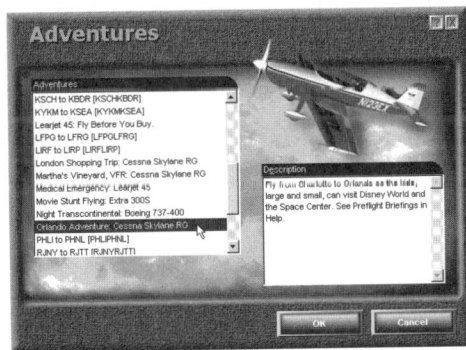

Click OK to continue. To make the flight realistic, select the **Aircraft | Aircraft settings...** command. Select the Reliability tab and make sure "Aircraft reliability" is set to the "Reliable " setting (for maximum reliability). Also select the Engines tab and make certain to enable the "Magnetos" and "Mixture control" options. Finally, select "Manual" for the Prop advance" option.

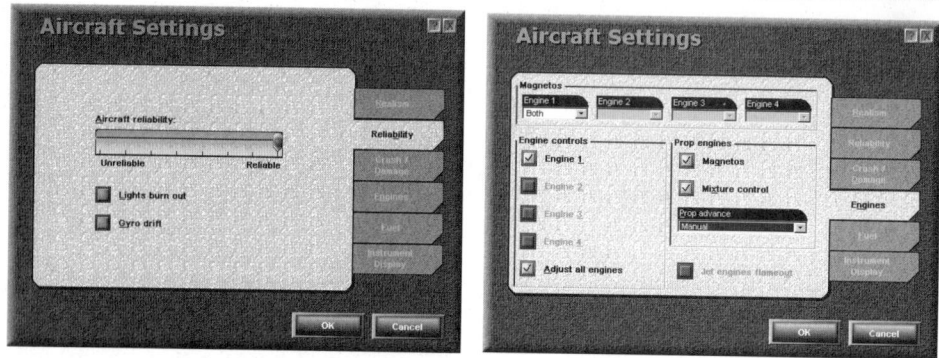

Make certain to have these settings if you want to have a more realistic adventure.

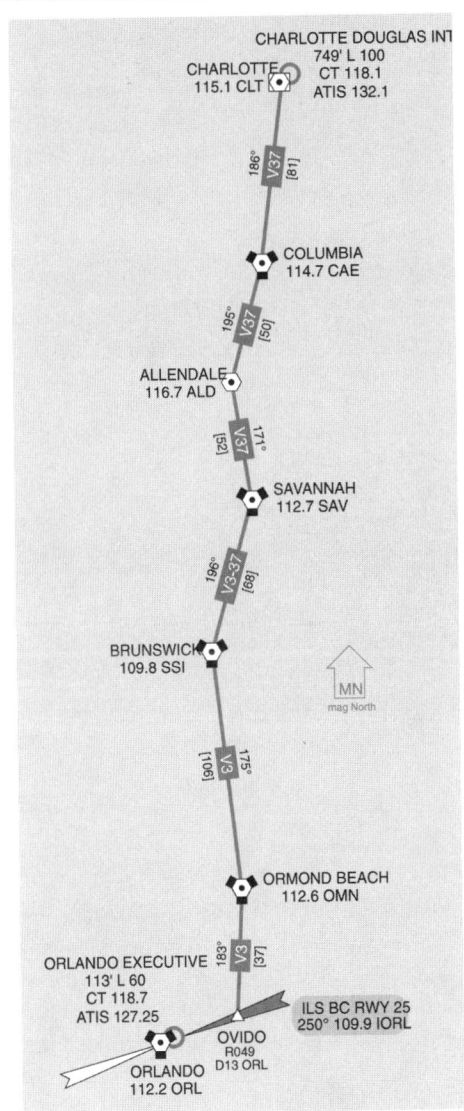

CHARLOTTE DOUGLAS INT
749' L 100
CHARLOTTE
115.1 CLT
CT 118.1
ATIS 132.1

186°
V37
[81]

COLUMBIA
114.7 CAE

195°
V37
[50]

ALLENDALE
116.7 ALD

171°
V37
[52]

SAVANNAH
112.7 SAV

196°
V3-37
[68]

BRUNSWICK
109.8 SSI

MN
mag North

175°
V3
[90]

ORMOND BEACH
112.6 OMN

ORLANDO EXECUTIVE
113' L 60
CT 118.7
ATIS 127.25

183°
V3
[37]

ILS BC RWY 25
250° 109.9 IORL

OVIDO
R049
D13 ORL

ORLANDO
112.2 ORL

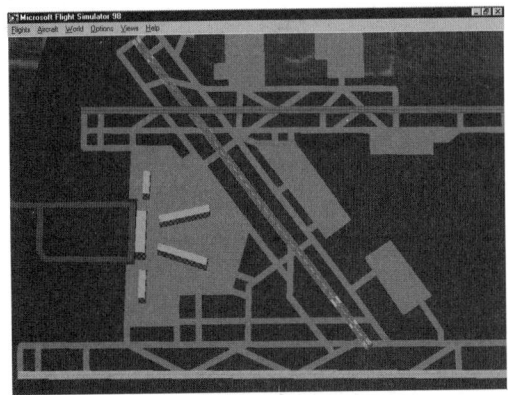

Checks before the flight

Before the flight, take a look at the Cessna Skylane in the Aircraft Handbooks section in FS Help. The Aircraft Handbooks section contains background information about each aircraft in Flight Simulator. It also has checklists and detailed information about basic flight maneuvers.

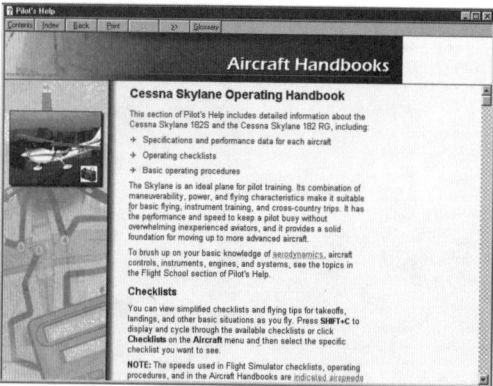

The Aircraft Handbooks in FS Help has information about each aircraft in Flight Simulator.

Furthermore, you need to be familiar with the following procedures:

→ VOR navigation on airways

→ ILS and Back Course approaches

The American World Aeronautical Charts CG-21 and CH-25 are available as basic material for route planning (contact NOAA National Oceanic and Atmospheric Administration: 1-800-638-8972). These charts record the middle and southern part of the east coast — including the two states in this adventure. The carefully prepared flight plan includes airways V37, V3 and V57 as the route between Charlotte and Orlando. The airways are determined by VOR stations that appear in the flight plan as waypoints. The directions and distances between the VORs and the expected flying time—at a cruising speed of 130 kts—are listed in the following table:

Wpt	Ident	Freq	Hdg	Dist	ETE	ATE
Charlotte	KCLT	132.1				
Charlotte	CLT	115.0				
Columbia	CAE	114.7	186°	81	35'	
Allendale	ALD	116.7	195°	50	21'	
Savannah	SAV	112.7	171°	52	22'	
Brunswick	SSI	109.8	196°	68	29'	
Ormond Beach	OMN	112.6	175°	106	45'	
	OVIDO		183°	37	16'	
Orlando	ORL	112.2	249°	13	5'	
	BC 25	109.9	250°			
Orlando Exec		127.25				
Total				407	173'	

Clearance

Once the VFR flight plan (with navigational support) has been submitted to the responsible checkpoint, it will be incorporated into the route monitoring of the air traffic control. The clearance for the Cessna 2001 Zulu then is:

> *Cleared to Orlando Executive Airport via Charlotte direct, V37 Brunswick, V3 Ormond Beach, V51 Intersection OVIDO, direct. Maintain 6.500 and squawk 3343.*

The start for all VFR flights takes place from takeoff runway 23 in Charlotte. The Cessna gets the final clearance for takeoff here from the tower, which also instructs the pilot to fly directly via Charlotte VOR after takeoff and to climb to the cruising altitude of 6,500 feet. The CLT VOR lies in direct extension to Runway 23 and is reached immediately after flying over the end of the takeoff runway.

From the Charlotte VOR, the commercial flight also begins on airway V37, on which the Cessna climbs up to 6,500 feet. The autopilot is fed with data for the altitude and the climb rate: after less than ten minutes autopilot has steered the airplane to VFR altitude at a climb rate of 700 feet per minute.

You'll also need to consider some economy measures during this adventure. Keep in mind the flight goes over 400 nautical miles so the flight will last about three hours, depending on the speed over ground. So, remember if you race your plane at full throttle, not only are you straining the engines, but you're also using a lot of fuel to maintain that speed. Therefore, after reaching cruising altitude, use the black throttle slider knob to lower the manifold pressure about 20". The average fuel flow drops immediately below 15 gallons per hour. The blue prop advance knob regulates the speed of the engine and is lowered to about 2,100 RPM.

Finally, the mixture of fuel and air that allows combustion in the cylinders is set to a more favorable ratio. Unfortunately, the C182 RG does not have an EGT measuring instrument that could display the optimum mixture of gasoline and air. Thus, the adjustment can only be determined here by comparing consumption and achievable performance and/or speed. This happens by slowly pulling out the red mixture control knob and observing the fuel flow and the air speed indicators. With an optimum mixture of gasoline and inflowing air (here at 6,500 feet the air is somewhat thinner than at sea level), the consumption levels out at about 11 gallons and a displayed speed of IAS (indicated airspeed) 127 kts. This reduces the consumption by a good four gallons per hour and increases the speed by about four to five knots. This is all at 20" manifold pressure and 2,100 RPM.

Now the displayed speed can be multiplied by 1.1 (IAS-TAS corrective factor for 6,500 feet) to determine the true air speed (TAS) of the airplane. This results in a TAS of about 140 knots. Since there is no appreciable wind in the adventure, the calculated TAS is also the speed above ground (GS) that is used for the scheduling. In the flight plan above the ETE is determined using the following formula:

```
ETE = Dist / TAS * 60 or ETE = Dst / GS * 60
```

for example:

```
ETE = 106 NM / 140 kts  * 60 = 45.4 min
```

It's also converted into minutes at the same time. The individual distance and time segments are added to the sum at the end of the table and should be offset for verification:

```
ETE (total) = 407 NM / 140 kts * 60 = 174 .4 min = 2h 54min
```

Reception of the Brunswick VOR (109.8 SSI) causes some problems in the approach—it doesn't reach the normal VOR range of 40 NM. Also, the departure from SSI VOR to Ormond Beach VORTAC is only supported for a short time. However, this is where the most interesting part of the trip begins. You'll fly along the gorgeous eastern coast of Florida, past Jacksonville with eight airfields, St. Augustine and Daytona Beach. The coast between Brunswick and Jacksonville, at first thick with estuaries and bays, slowly changes into the virtually straight, very long beach of East Florida.

Beginning at Brunswick, you can see the coastline out the starboard windows. Precisely at a right angle to the Flagler County airport—recognizable by the five crossed runways—you fly over the coastline again. The last big route segment on the V51 towards OVIDO intersection (R183 D37 OMN) starts exactly over Ormond Beach. Shortly before this airway crossing is the Sanford Regional airport, which maintains an NDB station. With the ADF set to frequency 408, one can also track the flyby "by instrument."

At the flyby, the responsible controller points the airplane to a new intermediate altitude of 3,000 feet. Beginning at OVIDO intersection, all the radar vectoring to the sighting of the localizer beacon/LOC is performed by Orlando Executive (109.9 IORL Rwy 07).

ILS Back Course

If the needle swivels to the right, you must make a course correction to the left on the back course to move the needle back to the middle. If the needle drifts to the left, a curve to the right on the back course of the needle will move the needle back to the middle.

However, the back course of the ILS (Back Course 250°) to landing runway 25 is used here, which only specifies the localizer course direction, but does not send any glide path information. Therefore, in the VOR device the needle movements from the back course signal are to be interpreted exactly the opposite.

With Adventure Autopilot enabled, the end approach phase is automatically controlled to the MDA (minimum descent altitude) of 480 feet. That means you can concentrate on watching the instruments and the airspace over Orlando.

Since the weather is perfect—with a blue sky from horizon to horizon—the landing is executed visually until touchdown.

However, don't forget to push the mixture control unit back to full rich no later than 2,000 feet, bring engine speed up to 2,400 RPM and lower the speed with the throttle to 90 knots. When landing runway 25 on the back course is in view, lower the landing gear and gradually put the flaps into position at 40°. Once you safely fly over the little lake at the edge of the airport at 70 to 80 kts, you're set for your vacation.

Adventure Flights With The Learjet 45

The previous adventure with the Cessna suggests the obvious: longer distances take correspondingly longer to travel. However, some people and most simulator pilots simply don't have that much time. The default jets of the Flight Simulator—Learjet 45 and Boeing 737—shorten flying times tremendously because of their faster speeds. What remains is the careful planning of the flight, which is usually done according to instrument flight rules.

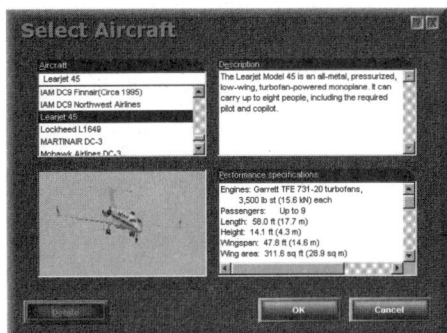

One-armed bandit

This flight adventure takes us from the sandy beaches of Santa Monica, in southern California, to the desert streets of Las Vegas, Nevada. We'll take the Learjet 45 since important people travel in style. This flight adventure requires the LJSLOTS.ADV and LJSMO21.STN files in the Adv folder of Flight Simulator 98. Load "Hit the Slots: Learjet 45" from the **Flights | Adventures...** dialog box to fly this adventure.

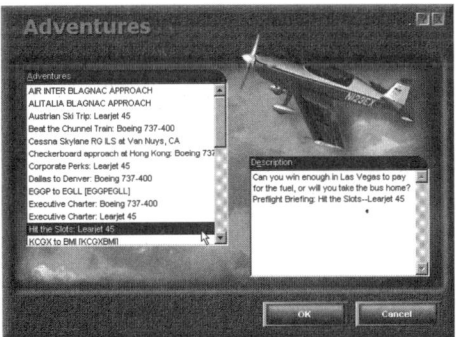

The checks prior to the flight involving the machine, planning of the IFR route, and programming of the autopilot are all important aspects for a smooth flight.

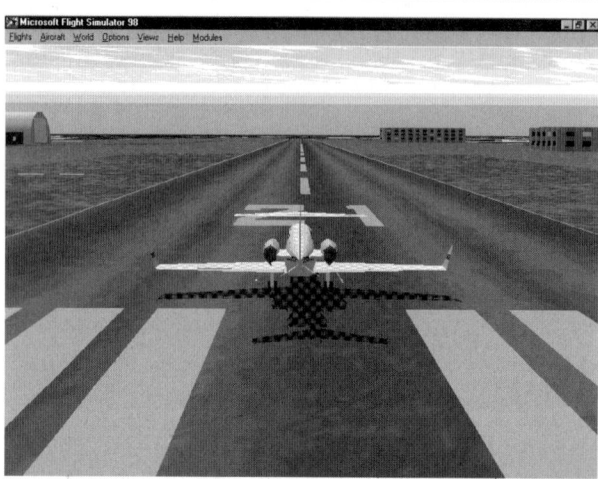

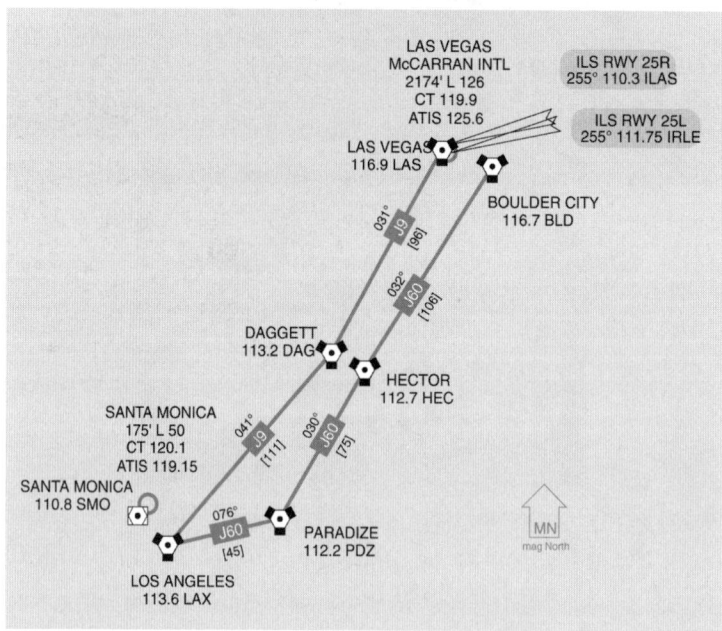

This relatively short flight for a Learjet is done in the adventure using airway J9 in upper airspace. It's detailed in the following flight plan:

Wpt	Freq	Hdg	Dist	ETE	ATE
Santa Monica	120.1				
SMO	110.8	210°			
LAX	113.6	060°	25	6'	
DAG	113.2	041°	111	16'	
LAS	116.9	031°	96	14'	
ILS 25L	111.75	255°			
ILS 25R	110.3	255°			
Las Vegas	132.4				
Total			**232**	**36'**	

However, the adventure flight coordinator wants to change things slightly. Therefore, the clearance of the air traffic control for this flight is:

Learjet 45 Lima Juliett is cleared to Airport McCarran via Los Angeles VOR direct, J9 Las Vegas VOR direct. Climb and maintain flight level 270 and squawk 4135.

You'll find information along the route about the airports, VORs and NDBs by clicking **World | Airport/ Facility Directory...** and clicking on the region over which you'll be flying. Furthermore, maps for the areas should also be available. For example, look for the Jeppesen High Altitude Enroute Chart US(HI)-1 and -2, the Low Altitude Chart US(LO)-3 and -4 for the western areas of the USA and the departure and approach maps of Los Angeles and Las Vegas. For more information, contact Jeppesen at 1-800-621-5377.

ILS Back Course

1. The Daggett VOR (113.2 DAG) is declared in the maps as a Low Altitude Station and therefore broadcasts only at low power for short distances. Reception over greater distances is not even guaranteed in Flight Simulator.

2. Flying over airway J60 from LAX, which runs to VORTAC Boulder City (116.7 BLD), would definitely be better. The BLD VORTAC serves as an IAF (initial approach fix) for ILS approaches to landing runways 25L/R from Las Vegas, in most cases when there are prevailing westerlies.

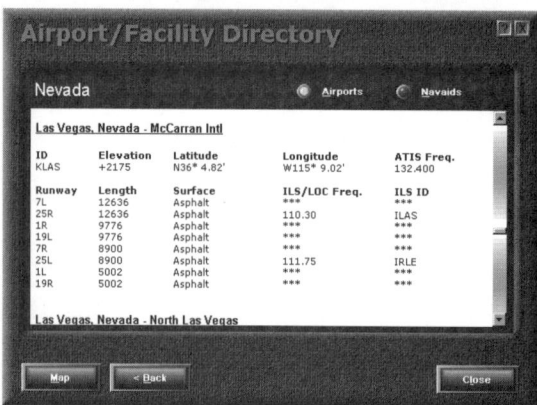

The reporting of the flight from SMO to LAS summarizes the most important moments:

After the start from takeoff runway 21 in Santa Monica, the flight first heads 240° over the Pacific Ocean up to 7,000 feet. This frees the approach and takeoff area of the large Los Angeles airport, and one can use a left turn to fly directly to the Los Angeles VOR (113.6 LAX). The approach course should then take place on radial 240 from LAX.

Airway J9 begins at LAX and runs northeasterly with radial 041 from LAX first to Dagget VOR (113.2 DAG). In the meantime, the clearance for the further climb to flight level 270 (= 27,000 feet) has also come, which is observed until further notice during the trip.

At DAG, J9 makes a very slight bend and continues on radial R031 DAG towards Las Vegas (116.9 LAS). In this route segment, we leave cruising altitude and drop to 10,000 feet as our new intermediate altitude. It is precisely at this altitude—not significantly higher and above all, not lower—that we must fly over the Las Vegas VOR. Otherwise, the adventure is canceled due to poor execution of the ATC instructions. For this reason, you must calculate the rate of descent from the beginning of the descent segment to LAS down to the last detail, and check it constantly. The current speed over ground and the distance to Las Vegas can be read from the DME, which is set to the NAV frequency 116.9 of LAS.

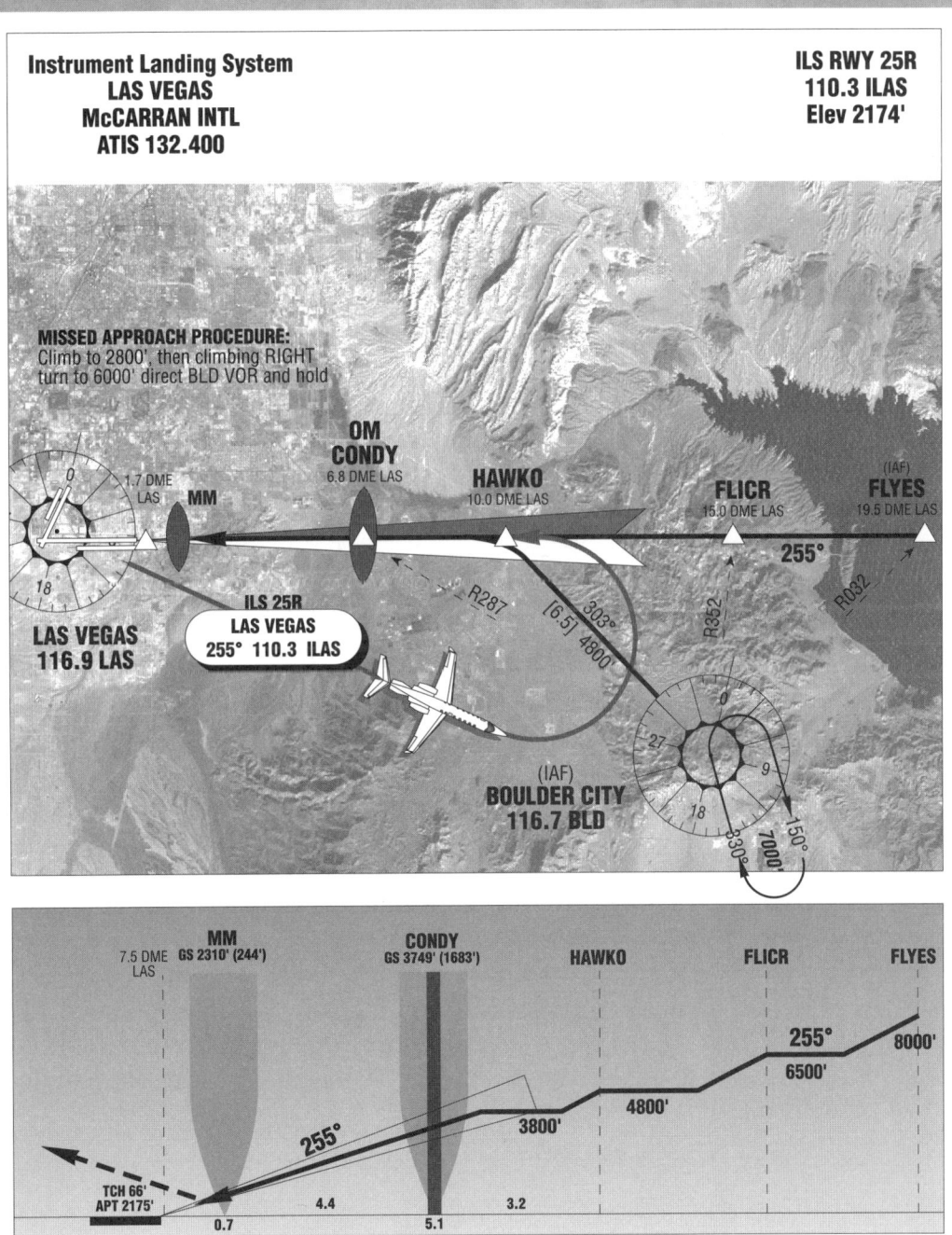

Instrument Landing System
LAS VEGAS
McCARRAN INTL
ATIS 132.400

ILS RWY 25R
110.3 ILAS
Elev 2174'

MISSED APPROACH PROCEDURE:
Climb to 2800', then climbing RIGHT
turn to 6000' direct BLD VOR and hold

OM
CONDY
6.8 DME LAS

HAWKO
10.0 DME LAS

FLICR
15.0 DME LAS

(IAF)
FLYES
19.5 DME LAS

1.7 DME
LAS
MM

255°

LAS VEGAS
116.9 LAS

ILS 25R
LAS VEGAS
255° 110.3 ILAS

R287

[6.5] 4800

303°

R352

R032

(IAF)
BOULDER CITY
116.7 BLD

150°

7000'

330°

MM
GS 2310' (244')

CONDY
GS 3749' (1683')

HAWKO

FLICR

FLYES

7.5 DME
LAS

255°

8000'

6500'

4800'

3800'

255°

TCH 66'
APT 2175'

0.7

4.4

5.1

3.2

The rate of descent (ROD) results from these calculations:

```
Rate of descent ROD = Difference in Altitude ALT / Time T (with ALT = 27,000
- 10,000)
```

```
Time T = Distance DIST / Speed GS * 60
```

60 nautical miles DME distance and a speed over ground of 400 kts results in the duration of descent:

```
T = DIST / GS * 60 = 60 / 400 * 60 = 9 minutes
```

and thus the required rate of descent

```
ROD = ALT / T = 17,000 / 9 = 1,888 feet/min, or around 1,900 fpm
```

If the rounded value for the rate of descent is programmed into the autopilot, all you need to do is make sure the speed over ground is kept somewhat constant, through sensible throttle control, so you do not reach the appropriate altitude too early or too late.

After the overflight, the approach controller will guide the airplane through a procedure turn at 110° toward the east. This is done to take a left turn over Lake Mead and the Hoover Dam and to prepare you to get bearings of the approach path to landing runway 25. The final approach to the edge of the landing runway goes over the gray brown, sandy surroundings of the airport into the glittery world of Las Vegas. Good luck!

Fresh fish from Boston

The assistant to the deputy director of an office in a large government agency has been assigned to gather certain facts. The delicate details of the facts are in an expensive sea food restaurant in Boston. You have to get the deputy there before the filets get cold...a job for the Learjet 45.

This adventure requires the LJSEAFUD.ADV and LJDCA18.STN files in the FS98\Adv folder. Load this adventure by clicking **Flights** | **Adventures...** and selecting the "Seafood dinner: Learjet 45" adventure.

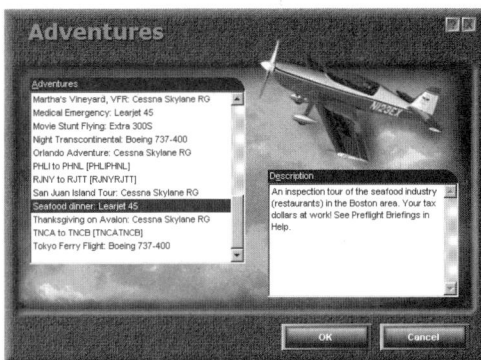

The clearance of air traffic control for this flight of Learjet 45 Lima Juliet is:

> *Learjet 45 Lima Juliet is cleared to Airport Boston Logan via Nottingham VOR direct, J42 Boston VOR direct. Climb and maintain flight level 330 and squawk 3235.*

After starting on takeoff runway 18, continue flying on the runway heading. Reduce power to 10 DME from Washington National (111.0 DCA). Expect a radar vectoring from the air traffic control for a left turn on heading 120° to reception of radial 270 in the direction of the Nottingham VOR (113.7 OTT) with approach course 090°.

Fly over OTT above 10,000 feet. Leave the Nottingham VOR on radial 071 and climb to flight level 330. You are now on J42. Turn at the GRACO intersection, the fix point 29 DME east of OTT, on to radial 235 from Woodstown VOR (112.8 OOD) with approach course 055°.

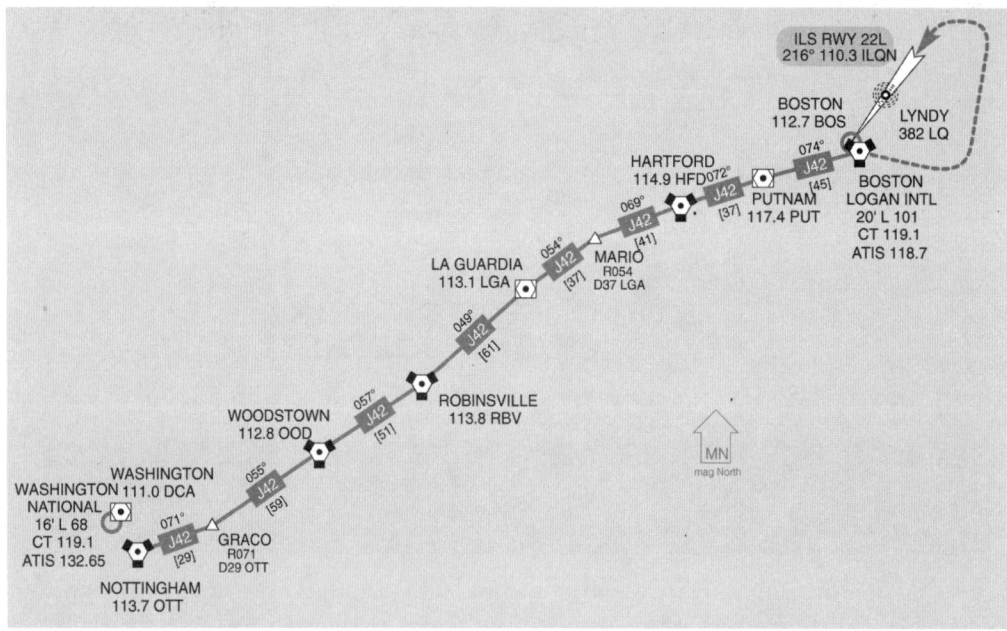

You achieve cruising altitude here and the subsequent flight until Hartford is determined solely by airway J42. Here the route guide changes to airway J225. The following table lists the important frequencies, reporting points and altitudes for the entire flight:

Wpt	Freq	Hdg	Dist	ALT	ETE	ATE
Washington DC	132.65					
DCA	111.0	180°				
OTT	113.7	270°	24	>10000	6'	
GRACO		071°	29		6'	
OOD	112.8	055°	59	FL330	9'	
RBV	113.8	057°	51	FL330	8'	
LGA	113.1	049°	61	FL330	9'	
MARIO	D37 LGA	054°	37	FL330	5'	
HFD	114.9	069°	42	FL330	6'	
PUT	117.4	072°	38		5'	
BOS	112.7	074°	45	<12000	6'	
ILS 22L	110.3	216°		3000		
LQ	382	216°		1700		
Boston Logan						
Total			**386**		**60'**	

After flying over PUT, the airplane continues flying 074° towards Boston (112.7 BOS). Here you can expect clearance, initiate the descent to BOS VOR, fly over this below 12,000 feet and then hold steady at 9,000 feet.

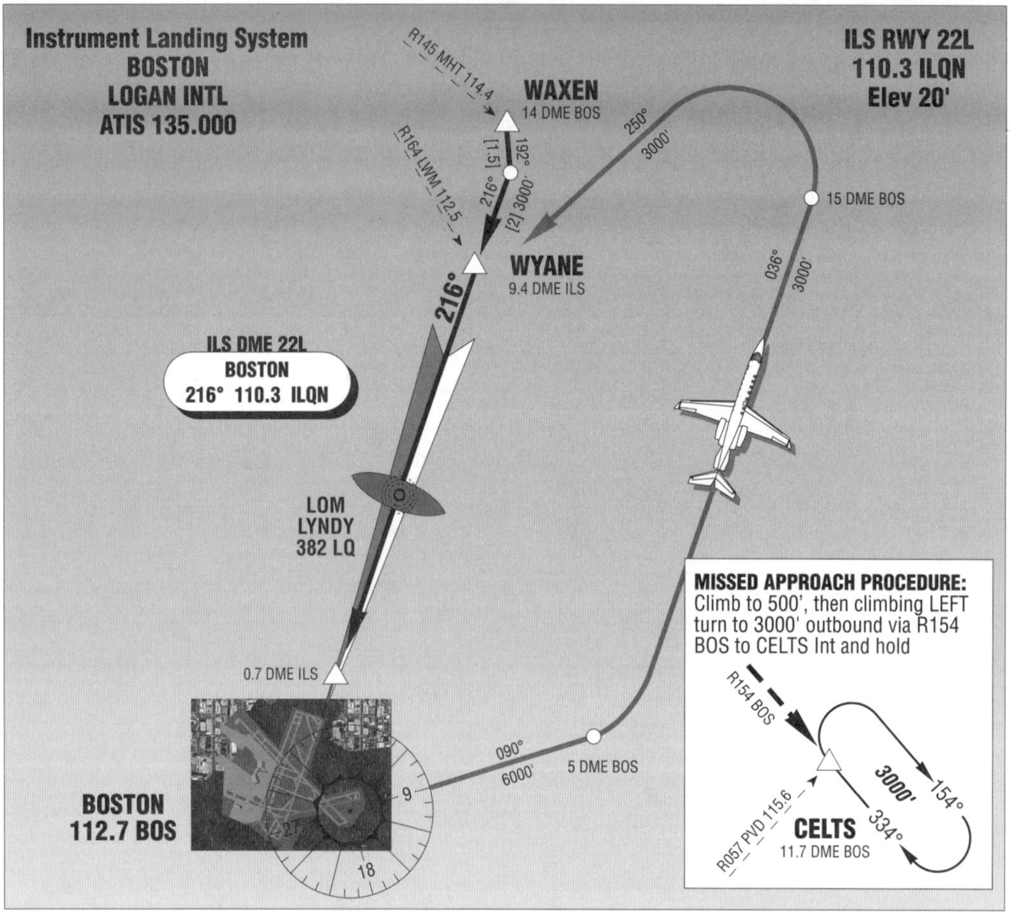

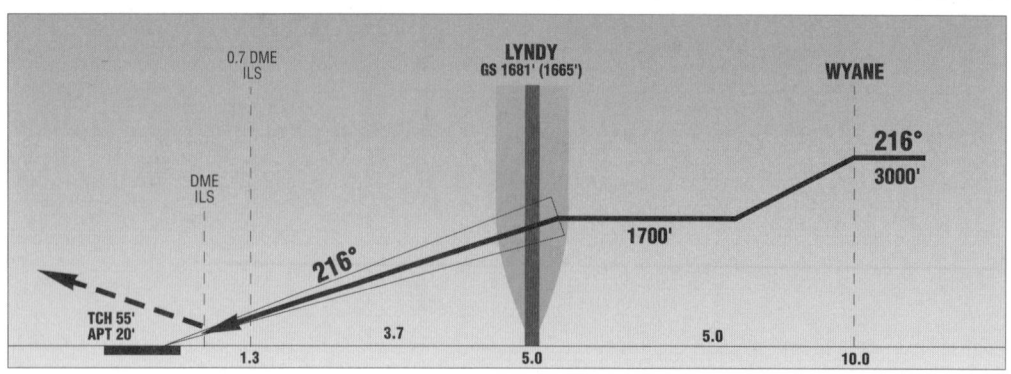

Instrument Landing System
BOSTON
LOGAN INTL
ATIS 135.000

R145 MHT 114.4

WAXEN
14 DME BOS

ILS RWY 22L
110.3 ILQN
Elev 20'

250°
3000

R164 LWM 112.5

192°
[1.5]
216°
[2] 3000

15 DME BOS

WYANE
9.4 DME ILS

216°

036°
3000'

ILS DME 22L
BOSTON
216° 110.3 ILQN

LOM
LYNDY
382 LQ

MISSED APPROACH PROCEDURE:
Climb to 500', then climbing LEFT
turn to 3000' outbound via R154
BOS to CELTS Int and hold

R154 BOS

3000'

154°

0.7 DME ILS

R057 PVD 115.6

334°

CELTS
11.7 DME BOS

090°
6000'

5 DME BOS

9

BOSTON
112.7 BOS

18

0.7 DME
ILS

LYNDY
GS 1681' (1665')

WYANE

216°

3000'

DME
ILS

1700'

216°

TCH 55'
APT 20'

3.7

5.0

1.3

5.0

10.0

Over the Boston VOR you will make contact with the Boston approach control. This air traffic control area gives a radar guide for the ILS approach to landing runway 22 left at Boston Logan. At the intermediate altitude of 6,000 feet, the airplane on heading 070° is first ordered away from the airport to the open Atlantic. Here, at 15 DME BOS, the plane reduces to an approach speed of 200 kts and makes another left turn to heading 260°. During this turn the airplane must also descend to 3,000 feet to start the approach course to runway 22L again at about 12 DME BOS.

During this turn back to the airport and to ILS 22L, clearance to the ILS approach is granted. Now, everything on board should be prepared for the final approach. Make certain to lower the flaps and landing gear and set the speed at about 140 kts. With the ILS clearance, the approach must now be continued on the approach course and glide path. At the Outer Marker LOM (LYNDY 382 LQ), the tower answers and gives the expected permission to land on landing runway 22L.

Charter flight for executives

On this flight you will take a group of executives from San Jose, California to a conference in Disneyland. You'll be flying a Learjet 45 to the flight to John Wayne Airport in Orange County (SNA).

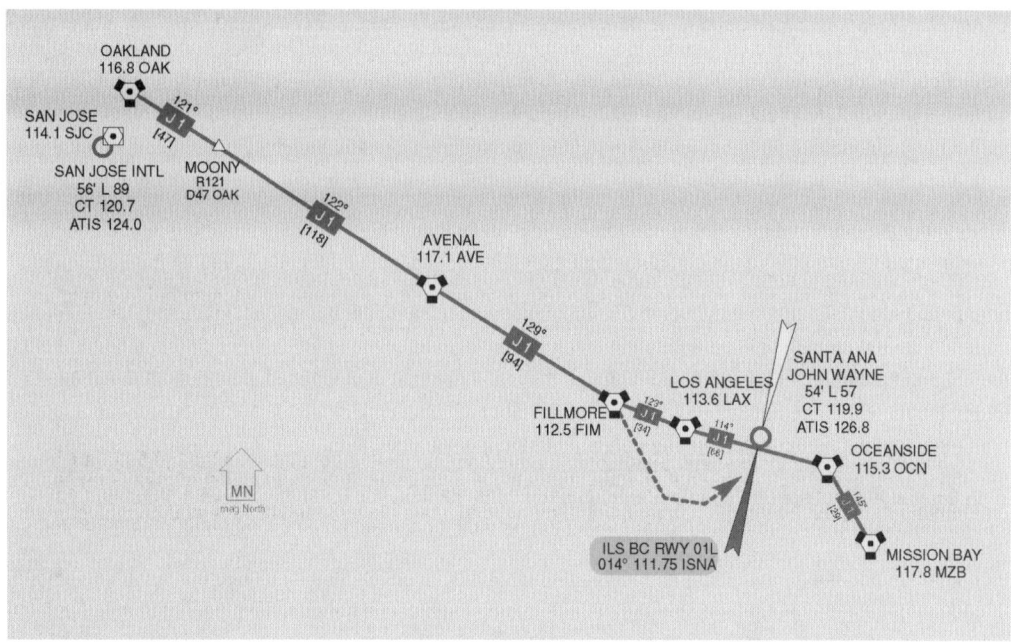

On this flight you will take a group of executives from San Jose, California to a conference in Disneyland. You'll be flying a Learjet 45 to the flight to John Wayne Airport in Orange County (SNA).

This flight adventure requires the LJEXECC.ADV and LJSJC30l.STN files in the FS98\Adv folder. To begin the adventure, select "Executive Charter: Learjet 45" from the **Flights | Adventures...** dialog box.

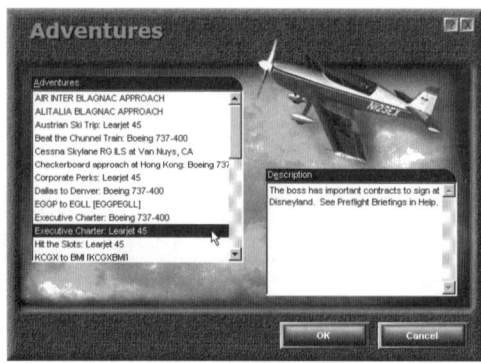

In the busy airspace around the San Francisco Bay, aircraft starting in San Jose must fly a narrow right turn in the climb immediately after starting. Upon your arrival at the John Wayne Airport, you must account for the famous strong Santa Ana winds. Make certain to follow the instructions of the air traffic control exactly. Otherwise, the adventure will immediately be canceled without further ATC support.

The route clearance for the Learjet 45 reads:

> *45 LJ is cleared to John Wayne Airport via San Jose, Departure SJC 8, J1 LAX, V16 PRADO, direct. Flight level 230. Squawk 4235.*

This much is clear. The tower clearance for the takeoff becomes a little more difficult since it contains some special instructions that you need to follow:

> *After departure fly runway heading until 1.8 DME San Jose VORTAC. Right turn to heading 110° within 4 DME SJC climbing to 5,000 ft.*

The instruction to turn to SJC VOR on the new heading of 110° within four miles after departure is a good one. The Learjet could be flown after departure beginning at 1,500 feet above ground at a maximum of 250 kts. However, then the turning radius at normal banking would be so great the required four mile area around the VOR would be overflown. In other words, the speed following departure cannot exceed 170 kts. At this reduced speed, the right turn at 110° will succeed within the required boundary.

Wpt	Freq	Hdg	Dist	ALT	ETE	ATE
San Jose	124.0					
(OAK	116.8)					
MOONY	R121 D47 OAK	121°	40			
AVE	117.1	122°	118	FL230		
FIM	112.5	129°	94			
BC 01	111.75	014°	35			
Santa Ana	126.8					
Total			**287**			

Beginning at 1,500 feet, the autopilot can be programmed to find and hold the altitude at 5,000 feet. This avoids the next trap in the clearance for takeoff: If the required intermediate altitude of 5,000 feet is exceeded by a few hundred feet, the task is ended and the ATC guide is canceled.

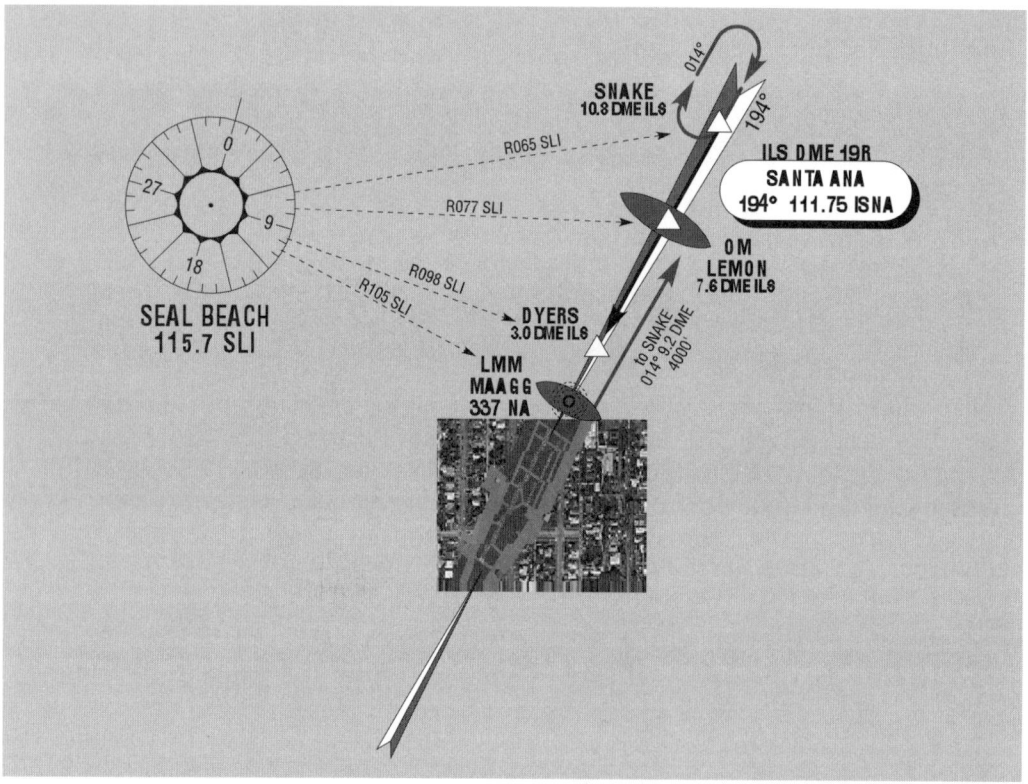

Then the cockpit can become a bit more relaxed. The autopilot is prepared in the NAV function on radial 121 from Oakland VORTAC (116.8 OAK). The clearance climb to flight level 230 with the additional instruction to fly over the MOONY intersection (R121 D47 OAK) above 12,000 feet starting at 30 DME from OAK.

Then you go on course 122° to Avenal VOR (117.1 AVE) and further on course 129° to the Fillmore VOR (112.5 FIM). The approach to the John Wayne Airport of Santa Ana from the Fillmore beacon begins on radial 148. At 48 DME after FIM, the radar control will prepare the airplane for the back course approach on landing runway 01 left of the John Wayne Airport. After that comes the instruction to take a left turn to heading 100° and to descend to 6,000 feet. Another left turn to 060° brings the plane to the back course of the landing transmitter. The approach clearance comes with the stabilized back course in the VOR1 display.

Adventure Flights With The Boeing B737

The Boeing B737-400 is the largest plane in Flight Simulator 98's default fleet of aircraft. It also has the most difficult task of flying the "checkerboard approach" in Hong Kong. The second adventure with the 737 is a domestic flight from Dallas to Denver.

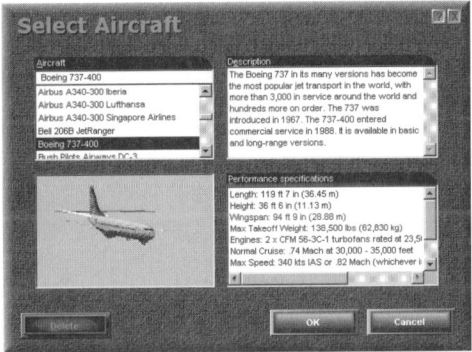

Checkerboard approach into Hong Kong

You're the captain of a Boeing 737-400 called the Blue Sky 737 on a routine flight into Hong Kong. However, there seldom is a routine flight into Hong Kong, an airport with the infamous and winding "Checkerboard Approach" on a short landing runway. Make certain the B3HKGIGS.ADV and B3HKG13I.STN files are in the FS98\Adv folder. Click **Flights | Adventures...** and select "Checkerboard approach: Boeing 737-400" to load this adventure.

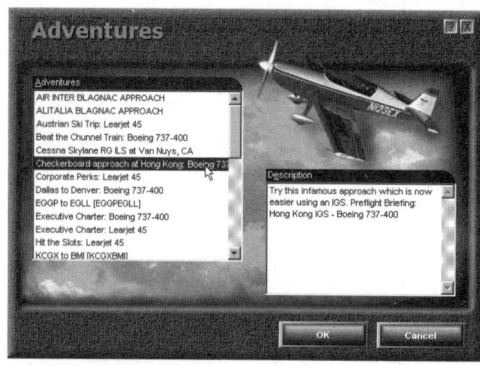

Your Boeing 737-400 is ready for takeoff.

The clearance for Blue Sky 737 reads:

> *Blue Sky 737 is cleared to Cheung Chau VOR via Intersection WHISKEY direct. Maintain 6,000 and squawk 3337.*

The ATC instructions for takeoff and the rest of the flight create the following picture: After departure from runway 13, continue along the runway course. At fixed point 23 DME to Hong Kong ILS-DME (HK), turn left on heading 330° to pick up radial 090 from Cheung Chau (CH) and approach on 270°. Over the CH VOR, reduce speed to 200 knots and hold 6,000 feet. At 7 DME from CH, turn right on heading 045° and descend to 4,500 feet. Clearance for the IGS approach is on landing runway 13. So far so good to this point.

The IGS approach to landing runway 13 doesn't occur on the extended line of the runway center line at 130° as is common practice. Instead, it occurs at an angle of approach twisted by 42°: 088° due to the special geographic location of the airport. The special IGS system sends an approach path signal for the direction of approach at 088° and normal glide path signal for a 3° glide angle.

The outer marker signal sounds at 5.8 DME to the IGS. The approach altitude here must be 2,000 feet. The crew has brought the airplane to the approach configuration: landing gear down, flaps to the outer marker in 30° position, load regulator to N1 55 to 60%, depending on landing load, speed 150 kts.

Use this configuration to steer the B737 to the middle marker. The altitudes are called out loud by the copilot at each full hundred as you fly. When you fly through the altitude of 1,000 feet, the landing configuration and the IGS with approach path and glide path must be absolutely stabilized. Aside from that, it's full tilt and pull up. At 650 feet altitude the middle marker signal sounds. The checkerboard grows threateningly large at this point.

Now the autopilot is completely turned off: The rest of the landing must be controlled manually and purely visually. And this is not exactly easy. The airplane is already flying far below the mountain peaks and very close over the skyscrapers of Hong Kong City. Directly with the middle marker signal the Boeing goes into a smooth right turn, which must negotiate the angular difference between the approach path and the actual direction of the runway. The bent chain of lights from the approach lighting marks the optimum flight path up to the edge of runway 13.

Do not under any circumstances decrease the speed during the turn or increase the rate of descent in the turn. However, if you do, you can correct both through sensitive load regulation. The glide path transmitter (in Flight Simulator 98) is designed so even in the turn a signal can be received up to the landing runway. This way, even the last part of the final approach can be optimized. Be careful, the right wing tip may come dangerously close to the ground or the surrounding houses.

As soon as the airplane is aligned with the runway, the landing runway edge is overflown. The touchdown, braking with the thrust brake and the wheel brakes and rolling off to the terminal building are routine procedures.

From Dallas to Denver

You're again the captain in this adventure of the Blue Sky 737 on a flight from Dallas-Ft. Worth International Airport (DFW) to Denver International Airport (DEN). This flight takes place in daylight and in the summer and requires the B3DFWDEN.ADV and B3DFW17R.STN files. Click **Flights | Adventures...** and select "Dallas to Denver: Boeing 737-400" to begin this adventure.

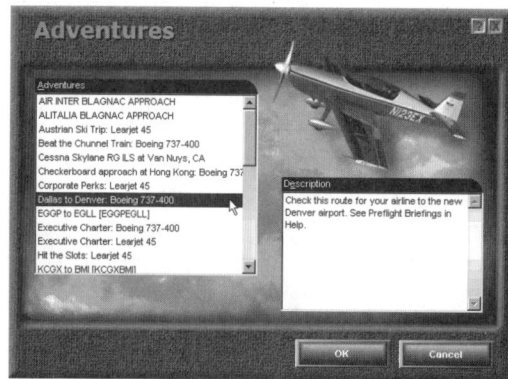

The clearance for the Blue Sky 737 reads:

> Blue Sky737 is cleared to Denver International Airport via Wichita Falls direct, J168 Lamar, J20 Falcon, direct. Maintain Flight level 350 and squawk 3327.

The following table lists the individual instructions of the control areas for your brief pre-flight planning:

Wpt	Freq	Hdg	Dist	Alt		
Dallas	117.0					
SPS	112.7	320°	111	FL310		
LAA	116.9	310°	321	FL350		
HGO	112.1	298°	58			
FQF	116.3	055°	70	<9000		
ILS 35L	108.5	350°		7000		
Denver	125.6					
Total			560			

32

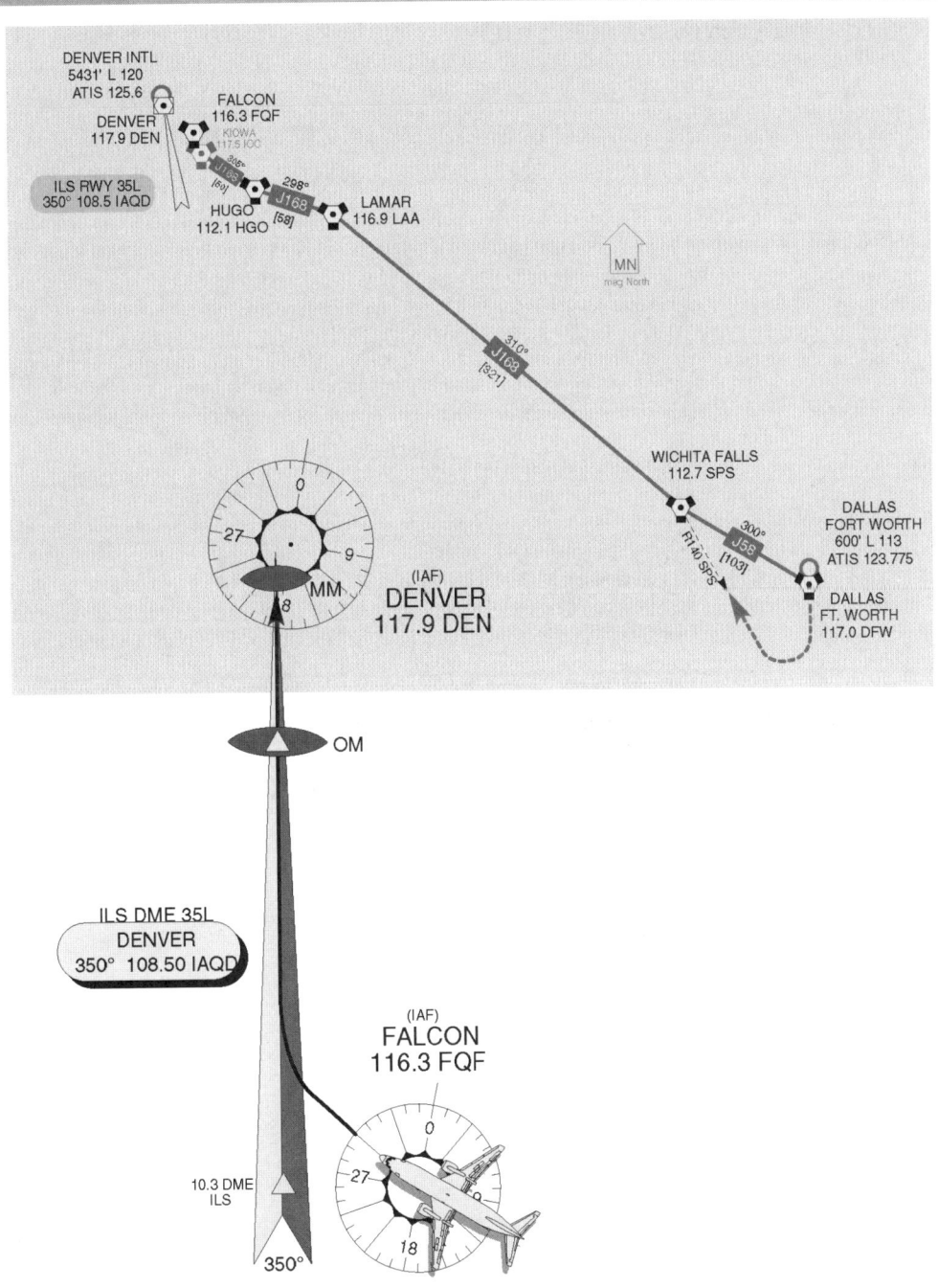

DENVER INTL
5431' L 120
ATIS 125.6

FALCON
116.3 FQF

DENVER
117.9 DEN

KIOWA
117.5 IOC

ILS RWY 35L
350° 108.5 IAQD

J168
[59]

298°
J168
[58]

HUGO
112.1 HGO

LAMAR
116.9 LAA

MN
mag North

310°
J168
[321]

WICHITA FALLS
112.7 SPS

(IAF)
DENVER
117.9 DEN

0

27

9

18

MM

DALLAS
FORT WORTH
600' L 113
ATIS 123.775

300°
J58
[103]

Rt 40 SPS

DALLAS
FT. WORTH
117.0 DFW

OM

ILS DME 35L
DENVER
350° 108.50 IAQD

(IAF)
FALCON
116.3 FQF

0

27

9

18

10.3 DME
ILS

350°

33

After departing from runway 17R, climb to 2,000 feet and turn right to heading 240°. At 20 nautical miles from Dallas (20 DME DFW), make another right turn to heading 270°, in order to join the radial 140 = Approach TO 320° to Wichita Falls VOR (112.7 SPS). Pass the SPS VOR at Flight level 310, and after that climb to FL 350.

On airway J168 the flight continues through Lamar VOR (116.9 LAA) to Hugo VOR (112.1 HGO). The clearance to descend to 7,000 feet towards Falcon VOR (116.3 FQF) comes at a distance of about 25 nautical miles from HGO comes. It has the restriction to reach the Falcon VOR at or below 9,000 feet. The air traffic control informs you that you can expect a radar vector for the ILS approach to landing runway 35 left in Denver. Some 16 nautical miles before FQF comes the instruction to fly to heading 300° and hold at 7,000 feet, to get bearings on the ILS approach path. The landing on runway 35L ends the business flight to the gigantic new airport of Denver, Colorado.

Keep in mind that Denver is the Mile High City; its altitude is 5,431 feet.

Film Stunts With The Extra 300

This is the only Flight Simulator adventure with the Extra 300 S. This small, one engine airplane is leaving the hangar to film a chase scene in Las Vegas. An on-board camera is installed on the aircraft so you can get the wildest possible film from different perspectives. In this adventure the video recorder in Flight Simulator is acts as the camera and switched to a short recording interval. The recordings from the cockpit can be checked after the flight by the video playback of the scenes.

The flight adventure with the Extra 300 requires the EXLSTWGS.ADV and EXLAS25R.STN files in the FS98\Adv folder. Click **Flights | Adventures...** and select "Movie Stunt Flying: Extra 300s" to load the adventure.

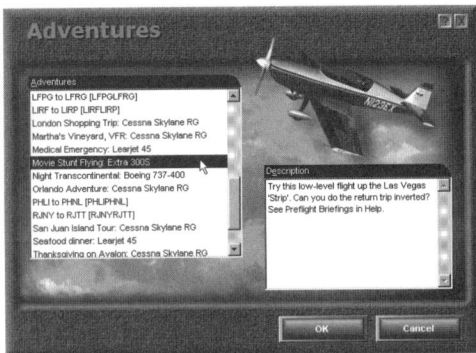

In this adventure the production manager works with the tower controller to track the stunt flight over Las Vegas. Their instructions come over the radio:

> *Extra 328 PW, fly west to the airport boundary and then north over the Strip. Pass the Luxor below 2,300 feet, and stay under 2,300 feet, until you pass Stratosphere Tower. Squawk 1232.*

The altitude of 2,300 feet may at first seem to be quite high and dangerous for a stunt. However, remember the area around the airport of Las Vegas is already 2,175 feet above sea level so the actual altitude above ground is only 125 feet.

Along with the extremely low altitude, the flight route will be discussed down to the last detail before the actual stunt, so that the flight path can be properly captured at each phase by all the cameras: The world famous strip of Las Vegas with its many hotels and casinos begins directly on the northern airport boundary next to the pyramid-shaped Luxor Hotel and the small obelisk. It then runs almost directly to the geographic north at about 345° (with a magnetic variation of about 13° west).

The adventure moves past the giant billboards of the Excalibur, the Tropicana Hotel and MGM and continues until the Aladdin. Soon the gates of Bally's Hotel open up with the stars Louie Anderson and Gordie Brown. On the other side of the street you'll see that the veterans of rock, the Moody Blues, will heat things up in Caesar's Palace. The Mirage Hotel, in which Siegfried and Roy play with their tigers two shows per evening, marks a slight bend of the strip (by 015°).

The second part runs by the Desert Inn, where Smoky Robinson and Buddy Greco are appearing. The Stardust follows on the left side. Next to the Stardust is the Circus Hotel-Casino with its Adventure Dome. The last hotel on the strip is the Sahara. The Stratosphere Tower, the high tower with the restaurant underneath its peak, marks both the northern end of the strip and the end of the stunt flight.

As soon as the aircraft has left the concrete of takeoff runway 25R, you may fly at only 125 feet above the ground—below the building roofs on the strip. Do not decrease the speed below 100 knots. Otherwise, the assistant director will continuously instruct you not to fly too slowly.

Chapter 2
Flying The Bell
206B JetRanger

In Chapter 2 we introduce you to the first helicopter included in Flight Simulator 98. The Bell 206B JetRanger is a popular helicopter that is used worldwide. You'll see it used on mobile drilling platforms, road supervision or as a rescue helicopter. This helicopter is the only acceptable solution in many areas of the world due to its maneuverability. Its ability to hover on the spot often makes it indispensable, particularly for rescuing injured people. Whether in the mountains or on the streets, this helicopter is often the only way to get to the scene of an accident quickly.

However, flying a helicopter is quite different from flying conventional aircraft. In this chapter, therefore, we won't send you on a big flight tour. Remember to set aside time for practice since you'll practice flight maneuvers during the flight. Disable crash detection for this practice exercise. Select the **Aircraft | Aircraft settings...** command and the Crash / Damage tab. Select the "Ignore crash" option. This will prevent Flight Simulator 98 from reloading the flight situation after each crash. Later, once you have got a handle on starts and landings, reset crash detection.

In this chapter you'll learn:

→ How to start the Bell 206B

→ How to execute flight maneuvers with the helicopter

→ How to coordinate the landing approach

→ How to safely land the Bell 206B JetRanger helicopter

38

Why The Helicopter Flies

The helicopter's rotor blades have a similar profile as the wings of the Cessna. These subtle curves provide the helicopter's lift. The rotor blades rotating around a common axis provides the upward lift. If the helicopter increases in speed, the lift is directed to the front. That is why the Bell 206B JetRanger takes off with its nose pointing down. This uses the lift for acceleration in a horizontal direction. To prevent the helicopter from revolving around its own axis, an additional rotor at its tail stabilizes the flight attitude.

Bell 206B JetRanger instrument panel

You'll need to be familiar with at least seven of the JetRanger's 21 panel instruments for the London tour (shown on the following page). The other instruments are important for longer flights or you want to test the circling capabilities of the Bell 206B JetRanger with extreme flights. (The London tour itself begins on page 56.)

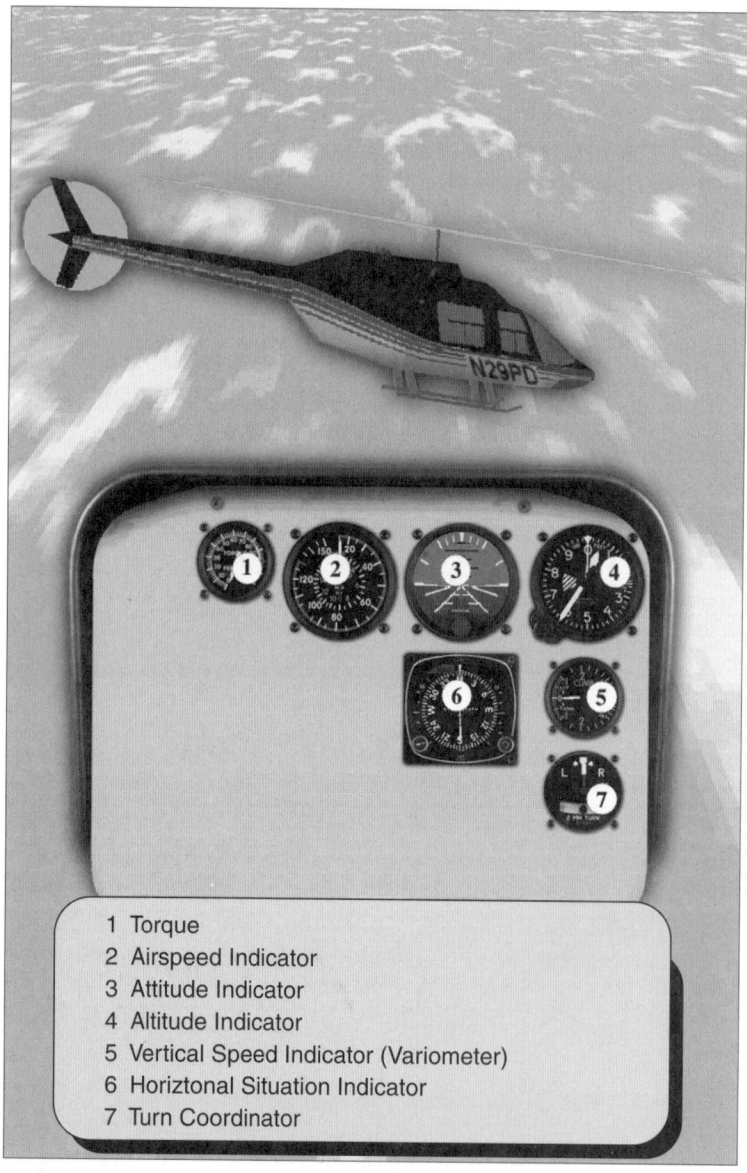

1 Torque
2 Airspeed Indicator
3 Attitude Indicator
4 Altitude Indicator
5 Vertical Speed Indicator (Variometer)
6 Horizontal Situation Indicator
7 Turn Coordinator

These seven instruments of the Bell 206B JetRanger are important for the London tour

The following pages explains these instruments in more detail.

Torque

This instrument shows the power generated by the engine. Although the torque can be as much as 100% at startup, the value should not exceed 90% during flight. The torque is controlled by the pitch control, which controls the rotor blades. Control the torque in FS98 by using the F2 key (reduce torque) and the F3 key (increase torque). If you have flown the Cessna, you could compare the pitch control to the throttle or the propeller pitch controls.

Airspeed Indicator

This instrument shows the speed in knots (1 knot = 1.852 km per hour or 1.15 mph). If a value is not shown, the helicopter is in hovering flight (or on the ground). When starting and landing the helicopter, you have to shift to hovering flight. However, since the helicopter is more difficult to control in hovering flight than it is when it is moving, shift only to hovering flight very briefly until you become more experienced as a helicopter pilot. The best way to practice this type of flying at the airport is to take off, climb to 1,000 feet and then immediately land again.

Attitude Indicator (also called the Artificial horizon)

Use this instrument to check the flight attitude. Notice the top half of the indicator is blue and the bottom half is gray. If the white bar is in the middle so the bar is almost on a line with the two small outer points, you can bring the Bell 206B to hovering flight. If the bar is below the middle, the helicopter is gaining speed, but losing altitude, in *most* circumstances. When the helicopter climbs, the white bar is *usually* above the two white outer points.

Now you're going to find out why we placed "most" and "usually" in italics. The climbing behavior of the helicopter depends on the elevator trim and the horizontal speed of the Bell 206B JetRanger. The higher the horizontal speed, the more likely the helicopter is to gain altitude.

Elevator trim

Set the elevator trim using the 7 and 1 keys on the **numeric keypad**. Make certain that Caps Lock mode is not active (the green Caps Lock light should be off). Toggle the numeric keypad on and off by pressing the Num Lock key on the keyboard.

This is true even when the artificial horizon shows the helicopter should be descending. The trim causes the helicopter to remain in horizontal flight in this situation. You can set the elevator trim so the helicopter maintains altitude even without control corrections.

Altitude Indicator

 This instrument displays your altitude in feet. The small pointer shows the altitude in thousands of feet and the large pointer shows hundreds of feet. The London City Airport is slightly above sea level. This is why the altimeter on the runway is about one point in front of the zero mark. That also means that during landing, the helicopter will touch down at the airport one point before the zero mark. This is not so serious for the London City Airport since it only lies 17 feet above sea level. However, miscalculating the altitude can be disastrous if you land at an airport that is several hundred feet above sea level.

Variometer (Vertical Speed Indicator)

 This instrument indicates how quickly the Bell 206B JetRanger climbs or descends. The display occurs in 100-feet-per-minute increments. If the pointer is pointing at the upper four, then the helicopter is climbing at 400 feet per minute. If the pointer is on the lower four, the helicopter is descending at a rate of 400 feet per minute. The variometer is an important gauge, especially for landing. It's tough to land a fixed wing aircraft with a descending speed of 600 feet per minute, but the landing can still succeed. However, this would end in catastrophe with a helicopter. The variometer should point at the zero mark shortly before touch down.

Horizontal Situation Indicator

 This instrument is more precise than the magnetic compass because it isn't influenced by magnetic fluctuations. During the London tour you'll first fly in a westerly direction (approximately 280°). After the 180° turn, the return flight takes place in the opposite, easterly direction (approximately 100°). Use the Horizontal Situation Indicator to precisely determine the exit from the 180° turn. However, since you're getting your bearings from the Thames, the Horizontal Situation Indicator doesn't play a dominant role in our practice session. We're only using it for information about the current course.

Turn Coordinator

 This instrument shows the bank during the turn. The small ball between the two lines at the bottom of the instrument should remain in the middle during a turn. If the ball slips to the side, it means the speed of rotation is too high. In aviation jargon this is referred to as *crab* or *drift*. During the turn, the pointer with the white tip will move to either the right or the left. If the white tip points directly at R or L for about 15 seconds, you have flown a 180° turn.

> **Elevator trim**
>
> The autocoordination in Flight Simulator 98 is disabled for the Bell 206B JetRanger helicopter. This means that flying turns is more difficult than with the Cessna. During a turn, keep your eyes on the variometer and the turn coordinator. If you maintain altitude during the turn and the turn coordinator doesn't move past the outer limit (the R or the L), then your turn will be successful.

Flight Preparations

After you learn the basics, you can practice your skills on a sightseeing tour over London (see page 56). The following figure shows the basic settings for the practice flight. Make all the settings in your Flight Simulator configuration exactly as shown.

The settings for the flight from London City

Select the **World | Go to | Airport...** command. Select the "Search places" option. Then type "London" in the "Type an airport name or select from the list" field. Click "London City" in the "Search results list" and select "28" in the "Runway" field. The dialog box should have the following settings:

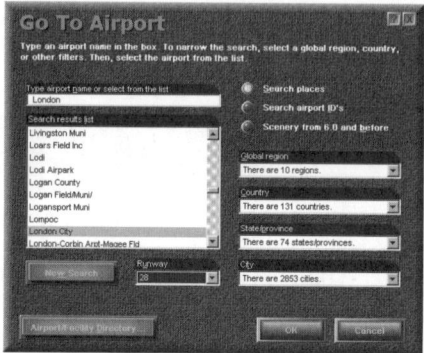

Click (OK) to continue.

Select the **Aircraft** | **Select Aircraft...** command and the "Bell 206B JetRanger".

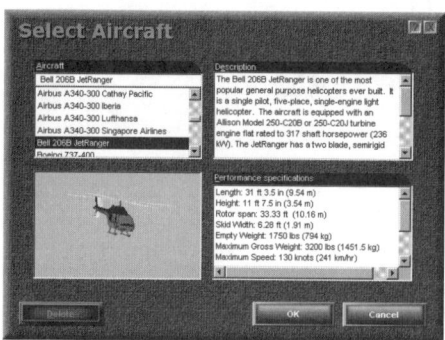

Click (OK) to continue.

Select the **World** | **Weather...** command to set weather values. Select to the following values: "Light Clouds" for "Clouds" , "Unlimited" for "Visibility" and "None" for "Wind".

Click OK to continue.

Next, select the **World** | **Time & Season...** command and set "Time of day" to "Day".

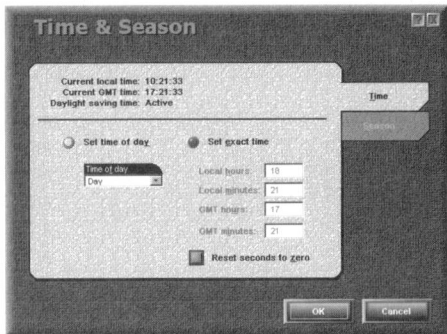

Before closing this dialog box, click the Season tab. Then select "Fall" in the "Season" list box. Click OK to continue.

Select the **Flight** | **Save Flight...** command from the mani menu to save these settings on your hard drive. Enter a name for the flight in the Title of Flight field (for example, "London Sightseeing Tour"). If you would like Flight Simulator 98 to automatically load this flight every time you start FS, click the "Make this the default flight" button.

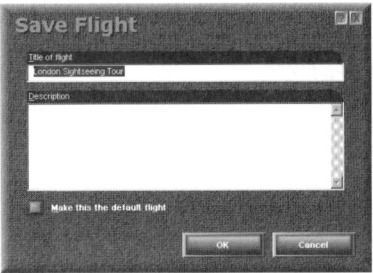

Finally, you'll need to turn off crash detection if you haven't already done so. Select the **Aircraft** | **Aircraft Settings...** command and click the Crash / Damage tab. Click the "Ignore Crash" option so whatever you do with the helicopter, it won't crash.

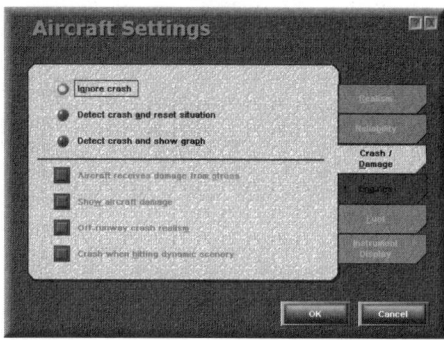

This option is very helpful for learning to fly the helicopter without waiting for Flight Simulator to restart after every crash. Don't set this option if you're looking for a realistic flight.

The Takeoff

You're probably already aware that taking off and landing a helicopter isn't easy. Therefore, we'll give you some valuable information in this section to help you with your takeoffs (the following section talks about landing a helicopter).

The following illustration shows how the helicopter should appear during takeoff (note the top row). The instruments show the values that you need for takeoff. The next six rows show what's involved in a takeoff. The last three images show various course corrections (needed to prevent the helicopter from swerving). You must steer in the direction opposite of the helicopter's swerve.

Note the small images with the mouse and the joystick. They show the steering direction. The graphics are not necessarily in any particular order because each takeoff could have a different appearance than those shown. It's very possible that a large course correction in steering will not be needed during takeoff.

Taking off with the Bell 206B JetRanger

Executing a perfect takeoff

Next, you'll learn how to execute a good takeoff with the helicopter. First, make certain you're familiar with the controls. Use your mouse and the joystick to perform the individual flight maneuvers. The F2 and F3 (pitch control) keys are important. Use these keys to control the rotor blades that influence the torque. For takeoff, gradually increase the torque using the F3 key. When you reach 60%, move your joystick or mouse slightly forward (away from your body). Make certain to move your joystick or mouse only slightly. The helicopter will now begin moving.

The torque may now have reached 90% or more. Maintain the helicopter so the attitude indicator is one to two points below the horizon. This means the blue region is above the two white outer marks. Maintain the helicopter in this position. Use the appropriate steering counter maneuver to compensate for any swerving. Proceed cautiously and be careful with any control adjustments. If everything worked, the Bell 206B will now begin climbing. The steering will be easier now since the flight attitude of the helicopter will be stabilized through the horizontal acceleration. Use the F2 key to reduce the torque at 500 feet to 70% or 80%. Then continue climbing to an altitude of 2,500 feet so you can practice the individual flight maneuvers.

The most frequent takeoff errors

If you have flown airplanes, you immediately switched to climbing flight after takeoff. The artificial horizon in the attitude indicator was pulled down and the blue field went below the two white outer marks.

However, you'll have to radically change your thinking if you want to pilot the helicopter successfully. Because the nose of the helicopter sinks down during takeoff, the blue region of the attitude indicator drifts toward the top. This is normal for flying a helicopter because it gains speed through this flight maneuver. The artificial horizon should never move to the middle position during takeoff under any circumstances. This would cause the helicopter to lose speed and it would crash immediately on the runway.

One way to track whether the helicopter behaves as we have described is to select the Spot Plane menu item from the **Views | New View** menu. You may also want to watch movies and TV shows that feature helicopters taking off and landing.

The optimal screen arrangement.

Here's what the screen should look like. We moved the instrument panel to the upper right of the screen during takeoff so the runway is clearly visible. The Spot Plane view appears in the upper left corner so you can watch the takeoff.

The Flight Maneuvers

We'll talk about flying turns, gaining or losing altitude, hovering flight and regulating speed in this section. You'll also learn how to recover when the helicopter begins spinning. The graphics show two sets of instruments. The top row shows the instrument readings before the maneuver. The bottom row shows the changes in the displays during the maneuver.

Regulating speed and altitude

You have two basic ways to regulate the JetRanger's altitude and speed. If you move the controls forward (away from you), the helicopter gains speed. If the torque is below 70% and the horizontal speed is below 100 knots, it also loses altitude.

The second method is if you pull the controls back (towards you), the helicopter loses speed and gains altitude. This maneuver is indispensable for going into hovering flight.

You can also change the altitude while the helicopter accelerates or reduces speed (as shown in the graphic on the following page). Press the F3 key to increase the torque during flight and to gain altitude. Alternatively, press the F2 key to reduce torque and lose altitude. However, do not increase the torque beyond 90% to avoid overloading the turbine.

Hovering

Hovering is possible when the white center line (artificial horizon) is located in the middle of the attitude indicator. The helicopter is very unstable when it is hovering. This is why it should hover only for short periods. Otherwise, you'll start with a minor correction and end with the helicopter going into a spin or crashing.

Intercepting spins

If the helicopter goes into a spin, put the controls in neutral for a moment and use the pitch control (F2 and F3) to stabilize the attitude.

Bell 206B JetRanger Flight Maneuvers

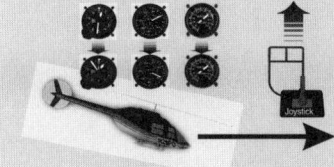

1. Move controls forward to gain speed

2. Pull controls back decreases speed and gains altitude.

3. Use the F2 (increase) and F3 (decrease) keys to regulate the torque during flight and increase or decrease altitude.

4. Hovering is possible if the white center line is centered.

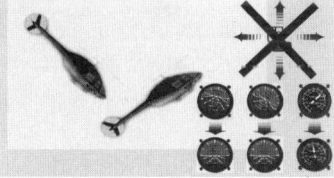

5. Put controls in neutral if the helicopter goes into a spin.

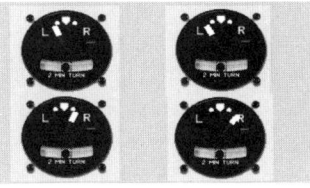

6. Check if the helicopter is flying left/right correctly. Check the turn coordinator frequently.

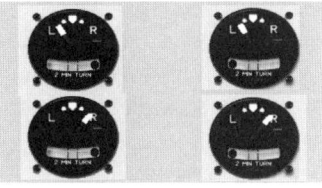

7. The helicopter "drifts" or "crabs" when you push the controls too hard.

Don't move the mouse if you're using it as the controller. If you're using a joystick, leave it in the middle position. It may seem strange but you'll usually be able to stabilize the helicopter with this maneuver (at least in Flight Simulator 98). However, this flight maneuver is not so easy if you're using a joystick with Force Feedback technology due to the kickback forces.

Flying turns

The turn coordinator shows how the turn is flown. Small dots on the left and the right indicate how quickly the JetRanger is turning. If the turn coordinator points at one of these dots for about half a minute, a 180° turn is flown. If the pointer is pointing at the L or the R, the turn will be completed in about 15 seconds.

Crab and drift

Drifting, or crabbing, occurs frequently when you push the controls too hard to the right or the left. If the pointer in the turn coordinator reaches the R or the L, do not continue moving the controls in that direction.

The helicopter can also go into a spin when you gain or lose altitude during a turn. If you're flying a right turn at 12° per second (the pointer of the turn coordinator is pointing to the L or the R during the turn) and at the same time the helicopter climbs or descends at more than 2,000 feet per minute, then the 206B can fall into a spin very quickly.

Avoiding descent

Making a coordinated descent with a helicopter is much more difficult than with airplane models, which have wings. After you have had some practice flying turns in the helicopter, then you can simultaneously lose altitude at 2,000 feet per minute or more. If you fly a narrow right or left turn (the turn coordinator points to the L or R during the turn), then you can circle the landing field losing altitude and speed until you can touch down for a landing.

The Landing

If you think taking off and flying were difficult with the Bell 206B JetRanger, we don't want to scare you, but landing is probably the most difficult maneuver. You must accomplish two things for a perfect landing: The horizontal speed (displayed by the airspeed indicator) and the speed of vertical descent (displayed by the variometer, or VSI) must be nearly at zero when touching down. This is difficult, since the Bell 206B JetRanger is very hard to control when it is hovering. Remember the takeoff? Right after takeoff many control corrections were necessary. This is also true with the landing. Corrections are harder to make at decreasing speeds since the helicopter tends more to swerve.

Disable Crash Detection for your first landing attempts but keep this setting only until you can land the Bell 206B JetRanger. Even if Crash Detection is enabled, you may still get a message that the helicopter crashed despite your "clean" landing. This is because the helicopter has no wheels. For example, if your Cessna touches down on the runway at 80 knots, the airplane will roll along the runway. If you touch down on the runway at 80 knots in the Bell 206B JetRanger, you'll be doing somersaults. The same is true for the speed of vertical descent. With the Cessna, landing on the runway with a vertical descent speed of 600 feet per minute will be very hard but not impossible. However, you're likely to crash at 600 fpm with the helicopter. We'll illustrate this with arithmetic:

An impact on the runway at 600 feet per minute means:

```
600 feet per minute * 60 = 36,000 feet per hour

1 foot = 0.3048 meters
-> 0.3048 meters * 36,000 feet = 10.97 km/h.

1 foot = .000189 miles
-> .000189 miles * 36,000 feet = 6.8 mph
```

Seven miles per hour doesn't sound like much. However, anyone who has ever crashed a bicycle at this speed knows that an accident can cause considerable injuries. Plus, the Bell 206B JetRanger would be seriously damaged in such a landing. We assumed in the problem the horizontal airspeed of the Bell 206B JetRanger was zero. However, the facts are no different if the horizontal speed is greater than zero. Increased ground speed will also increase the impact on the ground.

For the landing, first circle over the landing field or attempt a traditional straight-line descent. However, this is difficult to manage with the helicopter since the flight attitude must be corrected often. If you're quite high above the runway, try to lose altitude by circling around the airport and simultaneously losing altitude. You can control the vertical rate of descent with the pitch control (for rotor blade control). Press F2 to increase the vertical rate of descent or press F3 to decrease the vertical speed of descent and increasing the airspeed at the same time.

A perfect landing

First, approach the runway at an altitude of 800 feet and 50% for the torque. At this altitude, reduce the vertical rate of descent to a maximum of 100 feet per minute. Use the pitch control (F2 and F3 keys) to control the descent. The horizontal speed cannot exceed 20 knots. About 10 feet before touchdown, pull the controls back slightly (toward the body) so the horizontal speed and the vertical rate of descent go to zero. Use the F2 or F3 key to control the rate of vertical descent. Increase the torque to about 70%. In the following figure, we show you the landing in the top graphic. In the other graphics we are performing the landing, recording the instrument data. The readings are not "must" values but only serve to help you get your bearings. The instrument readings will look slightly different with each landing. Pay special attention to the attitude indicator. Depending on which position this is in, you'll have to steer in the opposite direction. The small graphics with the mouse and the joystick indicate the steering direction. No more corrections were made with the bottom graphic since the helicopter is in the process of touching down.

Making The Perfect Flight

We hope the information in this chapter will help you master individual flight maneuvers with the Bell 206B JetRanger. In your first flying lessons, concentrate on getting the knack of the basic flight maneuvers. One important way to check this is to use FS's course tracking. You can enable course tracking in the **Options | Flight Analysis** menu.

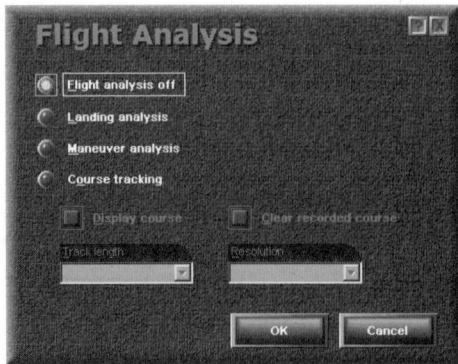

Starting the Bell 206B helicopter.

The Flight Analysis menu is a very useful resource for tracking your exact flight path. The flight path is marked with a red strip in the sky. When you work with course tracking, pay attention to the way the helicopter climbs and descends.

Keep in mind it should not look like this figure. You or your passengers would likely be very sick and this would be the last time your passengers would fly with you. Always make sure that the climbs and descents, as well as all other flight maneuvers, are executed smoothly and not abruptly.

Helicopter Exercise #1: Sightseeing Over London

The London tour starts at the London City Airport and flies along the Thames. You will be able to admire several sights of London during this sightseeing tour: Tower Bridge, London Tower, Westminster Abbey, Big Ben and many other famous buildings in London.

Other aircraft

Naturally, you can also take the sightseeing tour in London with the Cessna 182 RG/S or with any other aircraft of Flight Simulator 98.

You can deviate from the tour if you like. Although we recommend flying along the Thames to London Bridge before turning and landing at London City Airport, you could also turn towards London City and fly to the downtown area. If you take a slight right turn in front of Big Ben, you can visit Hyde Park. For the return flight, climb to an altitude of approximately 2,500 feet. Then find the Thames again and fly along it to London City Airport.

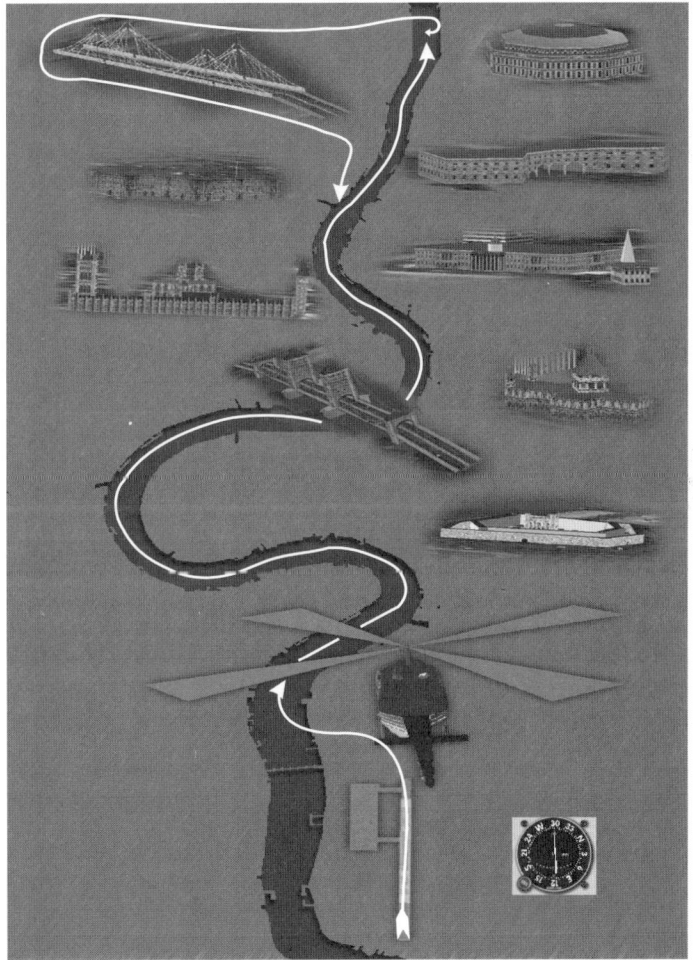

The route along the Thames.

We've planned this tour so you won't have to follow any course and you won't have to fly by ADF or VOR frequencies. Use the Thames to get your bearings during the flight. Fortunately, it's good that you won't be following a course or flying by ADF or VOR frequencies; you'll have your hands full controlling the helicopter.

For the flight, make certain to press (Shift)+(]) to open the Map window so you don't leave the flight route along the Thames. After departing from London City Airport, you'll first come to a small body of water, which is not yet the Thames. After that, you enter into the correct flight route. On the way back, the Map window will also help you discover the airport in time. You may also want to open a spot window so you can visually check whether the individual flight maneuvers are working properly with the Bell 206B JetRanger.

Sights you'll encounter on the sightseeing tour along the Thames.

The course of the flight

The flight begins on runway 28 at London City Airport. During the climb to an altitude of 2,500 feet, you're already flying in the direction of the Thames. It appears on the horizon shortly after the takeoff. Now follow the course of the Thames, swinging to the left and then back to the right. This section is ideal for experimenting with flying circles.

The first building you then see on the right side is the Tower Bridge, which is followed by the Tower. Next you'll see St. Paul's Cathedral and Cleopatra's Needle. The Thames next makes a small swing to the left. Big Ben and the houses of Parliament soon appear followed soon by Westminster Abbey. Finally, you'll see the Royal Albert Hall, which lies away from the Thames on the right side. After that, continue flying along the Thames until you reach London Bridge.

Now it's time for the return flight. After a 180° turn you find you're on the way back. It's time to practice the flight maneuvers for climbing and descending, since the airport is closer than you think. Finally, the landing takes place at the London City Airport. When you have successfully accomplished all of that, then there is nothing more standing in the way of getting your pilot's license for the helicopter.

Practicing banking (turns)

The Bell 206B JetRanger is an extremely maneuverable helicopter, which, naturally, is an invitation to banking. To gain some more flight experience, fly around one of the sights with the helicopter. To do this, fly at eye level to the selected sight and then circle it. This will improve your skill at banking. You'll notice the objects are very detailed 3-D objects that can be viewed from all sides.

Helicopter Exercise #2:
Using The Horizontal Situation Indicator

In this practice session you'll fly using the Horizontal Situation Indicator (HSI). Since you'll be flying over the ocean, it is very important to follow the course exactly. At the end of the practice session, you'll land using descent. Therefore, prior to this practice session make certain to practice the most important flight maneuvers for the Bell 206B JetRanger.

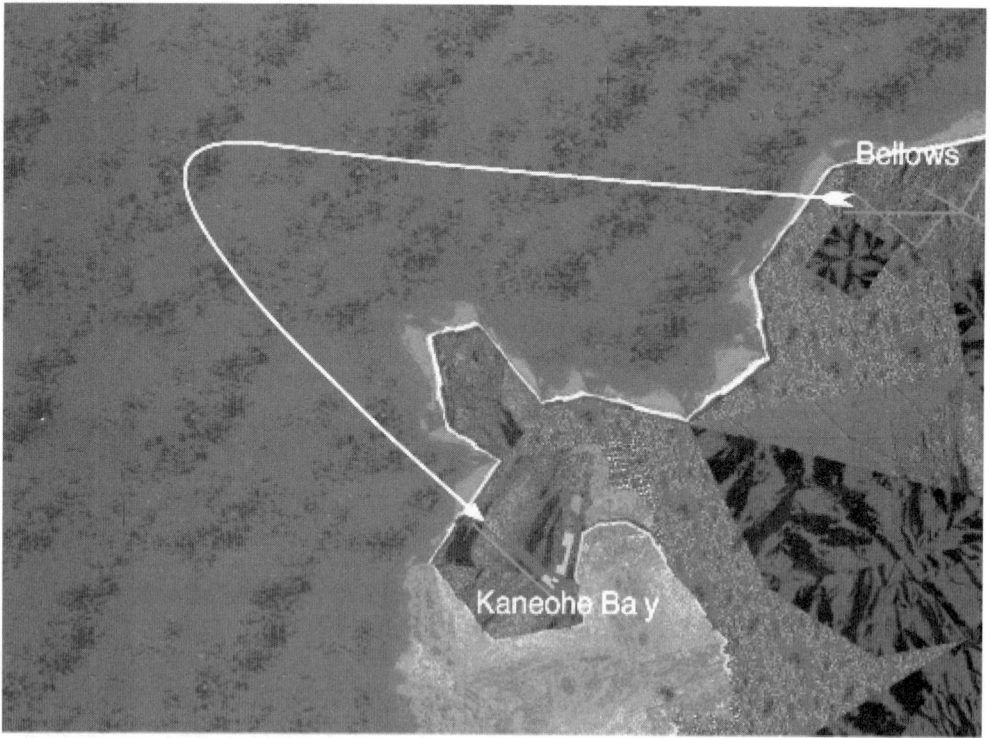

This is what the Bellows and Kaneohe Bay airports look like from above. You will take off at 9 o'clock in Bellows and land in Kaneohe Bay at 9:12. The course is drawn on the map.

Our flight training begins at the idle Bellows airport on one of the Hawaiian islands and ends at Kaneohe Bay airport. We chose these airports because Bellows and Kaneohe Bay are slightly above sea level so the altimeter reads nearly zero at ground level. This is easier than flying to and from airports that are several hundred feet above sea level. These airports require you to convert the altimeter reading so you can make safe landings.

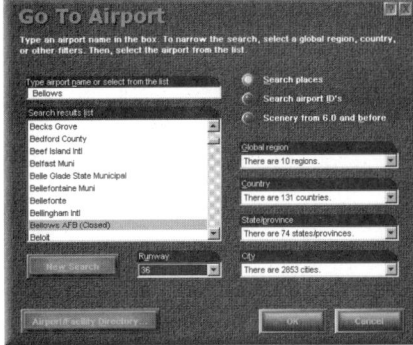

FS flight preparations

First you need to load the Bellows airport and specify clear weather with no winds. Select the **World | Go to | Airport...** command. Select the "Search places" option. Then type "Bellows" in the "Type an airport name or select from the list" field. Click "Bellows AFB (closed)" in the "Search results list" and select "36" in the "Runway" field. The dialog box should have the settings in the image on the right.

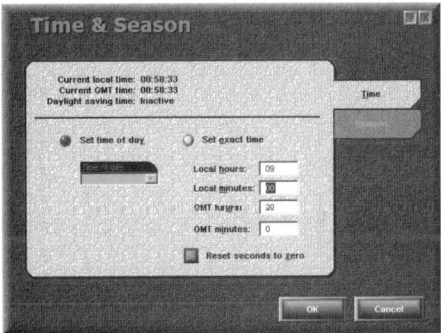

Click OK to continue. If you only see the instrument panel and a dark screen at Bellows, it's still nighttime in Hawaii. If so, go to the **World | Time & Season** menu. Set the exact time to "09" local hours and "00" local minutes (see the image on the right).

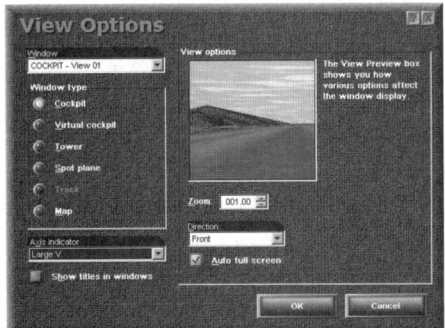

Enable the Axis Indicator from the **Views | View Options** menu. Choose *Large V* in the Axis Indicator list box. The Axis Indicator will help you align the helicopter to the horizon and coordinate the landing better (see the image on the bottom right).

Click OK to continue. The normal weather at Bellows includes high winds that are treacherous for helicopters. We prefer a calm morning for this exercise, so click **World | Weather...** and set the winds to *None*.

61

Click OK to continue.

Then it's time for takeoff. Your assignment is to take off from Bellows airport, climb to an altitude of 1,000 feet and turn to a 110° heading. Then begin the approach to the destination airport at Kaneohe Bay. In this exercise, it's a good idea to save the flight situation after the takeoff and climb before the landing approach.

The Bell 206B JetRanger starts in Bellows on runway 36 and lands in Kaneohe Bay on runway 22. Therefore, you'll start facing exact north (N=36=360 degrees) and will land in a southwesterly direction (22=220 degrees).

The runways are numbered by the direction in which takeoffs or

What runway numbers mean

Runway names may seem a bit peculiar. Bellows airport has six runways for takeoffs and landings. However, they are not numbered 1 through 6 as you might think. Instead, they're numbered 12/30, 7/25, 3/21, 13/31, 18/36, 4/22.

The numbers reflect the magnetic compass orientation for each runway with the last digit in the degree number removed. So, airport runway numbers range from 1 (=10°) to 36 (=360°). Runway 3 has a 30° heading and 33 has a 330° heading. North on the compass (N) stands for 000° (also for 360° since it's a great circle).

Compass Degrees	Direction
36 or N 360°	North
9 or E 090°	East
18 or S 180°	South
27 or W 270°	West

landings occur. Therefore, runway 36 is also runway 18, depending upon which direction you're flying. Once again, the last place of the degree number is not used. If you see the number 36 on the runway, it means you're taking off exactly towards north. The 18 faces in the opposite direction (to the south). If an L or an R appears on the runway, it means two runways, a right and a left one, have the same orientation.

Since Bellows airport is already shut down, runway markings are no longer appropriate. This is why you don't see a 36.

Takeoff And The 110° Turn

We've already talked about the takeoff maneuver so we won't describe this maneuver here.

We'll once again follow the route shown on page 60. Press [Shift]+[]] to display the Map window so you can compare the current flight position with the illustration. It's very important that you click the instrument panel with the left mouse button after displaying the map window.

After takeoff we'll climb to an altitude of 1,000 feet and remain there for approximately four minutes. During the climb, keep your eyes on the direction gyro and the attitude indicator. The direction gyro must always point north.

When the altimeter reads 1,000 feet, change to straight, horizontal flight. The white center line in the attitude indicator is again almost in the middle between the two white lines. The vertical speed indicator (VSI) is moving to zero. Now check the course. It has probably deviated slightly from the northerly direction (N). However, that's not serious. If so, correct the deviation by moving the joystick or mouse slightly to the left or the right. However, if you deviated from the course by more than five degrees, don't correct it. In this case, we will end the 110° turn a little earlier or later, depending on in which direction the aircraft drifted. There's no reason to panic. We will now continue flying a few minutes on heading 360° (N). Hold the airspeed at 100 knots.

You should begin the turn to a 110° heading at around 9:06. Move the controls (meaning the joystick or the mouse) to the left. Watch the turn coordinator. The white tip should be pointing at the small white dot on the left. Keep the helicopter in this position until the HSI is on 21. Now go back to the straight flight. The HSI should read 20 after you resume the straight flight. Now your approach to the destination airport of Kaneohe Bay begins.

The Approach And The Landing

We already described the landing maneuvers in our exercise for the sightseeing tour over London. If you haven't yet done this exercise or still having problems landing, reread those steps.

1. Before the descent, reduce speed to around 50 knots.

2. You need to be at an altitude of 1,000 feet.

3. Locate the Kaneohe Bay airport. It should be directly in front of you if you accurately followed the Bellows takeoff and 110° turn. (Adjust the zoom under **View | View Options** if necessary.)

4. Press ⓘ to save the flight situation so you can repeat the approach and the landing in case your first attempt crashes.

    Select a small approach angle for the landing so the helicopter doesn't come down for a landing at 140 knots, which would mean an abrupt end to the flight. We will calculate the time required for the descent. The speed of vertical descent should amount to a maximum of 700 feet per minute from an altitude of 1,000 feet.

    1,000 feet / 700 feet/min = 1 minute and 26 seconds, which we will figure for the descent.

5. We begin the approach 300 meters before the coast. We have specified a point in the sketch where the descent should begin. During the descent, fix the axis coordinator on the rear third of the runway.

6. You should descend at about 700 feet per minute (the vertical speed indicator should move to the lower seven).

7. Maintain the speed between 60 to 70 knots by adjusting the pitch control (using the F2 and F3 keys).

At an altitude of about 800 feet, adjust the rotor torque to about 40% using the pitch control and prepare for a landing. Shortly before the landing, the helicopter should descend only slightly and must be hovering when it touches down. This means that the turbine performance should be increased to about 60% shortly before touching down to reduce the rate of vertical descent.

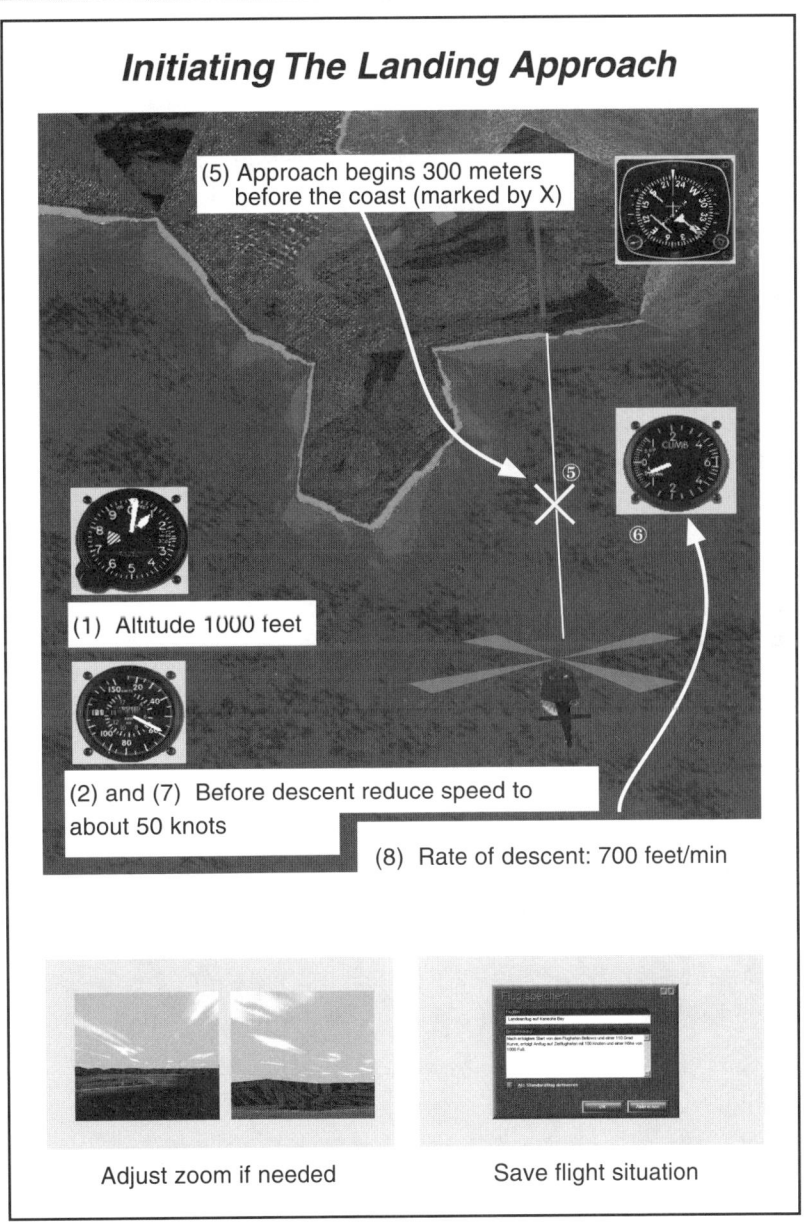

Initiating The Landing Approach

(5) Approach begins 300 meters before the coast (marked by X)

(1) Altitude 1000 feet

(2) and (7) Before descent reduce speed to about 50 knots

(8) Rate of descent: 700 feet/min

Adjust zoom if needed

Save flight situation

1 Oil Temperature
2 Torque
3 Indicated Airspeed
4 Outer Marker
5 Middle Marker
6 Inner Marker
7 Outside Air Temperature
8 Attitude Indicator
9 Altitude Indicator
10 Vertical Speed Indicator
11 Horiztonal Situation Indicator
12 Rotator (NR)/Turbine (N2) Speed
13 Turbine Temperature

14 Transmission Oil Temperature
15 Fuel Quantity
16 Gas Producers
17 Turn Indicator
18 Open Radio Stack
19 Left/Right Cyclic
20 Fore/Aft Cyclic
21 Anti-Torque Rotor Indicator
22 VOR 2 Indicator
23 ADF Indicator
24 Clock
25 Fuel Pressure

The computer instrument panel of the Bell 206B JetRanger

Bell 206B JetRanger Background Information

For nearly 50 years, Bell Helicopter, the world's most experienced helicopter manufacturer, has been dedicated to designing and building the best aircraft in the industry. An example of that is the legendary 206B JetRanger.

This helicopter has accomplished more missions has flown more hours, and has set (and broken) more industry records than any other aircraft in the world. Ever.

The Bell 206B JetRanger is one of the most popular general purpose helicopters ever built. It's used in many areas from corporate to construction, airborne law enforcement to electronic news gathering, military training to scenic tours.

It features a two blade, semirigid main rotor. A tail rotor provides directional control. It's equipped with an Allison Model 250-C20B or 250-C20J turbine engine flat rated to 317 shaft horsepower. The fuselage is covered by metal and fiberglass. An all-metal tailboom supports the vertical fin, fixed horizontal stabilizer, tail rotor and tail rotor drive system. The landing skids can be equipped with pop-out or fixed floats for landing on water.

Bell 206B JetRanger Specifications	
Length	31 feet 3.5 inches
Height	11 feet 7.5 inches
Rotor span	33.33 feet
Weight (empty)	1,780 pounds
Maximum weight (in-flight)	3,200 pounds
Maximum speed	241 km/h
Ceiling	4,115 miles
Maximum climb rate	396 m/min
Normal operating speed	0-241 km/h
Fuel capacity	91 gallons

Choose between five flights

Besides your original flights, you may also pilot the JetRanger on many flights provided by Microsoft especially for the Bell 206B. Click **Flights | Lessons...** to practice takeoffs and landings at Meigs field (FS's Preflight Briefings have more information on these lessons). Click **Flights | Challenges...** to push your skills to the limit flying inside of an aircraft carrier.

Five additional JetRanger situations are available by clicking **Flights | Select Flight...** and selecting one of the Bell 206B situations:

Bell206B - Hop, Skip and Jump

Depart from the municipal heliport in the center of Manhattan, fly to Wall Street and land on top of Wall Street 111, then continue your flight to the helipad atop the World Trade Center.

Starting the "Bell 206B - Hop, Skip and Jump" flight.

Bell206B - Oakland Rooftop

The Bell 206B JetRanger is ready for departure on the roof of the Oakland Convention Center.

Starting the "Bell 206B - Oakland Rooftop" flight.

Bell206B - San Francisco Roof

Start from the roof of the San Francisco Hall of Justice and fly to Alcatraz, where you can practice takeoffs and landings on the heliport. The weather can become very unpleasant on this flight.

Bell206B - Vegas Strip

Fly around the famous, magnificent buildings of the Las Vegas strip. You can increase the difficulty by hovering to read the marquees and billboards.

Flying the "Bell 206B - Vegas Strip" flight.

Bell206B - World Trade Center

Depart from one of the towers of the World Trade Center for a tour through the streets of New York City.

Starting the "Bell 206B - World Trade Ctr" flight.

Flying the JetRanger in other flight situations

In addition, you can fly the JetRanger with almost any flight situation by loading the flight and selecting the Bell 206B in the **Aircraft | Select Aircraft...** menu

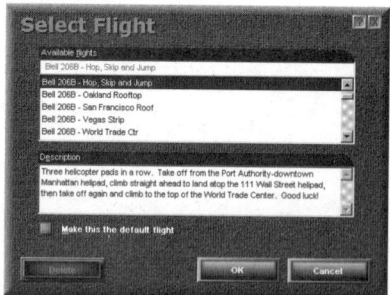

*Select the **Flights | Select Flight...** command*
for additional JetRanger situations

Chapter 3
Putting Multiplayer
To The Test

C hapter 3 describes the new multiplayer mode which can lead to a totally new simulator experience for you. Chapter 3 talks about the basics of connecting two or more computers as well as using Flight Simulator on networks and online. We'll also look at the Fly-ins that invite simmers around the world and that occur several times a year.

Multiplayer

A lthough a popular feature with Flight Simulator version 5/5.1, multiplayer features were not included in Flight Simulator for Windows 95 due to the changeover to DirectX technology. Now, however, it's fully integrated in Flight Simulator 98. This means you can use FS98 on two computers that are connected, on a network or fly the Internet with an almost unlimited number of sim pilots.

If you're not satisfied with normal flights—by yourself and without any communication—you can use several Flight Simulator "player" options, along with flight hours, flight lessons and flight adventures. You can participate in various flight competitions and stunt flights. You can even risk your neck in aptitude tests

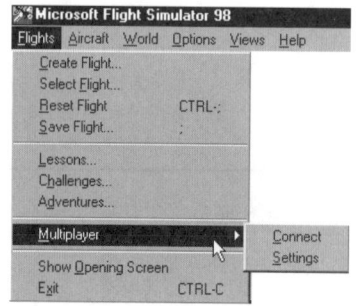

above and below obstacles. The most interesting option, however, is the multiplayer mode. It lets two or more connected computers fly with one another.

Multiplayer mode provides several options for filling the virtual sky of Flight Simulator:

✈ Direct cable connection using the serial port.

✈ Network connection on a local computer network.

✈ Telephone connection between two computers with modems.

✈ Connection to the Internet with a modem or ISDN.

The direct cable connection

You can connect two computers to each other through the serial ports COM 1, 2 or 3. The program exchanges data through this port with the second computer running Flight Simulator 98.

If both computers are in the same room, you can connect them directly to each other using a simple cable. The null modem cable has at least five conductors and has a 9-pin or 25-pin connector on both ends.

Plug the two cable ends into the serial ports of both computers and start Flight Simulator 98 on both computers. The data transfer between the computers starts from the **Flights I Multiplayer** menu. You'll first see the welcome screen to the multiplayer connection. Then a dialog box opens where you'll enter your name, call signal and the ID by which your airplane will be detected in the scenery.

Telephone connection

If the computers are too far from each other to be connected with the null modem cable, you'll have to use a normal telephone line. Both computers should be connected to the telephone using modems to send and receive data.

Besides a normal telephone connection, you can also use an ISDN line that transmits data at a much higher rate. Today's modems can transmit up to 33,600 bits per second, an ISDN connection increases the data transfer rate to 64,000 bits per second on one channel.

Local network connection

As soon as several computers are connected to each other on a network, they can exchange data of any type using the IPX or TCP/IP transmission methods. These are the standards in almost every computer network. A local network connection is usually used for exchanging texts, graphics, tables, spreadsheets and other office tasks. However, you could also have Flight Simulator 98 installed on two or more computers—and then it's up, up and away.

The Internet connection

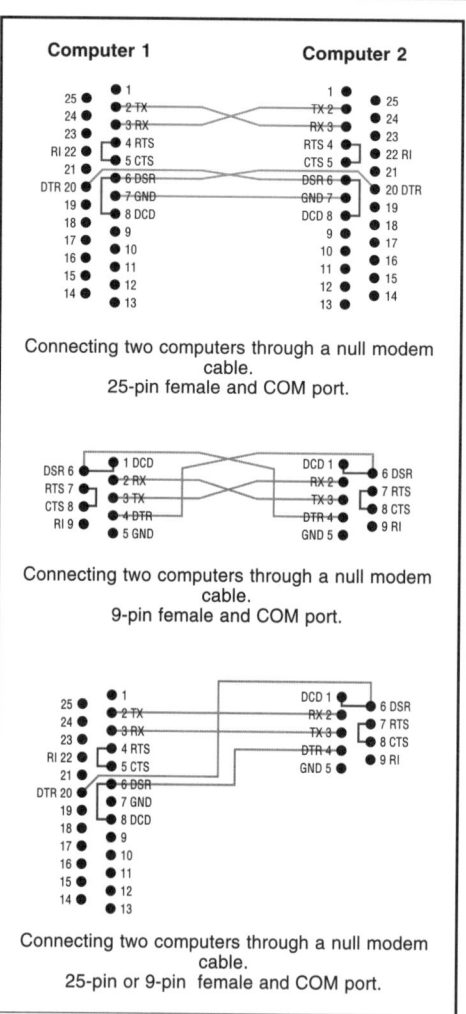

Connecting two computers through a null modem cable.
25-pin female and COM port.

Connecting two computers through a null modem cable.
9-pin female and COM port.

Connecting two computers through a null modem cable.
25-pin or 9-pin female and COM port.

A long distance telephone connection between two computers can become quite expensive. Network connections are usually limited to an office building. So how can you meet other flight simmers cheaply from home? Do your flying on the Internet.

The Internet has many options for virtual pilots. Online information services such as CompuServe or AOL have also opened forums and libraries of virtual aviation and are creating "airspaces" with almost unlimited opportunities.

An Internet connection, like telephones, is done using a modem or an ISDN adapter. The great advantage of the Internet is you probably only need to pay for the Internet service provider.

Multiplayer connection

If you have the simple direct cable connection between two computers, you can join an existing session as a *Guest* on the second computer. You can also create a new connection yourself as the *Host* and define the connection as a *New Session*. Enter a session name in the dialog box that follows. This name in a manner of speaking is declared as "airspace" for the other computer. After specifying the number of participants (with this direct connection, the only possible number is two), you can exit this dialog box by choosing *Continue* to specify the conditions of the connection.

Follow these steps to determine the transfer configuration by null modem cable (serial connection):

✈ Choose the serial port of computer No. 1 as the Port. The list box shows some of the possible ports (COM1, COM2, etc.).

✈ The baud rate determines the speed of the data transfer (1 baud = 1 bit per second). Therefore, choose the maximum baud rate allowed by the ports of both computers. Try the transfer with 57600 baud or more.

75

→ The default settings of Flight Simulator 98 are generally suitable for specifying stop bits, parity and protocol.

→ All the settings of the serial connection must be identical on both computers. The only exception is the COM port address.

Multiplayer connections on an existing computer network occur through IPX or TCP/IP, depending on which method is used within the local network. If you aren't sure which method is used, the network administrator will be able to tell you. With an existing connection on the local network, the Flight Simulator will search for other computers that also have the simulator started. The connection

Other aircraft

Make the following settings for a modem connection using a telephone:

1. Select the modem connected to the computer in the Modem connection dialog box.
2. Enter the telephone number of your flying partner.

It's as easy as making a phone call!

to the Internet is made by the Internet TCP/IP connection. To jump into an existing session, you have to enter the address of the host Internet computer.

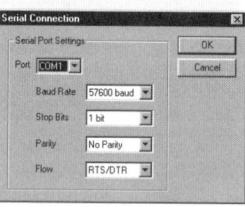

This is normally the name of the computer, such as myflyin.com, or the Internet number, for example, 112.233.45.67. If you do not know the address, in either Enter a session name, case you could call the host pilot. He will readily tell you his Internet name and/or Host IP number.

After setting the parameters, you can begin. The next dialog box is used to enter an existing session or—as in the mentioned example—to open a session as a host. The selected session name, the number of participating pilots and any spectators appear in the text window. With a successful connection to the second computer, the (Connect) button becomes active, and the show can begin.

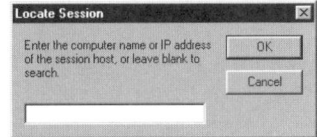

In contrast to the direct cable or modem connection between two computers, up to 255 pilots and as many spectators can participate on a local network or the Internet.

The first meeting

A few seconds after going online, the coordinates of the other airplane are received in the computer and your own coordinates are sent to the other computer. At the same time, both computers exchange aircraft types during the data transfer when the "Visual Details" option is enabled in the Session Setting dialog box. Another window also appears on the screen that lists all the participants with their names and IDs. This window is also used for communicating between pilots since it has an area for inputting text and a (Send) button.

If both FS98 programs are started up with the airplanes in the same position (for example, with one of the default flight situations), there won't immediately be much new to see. Both airplanes will be drawn on the screen from the internal perspective, as normal. However, if you switch to spot plane view (by pressing (S) three times), you will probably see both airplanes next to each other (or one on top of the other).

Have one of the two airplanes taxi forward slowly over the runway. Watch the procedure with the different cockpit views from the front and the rear (press `Num Lock` key for view mode and the appropriate direction key `2` or `8` on the numeric keypad). Once the planes have released themselves from their "Siamese connection," you can see them in a cockpit view. Depending on the configuration in the Settings dialog box, you will also be able to read the name or the marker of the airplane in the form of a text banner on the tail.

To familiarize yourself and to check for secure data transfer between the computers, do a couple taxi exercises on the ground with your fellow pilot. Use the taxiways, the apron and the runways to gather your first experiences. Also, try to estimate the distance to the other airplane and its size when you approach it on the runways. This is valuable help in estimating your own speed and size.

Exercises And Flying A Duet

Now taxi together (one after the other, please) to the starting point, get clearance for takeoff for each plane from the tower and take off. During the takeoff, use the view mode buttons and remain in visual contact with the other plane from the cockpit. The second (referring to the takeoff sequence) plane will definitely have a harder time following the first one.

This is why constant communication between pilots must occur. The values for speed, altitude and heading are the most important. If the pilots are not in the same room, this data exchange will occur using the program's internal text transmission.

Type the text to be transmitted into the message field and click the `Send` button to transmit this text to your fellow pilot. Your message is displayed on his screen.

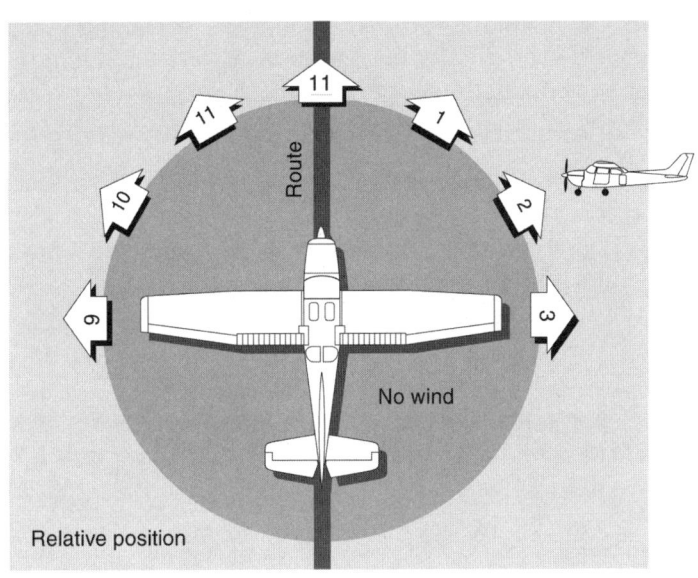

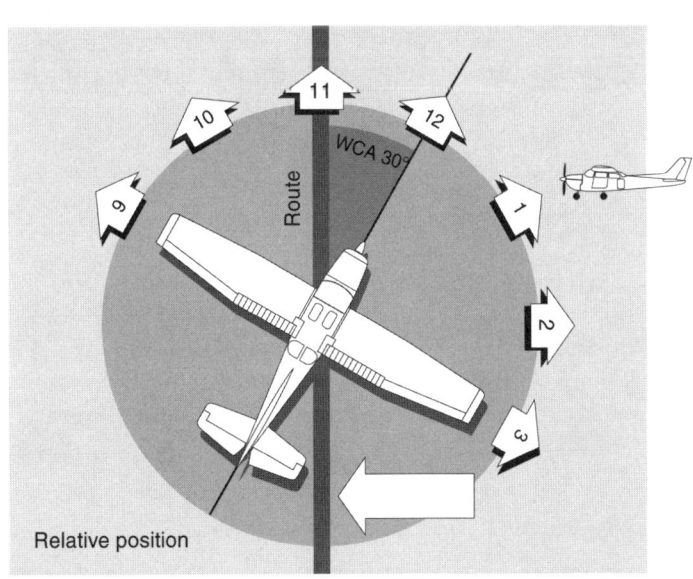

If one of the spectators or another pilot observes what is happening in the sky, he can track the movements of the aircraft and if necessary, respond to a possible collision course. He reports the potentially dangerous situation to one of the pilots and gives him a direction reference to the other aircraft.

The information about the direction for the pilot refers to his own line of vision and is not specified as an angle in degrees, but rather as a time position. This time specification corresponds to the position of the hour hand on a clock face, with the twelve o'clock position straight in front of the cockpit.

For example, if a second airplane is spotted at an angle to the first airplane, the controller reports:

> *D-E... there is traffic in your three o'clock position, three miles.*

The pilot then knows that another plane is on his right side, three miles away, and is possibly flying on a collision course.

By the way: The time specification always assumes the winds are calm. When the winds are calm the airplane will fly straight on its way above ground, uninfluenced. However, when there are crosswinds, the pilot will fly a correction angle into the wind, which keeps the airplane on the air route. The observer does not know this angle, he only knows the path above ground. Let us assume that the wind is so strong that the correction angle amounts to 30° to the right, then the controller would report a 2:00 position, but the pilot finds the other airplane in the 1:00 position. This is because the pilot has steered into the wind, changing his relative position.

Settings

Multiplayer mode provides additional resources for tracking the other plane. For example, if you set the Automatic Direction Finder (ADF) at the frequency of 000.0 KHz, the pointer will immediately point in the direction of the other airplane. Use the pursuit plane view mode, which you can reach by pressing Ⓢ, or press the zoom key ⊞ to "catch" the other airplane.

You can also use the Distance measuring Equipment (DME) device in your search for a potential partner in the sky. Its data will then refer to the direct distance between the two airplanes. This resource can even serve as an anti-collision warning device.

The autopilot is your third method for locating another nearby airplane. If the HDG (heading) and ALT (altitude) functions are enabled, the airplane will automatically steer in the direction and altitude of the second airplane.

Seeing and being seen

To prevent problems during a multiplayer event, certain rules of aviation must be observed. The VFR pilot, that is, the purely visual flier, must constantly monitor his air space to avoid dangerous approaches or a collision with another airplane. It is his task to watch the outside. To be seen in the twilight or at night, the airplane must have clearly visible lighting. The legally required navigational lights must be switched on at these times.

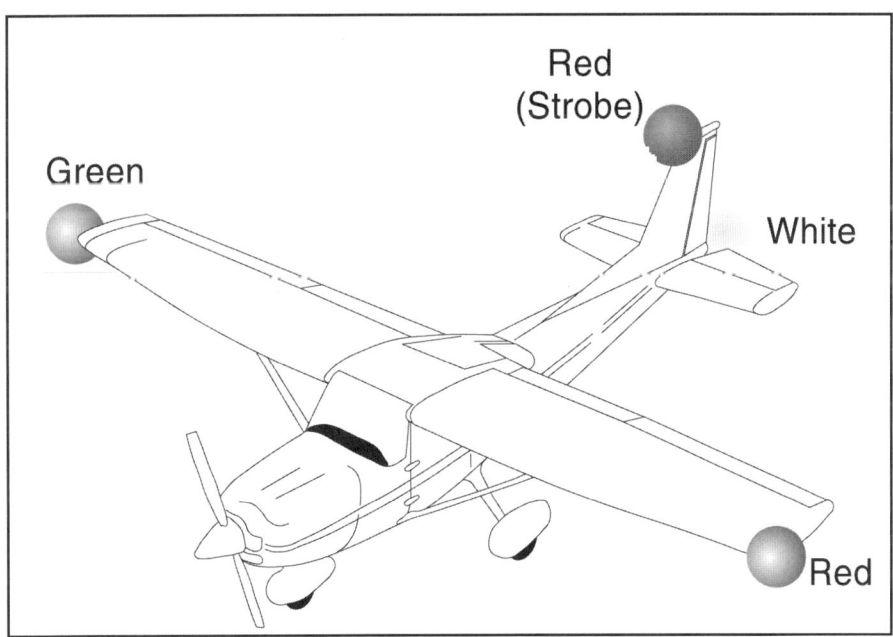

The location of the navigation lights

The navigation lights are on the wing ends (a red position light on the left side and a green position light on the right side) and on the tail (a white strobe light) of the airplane. Larger airplanes also have anticollision lights above and below on the fuselage.

Obviously you're in deep trouble if you see a green light on the left, a red light on the right and both collision lights. In this case, the other plane is flying directly at you!

Be a good host

The multiplayer function in Flight Simulator 98 automatically oversees data exchange between computers. So, it is also possible to arrange a meeting yourself. To do this, declare yourself the host in a new session and create the connection parameters:

The Host Options dialog box follows and prompts you for a session name.

The maximum number of active pilots and the number of spectators depends on the connection type and on your computer's performance. Too many participants can cause a data jam at the transmission interfaces or simply overstrain the multiplayer function.

It's easy to find out your own address on a network, especially on the Internet. Click the Windows 95 [Start] button and select **Run...** Type "C:\Windows\Winipcfg.exe" into the dialog box. This file contains the IP configuration of the connected network card and the host information, with the host name and the DNS server number.

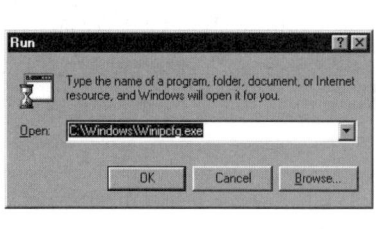
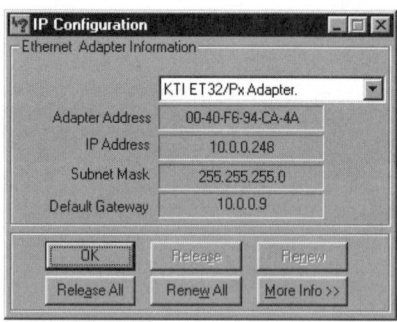

To ensure that your flight is a success, you will have to do the proper advertising. That means announcing the meeting with a date, time and connection type (telephone number, Internet address or the like). At the time agreed upon, the host opens the event.

Here are two examples from the Multiplayer Club of the Flight Simulator Forum in CompuServe that have advertised as hosts for specific meetings on the network:

> *Flight plan / details for the FS98 multi-pilot (MP) flight on Saturday November 1st, at 17:00 EST / 23:00 CET / 22:00 UTC (GMT) or 14:00 PST.*
>
> *Host IP address will be posted one hour prior to start in the Club Multiplayer (sec 16) message board at 16:00 EST / 22:00 CET / 21:00 UTC / 13:00 PST. Uploaded by Kemal Danisman.*

The second host specifies the upcoming meeting for specific, very fast military airplanes and gives a reference to the sceneries he is using. He concludes his ad with the specification of his IP host number:

> *Hi Multipilot fliers,*
>
> *I will be hosting a flight tonight at 19:00 EST. This flight will start at KRME, Griffiss AFB and hopefully end at CYYQ Churchill Manitoba. I don't have a neat theme for this flight like Kemal would, it is just a flight mission from point A to point B. I will be flying an F105 and would like to see other high performance jets as well. I could use a C17 or two in the flight and I need a KC135 to refuel us at YMO, Moosenee.*
>
> *If interested in flying tonight I will be online at 18:30 EST to set up the flight. I recommend using both NNYS2V.ZIP and CHURCHIL.ZIP for scenery. And here is the IP: 206.175.185.43. Hope to see you out there*
>
> *... Joel*

Off to the Internet

The Internet has become the meeting place for Flight Simulator enthusiasts. Using this kind of connection, up to 255 fliers from the entire world can convene and exploit the multiplayer function. Select the **Flights | Multiplayer | Connect** command.

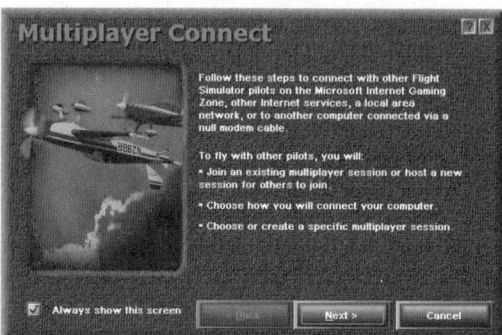

Then click the (Next>) button to open the following window:

Click the "Find other pilots to fly with on the Internet" option.

The operating expenses for a session depend on access to the Internet. If the dial-up site to the network is favorable, only charges for a local telephone call will be due.

Also, there are the fees for the Internet service provider. It can become more expensive if the Internet service charges by the amount of data transmitted. Flight Simulator 98 will have transmitted about 2 MB of information with an hour of multiplayer operation. A comparison of costs among the providers can help you save more than a couple dollars.

If you wish to click into any existing event, you can have Flight Simulator 98 automatically perform the search for you. Microsoft offers a special Web site for this purpose called the Internet Gaming Zone (http://www.zone.com).

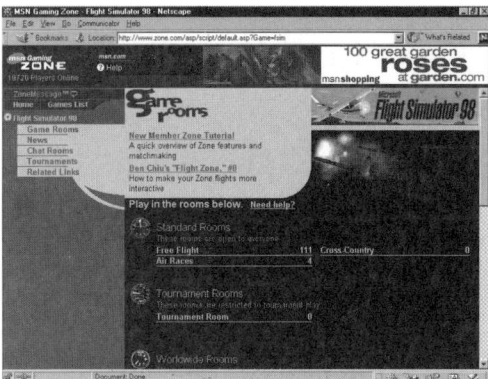

Meanwhile, knowledge about this address has gotten around, so the page is hopelessly overcrowded almost all the time. Waiting lines are not out of the ordinary.

The data and flight traffic run a bit more smoothly in the forums of CompuServe or AOL with specialized Flight Simulator homepages. One especially interesting address belongs to SimFlight (http://www.simflight.com). It also has software for virtual pilots.

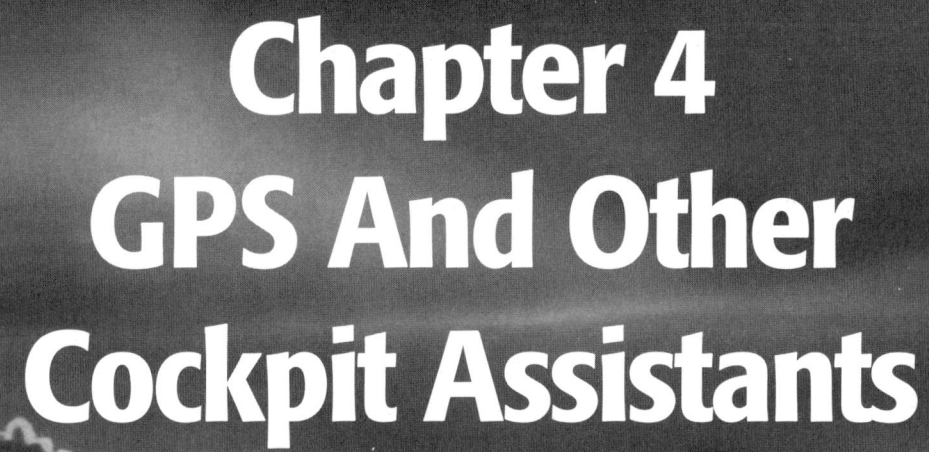

Chapter 4
GPS And Other
Cockpit Assistants

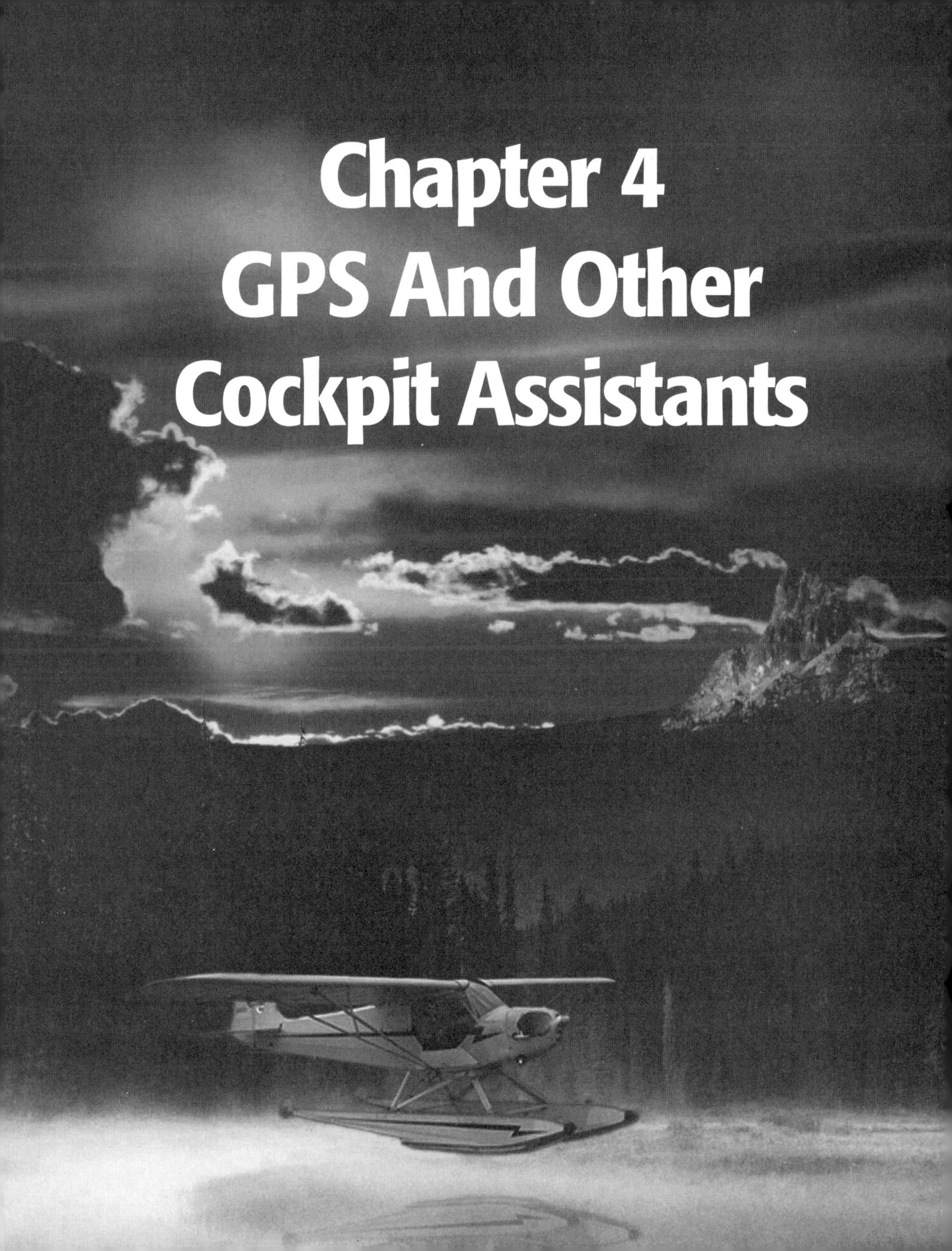

Chapter 4 opens by exploring satellite navigation using the Global Positioning System. Then we explore the CoPilot flight planning/GPS program from the onboard features to using it in flight. The following section discusses the weather, specifically the weather messages that can be so important for the pilot. Finally, we present a series of checklists that can be an indispensable help before taking off and while enroute.

GPS (Global Positioning System) is a hot topic of conversation everywhere today. Military aircraft, for which this project was designed several years ago, use this system to determine their flight routes and target objects. Today, commercial pilots and general aviators use GPS just as routinely. Even gliding—especially in competitive events—now relies heavily on GPS technology.

Using satellites for navigation has long been common on the ground and the water. Even automobiles are already being guided across the country with the help of GPS. The captains and navigators aboard countless ships are relying more on the "artificial stars" of the GPS. It seems likely that GPS will replace all other conventional navigation systems—primarily NDB and VOR—within a few years. GPS provides all the necessary data and facts, from takeoff to landing, for flawless navigation.

How GPS Works

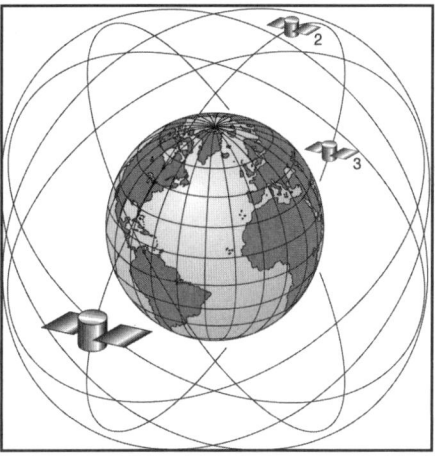

The position of an object in three-dimensional space—whether it's a glider, business jet, ship or automobile—is calculated according to trigonometric rules. To accomplish this, you need at least three arc-shaped lines from three precisely known measuring points that intersect at a point in space. With at least two measuring points, a single location can be determined in a single plane without altitude data. To meet these requirements, the USA and Russia have placed a ring of satellites around the earth. The American-named Global Positioning System (GPS) uses 24 satellites (21 navigational and three active spares) in six orbits. The Russian Global Orbiting Navigation System (GLONASS) also uses 21 satellites, but in three orbits.

This large number of measuring satellites provides virtually optimum conditions. The GPS receiver can filter from the given signals precisely those that are best suited for determining position. The distances from the receiver to the satellites lie on ellipsoids which should intersect at as obtuse an angle as possible.

The time that a GPS signal requires to travel from the satellite to the receiver is measured to calculate that satellite's distance. Electronic signals are assumed to move at the speed of light (300,000 km/second). This requires very precise time measurement, which is accomplished by the satellites with astounding accuracy through the use of atomic clocks (each satellite carries four atomic clocks). A measuring error of only 1/100 second would throw off a position calculation by 3,000 km.

Time measurement errors				
1 sec	=	300,000 km	=	161,987 NM
1/100 sec	=	3,000 km	=	1,619 NM
1/10,000 sec	=	30 km	=	16.2 NM
1/1,000,000 sec	=	300 m	=	0.16 NM

The accuracy of the military system, in which each receiver contains a computer to interpret the signals of a minimum of three satellites, is within nanoseconds. This results in a three-dimensional accuracy of an incredible 30 centimeters and puts even precision landing procedures using conventional ILS to shame. However, the CA (Coarse Acquisition) signal contains a deliberate error in its transmission that makes the signal most civilians can receive accurate to about ± 100 meters (although in practice the error is closer to 50 meters) 95% of the time. The accuracy is ± 300 meters the rest of the time. The Precise Positioning System (PPS), only available to the military), doesn't contain this error

The geometric positions of the satellites with respect to each other and the deflection of signal paths as they pass through the atmosphere, which causes time delays of different magnitudes, can also cause errors. A multipath error is caused by signals reflected from surfaces near the receiver, which can either interfere with or be mistaken for the signal that follows the straight-line path from the satellite. Multipath errors are difficult to detect and sometimes hard to avoid.

To eliminate the "naturally caused" errors as much as possible, sophisticated GPS receivers always use multiple signals from as many satellites as possible. This permits delay errors to be detected and filtered out, creating optimum reception conditions.

Flight Simulator isn't affected by these technical problems. By virtue of its programming, it always knows its position precisely and readily displays it on the screen. For flight planning using various position points, an additional utility is available called CoPilot by Abacus.

Using A Trial Version of CoPilot

You can download a trial edition of CoPilot from the Abacus website (www.abacuspub.com) to use with FS98, FS95 or FS5.1. Although it doesn't have the enhanced GPS of V2.0, it will give you an idea of how useful a flight planning utility can be.

At the Abacus website, click the "Download Trial Version!" button (shown on the right). This will open the following window:

Download
Trial Edition!

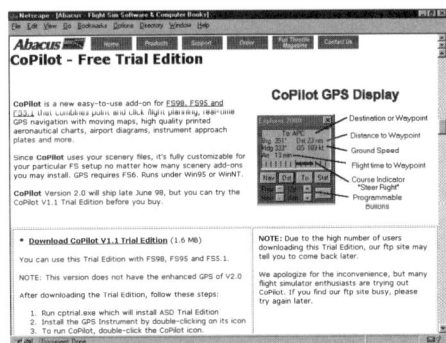

Then follow the online instructions downloading the CoPilot trial version.

Before using the trial version of CoPilot, you must first install the GPS instrument. Double-click the GPS Install icon in the CoPilot folder (see image top of next page). The install is almost instant. When the installation is completed press [Enter] to close the window. The GPS Installation copies a file called fs6ipc.dll to your Microsoft Flight Simulator \Modules folder. We're almost ready to start CoPilot.

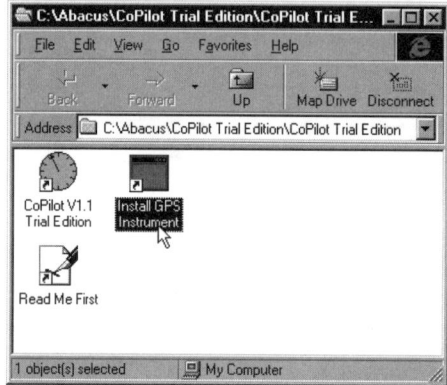

CoPilot displays navigational aids and airports by reading the same scenery data files that your Flight Simulator does. To do this, CoPilot must know:

1. Which version of FS you installed and where it was installed. Select the appropriate FS version - FS98, FS6 or FS 5.1. (Since you're using FS98, all the installation information here for CoPilot is for FS98.)

2. The drive letter for your CD-ROM drive. Many FS98's airports are kept on your CD-ROM (called *booster files*) and are not installed on your hard drive.

3. The path for your FS scenery.

CoPilot attempts to find the Scenery directory for your version of Microsoft Flight Simulator. The "FS SCENERY Path" edit box should contain the path to the SCENERY folder of your FS98. If not, click [...] to choose your directory. For example:

C:\FS98\SCENERY

Making aircraft compatible

You may need to insert the FS98 booster CD into your CD-ROM drive before you click the [Finish] button. Otherwise, none of the airports for the US Northwest will be displayed.

CoPilot will verify the information before you can continue. If it is incorrect, you can correct it or continue. If the information is not correct, CoPilot will be unable to automatically construct scenery file data sets.

After you've clicked the [Finish] button, CoPilot will construct several default scenery sets from the scenery data files included with FS98. It will also construct scenery sets for many of the popular commercial add on sceneries that you may have installed.

Using CoPilot

This section shows how to create and then fly your own flight plans using CoPilot's flight planning and GPS features. When you start CoPilot, you first normally select a map and scenery of the graphical area you'll want to fly. However, this trial version of CoPilot works only with the Washington state map and scenery area. Therefore, the **File | Open Scenery Files...** command remains ghosted.

Before you instruct CoPilot to create your flight plan (and after the Washington scenery map appears on the screen), select the **Navigation | Auto Route** command. Make certain a checkmark appears to indicate the Auto Route is active.

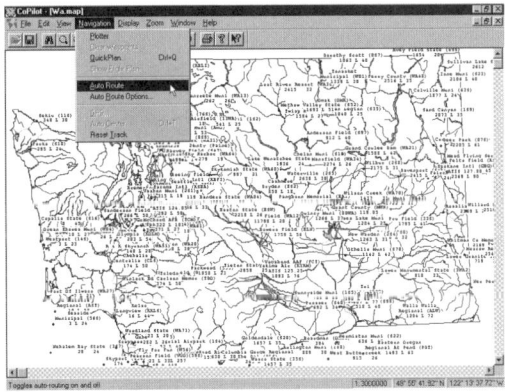

Creating a flight plan

CoPilot lets you create (and print) realistic flight plans quickly and easily from the scenery and airport data in your Flight Simulator's Scenery directory. Although three methods are available to create your custom flight plans, we will show you how to create your first flight plan using CoPilot's QuickPlan.

If you want to learn how to create flight plans using the other two methods (QuickPlan icon and quick Find icon), select **Help | Help Topics | CoPilot commands...**.

Select the **Navigation | QuickPlan...** command to open the QuickPlan window. In the area below the "Depart From:" box, use the scroll down bar to select "Arlington Muni" airport. Then click it one time. Notice that "Arlington Muni" appears in the "Depart From:" box.

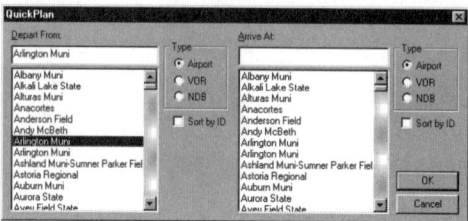

In the box below "Arrive At:" use the scroll down bar to select "Sanderson Field" and click it once. Notice "Sanderson Field" appears in the "Arrive At:" box.

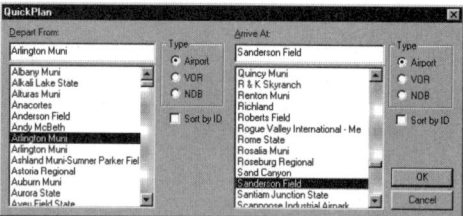

Click OK to continue. Click **File | Print...** to print a copy of your first flight plan. This is a simple flight plan to show you how the capabilities work.

Waypoint	ID Freq	Elev	Position	To Next Waypoint		
				Course	Distance	Comments
Arlington Muni	AWO	135	N 48° 09.7'	198T	15.2 nm	
			W122° 09.7'	178M		
PAINE	PAE	669	N 47° 55.2'	221T	54.2 nm	
VOR	110.60		W122° 16.7'	201M	15.2 nm	
Sanderson Field	SHN	266	N 47° 14.0'			
			W123° 08.9'		69.4 nm	

You can use the Zoom Tool (the magnifier icon on the tool bar) to increase the magnification of the flight path. The flight path is represented by a green line on the map connecting the Arlington Muni and Sanderson airports.

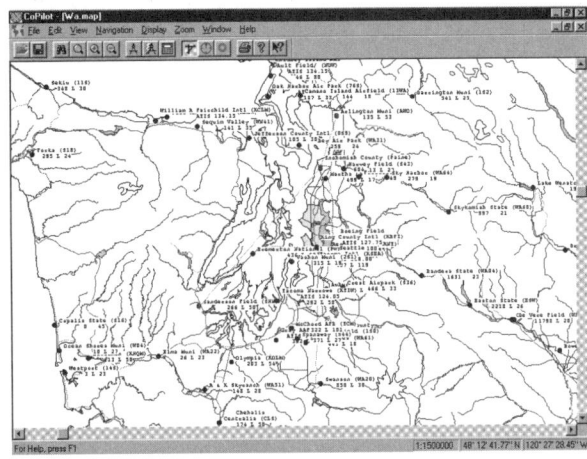

Flying a flight plan created by CoPilot

Now start Flight Simulator. Select the **World | Goto Airport...** command. (You may also want to click the New Search button.) Make certain "United States" is selected for the "Country" and

Making aircraft compatible

To increase the viewable area of the CoPilot map, you can turn off the Toolbar and Status Bar by selecting **View** on the toolbar and unselect them.

"Washington" is selected for the "State/province". Select "Arlington Muni" from the "Airport" scroll box and "Rwy 34" from the "Runway" scroll box. The window should like the following:

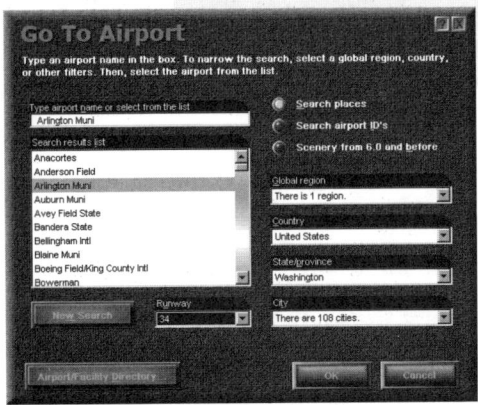

Then click OK to position yourself at the Arlington airport.

You're now ready to use the GPS Explorer 2000 instrument.

Running FS and CoPilot's GPS

Now you will need to turn on the GPS. Hold down the `Alt` key and press the `Tab` key until you're back to the CoPilot window. In the CoPilot graphic map window select the **Navigation | GPS** command (see image to the right).

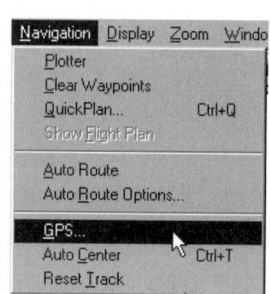

Next select the **Display | GPS Options** command and select **Both** (see image to the right).

This will display a '+' sign at your location (Arlington Muni in this example). It will also track your location on the **CoPilot** graphic map. In this exercise the complete flight is displayed in the window on your desktop. If the flight path goes beyond the viewing area displayed in the window, you may want to set the auto tracking to center the map based on your location. This will always keep your +' in the center, even if you fly past the window's border. Set it by selecting **Navigation | Auto Center**.

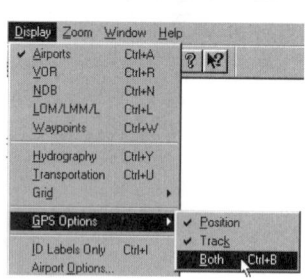

Using the GPS Explorer 2000 with your new flight plan

The Explorer 2000 is a GPS navigational aid that will help you easily reach your destination. It displays your plane's current position (longitude and latitude), altitude, heading, ground speed, bearing, distance remaining and arrival time to a specified destination. The destination in this example is Sanderson.

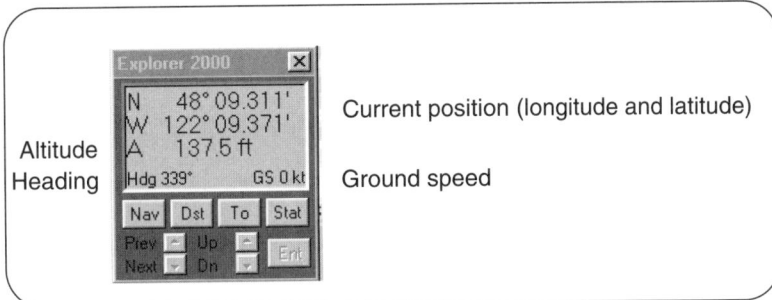

Before you begin your flight from Arlington to Sanderson using the GPS, you need to set your destination (Dst) in the Explorer 2000. When you turn on the GPS it automatically finds your location. For a more detailed explanation of the GPS Explorer 2000 and its many features select the **Help** command.

Click To on the Explorer 2000 panel and click the down arrow button beside **"Next"** until **"VOR"** is highlighted in the GPS window. This will be the VOR named PAE (the Paine VOR) which is displayed in the flight chart printout. Click Ent to select it.

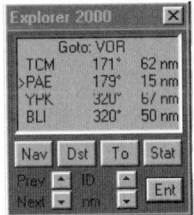

Click the down arrow button beside **Next** until PAE is highlighted and has a greater than sign to its left. Click Ent.

Click Dst (for destination) again. Notice the red slider bar. This is the CDI (Course Deviation Indicator) that represents the direction you need to fly to reach your destination (Sanderson in this exercise). If the red slider is to the left of the center line, you need to turn left. If the slider is to the right of center, fly right.

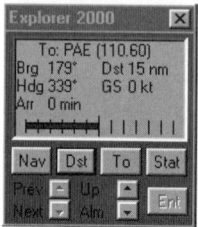

Now you're now ready to fly! By following the information in the GPS, you will arrive at the PAE VOR quickly.

You can also print aeronautical charts from map view. To view your flight on the CoPilot moving map, resize your windows so both FS and CoPilot are on the screen at the same time. You can also keep both CoPilot and FS in full screen and use the Alt + Tab key combination you can open the options menu in FS and remove the check from the box of front of Pause on Task switch.

By clicking on an airport (blue circle), you can view and print airport diagrams.

Seattle-Tacoma Intl (KSEA)

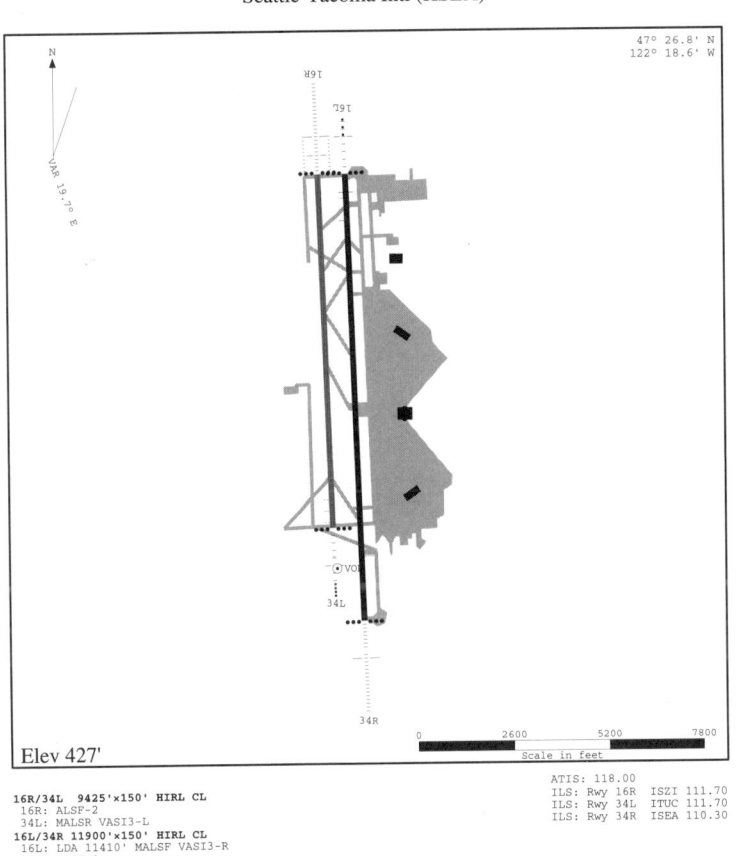

| 16R/34L 9425'x150' HIRL CL |
| 16R: ALSF-2 |
| 34L: MALSR VASI3-L |
| 16L/34R 11900'x150' HIRL CL |
| 16L: LDA 11410' MALSF VASI3-R |
| 34R: ALSF-1 |

ATIS: 118.00
ILS: Rwy 16R ISZI 111.70
ILS: Rwy 34L ITUC 111.70
ILS: Rwy 34R ISEA 110.30

By clicking on one of the runways at a larger airport that contains an ILS (e.g., Boeing Field - make sure to select **Display | ILS Transmitters**), you can view and print instrument approach plates.

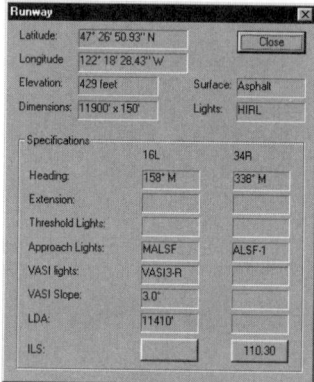

If you have a flight plan set, you'll need to use the **Display** menu to turn off the waypoints to view the airport diagrams. To turn the display of the waypoints on or off, use the Ctrl + W key combination or click the **Display** menu and chose **Waypoints**.

We've designed this trial copy of CoPilot to give you a good idea of its capabilities. If you'd like to order CoPilot, you can order from your local dealer or directly from Abacus.

GPS-VFR Maps

Air traffic control centers and commercial vendors have developed new map materials for the visual pilot that consider the special features of GPS navigation. For example, the required checkpoints in the control zones of larger airports are entered with their coordinates, speeding up the process of loading them into your own database. In addition, they also include all the other important entries that can be necessary for the VFR pilot:

- ✈ Frequencies of the flight information services and weather advisory
- ✈ Airspace classification and division
- ✈ Tables for the checkpoints and navigation beacons
- ✈ Conversion tables and graphics for various units
- ✈ Radius altitude rules

→   International alphabet and Morse code

These VFR maps are one alternative to the usual IFR route maps that are often included with add-on programs for Flight Simulator, since they also provide information about landscape details and teach you a little geography in the process. One of these vendors is the Jeppesen company, which publishes a complete VFR+GPS map series in a uniform scale of 1:500,000. The map set currently comprises Europe and is divided into several ICOA areas:

ED-1 to ED-6	Germany and adjoining countries
EG-1 to EG-4	Great Britain
EI-1	Ireland
EB/EH-1	Belgium and Holland
LF-1 to LF-7	France
LE-1 to LE-5	Spain
LP-1	Portugal
LO-1	Austria
LS-1	Switzerland
LI-1	Northern Italy

Sectional charts (United States)

The maps contain topographic detail with colored contours and altitude numbers, bodies of water, infrastructure, and city and settlement representations. The air traffic control imprint on the card contains airports (including glider and ultralight facilities) with their radio frequencies, altitudes, runway lengths, ICAO identifiers and coordinates, radio navigation aids with frequencies, identifier and coordinates, checkpoints and special air traffic obstacles, such as high smokestacks, towers, etc.

FS98 Checklists

You can call up checklists in FS for each aircraft type and for every standard flight condition. Checklists appear as "reminders." Of course, you must also be able to control your aircraft without checklists. However, these lists are indispensable checks for actions in the cockpit. In a short form, the pilot (or copilot) is shown the important points to check for takeoff, climb, cruise and descent, as well as for the landing.

You can customize the checklists in Flight Simulator 98 since they're simple text files in the corresponding Aircraft directory of FS98. The checklist for the Cessna 182S, for example, is the C182SCHK.CFG file in the \Flight Simulator98\Aircraft\C182 directory.

Use a simple text editor (like WordPad) to change the contents. Keep in mind, however, the number of characters you can use in your custom checklist is limited. Otherwise, there won't be enough space on the checklist sheet. Also, the aircraft model whose checklist you want to modify must be reloaded in order for the corrections to become effective. Only then will the corrected version of the checklist be initialized and displayed.

The first section of the checklist document, under [lists], shows the number and title of the checklists that will appear in FS's **Aircraft | Checklists** menu. The ampersand '&' character in front of a letter indicates that it will appear in the **Aircraft | Checklists** menu as an underlined entry representing a standard Windows keyboard shortcut. The text following the comma is the title of the checklist.

```
[lists]
0=&Takeoff, Takeoff Checklist
1=&Cruise, Cruise Checklist
2=&Descent, Descent Checklist
3=&Landing, Landing Checklist
```

The checklist points for the first checklist (Takeoff) are declared under [0]. The next checklist, Cruise, is identified by the numeral 1, and so on. The following lines show the predefined text of the checklists for the Cessna 182S:

```
[0]
0=Check flight controls.
1=Release brakes (Period [.]).
2=Smoothly increase throttle to full power (F3).
3=At about 60 knots, ease back on the stick and then relax the back
pressure.
4=Adjust pitch attitude to climb at 80-90 knots.
[1]
0=Establish level flight.
1=Set throttle at about 23 in. manifold pressure (F2 or F3) and prop at
2100-2400 RPM (CTRL+F2 or CTRL+F3).
2=Adjust elevator trim (NUMPAD 7 = nose down, NUMPAD 1 = nose up).
[2]
0=Reduce power to about 15 in. of manifold pressure (F2).
1=Relax pressure on the controls and the airplane will descend.
2=To level off, increase power to original cruise setting (F3).
[3]
0=Set power at about 15 in. of manifold pressure (F2 or F3).
1=At airspeed less than 95 knots, set flaps at 10 degrees (F7).
2=Continue descent. Set flaps at 20-30 degrees (F7).
3=Adjust pitch attitude to maintain 65-75 knots.
4=Smoothly increase or decrease throttle to adjust descent rate (F2 or F3).
5=Over runway, establish slight nose-up attitude. Reduce throttle to idle
(F2).
```

Almost any number of different checklists is possible, which you can then number sequentially from 0 to n-1. Each individual sheet can then incorporate as many checklist items as the length of the sheet permits. In this way, every Flight Simulator pilot can create personal reminders and notes for the respective aircraft. And since the checklist in Simulator gives more the impression of a shopping list than a technical instruction, you may be tempted to use some space for reminding yourself to get a few items from the duty-free shop.

Sample Learjet 45 checklist

Here is a sample checklist for the Learjet 45:

Learjet 45

Prestart Checklist

Preflight inspection	COMPLETE
Passenger briefing	COMPLETE
Seats, belts, shoulder harnesses	ADJUST and LOCK
Instrument lights	AS REQUIRED
Flight controls	FREE and CORRECT MOVEMENT
Landing gear switch	DOWN
Brakes	TEST and SET
Electrical equipment	OFF
Landing gear lever	DOWN
Autopilot	OFF
Fuel quantity	CHECKED

After Takeoff Checklist

Landing gear	RETRACT
Flaps	UP
Thrust levers	CLIMB POWER SET
Speed	250 KIAS below 10,000 ft MSL

Engine Start Checklist

Lights	ON
Thrust levers	CLOSED
Engine area	CLEAR
Engine start switches	START
Radios	ON

Climb Checklist

Altimeter	SET 29.92" (1013 mb) at transition altitude (FL 180 in US)
Autopilot	CHECKED and SET

Taxi Checklist	
Brakes	CHECK
Flight instruments	CHECK and SET
Speed brakes/spoilers	RETRACTED/LIGHT OUT
Flaps	8–20°
Trim	SET FOR TAKEOFF
Engine instruments	CHECK
Radios/Transponder	SET and CHECKED
Clearance	VERIFY

Cruise Checklist	
Power	SET
Elevator trim	ADJUST
Engine instruments/Ammeter	CHECK
Fuel quantity	CHECK
Altimeter	SET and CHECKED
Radios	TUNED and SET
Autopilot	CHECK and SET
Lights	AS REQUIRED

Before Takeoff Checklist	
Seats, belts, harnesses	SECURED
Transponder	ON
Pilot heat	ON
Lights/Strobes	AS REQUIRED

Descent/Approach Checklist	
ATIS/Airport information	CHECK
Approach briefing	COMPLETE
Altimeter	SET and CHECKED
(local setting below transition altitude)	
Nav/Com radios	TUNED and SET
Fuel quantity	CHECK
Power	SET
Lights	AS REQUIRED
Landing speed (Vref)	COMPUTED
Vref=IAS 125 kts at 14,500 lbs/6600 kg	
Spoilers	RETRACTED
Flaps	8° max IAS 200 kts 20° max IAS 185 kts 40° max IAS 150 kts

Descent/Approach Checklist	
ATIS/Airport information	CHECK
Approach briefing	COMPLETE
Altimeter	SET and CHECKED
(local setting below transition altitude)	
Nav/Com radios	TUNED and SET
Fuel quantity	CHECK
Power	SET
Lights	AS REQUIRED
Landing speed (Vref)	COMPUTED
Vref=IAS 125 kts at 14,500 lbs/6600 kg	
Spoilers	RETRACTED
Flaps	8° max IAS 200 kts 20° max IAS 185 kts 40° max IAS 150 kts

Before Landing Checklist	
Seats, belts, harnesses	SECURE
Autopilot	OFF
Landing gear	DOWN (max IAS 200 kts)
Flaps	DOWN
Airspeed	Vref=IAS 125 kts at 14.500 lbs/6600 kg)

Engine Failure After Takeoff	
Airspeed (IAS 134 kts at 16,900 lbs = 7650 kg)	CLIMB at V2
Landing gear	UP
Airspeed (IAS 164 kts at 16,900 lbs = 7650 kg)	Accelerate to V2+30
Flaps	RETRACT

Emergency Checklists	
Aborted Takeoff	
Brakes	APPLY
Speed brakes/spoilers	EXTEND
Thrust levers	REVERSE
After Takeoff Checklist	
Landing gear	RETRACT
Flaps	UP
Thrust levers	CLIMB POWER SET
Speed	250 KIAS below 10,000 ft MSL

Emergency Landing Without Power	
Airspeed (IAS 185 kts at 14,500 lbs = 6600 kg)	Vref+60
Landing gear	DOWN
Flaps	DOWN

In these descriptions, we are dealing with the flight simulator, and are therefore forced to adapt the procedures and checklists. For example, you can't actually carry out the Pre-Flight Check unless you crawl into your monitor and walk around the aircraft wiggling all the rudders, checking the oil level and tire treads or making sure all the covers and flaps are closed.

Flight Simulator-specific notes follow only for the Before Engine Startup Check.

Boeing 747 sample checklist

You don't exactly just climb into a B747 and take off. You must consider to where you're flying, how much fuel you need to get there and make the appropriate settings in FS. This applies to the flight planning, the fuel calculation and the actual flight. In any case, there are plenty of very good programs available via shareware as well as commercially.

Check the following points before starting a flight:

Flight Plan Check	
Aircraft, panel and sound select	AS REQUIRED
Enroute charts and other maps	AS REQUIRED
Maps for alternate airport	AS REQUIRED
Fuel calculation	AS REQUIRED
Flight Sim start	CHECK
Weather	CHECK
Departure airport set	CHECK
WEIGHT, T/O FIELD LENGTH	CHECK
Before Engine Startup Check	
PARK BRAKE	SET
Panel switch to FUELMANAGEMENT	SET
Overhead panel switch to ENGINES	SET
Fuel quantity (with menu)	SET
All fuel valves ON	SET
Panel switch to ENGINES	SET
Engines Startup	
MAIN-VALVE (overhead panel) ON	SET
ENGINE 1 startup ON	SET
ENGINE 1 FUEL FLOW	CHECK
ENGINE 1 startup OFF	CHECK
ENGINE 4 startup ON	SET
ENGINE 4 FUEL FLOW	CHECK
ENGINE 4 startup OFF	CHECK

Engines Startup	
ENGINE 2 startup ON	SET
ENGINE 2 FUEL FLOW	CHECK
ENGINE 2 startup OFF	CHECK
ENGINE 3 startup ON	SET
ENGINE 3 FUEL FLOW	CHECK
ENGINE 3 startup OFF	CHECK
MAIN-VALVE (overhead panel) OFF	CHECK
ALL ENGINES SAME VALUES	CHECK

For the following checklists, we assume that you have good familiarity with the instrument panel and know which panel you need to make the required settings.

The required keys or key combinations, such as the period (□) for brakes or Ctrl+H for Heading Hold On, etc., can be found in the original Flight Simulator manual or Flight Simulator 98's on-line help program.

We also assume that you have mastered how to use and operate the basic features of Flight Simulator 98, including the essential flying skills (e.g., navigation, takeoff, landing, etc.).

TAXI	
BRAKE LEFT	CHECK
BRAKE RIGHT	CHECK
BRAKES BOTH	CHECK
FUEL QUANTITY	CHECK
ENGINES	CHECK
ELEVATOR TRIM	CHECK
FLAPS (set as required)	CHECK
THRUST REVERSERS	CHECK/STOW
SPEEDBRAKES (SPOILERS)	CYCLE
TRIM	SET FOR T/O
TAKE OFF DATA	CONFIRM/SET
CREW BRIEFING	COMPLETE

BEFORE TAKEOFF	
LIGHTS	AS REQUIRED
TRANSPONDER	SET/ON
COMPASS SYSTEM	CHECK
NAV 1 FREQUENCY/RADIAL	CHECK
NAV 2 FREQUENCY/RADIAL	CHECK
BEFORE TAKEOFF	
ADF FREQUENCY	AS REQUIRED/SET
COM 1 / ATIS	CHECK/SET
CLEAR FOR T/O	RECEIVED
AFTER TAKEOFF - CLIMB	
LANDING GEAR	UP
LANDING LIGHTS	OFF
FLAPS	UP
CLIMB RATE	CHECK
RADAR ALTIMETER	CHECK
POWER SETTING	
250kts, max. 95% N1	CHECK
CRUISE	
AUTO-THROTTLE (CRUISE POWER)	CHECK/SET
AUTO-BRAKE	OFF
BRAKES	RELEASED
FLIGHT LEVEL	AS REQUIRED
AUTOPILOT	AS REQUIRED
DESCENT	
AUTOPILOT	TEST
AUTO-THROTTLE	AS REQUIRED
ALTIMETER (QNH)	CHECK
ATIS (CLEARANCE)	AS REQUIRED

APPROACH - IN RANGE	
AUTOPILOT	TEST
AUTO-THROTTLE (below 250 kts)	CHECK
AIRSPEED	CHECK
RADAR ALTIMETER	SET
DECISION HEIGHT	SET
ALTIMETER	CHECK
BEFORE LANDING	
FLAPS	T/O and APPROACH
ENGINES SYNC	ON
AUTO COORDINATION	OFF
EFIS	ON
FUEL CROSS FEED (ALL)	SET
LANDING GEAR	DOWN (GREEN)
BEFORE LANDING	
FLAPS	LAND
SPEED BRAKES	RETRACTED
AUTO-BRAKE (value)	ON/SET
FINAL AUTOPILOT	OFF
AFTER LANDING	
AUTO-BRAKE	CHECK
THRUST REVERSERS	CHECK
FLAPS	UP
SPOILERS	UP
TRANSPONDER	STANDBY

AFTER LANDING - TAXI BACK	
AUTO-BRAKE	OFF
THRUST REVERSER	STOW
FLAPS/TRIM	SET FOR T/O
SPOILERS	DOWN
TRANSPONDER	STANDBY
FLIGHT INSTRUMENTS	CHECK
TAKE OFF DATA	SET
CREW BRIEFING	COMPLETE
SHUTDOWN	
FLAPS	T/O - APPROACH
MAIN-VALVE	OFF
TANKSELECTOR	OFF
THROTTLES	CUTOFF
STROBES	OFF
LIGHTS	OFF
PARKING BRAKE	SET

Sample emergency checklists

The checklists in Section 3 describe emergency procedures, for example, loss of an engine or which displays have to be checked when the various Master Cautions come on.

One Engine CUTOFF in the air		
AUTOPILOT	CHECK	
AUTO-THROTTLE	OFF	
FUEL-VALVE (engine x)	OFF	
N1 RPM = 0%	CHECK	
EGT	CHECK	
N2 RPM = 0%	CHECK	

All Engines CUTOFF in the air		
AUTOPILOT	CHECK	OFF
AUTO-THROTTLE	CHECK	OFF
FUEL VALVE ENGINE 1	CHECK	OFF
FUEL VALVE ENGINE 4	CHECK	OFF
FUEL VALVE ENGINE 2	CHECK	OFF
FUEL VALVE ENGINE 3	CHECK	OFF
MAIN-VALVE (fuelpanel)	CHECK	OFF
TANK SELECTOR LIGHTS	ON	ORANGE
Engine(s) FAILURE in the air		
FUELFLOW	CHECK	POSITIVE
FUEL QUANTITY	CHECK	NOT 0
TANKSELECTOR	CHECK	ALL
ENGINE VALVE	CHECK	ON
Engine RESTART in the air		REQD.
FUEL SELECTOR	CHECK	All
MAIN-VALVE (overhead)	SET	ON
ENGINE STARTUP ON	SET	
ENGINE FUEL FLOW	CHECK	
MAIN-VALVE (overhead) OFF	CHECK	
N1 - N2 - EGT	CHECK	
FLAP MASTER CAUTION		
AIRSPEED ABOVE 270 kts TAS	FLAPS	UP
AIRSPEED BELOW 220 kts TAS	FLAPS	DOWN
GROUNDSPEED BELOW 40 kts	FLAPS	DOWN
STALL WARNING - MASTER CAUTION		
AIRSPEED	CHECK	>
THROTTLES 100%	SET	100%
SPOILERS	CHECK	DOWN
GEAR	CHECK	UP
FLAPS	CHECK	FULL
GO AROUND		AS REQUIRED

GEAR WARNING - MASTER CAUTION		
AIRSPEED ABOVE 240 kts TAS	GEAR	UP
RADAR ALTITUDE BELOW 50 meters	GEAR	DOWN
R-ALT. BELOW 150, CLIMBRATE NEG.	GEAR	DOWN
VERTICAL SPEED WARNING		
RADAR ALTITUDE	CHECK	
GS SIGNAL RECEIVED	CHECK	
VERTICAL SPEED POSITIVE	CHECK	
GEAR DOWN	CHECK	

METAR and TAF

We mentioned weather in the preceding sections on GPS navigation. You can control the weather in FS98 with the options of the **World | Weather** command. Real world pilots have various information sources to give them all types of data on the weather conditions at the takeoff location, for the flight and at the destination. The most important information is provided by the TAF and METAR services.

TAF Aerodrome Forecast

An airport provides the pilot with a forecast for weather conditions. This includes a summary of the local weather conditions expected over a period of time, generally for the next nine to 24 hours. The usual nine-hour TAF is updated every three hours.

METAR Aviation Routine Weather Report

A METAR report contains the current weather conditions at the airport at the time of issue. The report is updated and issued hourly. An excerpt of the METAR is contained in the ATIS (Automatic Terminal Information).

The European METAR consists of special coding with up to ten elements and three identifiers. These identifiers contain the following features:

The following is an example of a METAR from Kent County International Airport (KGRR) in Grand Rapids:

TYPE	ID	TIME	WIND	VIS	WX	SKY	T/TD	ALT	REMARK
METAR	KGRR	161456Z	16012KT	6SM	HZ	SCT100	06/02	A2969	RMK AO2

Note that not all ten elements must necessarily appear in the METAR. If there were no corresponding data to gather at the time of the observation (no precipitation or wind shear, for example), they are omitted.

ID

In this example, K refers to a North American Station and GRR is the three letter id for Kent County International (from Grand Rapids, its home city). Other examples are KORD (O'Hare in Chicago), KAMA (Amarillo, TX) and KDEN (Denver, CO).

Time

This refers not only to the time but also the date. In this example:

161456Z
>The 16 represents the day of the month
>The 1456 represents the time at which the observation went out
>The Z represents that the time is in ZULU or UTC (Universal Time Code).

Wind

The first three numbers refer to the direction of the winds in degrees from 0 to 360 degrees (you won't see 360 because it goes back to 0 after 350). The wind is always shown in degrees for the direction from which it is coming. The next two numbers refer to the average speed of the wind. The KT simply means knots and always appears at the end.

Example: 16012KT
>The wind is coming from 160° at 12 knots.

You might also see a "G" listed (such as 24015G25KT). The G25 represents the wind gusts. In this case the gusts are 25 knots. Gust may not be listed because criteria must be met to have a gust. Basically, unless it's windy, you won't see gusts in the observation.

Example: 24015G27KT
>The wind is from 240° at 15 knots, gusting up to 27 knots.

Wind that is constantly swirling and blowing from various directions but at low speeds (six knots or less) is called *variable wind*. This is the idea of "light and variable" that you might see in a forecast.

Example: VRB02KT
The wind is variable at 2 knots

Variable wind speeds above six knots require more precise description.

Example: 31015G27KT 280V350
The wind is from 310° at 15 knots, gusts up to 27 knots, but the direction is actually variable from 280° to 350°. To be variable above 6 knots, the winds must have at least a 60 degree variation.

Calm air is indicated as 00000KT.

Visibility

The visibility is listed in statute miles. It may also listed as fractions so, for example, 3/4SM means ¾ statue mile visibility. Miles and fractions are also reported (for example, 2 3/4SM for 2¾ statue miles visibility). You might occasionally see visibility up to 20 or 30 SM but it's usually listed from < 1/4 (visibility below ¼ SM) up to 10 SM.

Example: 6SM
Means visibility up to 6 statute miles

Present Weather and Obscurations

The type of precipitation is indicated by two letters.

Example: HZ
Present weather is haze.

The following table lists the most important of these precipitation factors:

BR	Mist	IC	Ice crystals
DS	Duststorm	PE	Ice Pellets
DU	Widespread dust	RA	Rain
DZ	Drizzle	SA	Sand
FC	Funnel Cloud	SG	Snow Grains
FG	Fog	SN	Snow
FU	Smoke	SQ	Squalls
GR	Hail	SS	Sandstorm
GS	Small Hail	VA	Volcanic Ash
HZ	Haze		

Supplementary code letters define the precipitation more precisely:

MI	Shallow	BL	Blowing	TS	Thunderstorm
BC	Patches	SH	Showers	FZ	Freezing
DR	Low drifting				

Precipitation is also indicated as light (-), moderate ( ) or heavy (+) based on certain criteria that must be met.

Example: -DZ
   Light Drizzle,

Example: +SHSN
   Heavy snow showers

Example: -SHRA
   Light rain shower

Example: FZFG
   Freezing fog

Sky conditions

Cloud formations are generally described using six characters and are categorized based on eighths (octas) of the sky. Three letters describe the degree of cloud cover, and three digits indicate the cloud height over the airport.

Example: SCT100
Means scattered at 10,000 feet

The cloud height is indicated by three digits and is measured in feet above the ground. The two last places representing tens and ones is not used.

Other examples:

SCT020
Scattered at 2,000 feet

BKN005
Broken at 500 feet

OVC250
Overcast ceiling at 25,000 feet

SKC
Means cloudless sky (Sky Clear)

CAVOK
means no clouds below 5,000 feet and visibility is greater than 10 kilometers (Clouds and Visibility OK) .

BKN
Means a broken sky. (The clouds cover 5/8 to 7/8 of the sky)

T/TD

The air temperature and dewpoint are measured in degrees Celsius. Minus values are prefixed with "M" for minus.

Example 06/02
06 represents the temperature in Celcius
02 represents the dewpoint in Celcius

Runway Visual Range (RVR)

The actual visibility on the runway in the takeoff/landing direction is shown for visibility conditions less than 1,500 meters. The prefix "R" is used with these components.

Example: R24/1,200
> Means visibility on runway 24 is 1,200 meters.

The RVR value is used mainly to evaluate the approach procedure. If visibility is below a limit approved for the airport, landing from an approach is not permitted. The approach is then aborted and if necessary an alternate is found.

ALT

ALT is the barometric pressure in inches of mercury. The code letter is "A" for Altimeter; International uses the letters QNH, measured in hectopascals (hpa).

Example: A2969
> 2969 means 29.69 inches of mercury for the pressure.

REMARK

Example: RMK AO2
> RMK simply means REMARKS and marks the end of the standard metar observation and the beginning of the remarks that are put in as necessary.
>
> A02 means that the site is automated and HAS a precipitation sensor. (AO1 indicates no precip sensor.) This does not mean the site is unmanned. If there is an AUTO after the ID in the metar ob, then there is no observer.

Many remarks are possible and you'll find a complete listing in the FMH-1 (Federal Meteorological Handbook-1). Here are only a few of the important and common remarks:

Recent Weather

Marginal or just-arriving weather conditions are also indicated by the code letters "RE." Example: RERA—for recent rain.

Wind Shear

Wind shear is indicated by "WS." Frequently, the runway affected by the wind shear is also indicated. Examples: WS LDG RWY28L or WS TKOF RWY08.

Trend

The anticipated weather development for the next two or three hours is indicated in the last group of elements. Examples:

TEMPO 3000 SHRA
> Temporary visibility 3,000 meters with rain showers

BECMG 33035KT
> Becoming wind 300° at 35 knots

NOSIG
> No significant changes

Finding current FAA weather

GTE Direct User Access Terminal Service (GTE DUATS) provides current Federal Aviation Administration (FAA) weather and flight plan filing services to all certified civil pilots. The service is available 24 hours a day, seven days a week, at no charge to the user. Fees to operate the basic GTE DUAT Service (weather briefing, flight plan filing, encode/decode) are paid by the FAA.

Another alternative for non-licensed pilots is the Worldwide Airport Pathfinder Web site. You'll find a lot of weather and flight planning information at their location (http://www.fallingrain.com/air/).

GAMET and AIRMET

GAMET reports are regional forecasts for the lower airspace for a flight information region (FIR) or a part of it. Significant weather conditions are forecast. In the Federal Republic of Germany, GAMETs are routinely generated four times daily at 02, 08, 14 and 20 hours UTC. GAMETs are amended if predicted conditions are no longer expected.

AIRMET reports are warnings before significant weather conditions occur that have effects on air travel in the lower airspace. The weather conditions correspond to those in GAMET. AIRMETs replace the previously issued ADVICEs FOR GENERAL AVIATION. They are issued only as needed. The reporting structure corresponds to the popular SIGMET format.

Note the following conventions:

→ No references to icing and turbulence when thunderstorms are reported.

→ Whenever possible and necessary, a locale is indicated.

→ Whenever possible and necessary, information about shift direction and speed is provided.

→ For all events, intensity changes and tendencies are described.

→ The time of validity is limited to maximum four hours (although six hours is allowed in exceptional cases.

→ AIRMETs are sequentially numbered each day.

→ AIRMETs are lifted when the causing event is no longer expected.

GAMET/AIRMET are formulated in the English clear text of the ICAO. They are exchanged internationally and are valid for the lower airspace up to FL 100, or up to FL 150 in the FIR Munich.

The GAMET/AIRMET reports are made available to pilots as part of individual advisory and in the context of the self-briefing procedure offered by DWD such as telefax (GAMET), INFORMET-phone, pc_met and BTX. AIRMET information is also conveyed by radio by the DFS to controlled flight pilots when entering an FIR. VFR pilots who are flying without regular contact with the DFS are encouraged in their own interest to contact air traffic control for any AIRMETs that may have been issued.

Due to the limitation of the forecast to significant weather events of moderate intensity, GAMET/AIRMET reports must be used in close connection with issued SIGMETs. Their use does not relieve the pilot of his or her responsibility to stay informed.

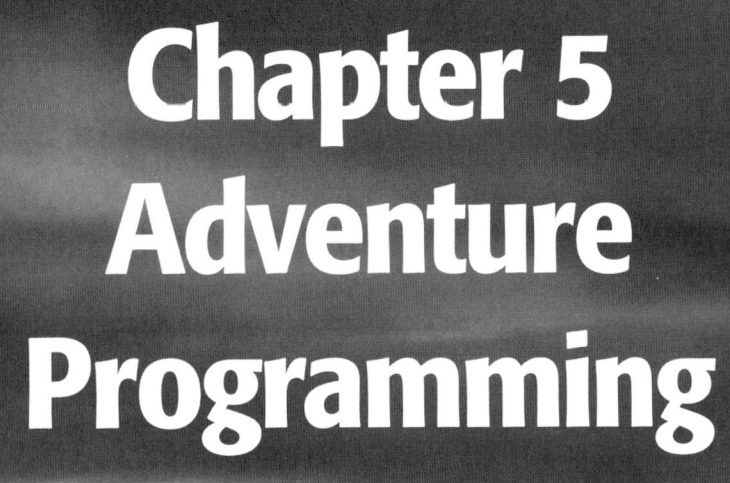

Chapter 5
Adventure
Programming

Chapter 5 explains how to program Flight Simulator adventures using APLC.EXE from FlightShop. The basics and the command syntax will be illustrated in various programming examples. Finally, we will take a look at the ATC Flight Planning program module in FlightShop, which can be used to create a complete FS adventure in just a few steps.

Flight Simulator Adventures

Besides accurate flight models and pretty scenery, Flight Simulator offers several more options to increase the realism. The FS adventures, for example, recreate entire flight environments, even including voice commands from the air traffic controller (ATC).

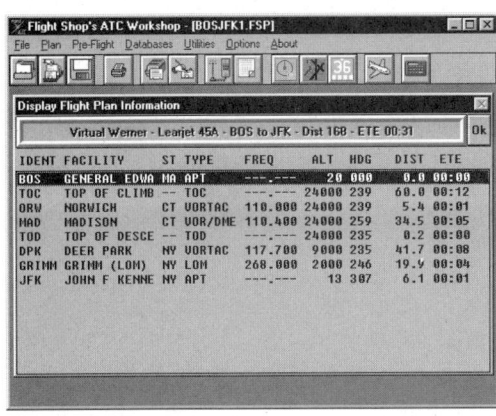

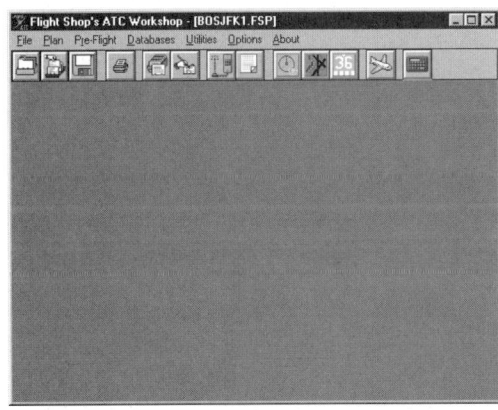

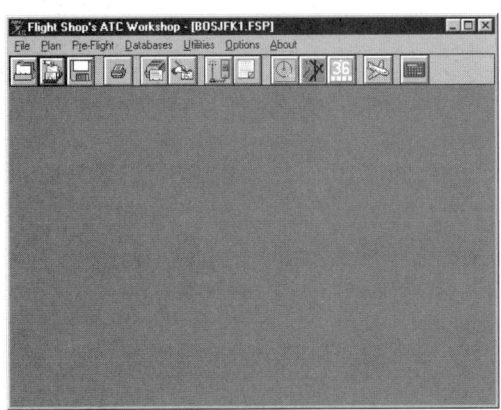

The adventures are simulated ATC flights that become very realistic due to the direct radio contact with the Air Traffic Control/Flight Service. In the preprogrammed sequence of flight events, the pilot receives advisories and flight information from the control stations. The ATC Workshop in the Flight Simulator FlightShop (FSFS) program generates this type of air-route programming almost automatically.

Using the Adventure Programming Language (APL) integrated into the FSFS (which closely resembles Basic), you can build additional elements into the simulation, which can greatly improve the performance range of Flight Simulator.

This expansion may include simple things, such as an extra radar altimeter, and more complicated elements, like a highly complex GWPS with a warning system, voice output of the checklists and a completely automatic Flight Management System (FMS), which monitors and controls that leg of the flight from takeoff to landing.

The ATC Workshop Adventure Generator

The ATC Workshop in FSFS contains everything needed to generate simple flights with ground and radar support and print them as complete flight plans. As usual under Windows, most of the menu options can be accessed from the keyboard and/ or by on-screen icons. The following sections explain the program functions.

File	
New Flight Plan	Ctrl+N
Open Flight Plan...	Ctrl+O
Save Flight Plan	Ctrl+S
Save Flight Plan As...	Ctrl+A
Printer Setup	
Exit	Ctrl+X

File

The **File** menu is where you'll create a new flight plan, open an already existing flight plan and save the current flight plan. In Printer Setup the printer can be set to print the flight plan document.

Plan

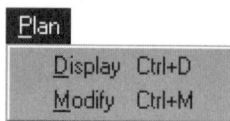

The short **Plan** menu permits the display or modification of an open flight plan.

Preflight

The **Preflight** menu converts the data of a planned leg of the flight into several types of flight plans. The most important command here is **File Plan with Flight Service**, which simulates delivering a flight plan to the Flight Service in order to generate a

Flight Simulator flight adventure. A printed plan for the flight, including route markers, radio frequencies, and airport and runway information for the takeoff and destination airports, serves as an indispensable aid during the flight.

The flight plan for a CompuServe Fly-in will ease the registration for a CServe-sponsored multiplayer event. The **Summary Flight Plan** is modeled after the official FAA flight plan.

Databases

The standard FSFS database contains all airports in North America, listing their takeoff and landing runways and radio-navigation equipment (VOR and NDB). This database can be expanded with add-ons, which permit flights in European airspace with ATC support, for example.

Utilities

The FSFS utilities provide a small, on-screen computer suitable for calculating certain flight data, such as climb or descent rates, turn radius or for converting geographical latitude/longitude data into decimal numbers (though this last function has a strong tendency to crash the computer since the last version of FSFS, so do not use it if possible). It is also possible to run Flight Simulator (still referred to as FS5 here) with the **Run FS5** command. The path to FS can be set in the **Options | Set path to FS5 m**enu.

Options

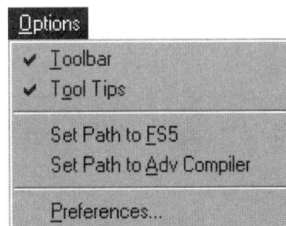

The options define the work environment of the ATC Workshop, including the paths to Flight Simulator and to the internal Adventure Compiler APLC, which generates flight adventures from the user data. The Preferences contain data that will be included in the flight plans, such as the pilot's name, the performance data of the aircraft or the frequently encountered navigation frequencies.

About

The last menu shows the program version of the ATC Workshop within the FSFS. Version 5.0, the first official version, contains a few small errors which were eliminated with a bug fix called FSUPDATE (FSFS501.EXE). Meanwhile, version 5a, from which these errors have been cleaned, is also available.

The FSUPDATE file can be obtained free of charge from the Apollo Internet page: http://www.apollosoftware.com.

The Tools

The most important menu commands have been grouped together as icons in a toolbar, giving the user one-click operation of the ATC Workshop. We find the following buttons on the toolbar:

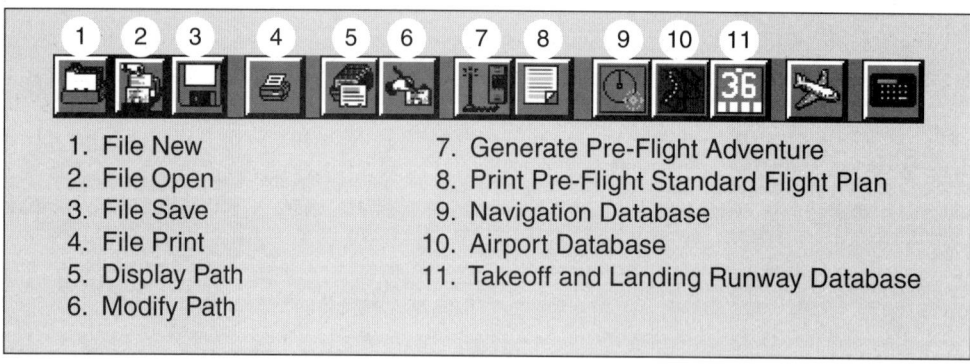

1. File New
2. File Open
3. File Save
4. File Print
5. Display Path
6. Modify Path
7. Generate Pre-Flight Adventure
8. Print Pre-Flight Standard Flight Plan
9. Navigation Database
10. Airport Database
11. Takeoff and Landing Runway Database

Creating Standard Flight Plans

The Options | Preferences dialog box requires the name of the pilot, the call sign of the aircraft, its flight data, and the data of the radio frequencies anticipated from all ground stations. The Default Frequencies are the values to be entered during the flight in order to maintain constant contact with the correct controller.

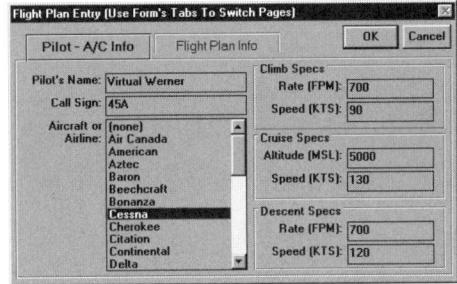

The individual control stations for the adventure are the Clearance Delivery, for the general clearance of the entire flight plan; Ground, as ground control; and Tower (Dep), at the takeoff airport. Departure takes charge of the aircraft immediately after takeoff and in most cases takes it up to the first checkpoint. Center represents the first control station of the flight stage up to the traffic zone of the destination airport. Once there, Approach takes charge of the aircraft until the landing course is reached, when it transfers control to the tower at the destination airport. After a successful landing, the ground station welcomes the pilot and allows him to taxi to the terminal.

All the necessary COM frequencies in the band from 118.000 to 136.975 MHz can be read from the official chart (for example, Jeppesen Airport Charts, Approach Charts, etc.) or made up arbitrarily. In that case, record these frequencies for yourself and for others, to prevent unnecessary stress during the adventure flight. The last frequency entry refers to the Flight Information Service, which broadcasts (in the USA) the current weather (wind, cloud cover, temperature) for the Flight Simulator on the frequency 122.2 MHz.

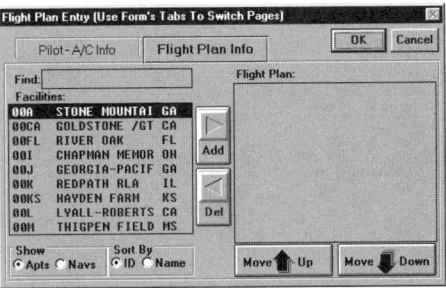

The six flight parameters for climbing, level and descending flight are the values the pilot aims to maintain during the flight. Not only does the program use these flight characteristics to compute the flight data, but the simulated controllers also use them, for example, during the introductory phase of the descent or the control of circling.

So, it is important to work with realistic values here. For example, valid climbing and descending rates for the single-engine Cessna are between 500 and 1,000 feet per minute (fpm), and it has a cruising airspeed (TAS) of 120 to 140 kts at a flight altitude of 5,000 feet. Entirely different data are needed for the Learjet 45. This plane can climb at the rate of at least 1,800 fpm, and at flight level 350, it reaches a TAS of approximately 450 kts.

Creating An ATC Adventure

When you create a new flight adventure using the ATC Workshop, the default flight data appear in the Pilot A/C Info area of the Flight Path Entry dialog box. Here you may modify all the values and data, but these entries will not affect the previous entries in the Preferences, and are valid only for this newly created adventure.

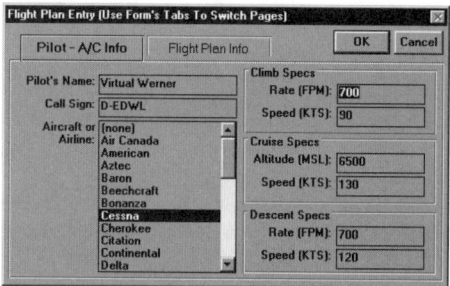

The painted recognition markings, found on the fuselage of light planes, are entered as the call sign. Flight Simulator's Cessna 182 S, for example, carries the marking "N9110E," and the Learjet has the marking "N45LJ" (carried over from the first prototype). Large aircraft employed by airlines and charters, in most cases, are called using the name of the airline (for example, Lufthansa) and the flight number of the route.

The flight data can still be changed at this point. It is best not to exceed or drop below the realistic values. It does not make any sense to attempt to fly at a cruising speed of five knots (in which case, you would merely put on your hiking boots and carry the airplane on your back) or operate with rocketlike climbing rates of 10,000 fpm.

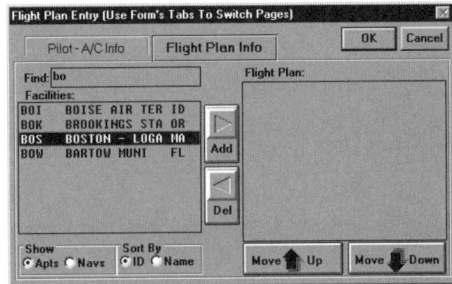

In the second registration chart, Flight Plan Info, is where you specify the flight route. Preflight planning also begins when using the ATC Workshop with a look at the big chart. The questions "Where am I?," "Where do I want to go?" and "How do I get there?" must be precisely answered by entering the starting point and destination—and in most cases, several intermediate points along the way.

The Flight Path Editor in the ATC Workshop lists the airports and navigation devices for that purpose. To find a point along the course, type in the first letter of the name (or route-marking characteristic) in the Find field to display all the Airports or Navaids beginning with that letter.

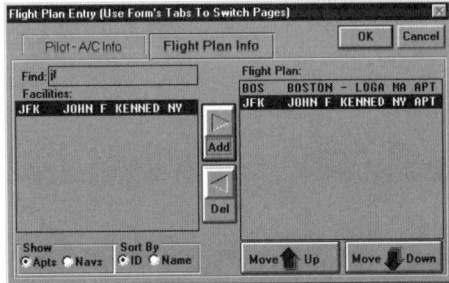

In the next steps, all the prominent navigation facilities marking the air lanes are entered into the list. Starting from the Boston VOR, the Victor Airway V16 with course 240° leads to the Norwich VORTAC (110.0 ORW), which can serve as the first route marker. The entry of ORW during the search for the Navs-ID and the inclusion of the found station in the Flight Path list sorts this waypoint behind the last one marked. If the sequence does not coincide, it is corrected with the [Move Up] or [Move Down] buttons. It is just as easy to remove a mistakenly entered point from the list using the [Delete] button. From the last waypoint entered ORW, the route proceeds toward New York, via airway V 475 to the Madison VOR/DME (110.4 MAD). At this point, you need to decide the rest of the route: either to continue along V475 to the La Guardia

VOR (113.1 LGA) or to turn over the V1 and proceed to the Deer Park VORTAC (117.7 DPK). These considerations could depend, for example, upon the wind conditions over New York. Flights from the north and west are normally carried out from the LGA VOR to runways 04 and 13, although pilots are guided to runways 22 and 31 when the winds are from the west.

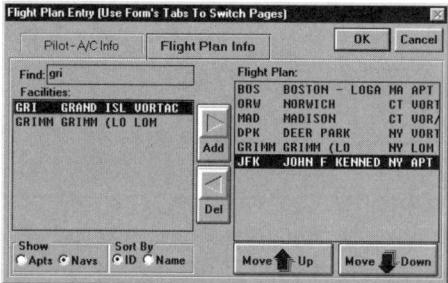

How the simulated controller in Flight Simulator will choose an approach is influenced by the winds, but also depends upon a certain arbitrariness of the internal programming of the ATC Workshop. To force the landing onto a specific runway, a further navigation facility should be inserted between the last navigation point (in the example, it is DPK) and the JFK airport. For this example, it happens to be the locator GRIMM (268 RT) on the ILS localizer to the 31R runway. With the addition of this NDB between DPK and JFK, the route planning of the flight is complete.

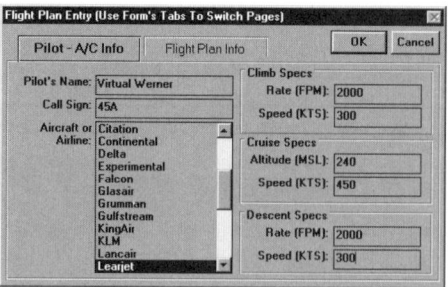

The entire route between Boston and New York can be read in abbreviated form: BOS - ORW - MAD - DPK - GRIMM - JFK. Conscientious people further expand this representation to include the data for the airways used, so that a detailed route description could appear like this:

```
BOS V16 ORW V475 MAD V1 DPK GRIMM JFK.
```

Now the preplanned route can be saved as a flight plan. Provided with an appropriately descriptive name (in this example Bosjfk1), the flight plan is saved as an .FSP file on the hard drive.

The entire flight plan can now be called with all routing data using the Plan | Display command. The top row of the table shows the route of the flight BOS-JFK, the total distance and the anticipated duration of the flight, which the ATC Workshop has calculated from the individual waypoints. In the first column of the main part of the list, we find the waypoints along the route, including the place of takeoff and landing. In the next columns are the cleartext names, the US state and the type of facility (APT (airport), VOR, VORTAC, VOR/DME, NDB, and LOM, among others) along with their radio frequencies. There is no need to worry about the courses and distances between the individual route markers when drafting the plan, because they are calculated here for each leg on the basis of the Nav/Apt database in the ATC Workshop and displayed in the columns Hdg and Dist.

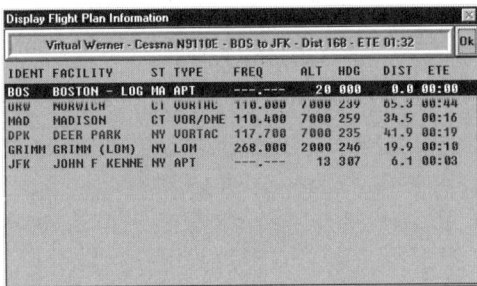

Two new points along the route with the labels TOC and TOD are inserted between the actual points. These imaginary points represent where you reach the planned cruising altitude with the climbing rate entered as Top Of Climb and the beginning of the descending flight as Top Of Descent at the indicated rates of descent and speed.

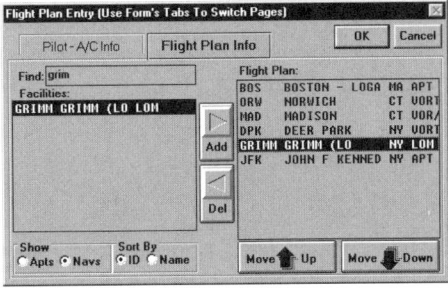

These last calculation are always based upon a constant forward movement of the aircraft during climbing or descending. This speed changes continuously for fast aircraft, however. The goal up to 10,000 feet is normally a maximum IAS of 250 kts (for noise reduction). At 10,000 feet, however, this IAS yields (at standard atmospheric pressure) a true speed (TAS) of approximately 290 kts. From 10,000 feet to 24,000 feet, the result, at a constant IAS of 300 kts, is already a true air speed between 350 and 440 kts. From 24,000, flight is then by Mach number, in which case the underlying speed of sound depends upon the ambient temperature. At flight level 250, the external temperature under standard conditions lies at approximately -35 °C. A Mach number of M 0.70 yields approximately 429 kts at this altitude. At an altitude of FL 390 and at a temperature of -57 °C, the true speed is reduced to about 400 kts.

The numerical examples make it clear that the entry of a specific speed can produce merely an average in the corresponding phase of the flight (climbing, cruising or descending), which can be determined only from precise observation and recalculation for each type of aircraft.

Printing The Flight Plan

You may print a newly created or modified flight plan in uppercase format using virtually any type of printer (dot-matrix, inkjet or laser).

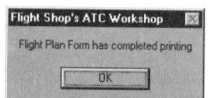

The printout should only be in uppercase using a monospaced font (LinePrinter, Courier or the like). This will preserve the table character of the document. The standard flight plan will than have the appearance of a form used in real flying.

The first six items list the type of flight (IFR or VFR), the aircraft model, the targeted cruising speed, the takeoff airport, the anticipated takeoff time and the proposed cruising altitude.

Section 8 lists the entire route of travel, from takeoff to arrival, with all the waypoints, as entered during the preliminary planning. The remaining sections of the form contain the destination, the total flight time and optional remarks.

Sections 12 and 13 list the detailed data of the two airports, including geographic position, radio frequencies and the takeoff and landing runways.

```
+---------------------------------------+
| FS DEPARTMENT OF TRANSPORTATION | FOR FLIGHT SIMULATOR(R) USE ONLY   |
|      F L I G H T   P L A N      | NOT TO BE USED FOR REAL WORLD FLIGHT |
+---------------------------------------+
|1.TYPE|2.AIRCRAFT IDENT |3.CRUISE|5.DEPARTURE POINT|6. DEP TIME    |7.CRUISE|
|_|VFR | Learjet        | SPEED  |      BOS        |PROPOSED|ACTUAL|  ALT   |
|_|IFR | 45A            |  450   | GENERAL EDWARD  |        |      | FL240  |
| |DVFR|                |  KTS   |                 |        |      |  MSL   |
+---------------------------------------+
|IDENT|FACILITY NAME |TYP| FREQ   | ALT |HDG| DIST|DISTREM| GS | ETE  | ATE  |
+---------------------------------------+
| BOS |GENERAL EDWARD|APT|-.-|  20  |000|  0.0| 168.1| 300 |00:00|      |
| TOC |TOP OF CLIMB  |TOC|-.-|FL240|239| 60.0| 108.2| 300 |00:12|      |
| ORW |   NORWICH    |VOR|110.000|FL240|239|  5.9| 102.3| 450 |00:01|     |
| MAD |  MADISON     |VOR|110.400|FL240|259| 34.5|  67.8| 450 |00:05|     |
| TOD |TOP OF DESCENT|TOD|-.-|FL240|235|  0.2|  67.6| 450 |00:00|      |
| DPK |  DEER PARK   |VOR|117.700|9000 |235| 41.7|  26.0| 300 |00:08|     |
|GRIMM| GRIMM (LOM)  |LOM|268.000|2000 |246| 19.9|  6.1 | 300 |00:04|     |
| JFK |JOHN F KENNEDY|APT|-.-|  13  |307|  6.1|  0.0 | 300 |00:01|      |
+---------------------------------------+
|9.DESTINATION   |10.TOT ETE|11.REMARKS          |
|     JFK        |  00 hrs  |                     |
|JOHN F KENNEDY  |  31 mins |                     |
+---------------------------------------+
|12.DEPARTURE AIRPORT INFORMATION                 |
| BOS - GENERAL EDWARD - ST/CO:MA   UNICOM: 122.95   CTAF: 121.3   |
| LAT:N42-21-51.65 LON:W071-00-18.64 ELEVATION: 20MSL   MAGVAR: 16W  |
| 04L/22R  - 7860 x 150 [04L HDG-036  -    ][22R HDG 216       ]|
| 04R/22L  - 10005 x 150 [04R HDG-036 ILS-110.3 ][22L HDG-216 ILS-110.3 ]|
| 09/27    - 7000 x 150 [09 HDG-093  -    ][27 HDG-273 ILS-111.3 ]|
| 15L/33R  - 2557 x 100 [15L HDG-151  -    ][33R HDG-331  -     ]|
| 15R/33L  - 10081 x 150 [15R HDG-151 ILS-110.7 ][33L HDG-331 ILS-110.7 ]|
+---------------------------------------+
|13.DESTINATION AIRPORT INFORMATION               |
| JFK - JOHN F KENNEDY - ST/CO:NY   UNICOM: 122.95   CTAF: 121.3   |
| LAT:N40-38-24.87 LON:W073-46-40.38 ELEVATION: 13MSL   MAGVAR: 13W  |
| 04L/22R  - 11351 x 150 [04L HDG-044 ILS-110.9 ][22R HDG-224 ILS-109.5 ]|
| 04R/22L  - 8400 x 150 [04R HDG-044 ILS-109.5 ][22L HDG-224 ILS-110.9 ]|
| 13L/31R  - 10000 x 150 [13L HDG-134 ILS-111.5 ][31R HDG-314 ILS-111.5 ]|
| 13R/31L  - 14572 x 150 [13R HDG-134  -    ][31L HDG-314 ILS-111.35 ]|
| 14/32    - 2560 x 75 [14 HDG-138  -    ][32 HDG-318  -     ]|
+---------------------------------------+
|14.PILOT'S NAME, ADDRESS, TELEPHONE NUMBER, & AIRCRAFT HOMEBASE      |
| ** On file with Flight Shop's Flight Service Station (FSS) **       |
+---------------------------------------+
|CIVIL AIRCRAFT PILOTS. FAR Part 91 requires that you file an IFR flight plan |
|to operate under instrument flight rules in controlled airspace. Failure to  |
|file could result in a civil penalty not to exceed $1,000 for each violation |
|(Section 901 of the Federal Aviation Act of 1958, as amended). Filing of a   |
|VFR flight plan is recommended as a good operating practice. See also Part 99|
|for requirements concerning DVFR flight plans.                       |
+---------------------------------------+
|FSFS Form 7233-1 (4-94)      CLOSE VFR FLIGHT PLAN WITH FSS ON ARRIVAL|
+---------------------------------------+

     FLIGHT PLAN CREATED BY THE FLIGHT SIMULATOR(R) FLIGHT SHOP(TM)
```

The printout is not only used during the flight, but is now above all a means for controlling the generation of the adventure file. The route of the flight should now be examined once more for clarity. Are the waypoints in logical sequence? Are any of them omitted or listed twice? Has the flight altitude been selected correctly? If at least one waypoint is present between the TOC and TOD markers, the preliminary calculation was well done. If you see several route markers with long distances between them, the entered cruising altitude is too low. A turbine-driven aircraft (Learjet or Boeing) could operate much more cheaply at a greater altitude. If TOC and TOD lie directly behind one another, it will be necessary to resume descending flight shortly after reaching the cruising altitude, without the pleasant recovery phase of the cruising flight. When only the TOD appears in the flight plan, the preset cruising altitude cannot be reached at all, unless you want to make a very steep descent. In this case, you should recalculate the flight plan (by clicking **Plan | Modify**) using a lower cruising altitude.

Generating The ATC Adventure

In principle, an adventure is a sequence of specific commands that Flight Simulator converts into various actions. The flight plan created with the ATC Workshop is a good starting base for the adventure. The Workshop assembles a complete flight environment to accompany the pilot of the adventure from the start of the engine at the takeoff airport to docking at the destination airport. The adventure will also play digitized controllers' voices (directing the pilot to new courses and altitudes) and set the scene for dynamic weather, whose changes can submit a pilot to a true test.

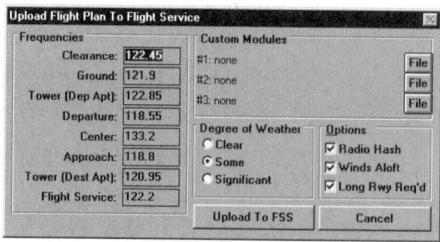

The final preparations for generating an adventure are encountered after selecting the **Pre-Flight | File Plan** menu command. A flight plan must be loaded, but not displayed (by clicking Display | Modify). The Upload Flight Plan dialog box enables the conditions of the simulated adventure to be created. The frequencies of various control points already entered in the Preferences can be adjusted here, only for this adventure, to the proper values. The Degree of Weather options, from Clear (no change) to Some (slight change) to Significant (marked change), control the weather conditions between the takeoff and landing locations.

The remaining options turn the Radio Hash on or off. That is the well known crackling noise generated when a microphone button is pressed. It is used in Flight Simulator for drawing attention to a radio message addressed directly to the simulator pilot. Without this crackling noise, sometimes an important message is not received, creating serious difficulty for the flight.

The Winds Aloft option activates winds during the cruising phase of the flight above 3,000 feet, which force the pilot to compensate his course by using a Wind Correction Angle (WCA), the lead angle toward the wind. The flight duration is also influenced by this wind, according to whether a tail-wind, which increases the speed over the ground, or a head-wind, which reduces the speed over the ground, results.

The third option causes the controller to select only the relatively long takeoff and landing runways, which in most cases are also equipped with ILS. This ensures that there will be sufficient runway length available for the takeoff and landing of large aircraft, like the Boeing.

The Custom Modules are subprograms, ranging from small and simple to highly complex, which—whether programmed by the user or obtained perhaps as a shareware program—can be built into the ATC adventure. In this way it is possible to program a radar altimeter into Flight Simulator or add another voice to announce the taxiing speeds during takeoff or count off the last 200 feet over the landing runway. A few brief examples will be presented in this chapter.

To integrate such a Custom Module, you first have to find the desired file on your hard drive using the File button. The module, which must be available as a pure text file, is then incorporated into the flight plan from the selection box:

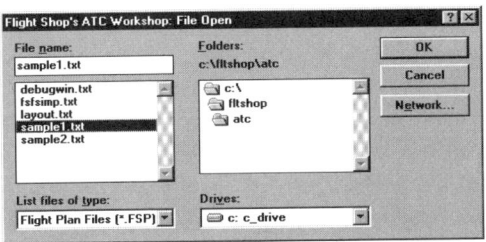
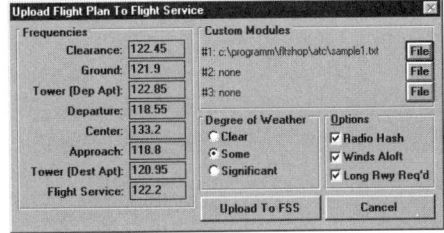

To develop your own submodule for the ATC Workshop, you have to mind a few things to avoid colliding with the main module. The home-brew module must not contain any variables declared with the name A to Z; likewise, none of the following names may appear:

```
vHdg, vAlt1, vDig1, vDig2, vDigit, vTemp, vTemp2, vRadio, vCldBot, vCldTop,
vCldCvr, vVis
```

Moreover, no Ctrl key combinations may be used that are already used in the main module of the ATC adventure. Included are the keys:

Keys			Function
Ctrl	+	W	Radio report only as voice message
Ctrl	+	X	Radio report only as text message
Ctrl	+	Y	Radio report as voice and text message
Ctrl	+	X	List of the adventure key combinations
Ctrl	+	K	Establish contact with the current control station over the correctly entered COM frequency
Ctrl	+	R	Repeat last instruction
Ctrl	+	W	Monitor flying weather
Ctrl	+	G	Switch between IFR and VFR flight plan
Ctrl	+	G	Announce missed approach (go-around)
Ctrl	+	F	Switch on ADV internal autopilot
Ctrl	+	E	Switch off ADV internal autopilot

Possible Ctrl combinations for applications within the home-brew module include, for example:

Ctrl+D, Ctrl+G, Ctrl+J, Ctrl+M, Ctrl+P, Ctrl+Q, Ctrl+S, Ctrl+U

Already completed subroutines integrated into each adventure module can also be created quite easily using GOSUB-jumps. Here is a list of such small, auxiliary routines:

CHKHDGDIRECT

To use this subroutine, which computes a direct course to a choosen location, you must convert the W variable to the opposite direction of the course (for example, choose 90° if 270° is the course desired). The subroutine then returns the W variable, which contains the wind-dependent course value. The variable H of the subroutine contains the number of degrees of deviation from the desired direction of flight.

Example:

The speed of the aircraft is 130 kts and the wind is blowing 20 kts from the south. The aircraft is flying a steering course of 080°, though the intended direction of flight is 100°. The variable W will return the wind-corrected value of 100°+wca = 109° and H will contain the value 29°.

Subroutine call:

```
GOSUB CHKHDGDIRECT
```

PLAYDIGIT

This subroutine loads one of the .WAV files from FS's Adv\Wav folder and returns a spoken number from 0 to 9. This number is received from the vDigit variables.

Subroutine call:

```
 GOSUB PLAYDIGIT
```

PLAYALT

This subroutine loads one of the .WAV files from FS's Adv\Wav folder and returns spoken flight altitude data, rounded to the nearest 100 feet. This number is transmitted from the variable Y.

Subroutine call:

```
GOSUB PLAYALT
```

PLAYSPD

This subroutine loads one of the .WAV files from FS's Adv\Wav folder and returns a spoken value for the speed. This number is transmitted from the variable Y. Subroutine call: GOSUB PLAYSPD.

PLAYHDG

This subroutine loads one of the .WAV files from FS's Adv\Wav folder and returns a spoken value of the steering course, rounded to the nearest 10 full degrees. This number is transferred from the variable M.

Subroutine call:

```
GOSUB PLAYHDG
```

The following example for a very short custom module assumes some APLC-programming familiarity, but is easy to understand with basic knowledge. It allows the pilot to determine his precise altitude above the ground by pressing Ctrl+J. The subroutine itself provides these keys via the ADV_KEYS ADD function and monitors their activity. As soon as the pilot presses Ctrl+J, the value from the native Flight Simulator variable PLANE_ALT-GROUND_ALTITUDE is converted from meters into feet (MTOF) and stored in the variable X. If T=1 (meaning the aircraft is not on the ground), the altitude will be displayed in the text window of Flight Simulator as a whole number (INTeger) in feet AGL (**A**bove **G**round **L**evel). The variable V refers to the option in the adventure of having the ATC conversations delivered in text or voice form and triggers the playing of .WAV files at V=1. If V=1, the variable Y is loaded with the integer part of X and, on jumping to the PLAYALT subroutine, is spoken by a digitized voice.

```
SAMPLE1:
      ADV_KEYS ADD,KV(CTRL "j")  ;Ctrl-J

      WAIT 0
      IF KEY=KV(CTRL "j") THEN    ;Ctrl-J
        WAIT 0,KEYPRESS
        X=MTOF(PLANE_ALT-GROUND_ALTITUDE)
        IF T=1 THEN
            SCROLL "Altitude is ",INT(X)," AGL."
        ENDIF
        IF V=1 THEN
            Y=INT(X)
            GOSUB PLAYALT
        ENDIF
      ENDIF
```

Three such custom modules can be accommodated in the main module at the same time. When this ATC main module is compiled, these subroutines are generated in the manner correct for the simulator. During this compilation process, the transmission of the flight plan to the flight control stations is simulated in the form of a modem. The LEDs of the modem light up to show the 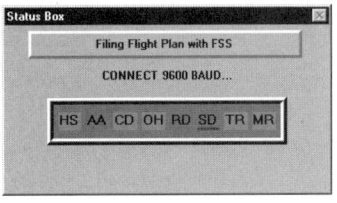 progress of the adventure generation. If all the modules were programmed free of errors, the ATC Workshop generates an .ADV adventure file, which carries the same name as the original flight plan, BOSJKF1.ADV in the example. This adventure is saved on the hard drive in the FS5\Adv folder, unless using APLC32 compiler.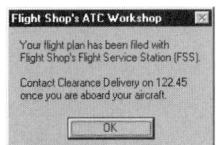

The last display confirms the successful compilation of the adventure and indicates the radio frequency (from Clearance Delivery) for the first contact.

Converting The FS5 .ADV

Unfortunately, the generated .ADV file is still not ready for use in Flight Simulator 98: it is readable only by version 5 or 5.1 of Flight Simulator.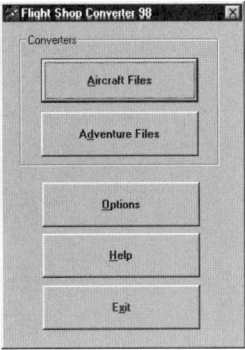

Further processing and conversion into a module capable of running on FS98 is accomplished using the conversion software AAFCONV98, which is available free of charge with nearly every add-on and in many Flight Simulator forums on the Internet, CompuServe or other services.

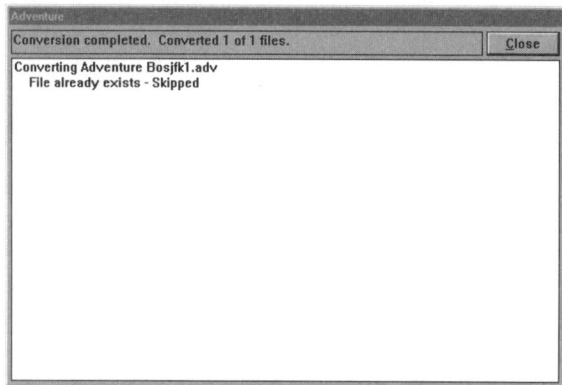

Using the converter, one click converts the new .ADV file into an FS98 adventure file. .WAV files that are missing or cannot be found are listed in the Error window and may be converted again by restructuring the sounds into the correct directory. The converter prefers a Wav subfolder to correctly enable the ATC sounds of the Workshop.

You have two ways to check whether an adventure has been properly converted for FS98. Open Windows Explorer, and look for your adventure in the FS98\Adv folder. Or, launch FS98 and click **Flights | Adventures...** If you see your new adventure in one of these locations, you're ready to go.

Starting An Adventure

A completed adventure is started from the Flights | Adventures... dialog box in Flight Simulator 98. ATC Workshop (and also AAFCONV) creates the file name based on the abbreviations of the takeoff and destination airports. In the present example, the file is titled BOS to JFK. In the description, ATC delivers a sharply abbreviated flight plan with a copyright notation:

BOS-GENERAL EDWARD LAWRENCE LOGAN INTL to JFK-JOHN F KENNEDY INTL, Created: 01-05-1998, Virtual Werner - Learjet 45A, Cruise Alt: 24000 MSL, Speed: 450KTS, Dist: 168.1, ETE: 00:31, [A Flight Sim Flight Shop generated ATC Adventure].

Pressing the OK button loads the adventure file, and it begins with a brief text message regarding setup and the selection for the display or reproduction of the radio messages.

Flight Service Station

The ATC Workshop equips the adventure with a Flight Service Station (FSS) (in Europe, this corresponds to the Flight Information Service). Contact can be made with this service at any time on the COM frequency 122.2 MHz, to check on the most recent weather, for example. This may be necessary under difficult weather conditions or to get the latest information at the beginning of the flight. Depending upon the option settings in the adventure generation, the weather can change considerably over the duration of the flight. Pressing Ctrl+W orders the appropriate Flight Service Station to report the current weather.

In addition to weather reports, the FSS is also responsible for the change from IFR to VFR flights (and back again). Changes from radar-guided and controlled flight to uncontrolled visual flight can be made under favorable weather conditions (no clouds, good visibility). With that is the possibility of deviating from the route of the flight plan as filed, for example, to fly to special landmarks in the scenery or to make an intermediate landing at a small airport in the region for a cup of coffee. You can resume the IFR flight plan by pressing Ctrl+I on the FSS frequency.

Clearance

Each ATC adventure begins with the flight clearance, which the pilot receives from the Clearance Delivery. When the flight plan is filed (which is simulated by the ATC Workshop), all the flight control stations responsible for the flight (Ground, Tower, Center, etc.) are notified and coordinated to ensure a run with the least possible friction.

On the basis of the data in the filed flight plan—IFR/VFR, speed, flight altitude and route—Clearance issues the clearance of the flight plan and also announces the transponder code to be set and the various COM frequencies of the participating FFS control stations, Departure and Ground.

The only problem with the flight clearance is receiving and understanding the report. Therefore, three things should be ready at the beginning of the adventure: the knowledge of what is expected of the pilot, paper and pencil. When the adventure begins, you are immediately bombarded with a clearance from the ATC, even if you are busy doing something else at the moment. Unfortunately, you have no stand-by key to ask the controller to wait a moment. However, you can repeat the message by pressing Ctrl+R and away you go:

> *Learjet 45A - General Edward Logan Clearance - Cleared to John F. Kennedy Airport as filed. Climb and maintain 4000' - expect FL240 10 minutes after departure - departure frequency 188.55 - Squawk 4331 - Check latest weather report on FSS 122.2 - Contact Ground 121.9 prior to taxi.*

The notation of an ATC flight clearance is very simple. Appearing first is the desired destination. Then comes the flight plan, precisely as you entered it. Then comes the first intermediate altitude after takeoff and the time until the requested cruising altitude is reached. Departure is responsible for the takeoff from the starting point. The Squawk is the four-digit transponder code that provides the controllers a reliable identification of the aircraft on their radar screens. Following this are the frequencies FSS, for the last weather report, and Ground, starting the engines and taxiing. The record of such a release could then look like this:

```
cl JFK R af          cl = cleared, R = Route, af = as filed
A 50 exp FL240 10'   A = Altitude, FL = Flight Level
D 118.55  T 4331     D = Departure Frequency, T = Transponder
W 122.2  G 121.9     W = Weather Info, G = Ground
```

The Flight Simulator pilot is relieved of the obligation to "read back" and confirm this clearance. The simulation would be truly authentic only if this important feature were built in. In FS's options, you select the Clearance report, to be delivered as running text or as a one-line text block. Pressing Ctrl+R causes the Controller to repeat its last report.

Ground

The Ground control of an airport monitors all the movements of aircraft on the ramp and taxi-ways from and to the takeoff and landing runways. Following the general flight clearance, Ground begins with the clearance for starting the engines and for taxiing up to the holding point before the active takeoff runway. If nothing unusual takes place on the taxiways, change the Tower frequency on the command of Ground.

Tower

The Control Tower (the only actually visible control station at an airport) has the job of monitoring aircraft that are taking off and landing. The first contact with the Tower clears you for departure. This is usually followed by the orders to continue the takeoff in the runway heading and to contact Departure. Only then is the actual clearance for takeoff granted: Cleared for take off.

Departure

The Departure controllers sit in front of radar screens in darkened rooms. The aircraft symbol appears on the screen along with the aircraft's transponder code. The unequivocal identification is confirmed to the pilot with the message "...Radar contact." Following a short time later are the instructions for the continued flight to the first route marker, sent with new course and altitudes, which must be read back and implemented by the pilot immediately.

Center

The heart of flight control (in American airspace) are the Centers, which monitor large areas of airspace. Each Center station is responsible for the air traffic within its sector. As long as the pilot has switched on the correct Center frequency, he will fly under radar control and receive information and instructions from the controller. The more precisely the aircraft is guided along the intended courses and altitudes according to the flight plan, the less you will hear from the Center controller. If the pilot makes large deviations from the filed flight plan, the controller will order new courses and altitudes, to return the pilot to the preset route. In real life, gross transgressions against the orders can result in significant penalties. The worst that can happen to a simulator pilot is that the controller will no longer speak to him, because the aircraft has flown out of the controller's range. With that, the ATC adventure ends and the pilot is on his own.

When all courses and altitudes are correctly maintained and the destination is approached, Center will hand off the aircraft to Approach control.

Approach

The Approach Control near an airport takes over incoming aircraft from the Center. Approach has the job of safely guiding aircraft to the field so that the pilot can successfully land. Depending on from where the plane arrives, Approach will direct the aircraft either straight to a runway or into a traffic pattern leading to final approach. If the aircraft is at the correct approach altitude and on the localizer course of the ILS, Approach then hands-off to the Tower.

Tower

The control tower of the destination airport notifies the pilot in final approach, usually on reaching the outer marker, of the landing clearance: Cleared to land. The controller precisely observes the path of approach during this last phase of the flight, estimates the speed, issues possible orders to correct the same, and calls the pilot immediately if he sees the landing gear has not been lowered for the impending landing.

Unfavorable conditions—parts on the runway from an aircraft which has met with an accident, wind gusts crosswise to the runway, flights of birds in the approach sector—can cause the tower controller to order the aircraft to perform a Missed Approach Procedure. On hearing that, the pilot must immediately abort the landing and initiate the missed approach procedures published in the approach charts or follow the special orders of the controller. In the ATC adventure, the pilot will transfer back to the Approach control, which will initiate a new approach attempt for the aircraft. Naturally, the pilot also has the option to break off the landing approach on his own initiative and carry out a missed approach. That can be justified under very poor visibility conditions, an inappropriate approach altitude or imprecise direction of approach. The key combination Ctrl+G orders the missed approach and the associated go-around from the tower. In this situation, too, the continued flight is monitored by Approach.

Following a successful landing, the tower controller orders the pilot to use the nearest possible taxiway, to clear the landing runway for subsequent traffic. Once on the taxiway, the aircraft is again within the sphere of responsibility of the Ground station, which guides the aircraft to the the terminal (gate, ramp, etc.). And so, the adventure ends.

Flight Plan Autopilot (FPAP)

For each adventure from the ATC Workshop, the aircraft is equipped with a modern autopilot, which steers the preset course via the radio stations and the controller's orders completely automatically. The operation of this autopilot can be switched on just after takeoff, starting at about 1,000 feet, and can remain active until reaching the final landing approach. This autopilot function can be switched on or off as desired during the flight.

The Ctrl+F key combination activates the FPAP; pressing Ctrl+E switches it off again. With FPAP engaged, flights in complete darkness or in clouds become child's play for the pilot, who only needs to monitor the activities of his electronic partner.

Flying An Adventure

Starting an adventure via selection in the **Flights | Adventures...** dialog box moves the last aircraft model activated with all its characteristics (from the aircraft settings) to the starting position of the ADV-program, and the takeoff airport within the adv-file, with which the aircraft is to be flown, is retained. Selecting the correct aircraft from the hangar must be taken care of by the pilot before starting the adventure. A further shortcoming involves the adventure's starting position. The ATC Workshop gets this starting point from its own airport data base. In most cases, the airport reference point (ARP) is on a takeoff runway, but it may be in the middle of a green meadow, on a lake's surface or on the roof of a house. In the latter cases, the adventure will terminate prematurely with a splash or crash. Such awkward circumstances frequently arise when the original scenery is supplemented or replaced by additional scenery areas, which aren't recognized by the ADV Workshop.

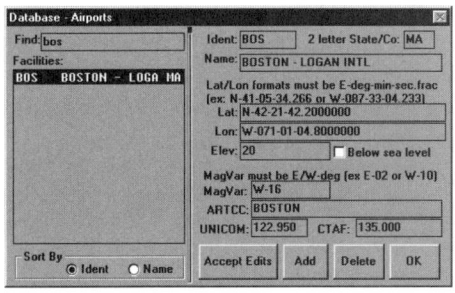

The best solution for the clean start of an Adventure is the advance briefing on the scenery environment and the positioning of the desired aircraft type with its characteristics on the apron, for example, in front of the terminal buildings. That takes place most simply via slewing the aircraft Y. If a suitable place is found on the concrete surface of the apron, a note is made of the exact position, either from the option Go to ... exact position or directly by entry of the position values in the viewing or map window Shift+Z.

The starting position is then saved in the Flight Simulator as the flight position and can be reloaded at any time in this constellation.

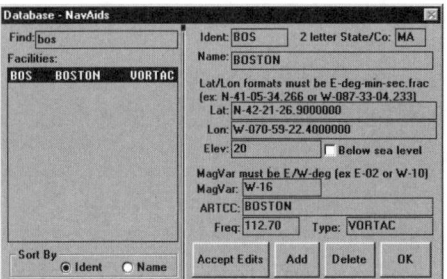 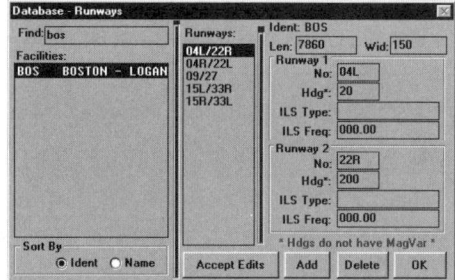

The latitude and longitude position values for the BOS-JFK adventure should—if the aircraft is parked at the south terminal of Boston Logan Intl.—read more or less as follows:

	FS98-Format	ATC-Workshop
Latitude	N42° 21.82'	N-42-21-42.20
Longitude	W071° 01.08'	W-071-01-04.80

The data are entered in the airport database for the Boston airport (waypoint BOS) in the corresponding entry fields and, using the [Accept Edits] button, written back to the Workshop database. The (re)compilation of the adventure flight plan will have the exact starting position available, as stored in the Flight Simulator flight situation.

With these two actions—creating the flight situation file BOSJFK.STN and the adventure file BOSJFK1.ADV—you now have both the desired aircraft type and the correct starting position in the adventure.

Importing Additional Navigational Data

In the original edition, the ATC Workshop of the FSFS contained the most important navigational data (airports, runways and NavAids) for the North American airspace. To use the remainder of the world for the application, one must integrate additional data into the ATC database. A Database Import Utility for the Flight Simulator FlightShop is available for that purpose. It can be obtained as freeware in most Flight Simulator forums on the Net as the file FSFSIMP.ZIP.

Check the MicroWings Web site (wwwmicrowings.com), CompuServe (go: FSFORUM), AOL (keyword: FSRC) orFTP.IUP.EDU

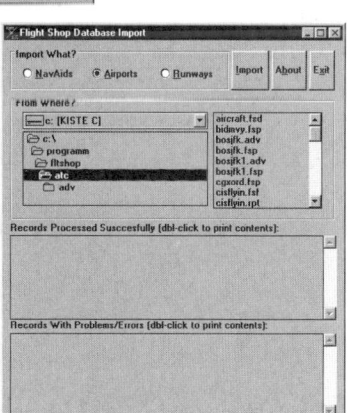

The unpacked import program is best stored in the FlightShop computer and can load the new data into the database from there.

Just as in the case of FSFSIMP itself, a large number of database collections for the ATC workshop are available in the forums and can be imported immediately after the download. Anyone willing to make the effort to build in his own data must know how the ATC Workshop processes these data collections and in what form they need to be prepared.

FSFSIMP data format

Each batch of data to be imported is first specified according to its data class. The ATC Workshop distinguishes the following classes:

✈ Airport information

✈ Runway and ILS information

✈ NavAids information (VOR, NDB, intersections, etc.)

Each of the three classes then contains a specific number of data batches (which have absolute lengths). Each data batch contains entries for names, waypoint characteristics, latitude, longitude and the like, the position within which the data batch is set. Unused areas must be filled with spaces. Special characters, such as the comma, semicolon or tabulator, separate the entries. The following three tables show the data structure of the individual classes.

Airport data

```
Field      Start Length Format
Ident      1    5    Text
Name       7    35   Text
Staat      44   2    Text (uppercase letters)
Latitude   48   14   Y-00-00-00.000 (Y = N or S)
Longitude  64   15   X-000-00-00.000 (X = E or W)
MagVar     81   3    X00 (X = E or W)
Elevation  86   6    000000
ARTCC      94   12   Text
UNICOM     108  7    000.000
CTAF       117  7    000.000
```

Runway data

```
Field        Start Length Format
Ident        1    5    Text
Rwy no       7    10   00X/00X (x=L/R/C)
Length       18   5    00000
Width        24   5    00000
Rwy1 no      30   3    00X (X=L/R/C)
Rwy1 direction 34  3    000
Rwy1 ILS type 38   9    Text (uppercase letters)
Rwy1 ILS freq 48   7    000.000
Rwy2 no      56   3    00X (X=L/R/C)
Rwy2 direction 60  3    000
Rwy2 ILS type 64   9    Text (uppercase letters)
Rwy2 ILS freq 74   7    000.000
```

NavAid data

```
Field    Start Length Format
Ident    1    5     Text
Name     7    35    Text
Staat    44   2     Text (uppercase letters)
Latitude 48   14    Y-00-00-00.000 (Y = N or S)
Longitude 64  15    X-000-00-00.000 (X = E or W)
MagVar   81   3     X00 (X = E or W)
Elevation 86  6     000000
ARTCC    94   12    Text (name <!von!> Center)
Freq     109  7     000.000
Type     117  7     Text (uppercase letters)
```

Adventure Programming Language (APL)

In the background of each adventure is a series of programmed commands that Flight Simulator processes at the appropriate time. In contrast to the event-controlled programming of Windows applications, all the commands of the Basic-like APL programming language are executed individually and in sequence. Thus, unfortunately, it is not possible to utilize a programming environment, like that offered by VisualBasic, for example. APL is, rather, a simple, line-oriented programming language, whose functionality can be best illustrated by an everyday example:

```
In _the_morning
      Print "Look out the window"
      If the_sun_is_shining Then
            be_happy
      Or if it_is_raining Then
            put_up-umbrella
      Or if it_is_snowing Then
            put_on_overcoat
      End Mit if
      Goto In _the_morning
      Eof
```

Chapter 5: Adventure Programming

The brief programming example devotes most of its time to the query structure If...Or...Then. It never leaves this structure, because a specific reaction will follow, according to the weather situation, but the entire story begins again from the top with the command Goto In_the_morning.

The brief programming example below, one surely more suitable for Flight Simulator, should explain a few basic commands and functions of the APL. The example will support a flight from Düsseldorf to Bremen, thereby simulating a very simple, preprogrammed GPS-INS device. In addition, a somewhat different version of the checklists has been integrated.

The APL module begins with the initialization section, which contains the adventure title in the first line and loads the appropriate flight situation in the next line. This flight situation (which was set up beforehand) places the aircraft on the Düsseldorf apron at the parking position 20 (N 51° 17.1′ E006° 46.2′). The situation file DUS20.STN must be stored in the Adv or Pilots subfolder of Flight Simulator.

The two commands north_latitude and east_longitude convert the ADV system for the later calculations in such a way that positive values are used for north latitudes and east longitudes, while south latitudes and west longitudes have negative values.

```
; Modul-Initialization————————————————

title "GPS Test Flight"
load_situation "DUS20.stn"
north_latitude
east_longitude

adv_keys add, kv("1"),kv("N")     ;1 and Shift-N

declare check, flight
declare gps,wpt,anz
declare qdm,qdr,dst,tim
declare lat,lon

check=0
gps=0
anz=6
wpt=-1
nav1_freq=114.3          ; OSN
vor_1_obs=064            ; R244=TO 064
nav2_freq=115.15         ; DUS
vor_2_obs=002            ; R002
```

```
adf_freq=284.5        ; DY
com_freq=123.77        ; DUS ATIS
trans_freq=4321         ; Squawk

season=3            ; Fall
hour =12            ; 12:00:00 hours
minute=0
second=0
```

New key combinations for this adventure are handled with the adv_keys command. This command is expanded with key words which can add new keys and delete them again. The new key combinations are attached to adv_keys in a list, with their key code (key value) as a parameter.

Examples	
adv_keys add, kv("1")	adds Key 1 to the adventure program
Adv_keys delete, kv(„1")	deletes Key 1 from the adventure program
Adv_keys clear	deletes all previosuly defined key combinations

Individual keys or key combinations are activated via a special code for the adventure. This code is very simple to create, because it directly addresses the respective key. "CTRL," "SHIFT" and "KeyPad" are in this case special, supplementary key words that are employed in specific key combinations.

Examples	
kv("q")	the small q
kv("Q")	the large Q, thus [Shift]+[Q]
kv(CRTL+SHIFT+Q)	[Ctrl] and [Shift] together with [Q]
kv(CRTL+KeyPad8)	[Ctrl] and [8] in the numeric keypad
kv(CRTL+PgUp)	[Ctrl] and [9] in the numeric keypad

The declare command defines the variables used in the program. A variable name can consist of letters, numerals and the underline '_', but it must begin with a letter. The APL-native variables (see later in the chapter) need not be defined beforehand.

Per definition, the variables for the starting conditions are provided using the declare command.

The following commands specify, according to their meaning, the season and time of day for the adventure. The season is characterized with numerals 0 through 3:

Seasons			
0	Winter	2	Summer
1	Spring	3	Fall

The time of the day is specified in hours (0 through 23), minutes and seconds (0 through 59).

The frequencies and courses of the navigation aids are set via the APL-native variables. They overwrite the data stored in the current flight situation.

The main program consists essentially of three large while…endwhile structures. The loop structures contain the phase of the flight on the ground prior to the start, during flight and back on the ground after landing. The while loop uses the APL variable on_ground, which returns the current status (on the ground or not).

So long as the aircraft stands on the ground or taxis, the program branches via the gosub calls into subroutines of the program. The subroutines contain entirely standard checklist texts that are displayed in a special window, the debug window of the APL. The variable check is employed to determine whether all the checks in the subroutine have been processed. After the last checklist, takeoff, the way is open for the start. The first loop is exited with check=1 and with the variable on_ground, which is no longer valid.

```
; Main program ───────────────────

print "This is a test..."
; play ATC-Sounds
wait 5
while on_ground          ; on the ground
      if check = 0 then
              gosub safety
              gosub startup
              gosub blockoff
              gosub taxi
              gosub takeoff
              check=1          ; all ground checks complete
      endif
endwhile
;
```

Program execution runs through the second while loop as long as the aircraft is in the air, i.e., no longer touching the ground. After the takeoff, which must be performed manually by the pilot, the autopilot is switched on at an altitude of 1,500 feet. The cruising altitude is set at 15,000 feet and locked in at this altitude. The steering course (HDG) in the autopilot is set to the takeoff course already programmed in the NAV2/ OBS2 unit, and the aircraft turns completely automatically onto the new course toward the north, climbing to the cruising altitude.

An if loop and a flag query the variable plane_alt to determine whether or not the intermediate variable of 1,500 feet has already been reached. Because Flight Simulator 98 and APL calculate the altitude internally in meters, the altitude value has to be converted.

```
;
while NOT on_ground        ; in the air
      if flight=0 then
            if plane_alt>ftom(1500) then
                  autopilot_master=1
                  autopilot_altitude=ftom(15000)
                  autopilot_altitude_hold-1
                  autopilot_heading=vor_2_obs
                  autopilot_heading_hold=1
                  flag=1       ; Departure complete
            endif
      endif
```

The Key 1, previously defined with adv_keys (on the main keyboard), will now be queried continuously within the while loop, that is to say, during the flight. If the key is pressed, the program branches into the gps_onoff subroutine, where it is noted whether the pilot has switched the GPS on or off. With the GPS switched off (gps=1), the pilot can call the next waypoint with the key combination [Shift]+[N], which is established in a way-point definition at the end of the program code. The geographical data of the waypoint are then read. The distance, course and flying time to this waypoint are displayed in the text line of the Flight Simulator via the subroutine show_gps.

After the last programmed waypoint (wp6), which lies on the landing approach to Runway 27 of Bremen, the signals of the outer and middle markers and the rate of descent are queried. Once both conditions have been satisfied, the corresponding messages are displayed in the text window. The while loop Not on_ground terminates when the wheels make contact with the runway.

```
        onkey kv("1") gosub gps_onoff
        if gps=1 then
                onkey kv("N") gosub next_wp
                if wpt>-1 then
                        gosub show_gps
                endif
        endif
        if omark and velocity_y < 0 then
                gosub final
        endif
        if mmark and velocity_y < 0 then
                gosub landing
        endif
endwhile
```

Once the aircraft again touches ground, the third while loop begins processing the after-landing checklists. The variable check is again used to monitor the outcome. The adventure automatically ends with the last checklist, blockon.

```
while on_ground         ; landed! Again on the ground
        if check = 1 then
                gosub landing
                gosub blockon
                check=2         ; all ground checks complete
        endif
endwhile

print "End of the Adventure ..."
wait 5
end
```

For greater clarity, the subroutines and other functions continuously needed by the program are noted after the main program ends. The first subroutine is a simple on/off switch for the GPS unit: If it is switched off (gps=0), it will then be switched on (gps=1) and vice versa. If you desire a longer display duration, a delay (in seconds) can be set using the wait command:

```
; Subroutine ———————————————

gps_onoff:
        if gps = 0 then
                print "GPS on"
                gps = 1
                ; wait 3
```

```
        else
                print "GPS off"
                gps = 0
                ; wait 3
        endif
return
```

The subroutine next_wp is then called by pressing the (Shift)+(N) key combination. It increases the value of wpt by one each time the key combination is pressed and branches with the on...gosub command to the corresponding waypoint definition. For wpt=0, the label wp0 is targeted; for wpt=1, the label wp1, and so forth. If the index wpt becomes greater than 5 (=anz-1), it is reset to zero. In this way it is possible for the pilot to fly directly to each of the predefined waypoints.

```
next_wp:
        wpt = wpt + 1
        if wpt > anz - 1 then
                wpt = 0
        endif
        on wpt gosub wp0,wp1,wp2,wp3,wp4,wp5
return
```

The geographical data are read into the waypoint definitions and stored in the variables lat and lon. Note the numerical format of latitudes and longitudes: Latitudes between -90° and +90° are in the format DD:MM:SS, and longitudes between -180° and +180° in the format DDD:MM:SS. The subroutine show_gps calculates the current position of the aircraft, the distance and the course from the waypoint definitions. The function ground_distance(lat,lon) calculates the true distance of the aircraft above the ground, in contrast to the function air_distance(lat,lon), which returns the distance through the air between the aircraft at that altitude and the waypoint. The distance is stored in the variable dst.

The variable qdr stores the result of the function radial(lat,lon)-magvar. This function calculates the bearing from the waypoint to the aircraft, which corresponds to VOR radial or FROM report. A bearing from a navigation point to the aircraft is designated as QDR. The bearing in the opposite direction, that is to say, the bearing from the aircraft to the waypoint, is designated as the QDM.

The variable qdm is accordingly reversed by 180°. The variable magvar contains the average local declination and corrects the magnetic course to the true course. The anticipated duration of the flight to the waypoint is computed via the ratio of distance, dst, and momentary speed, velocity and stored in tim.

```
show_gps:
      dst = ground_distance(lat,lon)
      qdr = radial(lat,lon)-magvar
      qdm = qdr + 180
      if qdm > 360 then
            qdm =qdm - 360
      endif
      tim = dst / velocity * 60
```

The contents of the variables wpt, dst, qdm, qdr and tim are then displayed in the single-line text window of the Flight Simulator.

Examples: precision left, min right, max right

Value	Command	Output
1	precision 1,0,0	1
1	precision 1,1,2	1.0
1	precision 1,2,2	1.00
1	precision 3,1,1	001.1

The format of a number is thus defined by the number of places to the left in front of the decimal point (left), the smallest number after the decimal point (min right) and the maximal number of places following the decimal point. (max right):

```
      precision 1,0,0
      print "WP",wpt+1,":",
      precision 1,1,1
      print " DST ",dst,
      precision 3,0,0
      print " TO ",qdm," FR ",qdr,
      precision 1,1,1
      print " TTG ",tim
      wait 5
return
```

Waypoint definitions, labeled wp0 to wp5 of the subroutine next_wp, follow the calculating subroutines. The geographical data are taken from the takeoff chart SID of Düsseldorf. The comments after the semicolon describe the definitions in cleartext, just as they are given on the map (wp0 to wp3) or even self-determined fixed points for the takeoff (wp4 and wp5):

```
; Waypoints-Definitions ─────────────
wp0:
        lat = 51:30:00                  ; DLW 0: R002 40 DME NOR
        lon = 006:40:00
return
wp1:
        lat = 51:51:00                  ; DLW 1: R028 38 DME DUS
        lon = 007:11:30
return
wp2:
        lat = 52:12:06                  ; DLW 2: R010 21 DME HMM
        lon = 007:47:54
return
wp3:
        lat = 52:46:18                  ; BASUM Intersection
        lon = 008:47:18
return
wp4:
        lat = 52:54:00                  ; 12 DME BMN
        lon = 009:00:00
return
wp5:
        lat = 53:03:00                  ; On final 10 NM
        lon = 009:03:00
return
```

The Checklist function of the adventure makes use of a function that was designed only for testing the program: debug_window on/off displays a window on the screen or deletes it again, and debug_print displays any desired text in this window. The checklists are then called by the main program in the form of this window and should reduce the workload of the pilot (and his co) in the cockpit.

```
; Checklist─────────────────────

safety:
        debug_window on
        debug_print "Safety: Landing gear ... down"
```

```
        debug_print "    Engine Master ... off"
        wait 5
        debug_window off
return
startup:
        debug_window on
        debug_print "Startup: Circuit breakers ... Normal"
        debug_print "      Logbook ........... Checked"
        debug_print "      Cabin signs ....... On"
        debug_print "      Emergency lights ... Armed"
        debug_print "      Ice Protection ..... Off"
        debug_print "      Air condition ...... Set"
        debug_print "      Electricals ....... Set"
        debug_print "      Hydraulics ........ Set"
        debug_print "      Instruments ....... Normal"
        debug_print "      Altimeter ......... Set"
        debug_print "      Fuel On Board ...... Checked"
        debug_print "      Gear .............. Down & Green"
        wait 5
        debug_window off
return

; You can use the standard checklist or make your own
;blockoff:
;taxi:
;takeoff:
;climb:
;transition:
;cruise:
;descent:
;approach:
final:
print "Outer Marker inbound ... Landing Checks Completed"
return
landing:
        print "Middle Marker ... Decision Height, Runway in sight"
return"
```

According to the type of aircraft, special checklists can be prepared for nearly any situation and called using special key combinations or in a certain phase of the flight. The above already contains place holders for various situations.

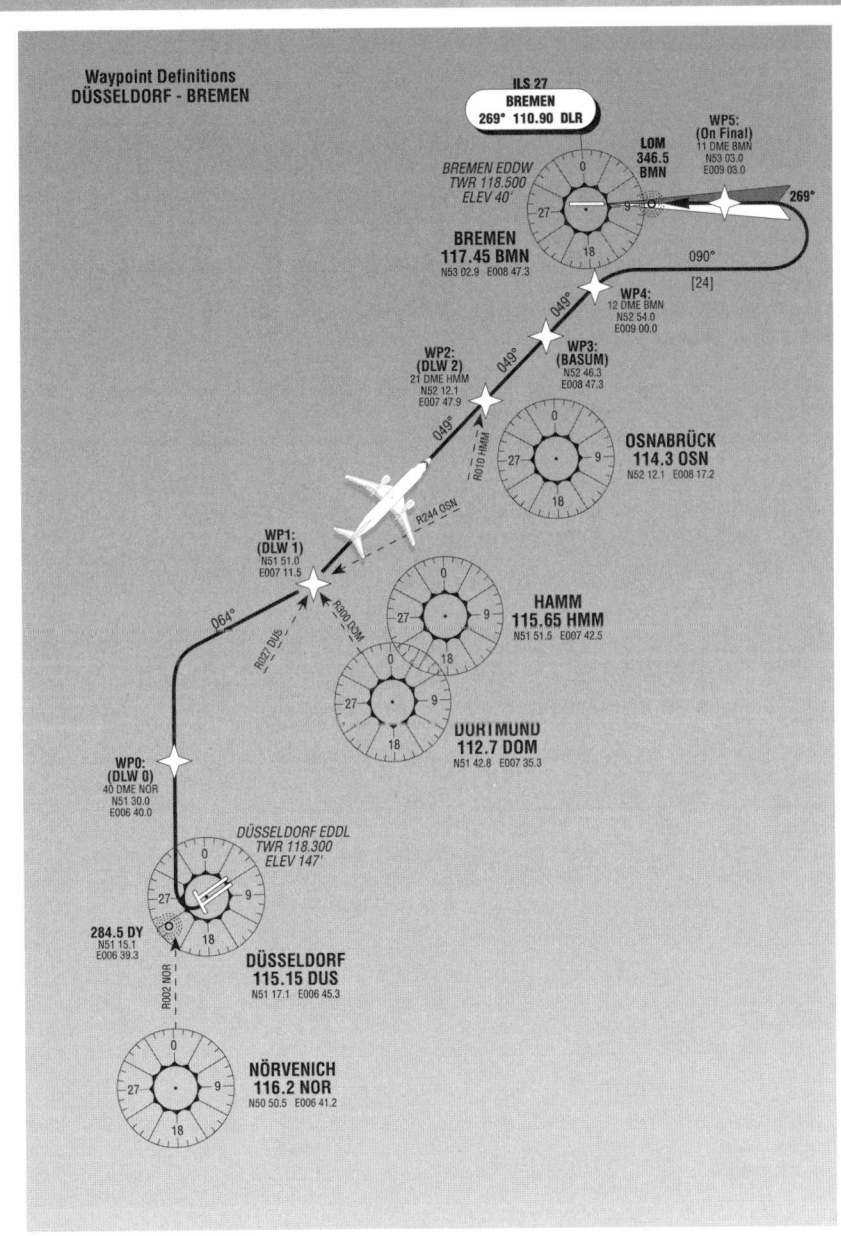

Chapter 5: Adventure Programming

Commands and functions

The structure of the Adventure Programming Language (APL) corresponds to that of the Basic programming language. For that reason, only the essential components of the language—commands and functions—are listed below and provided with a brief descriptive note or comment.

Condition: *IF structure*

```
IF expression THEN
ELSEIF expression THEN
ELSE
ENDIF
```

Counter loop: *FOR ... NEXT structure*

```
FOR variable=expression1 TO expresion2 [BY expression3]
      ... Program lines
NEXT variable
```

General loop: *WHILE structure*

```
WHILE expression
      ... Program lines
ENDWHILE
```

Branching

```
GOTO label
GOSUB label
ON expression GOTO label0, label1, label2, label3, ...
ON expression GOSUB label0, label1, label2, label3, ...

Label:
RETURN
```

Logical program end

```
END
```

Definition of variables

```
DECLARE
```

Screen output

```
PRINT liste
SCROLL liste
PRECISION left, min right, max right
PRINT_TIME zeit
```

Acoustic output

```
PLAY "*.wav"
```

Adventure - title

```
TITLE "character string"
```

Adventure - description text

```
DESCRIPTION "character string"
```

Adventure - break

```
WAIT time , KEYPRESS
```

Adventure - key combination

```
ADV_KEYS
ADV_KEYS ADD, key
ADV_KEYS DELETE, key
ADV_KEYS CLEAR
KV( )
```

Definition of the main hemisphere

```
NORTH_LATITUDE
SOUTH_LATITUDE
EAST_LONGITUDE
WEST_LONGITUDE
```

Movement of the aircraft to a new Position

```
SETPOSITION latitude, longitude, altitude
```

Reset to current Flight Situation

```
RESET_SITUATION
```

Loading a stored Flight Situation

```
LOAD_SITUATION
```

Restart of current Adventure:

```
RESET_ADVENTURE
```

Program braching during crashes, stalling and key input

```
ONCRASH [GOSUB label]
ONSTALL [GOSUB label]
ONKEY key [GOSUB label]
```

Weather functions

Each adventure can define its own weather situation in Flight Simulator. That takes place most expediently by defining an appropriate weather zone for a specific geographical region. The weather commands of the APL correspond to the dialogs in the Weather Areas menu of Flight Simulator:

```
WEATHER "name", lat1, lon1, lat2, lon2
WEATHER_CHAR winds, transition, course, speedin knots
```

Clouds are defined in layers with a lower and upper boundary according to type, degree of cover, etc.:

```
CLOUDS layer, base, top, type, cover, turbulence, deviation, eis
CLOUDS layer, DELETE
```

The predefined cloud types have certain characteristics, which are summarized in the following table. The boundaries should be observed to avoid producing any unnecessary error messages during the course of the adventure:

Cloud type	Base		Thickness		Cover		Turb.		Dev.
	min	max	min	max	min	max	min	max	max
Cirrus	4800	14000	3	100	clr	sct2	0	18	0
Cirrostratus	4800	14000	3	5	brk7	ovc	0	18	0
Cirrocumulus	4800	14000	5	300	sct2	brk6	36	109	0
Altostratus	1800	7000	15	300	brk7	ovc	0	18	0
Altocumulus	1800	7000	30	1000	sct2	brk6	36	109	0
Stratocumulus	100	1500	100	1000	sct2	ovc	36	109	100
Nimbostratus	100	1500	300	1200	brk6	ovc	0	18	20
stratus	100	1500	30	600	sct4	ovc	0	18	20
cumulus	100	1500	100	5000	sct2	ovc	36	109	200
cumulonimbus	100	6000	1500	9000	wide	dense	146	255	200
Userdefined	100	14000	3	10000	clr	ovc	0	255	200

The table contains abbreviated key words for the degree of cover. It is, however, necessary to use the cleartext formulations in the Clouds command:

Degree of cover	
clear	clr
Scattered1	sct1
Scattered2	sct2
Scattered3	sct3
Scattered4	sct4
broken5	brk5
broken6	brk6
broken7	brk7
overcast	sct8

The remaining commands, Winds, Temperature, Baro-Pressure and Visibility, correspond to the dialogs in Flight Simulator's Weather menu:

```
WINDS layer, base, top, type, direction, speed, turbulence
WINDS layer, DELETE
TEMPERATURE layer, altitude , temp, zone
TEMPERATURE layer, DELETE
BARO_PRESSURE air pressure, drift
VISIBILITY distance
```

Functions

The functions of the APL that very rapidly accept and convert complicated calculations—such as, distance and course between the aircraft and a certain geographical location—have already been mentioned several times.

Function and argument	Internal conversion
FTOM(Feet)	Feet to meters ft/3,2808 or 0,3048*ft
MTOF(Meters)	Meters to feet 3,2808*m or m*0,3048
FTOC(Temp F)	Fahrenheit to Celsius
CTOF(Temp C)	Celsius to Fahrenheit
MBTOINHG(Pressure mb)	Millibar to Inch Hg
INHGTOMB(Pressure inch Hg)	Inch Hg to Millibar
KMTONM(Dist km)	Kilometers to nautical miles
NMTOKM(Dist NM)	Nautical miles to kilometers
SMTONM(Dist SM)	Statute miles to nautical miles
GROUND_DISTANCE(lat, lon)	True distance over ground between aircraft coordinates and position (lat,lon)
AIR_DISTANCE(lat, lon)	Air distance between aircraft in the air and position (lat,lon) on the ground (corresponds to the DME-indication in the aircraft)
RADIAL(lat, lon)	Bearing from location Ort(lat,lon) to aircraft
GLIDE_SLOPE(lat, lon)	Glide angle to the position (lat,lon)
DEGREES(angle)	Angle in whole degrees
MINUTES(angle)	Angle in whole minutes
SECOND(angle)	Angle in whole seconds
INT(value)	Integer value
INRANGE(value, min, max)	returns 1 (true), if value lies between min and max (value >=min, value <=max)

Variables

All the variables used by APL are 32-bit, fixed-point numbers with 16 places before the decimal and 16 places after it.

User variables are defined using the DECLARE command, in which case there must be no variable names from A to Z, because these are already predefined.

Flight Simulator-internal variables serve to query the flight parameters and can be tested in the adventure, taken over or, in a few cases, even overwritten with new data.

Variable name	Unit	*	Description
ADF_ACTIVE	bool		True if ADF receives signals
ADF_ALT	meter		Altitude of the NDB
ADF_FREQ	kHz	*	200 ... 1699.9
ADF_LAT	degree		Latitude of ADF station
ADF_LON	degree		Longitude of ADF station
AUTOPILOT_ALTITUDE	meter	*	Alt. MSL for autopilot to maintain
AUTOPILOT_ALTITUDE_HOLD	bool	*	True if autopilot is to maintain altitude specified by AUTOPILOT_ALTITUDE
AUTOPILOT_APPROACH_HOLD	bool	*	True if autopilot is to follow localizer and G/S tuned to NAV1
AUTOPILOT_ATTITUDE_HOLD	bool	*	True if autopilot is to hold the plane's atitude steady
AUTOPILOT_BACK_COURSE_HOLD	bool	*	True if autopilot is to fly the back course tuned to NAV1
AUTOPILOT_HEADING	degree	*	Heading for autopilot to hold 1 ... 360° (magn)
AUTOPILOT_HEADING_HOLD	bool	*	True if autopilot is to maintain heading specified
AUTOPILOT_LOCALIZER_HOLD	bool	*	This should correspond to the check box on the LOC line in the autopilot dialogin FS5.1
AUTOPILOT_MASTER	bool	*	Autopilot master switch must be on for functions to be active
AUTOPILOT_NAV_HOLD	bool	*	True if autopilot is to maintain heading tuned to NAV1
AUTOPILOT_WING_LEVELER	bool	*	True if the autopilot is to keep the wings level
BAROMETRIC_DRIFT	bool		True if Barometric pressure drift is enabled

Variable name	Unit	*	Description
BAROMETRIC_PRESSURE	inch Hg		Current barometric pressure
BRAKE_LEFT_POSITION	int		0=off, 32767=full on
BRAKE_RIGHT_POSITION	int		0=off, 32767=full on
CLOUD_HIGH_ACTIVE	bool		True if there is high cloud layer active
CLOUD_HIGH_BASE	meter		Alt. MSL of base of high cloud layer
CLOUD_HIGH_ICING	bool		True if there are icing cond. In the high cloud layer
CLOUD_HIGH_TOP	meter		Alt. MSL of top of high cloud layer
CLOUD_HIGH_TURB	int		Turbulence of high cloud layer: 0 (calm) –255 (most turbulent)
CLOUD_HIGH_TYPE	int		Type of high cloud layer
COM_FREQ	MHz	*	Frequency to which COM radio is tuned.
COURSE	degrees		Wind-corrected course (mgn)
ELEVATOR_TRIM_POSITION	int		-16383 full nose down ... 16383 full nose up
EMERGENCY_FAILURE	bit	*	bit0=Oil temp too high bit1=Oil temp too low bit2=left tank leak bit3=right tank leak
ENGINE_TYPE	int		0=Piston engine 1=Jet engine
2=No engine			
FLAPS_LEFT_POSITION	int		0=Up
32767=Down			
FLAPS_RIGHT_POSITION	int		0=Up32767=Down
GEAR_1_POSITION	int		0=Up32767=Down
GEAR_2_POSITION	int		0=Up32767=Down
GEAR_3_POSITION	int		0=Up32767=Down
GROUND_ALTITUDE	meter		Altitude MSL of ground under plane
HOUR	hours	*	Current time 0 -23
IMARK	bool		True if inner marker indicator is on
KEY	int		Modified scan code of last key
LEFT_AUX_FUEL_LEVEL	gal		Fuel remaining in left aux. tank

Variable name	Unit	*	Description
LEFT_MAIN_FUEL_LEVEL	gal		Fuel remaining in left main tank
MAGVAR	degrees		Magnetic Variation
MINUTE	minutes	*	Current time minutes 0 ... 59
MMARK	bool		True if middle marker indicator is on
NAV1_FREQ	MHz	*	108.00 ... 117.95
NAV2_FREQ	MHz	*	Freq. Nav 2 is tuned to108.00-117.95
OMARK	bool		True if middle marker indicator is on
ON_GROUND	bool		True if plane is on the ground
OVERSPEED_WARNING	bool		True if overspeed warning is on
PARKING_BRAKES	bool		True if parking brakes are on
PLANE_ALT	meter		Plane Altitude MSL
PLANE_BANK	degrees		Plane's bank: 0 if level, positive values indicate bank to the left
PLANE_HEADING	degrees		Plane's magnetic heading
PLANE_LAT	lat		Plane's Latitude
PLANE_LON	lon		Plane's Longitude
PLANE_PITCH	degrees		Plane's bank: 0 if level, positive values indicate pitch up
RANDOM	frac		Random between 0...1
RETRACTABLE_GEAR	bool		0=fixed gear 1=retractable gear
RIGHT_AUX_FUEL_LEVEL	gal		Fuel remaining in right aux. tank
RIGHT_MAIN_FUEL_LEVEL	gal		Fuel remaining in right main tank
RUDDER_PEDAL_POSITION	int		-16383... +16383
SEASON	int	*	0=winter 1=spring 2=summer 3=autumn
SECOND	Sec.	*	Current time in seconds 0 ... 59
SLEW_SYSTEM_ACTIVE	bool		True if the user is in slew mode
SMOKE_SYSTEM_ON	bool	*	True if the smoke trail system is on
STALL_WARNING	bool		True if the stall horn is sounding

Variable name	Unit	*	Description
TEMPERATURE_HIGH_ALT	meter		Altitude of high temperature layer
TEMPERATURE_HIGH_TEMP	°C		Temperature of high temperature layer
TRANS_FREQ	int	*	Four digits transponder squawk value each 0 ... 7
VELOCITY	knots		True airspeed
VELOCITY_INDICATED	knots		Indicated speed
VELOCITY_Y	meters		Vertical speed
VOR_1_ACTIVE	bool		True if Nav1 radio is tuned to VOR
VOR_1_ALT	meter		Altitude of station tuned to Nav1
VOR_1_DME	NM		Distance to station tuned to Nav1
VOR_1_DME_AVAIL	bool		True if station provides DME and tuned to Nav1
VOR_1_GLIDE_SLOPE	degree		Glide slope indicated on VOR1
VOR_1_GS_AVAIL	bool		True if station to Nav1
VOR_1_LAT	lat		Lat. of station tuned to Nav1
VOR_1_LON	lon		Long. of station tuned to Nav1
VOR_1_LOCALIZER	degree		Localizer course indicated by VOR1
VOR_1_LOCALIZER_AVAIL	bool		True if station to Nav1 is an ILS station
VOR_1_OBS	degree	*	OBS value dialed in on VOR1
VOR_1_RADIAL	degree		Radial to station tuned to Nav1
WIND_LOW_BASE	meter		Altitude MSL base of low winds aloft
WIND_LOW_DIR	degree		Heading low winds aloft layer is blowing
WIND_LOW_TOP	meter		Altitude MSL top of winds aloft layer
WIND_LOW_TURB	int		Turbulence factor of low winds 0 ... 255 (most turbulent)
WIND_LOW_TYPE	int		0=steady; 1=gusty
WIND_LOW_VEL	knots		Wind speed of low winds aloft layer
YOKE_X_POSITION	int		-16383 full left +16383 fullright
YOKE_Y_POSITION	int		-16383 full up (nose down) +16383 full down (nose up)

The APLC Compiler

The source code for an adventure can be written with any desired text editor. The finished source code is stored on the hard drive as a text file in ASCII format, to permit the later insertion of changes or the correction of errors. The ASCII source code may not contain special characters, such as Ä, Ö, Ü, ß or °.

To generate an adventure for Flight Simulator 98, this source code must be compiled and then converted. The conversion handled by the well known AAFCONV98. The compilation is taken care of by the APL compiler. The compiler is included in the FlightShop package and usually installed in the Adv subfolder in the FlightShop ATC folder.

The APLC is a pure DOS-command-line compiler. With the MSDOS prompt under Windows 95, APLC.EXE expects the ASCII text of the adventure source code and generates the binary adventure file (.ADV). The APLC call and the subsequent compilation are started with the following command line:

```
aplc adventure..txt [adventure]
```

The name of the source-code file in the example is ADVENTURE.TXT. This file is converted into an .ADV file with the optional name Adventure and contains the file group adv. In the case of the source code generated for an adventure from Düsseldorf to Bremen, the compilation could take place more or less as follows:

```
aplc dusbmn.txt dusbmn
```

The source text DUSBMN.TXT is compiled and saved in the Adv folder of FlightShop under the file name DUSBMN.ADV.

Now the AAFCONV98 converter comes into play. Depending upon which options are enabled, it looks directly in FlightShop's Adv folder, or it must be guided to the source text. Along with this text, the desired situation file (in the example, DUS20.STN) must be present in the same directory. If the compiled adventure and all paths to the necessary files (*.STN and possibly *.WAV) are free of errors, the conversion takes place, and the ready-to-fly adventure is saved in Flight Simulator 98's Adv folder. The mentioned .STN and .WAV files must then be copied manually into the Fs98\Adv or \Wav folders. And then everything in the simulator will be ready to go.

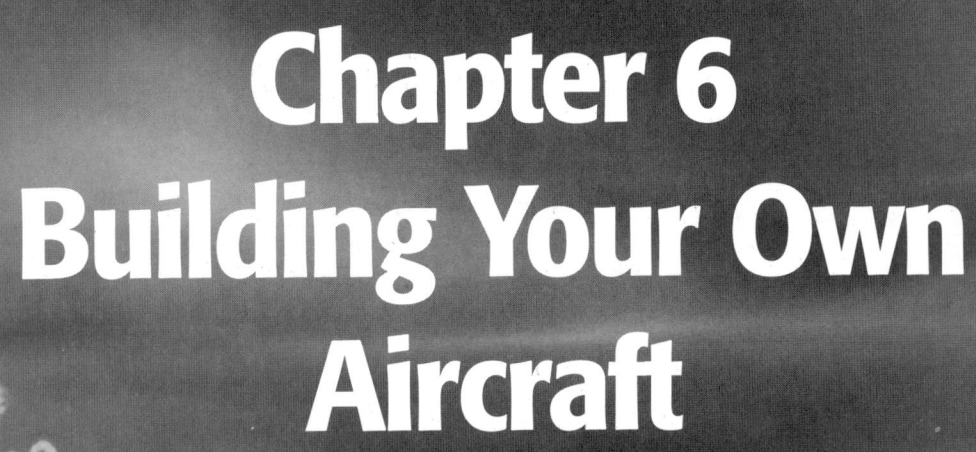

Chapter 6
Building Your Own Aircraft

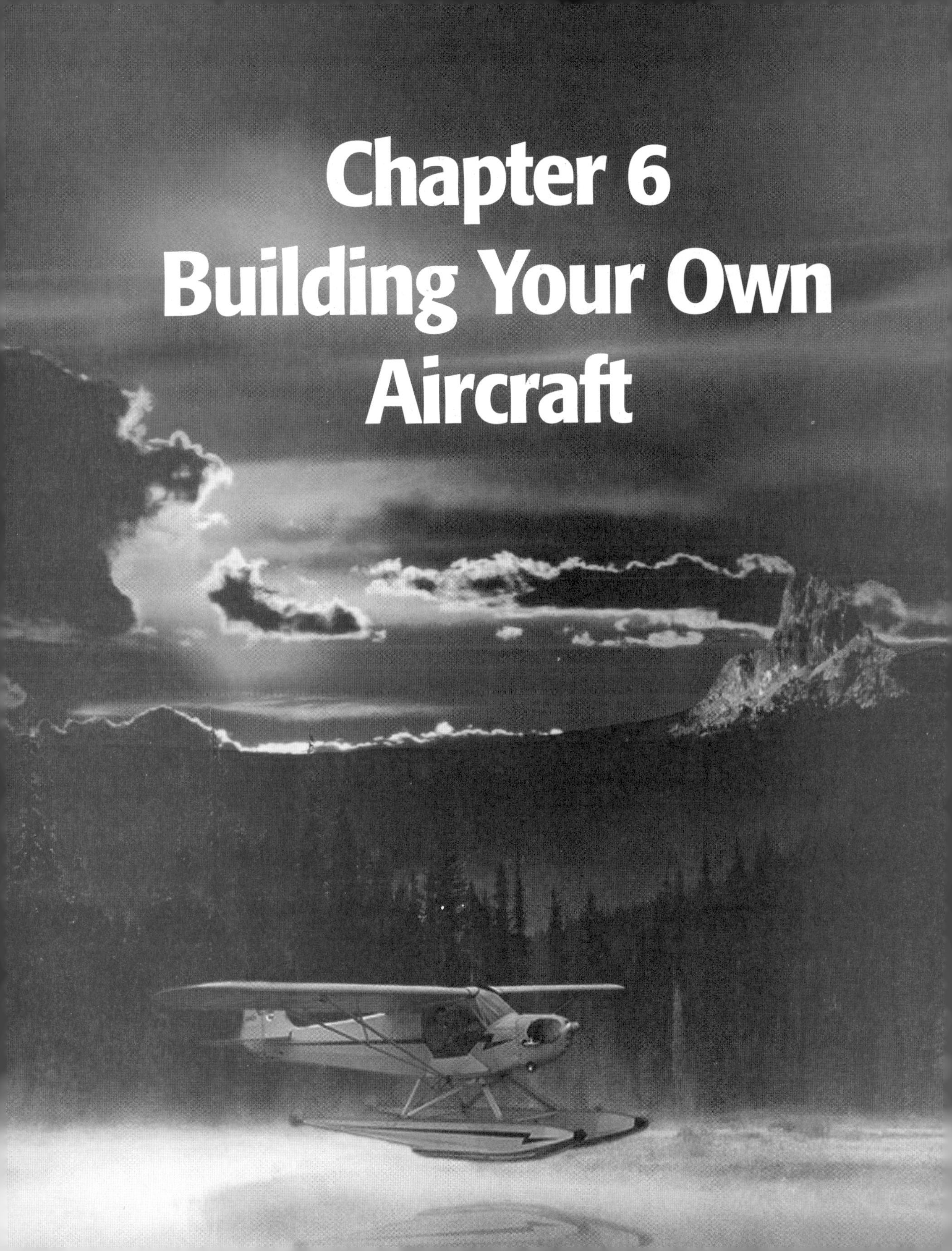

Chapter 6 explores the Aircraft Factory Designer (AFD) in the Flight Shop program. We start with an extensive look at real aerodynamics and how they affect flight dynamics with the Aircraft Dynamic Editor. We'll test the Beech Baron, DC 3 and Boeing 747 aircraft, and we'll use AFD to build, test and adjust the characteristics of an aircraft.

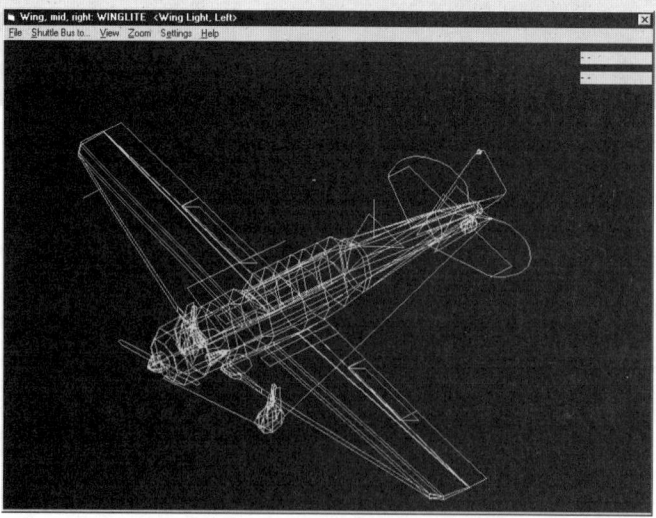

The aircraft that come with Flight Simulator 98 are wonderful models. But since Flight Simulator was introduced, professional developers and fans have developed new airplanes and modified the ones they had available. Since Microsoft gracefully stayed out of the picture, several tools have appeared on store shelves or on the Internet over the past years that help you build your own Flight Simulator airplanes. The best known of these programs is the Flight Simulator Flight Shop (FSFS) created by the Bruce Artwick Organization (BAO).

What runway numbers mean

BAO Flight Simulator Flight Shop requires Microsoft Flight Simulator version 5. It can be used to create elements for later versions of FS, but FS v.5 is required to create these elements.

The Aircraft Factory Designer in Flight Shop is an add-on for Flight Simulator (versions 5 and later). According to BAO, 80-90% of all third-party Flight Simulator aircraft are created using this program. The Aircraft Factory Designer, or AFD, is a design office with attached production facilities. Several departments in the Aircraft Factory Designer manage the internal operations:

Planning/Logistics			
Assembly Line	Parts	Components	Structures
Paint	Storehouse		Bulkheads
Blueprint			
Photo Lab			
Performance			
Production			
Test Flight			

Inspecting a Flight-ready Model

Aircraft Factory Designer includes six flight-ready aircraft models to familiarize you with the program:

- ✈ North American T6 Texan
- ✈ Ultralight
- ✈ McDonnell Douglas F/A-18
- ✈ Beechcraft Baron 55
- ✈ McDonnell Douglas DC 3
- ✈ Boeing B747 Jumbo

Unpacking the aircraft model

Each aircraft is made of small parts, components and structures, which are compressed in a "transport file." This insures that the aircraft remains complete after a copy procedure (e.g., from the hard drive to a diskette) and that no important piece gets lost in the process.

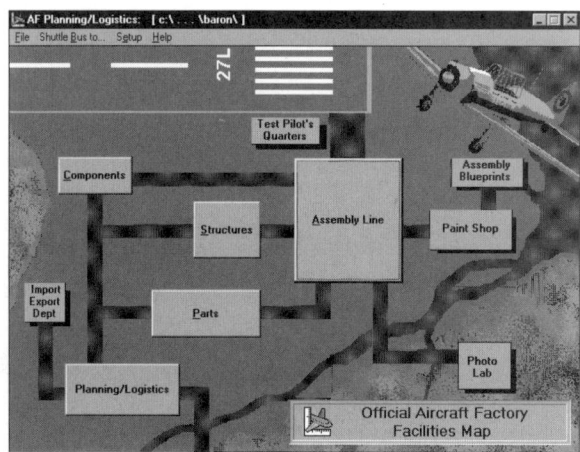

After starting the AFD, you see the "Official map of the AFD factory"—a site map of the aircraft plant. This map and the user menu guide you through the design departments and the production plant. When you select the desired aircraft in the **File** menu, it is extracted from its project directory. For example, the path to the project "T6 Texan" in the selection list is:

```
C:\  ...  \fltshop\af5\t6texan.
```

This makes it possible to bring the aircraft out of its transport crate (the filename extension .AFX stands for "Aircraft Factory Extract"). The third option in the **File** menu, **Unpack Project from Import Crate**, unpacks the model's parts and assemblies.

Breaking into parts, components and structures

Probably every aircraft built with AFD consists of multiple parts that can be combined to make components or structures. After a project file has been created, AFD stores each piece on the hard drive and identifies the piece by its file name and extension. The filename extensions are standard:

Item	Extension	Item	Extension
Part	.AFP	Assembly	.AFA
Component	.AFC	Packed File	.AFX
Structure	.AFC		
Assembly	.AFA		
Packed File	.AFX		

To look at an individual part of an aircraft, you need to find the Parts Shop that manages these pieces.

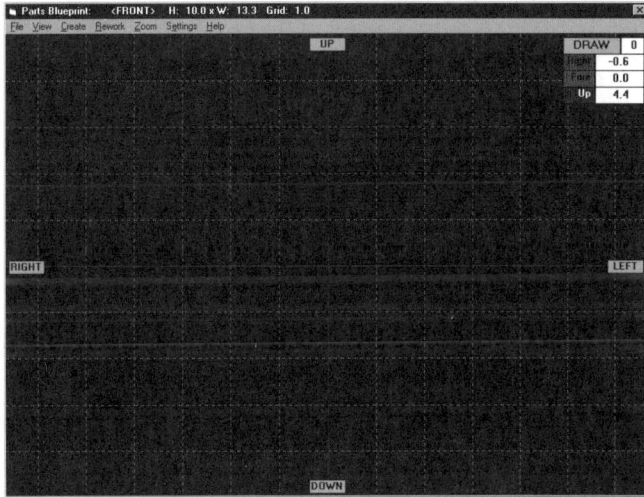

New parts can be planned and constructed on the blueprint in the Parts Shop, which is empty at first. You can also look at other finished parts and change or improve them if you want. Transfer a finished part from the T6 to the blueprint on the screen using the **File | Open Part for Rework** command. The selection list contains all the T6's individual parts, shown with the extension .AFP.

The file named CANOPY1.AFP is part of the canopy section of the T6. If you use the **Select** command to highlight this part, its technical drawing appears in the blueprint in one of three views: side, top or front. The function keys F2, F3 or F4 are the fastest way to switch between views. You can also use the **View** menu options.

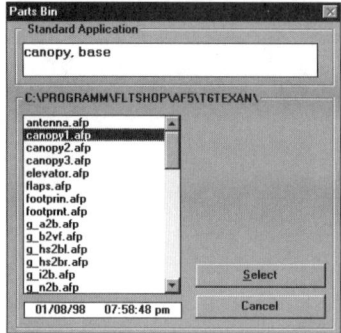

Correctly assessing a piece's size or proportion to another piece can be difficult in this situation, though. That's why an additional part, component, structure or assembly can be added into the drawing as a reference for each part. The selected part is shown in a brighter color to make it stand out from the other line elements.

You can center the part in the middle of the drawing or place it in any other spot you want within the screen area. To do so, place the mouse pointer or the cross-hair on the middle of the part. Move the part to the middle of the screen by right-clicking on it with the mouse.

The **Zoom Factor** (from the menu with the same name) determines how large the part is displayed or you may use the following key combinations:

Key	Description
2	Enlarge current display two-fold
5	Enlarge current display five-fold
Shift 2	Reduce current display two-fold
Shift 5	Reduce current display five-fold
Shift R	Reset to normal display size

The number box in the upper-right of the screen indicates the part's position along the three major axes. The main axes are oriented to the aircraft as follows:

Longitudinal axis	Front-Aft
Lateral axis	Left-Right
Vertical axis	Up-Down

The numerical values indicate the distance of the current mouse position from the center point (the intersection of the three major axes) in feet. The grid size will vary according to the zoom factor. In the normal display (**Zoom Reset**), the grid lines represent a distance of exactly two feet. By moving the mouse pointer/cross-hair across the screen while watching the number box and changing the viewpoint, you can gradually get a feel for the scale of the pieces on the blueprint.

Components

To make it easier and simpler to work with pieces in the later production stages, you can combine individual parts to form subassemblies called *components* and *structures*. The Components Shop manages these subassemblies, similar to the Parts Shop.

Since one component consists of at least two parts, you have to select these parts from a list and combine them. To be combined, the parts have to have at least two points in common. You can load existing components in the **File** menu of Components.

The component CANOPY.AFC, which can be selected from the list, contains all the individual parts that are needed for constructing the canopy of the T6: CANOPY1.AFP, CANOPY2.AFP, CANOPY3.AFP and INVU.AFP. The last-mentioned piece shows up seven times in the list, which is not an error. This part, the cockpit strut-work, is used in this component that many times so that it doesn't have to be reconstructed every time.

If a part is selected in the list, afterward the [View] button will display the entire component in the familiar blueprint. The selected part is shown in a lighter color so that it stands out. This part can now be grabbed with the mouse pointer or cross-hair and moved around, in contrast to the other parts, which are immobile. This way you can make a correction, if an inaccuracy in the positioning of the individual pieces has sneaked in.

No other construction activities are possible here, since this is not actually a construction department, but merely a place where finished parts are connected. The **Build | Blueprint** menu command also shows the three-sided view of the components, but there's no chance to make changes here. As in the Part Shop, you can select the view using function keys [F2] through [F4] in both component blueprints.

Structures

A larger unit—like the fuselage, the wings or the motor area—is prepared in AFD's Structure Shop. You create these structures by combining side and top views with a three-dimensional base form. Both views of a component are given a predefined cross-sectional shape, which is developed for the front view.

To invoke the side and top views of an already finished structured unit, click **File | Open** from the menu. For example, if the structure T6BODY.AFS is selected and opened, both views appear, although the display takes a little getting used to because it's squeezed together quite a bit:

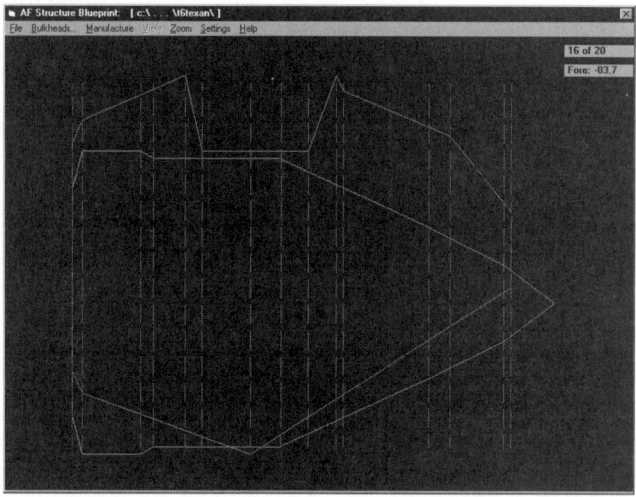

At the same time, AFD prompts you for the desired cross-sectional shape (bulkhead) in a dialog box. The cross-section is selected from a list:

✈ Diamond	✈ Hexagon
✈ Keytone	✈ Octagon
✈ Oval	✈ Pentagon
✈ Point	✈ Rectangle
✈ Triangle	✈ Vee

Once the desired cross-sectional shape has been selected, we have to specify where to insert this shape in the drawing. You can choose any position in the side/top view, though it's best to place it exactly at those locations where the outline of the component makes a crease in the side or top view.

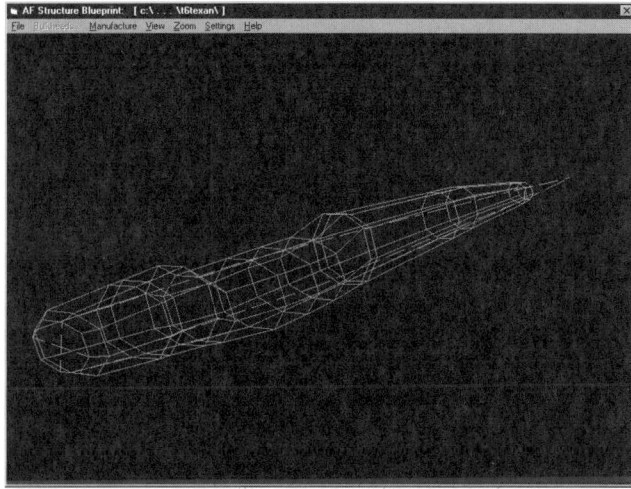

Place the bulkhead by clicking the left mouse button as soon you reach a folding point above or below the mouse pointer, when the mouse pointer changes to a vertical double arrow. If you make a mistake placing the bulkhead, you can delete it with the (Bksp) key.

With the T6's fairly long fuselage, you need to follow this procedure to place a total of 15 bulkheads at the folding points and corner points, starting at the front left side.

After that, you can transfer the workshop drawing to the production area, using the **Manufacture | Start** option. The AFD then automatically generates the three-dimensional, spatial structure of the body using the two preconstructed views of the body (side and top) and the assigned cross-sectional shape (octagon).

Assembly

At this point the parts, components and structures are still located in different shops of the AFD. All of the pieces are listed and combined in the company's Assembly Line. In addition, the Assembly Line also paints and decorates the airplane.

The AFD's Assembly Line, which is still empty at this point, is filled when you load an aircraft project; with the current example, that would be the T6 from the corresponding project directory:

```
D:\...\Fltshop\Af5\T6texan
```

AF Paint/Special Effects Shop: [c:\... \t6texan\ ]
File Shuttle Bus to... Add to Assembly Edit Help

North American T Objects	File	Assembly Group	Seq	Effects	Use as	Color	Techniq
step area	step	Wing, mid, right	002 P	Always	Above	Gray	Regular
pitot tube	pitot	Wing, mid, right	003 P	Always	Regular	[G]Gray, light	Regular
wing (right), trailing	w1124rt	Wing, mid, right	005 P	Always	Regular	Gray, light	Regular
Flap Up Fill	wfuf	Wing, mid, right	005 P	Flaps, retracted	Regular	[G]Gray, light	Regular
Wing Light, Left	winglite	Wing, mid, right	006 P	Lights, on	Fore, Right	[L] Red	Opposite
flaps	flaps	Wing, low, right	001 P	Flaps, extended	Regular	Gray, light	Regular
Wing structure (Right)	w1124s	Wing, mid, left	001 S	Always	Regular	[T][G]Gray, light	Opposite
step area	step	Wing, mid, left	002 P	Always	Above	Gray	Opposite
wing (right), trailing	w1124rt	Wing, mid, left	004 P	Always	Regular	Gray, light	Opposite
Flap Up Fill	wfuf	Wing, mid, left	004 P	Flaps, retracted	Regular	[G]Gray, light	Opposite
Wing Light, Left	winglite	Wing, mid, left	006 P	Lights, on	Rear, Right	[L] Green	Regular
flaps	flaps	Wing, low, left	001 P	Flaps, extended	Regular	Gray, light	Opposite
antenna	antenna	Tail	002 P	Always	Regular	Blue, light	Regular
Glue: antenna to body	g_a2b	Tail	003 G				Regular
body, rear	bodyd	Tail	004 S	Always	Aft bulkhead	[T][G]Gray, light	Regular
Glue Template for Tail	gluet1	Tail	005 G				Regular
Tail Tire (3D)	tailtire	Tail	006 S	Always	Regular	Black	Regular
Glue: body to vert stab	g_b2vf	Tail	007 G				Regular
vertical stabilizer, Top	vstabt	Tail	008 P	Always	Regular	[T]Red	Regular
Glue: hor stasb to body	g_hs2bl	Tail	009 G				Regular
Horizontal Stabiliser	hstab	Tail	010 C	Always	Collection	[T]Blue, light	Opposite
Glue: hor stab to body	g_hs2br	Tail	011 G				Regular
Horizontal Stabiliser	hstab	Tail	012 C	Always	Collection	[T]Blue, light	Regular
vertical stabilizer, bottom	vstabb	Tail	015 P	Always	Regular	[T]Red	Regular
Strobe Lamp	strobe	Tail, upper	001 C	Strobes, on	Regular	[L] Red	Regular
Wheel wells	wells	Gear, right	001 C	Gear, up	Below	Gray	Regular
Tire, 3D	tire	Gear, right	004 S	Gear, down	Regular	[T]Black	Regular
Glue: stuff to gear	g_s2g	Gear, right	007 G				Opposite
Lower gear strut	lowstrut	Gear, right	008 P	Gear, down	Regular	Gray	Opposite

The Assembly Line dialog box contains the name of the project, T6texan, the descriptive name North American T6D, and a brief description of the technical data, just like you can read later in the Flight Simulator.

The main function of this dialog box is to make the component list available to the Paint/Effect Shop, which is displayed using the **Shuttle Bus to**… option, via the (View List) button. This list controls almost all of the assembly work on the T6.

The visual control of the projects in the list makes it possible to display the blueprints for all of the views and a three-dimensional depiction of all the inserted and assembled components. The blueprint is opened directly from the Assembly Line via the (Blueprint) button, from the Paint/Effect Shop's job list with the **Shuttle Bus to**… option or by pressing the function key (F5).

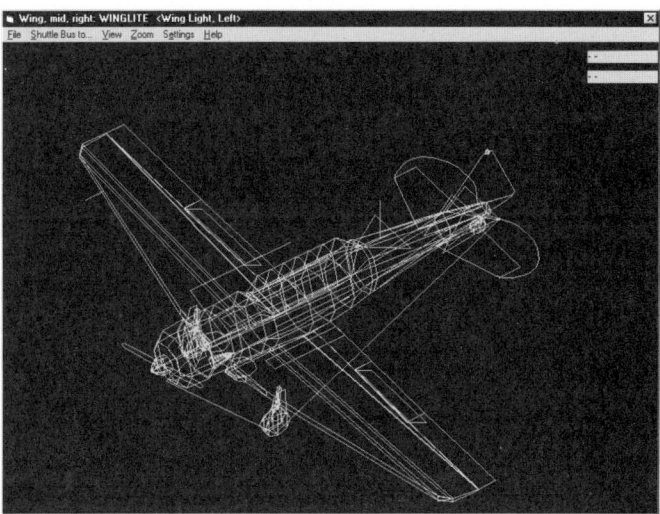

Modifications

If you have already converted the T6 for use in Flight Simulator using AAFCONV98 and you've taken it up for a spin or two, maybe you've noticed a small design flaw. If you use FS's external view from the spotter plane, it's obvious that the two navigation lights on the ends of the wings have been accidentally switched. It should have a red light on the left wing (port side) and a green light on the right wing (starboard).

The big parts table in the Paint/Effect Shop lists these two small parts, and the 3-D view in the blueprint shows these elements drawn in. You can correct the error in the table. First, highlight the line containing the left navigation light in the table.

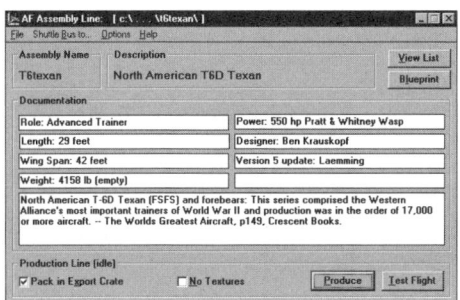

The part is named *Wing Light, Left*, and the file name is WINGLITE.AFP. For some reason, the light on the other wing has the same name and the same file name, which explains the erroneous placement. To determine exactly which line entry is for the red light on the left, simply switch to the blueprint view. The part highlighted in the table is shown in a lighter color in the blueprint. If the second Wing Light part is highlighted, the third column points to the Assembly Group of the left wing. Correspondingly, the blueprint makes the left navigation light stand out.

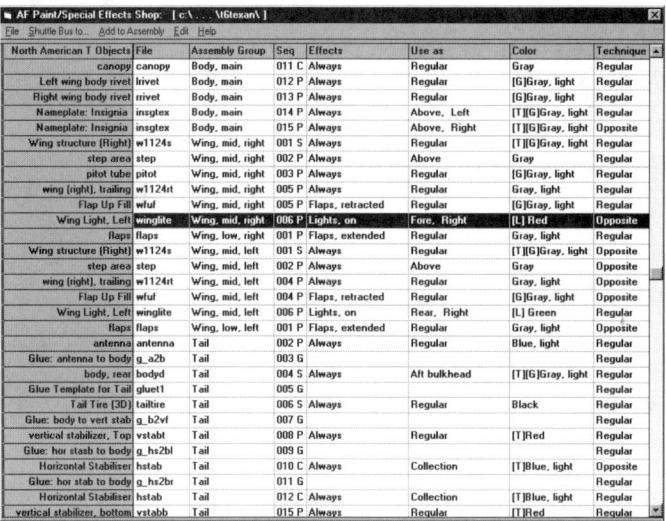

North American T Objects	File	Assembly Group	Seq	Effects	Use as	Color	Technique
canopy	canopy	Body, main	011 C	Always	Regular	Gray	Regular
Left wing body rivet	lrivet	Body, main	012 P	Always	Regular	[G]Gray, light	Regular
Right wing body rivet	rrivet	Body, main	013 P	Always	Regular	[G]Gray, light	Regular
Nameplate: Insignia	insgtex	Body, main	014 P	Always	Above, Left	[T][G]Gray, light	Regular
Nameplate: Insignia	insgtex	Body, main	015 P	Always	Above, Right	[T][G]Gray, light	Opposite
Wing structure (Right)	w1124s	Wing, mid, right	001 S	Always	Regular	[T][G]Gray, light	Regular
step area	step	Wing, mid, right	002 P	Always	Above	Gray	Regular
pitot tube	pitot	Wing, mid, right	003 P	Always	Regular	[G]Gray, light	Regular
wing (right), trailing	w1124rt	Wing, mid, right	005 P	Always	Regular	Gray, light	Regular
Flap Up Fill	wfuf	Wing, mid, right	005 P	Flaps, retracted	Regular	[G]Gray, light	Regular
Wing Light, Left	winglite	Wing, mid, right	006 P	Lights, on	Fore, Right	[L] Red	Opposite
flaps	flaps	Wing, low, right	001 P	Flaps, extended	Regular	Gray, light	Regular
Wing structure (Right)	w1124s	Wing, mid, left	001 S	Always	Regular	[T][G]Gray, light	Opposite
step area	step	Wing, mid, left	002 P	Always	Above	Gray	Opposite
wing (right), trailing	w1124rt	Wing, mid, left	004 P	Always	Regular	Gray, light	Opposite
Flap Up Fill	wfuf	Wing, mid, left	004 P	Flaps, retracted	Regular	[G]Gray, light	Opposite
Wing Light, Left	winglite	Wing, mid, left	006 P	Lights, on	Rear, Right	[L] Green	Opposite
flaps	flaps	Wing, low, left	001 P	Flaps, extended	Regular	Gray, light	Opposite
antenna	antenna	Tail	002 P	Always	Regular	Blue, light	Regular
Glue: antenna to body	g_a2b	Tail	003 G				Regular
body, rear	bodyd	Tail	004 S	Always	Aft bulkhead	[T][G]Gray, light	Regular
Glue Template for Tail	gluet1	Tail	005 G				Regular
Tail Tire (3D)	tailtire	Tail	006 S	Always	Regular	Black	Regular
Glue: body to vert stab	g_b2vf	Tail	007 G				Regular
vertical stabilizer, Top	vstabt	Tail	008 P	Always	Regular	[T]Red	Regular
Glue: hor stab to body	g_hs2bl	Tail	009 G				Regular
Horizontal Stabilizer	hstab	Tail	010 C	Always	Collection	[T]Blue, light	Opposite
Glue: hor stab to body	g_hs2br	Tail	011 G				Regular
Horizontal Stabilizer	hstab	Tail	012 C	Always	Collection	[T]Blue, light	Regular
vertical stabilizer, bottom	vstabb	Tail	015 P	Always	Regular	[T]Red	Regular

In the Color column, the table does indeed list the wrong color, i.e., luminous green (L green). Double-clicking in the line opens the Spec Sheet dialog box, where you can make changes to the part. Usually these changes will affect the placement within subassemblies and the color of a part.

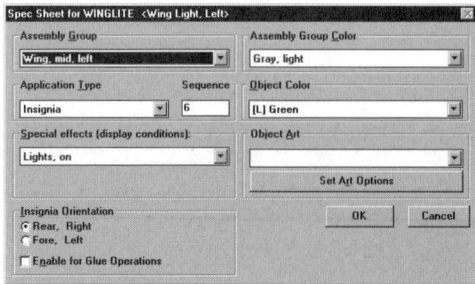

In the Spec Sheet of the left wing light, under Object Color, we change the color to luminous red (L red). At the same time, we specify that the light will always be visible when the Lights, On option is set as a display condition; in other words, when the switch for the navigation lights is turned on in the cockpit.

If we change the left wing light from green to red, naturally we have to fix the light on the right wing as well. The line we're looking for is exactly six rows higher in the table. Here, too, we just double-click on the Spec Sheet and change the object color from L red to L green.

Assembly and test flight

After this minor operation to correct the navigation lights, the assembly of the T6 is now complete. As long as no other in-depth modifications to the parts have been made which would significantly change the dynamics, the airplane can now go into production.

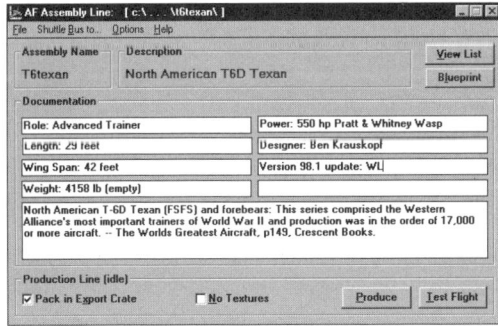

The Spec Sheet will travel over to the Assembly Line with the **Shuttle Bus** command. Before the assembly is converted into an airworthy model, you can make a special note in the dialog box to indicate the modification, for example: Version 98.1, with the author and a description of the change that was made. Then click on the (Produce) button, and the production process is complete.

Aircraft that have been manufactured by the Flight Shop AFD must be converted one more time for operation in Flight Simulator 98. AAFCONV98 performs this conversion in a just few seconds, as long as all of the file paths are correct. (These paths can be set after clicking AAFCONV98's (Options) button.)

The conversion performed by AAFCONV98 creates a new directory in the Aircraft folder of Flight Simulator 98, which contains the folders Model, Sound, Panel and Texture, along with the aircraft configuration file and the actual flight model file.

Designing And Producing Custom Aircraft

Creating, planning and producing a custom airplane for Flight Simulator is one of the most time-consuming jobs. So, we will not attempt to describe a project like building a new, complex, turbine-driven, long-distance airplane. Instead, we will demonstrate the basic procedures and methods of how to proceed from an idea to a flightworthy model. Using a quite simple model, which has only a vague similarity to an original aircraft, we will explain the necessary steps up to the production stage, and we will add a few savory tips here and there. The example we will use for this project is a bird perhaps best known to model airplane builders: the horned owl.

Finding information: pictures and performance specifications

The blank sheet of paper is the most difficult hurdle for an author or an artist to overcome at the start of his work. For the aircraft designer, this is the blank blue area of the AFD blueprint. After all, this is where the concept of an airplane model has to be converted into computer values and reasonable shapes for a 3-D simulation have to be developed.

The first challenge when making your own model in Flight Simulator is acquiring pictures (photos, prints, technical drawings, etc.) that uniquely characterize a particular type of aircraft. You can find these kinds of patterns in books, from the original aircraft manuals, in various trade journals and relevant publications. The best pattern for developing a model with AFD is a technical drawing with the usual three-sided view of an airplane from the top, the side and the front. If you can also get the original measurements from the drawing, like the wing span, length, height, etc., then nothing will prevent you from transferring the information to AFD's blueprint.

Drawing methods

One way to transfer the outline of an aircraft is to directly copy the three-sided view onto transparent film material with a photocopier. The most important (most distinctive) of the three sides should have its scale adjusted so that the film can be placed against the monitor screen as a reference over the AFD blueprint, so that the grids match up.

With this true-to-scale pattern in hand, we simply set the most important points using the mouse. All necessary corrections—for instance, to smooth out a curve—can be made afterward in the Data Sheet.

If an outline copy can't be made of the original picture, then you'll need to trace the original onto transparent paper and then recopy it onto film using a photocopy machine. Again, the outline taped to the screen helps you set the important points and connecting lines using the mouse pointer.

If you're not able to use the transparent film and the mouse to transfer the specifications, you'll have to input the outline points as individual numerical values. However, to do this, you must divide the original image into a grid suitable for the Aircraft Factory Designer by overlaying it with transparent paper. The corner points of the construction are then read from the values in the grid. Make sure that you place the grid on the image so that the geometric midpoint of the view represents the zero point of the grid.

The three-sided view has to show the airplane as described below to convert it for use in the Aircraft Factory Designer.

The side view should always show the airplane from the left side, i.e., with the nose toward the left and the tail toward the right. If the aircraft is built using a view from the other side, the airplane will fly backwards.

Envision the top view as a folded-down image of the side view. That way, the nose of the plane is still pointing to the left, and you see the actual top of the aircraft rather than the underside.

In the front view, the nose turns towards the front, facing the viewer, and the left wing is seen on the right side of the screen. All of the numerical values displayed in the box at the top right refer to these views: Values towards the front, above, and to the right of the midpoint are positive values, while those behind, below and to the left give negative values.

Building the individual parts

The first step in building the parts of an airplane is to create a project directory. To do so, click **File | Create Project Directory** on the startup page AFD Planning/Logistic directory. The AFD file clerk asks for the new project name and supplies a new directory in the AFD folder, in this example: the horned owl.

That takes care of the bureaucratic preparations. Work on the project can begin. We go into the Parts Shop, where the new parts of an airplane have to be drawn. Click the **Shuttle Bus to | Parts Shop**.

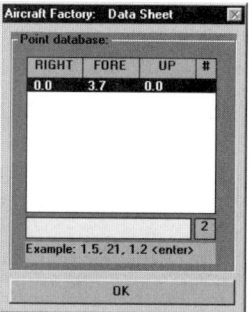

As the designer, you sit in front of a large, dark blue CAD screen: the Parts Blueprint. This is where the individual parts are constructed by setting image points. You can draw the image points with the mouse (cross hairs or pointer) or you can use **Create Data Sheet** to enter the construction points as numerical values.

The first part of the horned owl will be the side view of the body. If the drawing points are known, they will be placed in the corresponding mouse position on the screen. Each new point is automatically joined with the last one by a straight line. Bent curves are not possible, but can be simulated by a large number of intermediate points. The outline of a part should always be created by placing the points in a clockwise manner. In addition, you need to take care that no lines intersect, which would lead to unpredictable results.

The construction points are entered in the data sheet (Create Data Sheet) as relative coordinate values. In the two-dimensional side view of a part, the values for the longitudinal axis (Fore/Aft) and the vertical axis (Up/Down) are important, while the lateral axis (Right/Left) is ignored for now. Also, in the data sheet it is important to enter the points sequentially to prevent any lines from intersecting.

The side view of the first body part uses 17 construction points that describe the classic outline of the horned owl. The data sheet should contain the following values:

Point	Right	Fore	Up	Point	Right	Fore	Up
1	0.0	12.0	0.0	9	0.0	3.9	2.5
2	0.0	11.8	0.4	10	0.0	0.0	2.5
3	0.0	11.3	0.8	11	0.0	0.0	0.7
4	0.0	10.3	1.2	12	0.0	2.0	-1.6
5	0.0	9.2	1.3	13	0.0	4.2	-2.7
6	0.0	8.0	1.3	14	0.0	7.7	-2.7
7	0.0	7.3	0.5	15	0.0	10.0	-2.2
8	0.0	4.6	0.5	16	0.0	11.1	-1.6
				17	0.0	11.9	-0.7

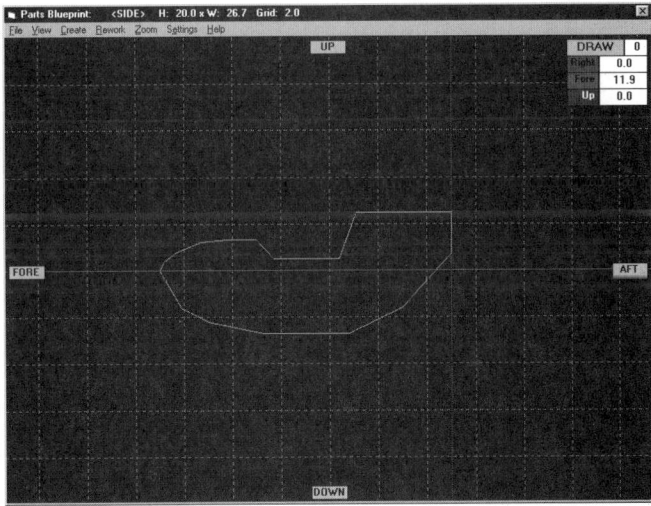

Naturally, a successful construction must be insured for the other departments. Click **File | Save As...** from the menu to give the part a unique file name, a descriptive plain text name, a category and function as it is saved to the hard drive.

For example, a good descriptive text here might be "Body Part 1 Side." The file name is an abbreviated form of this, like "S_body1." Aircraft Factory Designer will automatically append the file extension .AFP, so it doesn't need to be added.

So that the body can emerge later as a solid part with a closed outline, this part is declared as Solid. Now the side view of the body serves as a template which, along with the top view (which still needs to be drawn), forms the three-dimensional basic structure (Structure) of the body. Therefore, the function of this Side component within the total construction is declared here as Template: Side Structure.

The second part of the body is drawn in a top view (as a template for the body structure). This view is positioned as a new part (**File | New Part**). Display the side view on the screen to see just how this part has to be drawn. Naturally, in the top view, the Side component is seen only as a bright stripe, but that's sufficient to estimate the length of the part.

The points for the top view of the body are listed in the table below. Again, you can enter the points using the Data Sheet:

Point	Right	Fore	Up	Point	Right	Fore	Up
1	-0.3	0.0	0.0	6	0.0	12.0	0.0
2	-0.5	0.5	0.0	7	0.5	11.5	0.0
3	-0.5	11.5	0.0	8	0.5	0.5	0.0
4	0.0	12.0	0.0	9	0.3	0.0	0.0
5	0.0	5.9	0.0				

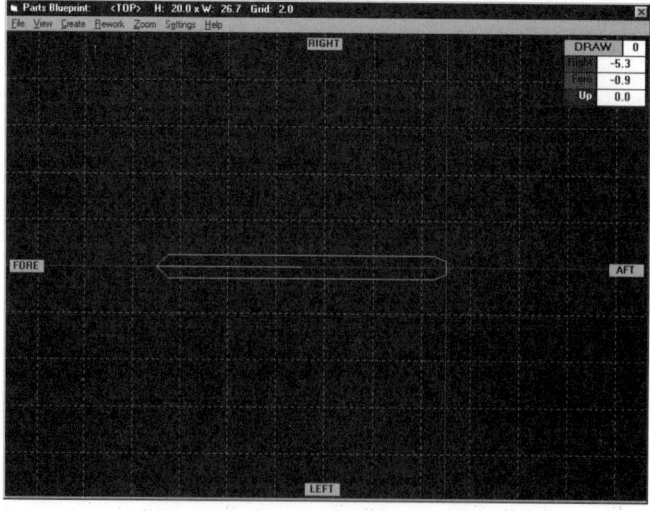

Save this part as well. This time use "t_body1" as a file name and "Body Part 1 top" as descriptive text. Declare the part as Solid and as a template (Template: Top Structure).

Draw the second, back end part of the body in a new partial construction, again in side and top views. The construction points for this part are entered in the two data sheets below and need to be saved in the corresponding files:

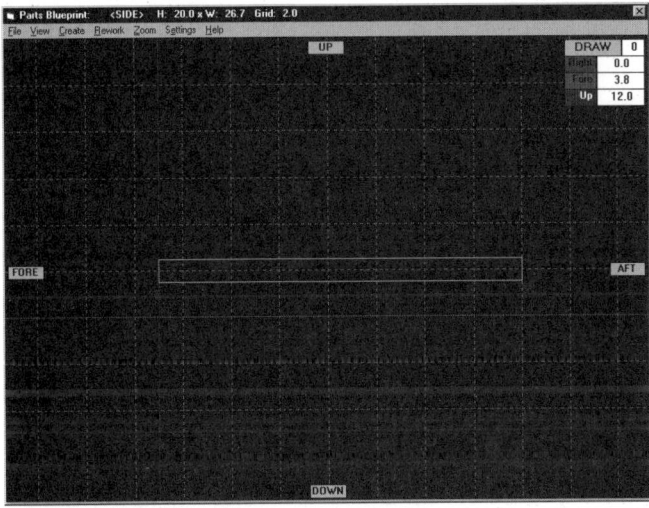

Body Part 2 Side: S_BODY2.AFP				Body Part 2 top: T_BODY2.AFP			
Point	Right	Fore	Up	Point	Right	Fore	Up
1	0.0	0.0	2.5	1	-0.1	-15.0	2.0
2	0.0	-15.0	2.5	2	-0.2	0.0	2.0
3	0.0	-15.0	1.5	3	0.2	0.0	2.0
4	0.0	0.0	1.5	4	0.1	-15.0	2.0

The cockpit is inserted into the area of the first body part, which is left open. Its construction data follow:

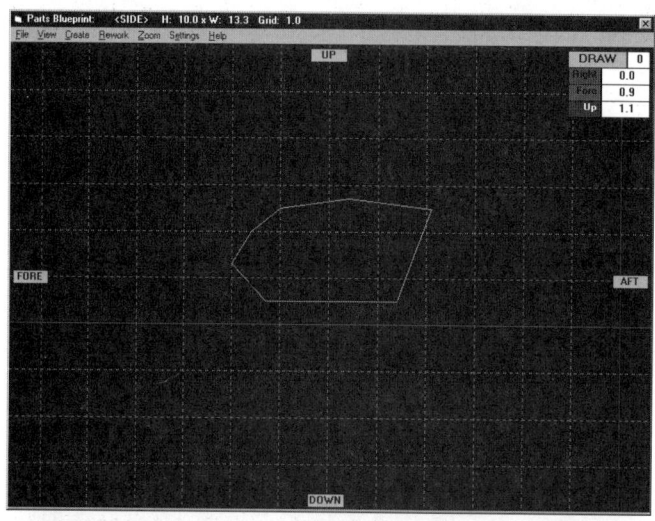

Cockpit side: S_CP.AFP			
Point	Right	Fore	Up
1	0.0	8.0	1.3
2	0.0	7.6	2.0
3	0.0	7.0	2.5
4	0.0	5.6	2.7
5	0.0	3.9	2.5
6	0.0	4.6	0.5
7	0.0	7.3	0.5

Cockpit top: T_CP.AFP			
Point	Right	Fore	Up
1	-0.3	3.9	0.0
2	-0.3	8.0	0.0
3	0.0	8.0	0.0
4	0.3	8.0	0.0
5	0.3	3.9	0.0

Create and save the other basic parts, like the rudder and the elevator and the elementary wings of the horned owl, as Standard Applications without a template function for a three-dimensional depiction. These components can be further polished later, and they can possibly be given volume. So, here are just the side and top views of these parts:

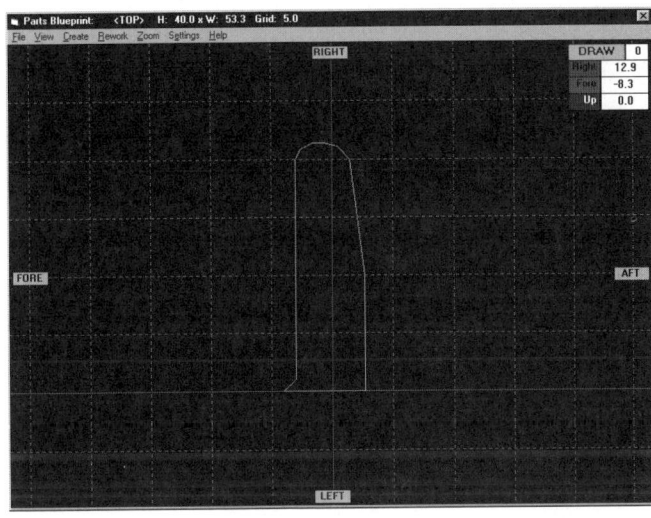

Wing: T_WING.AFP			
Point	Right	Fore	Up
1	0.0	4.0	0.0
2	1.0	3.0	0.0
3	20.0	3.0	1.0
4	20.8	2.6	1.0
5	21.4	1.6	1.0
6	21.4	0.6	1.0
7	21.1	-0.5	1.0
8	20.0	-1.5	1.0
9	10.0	-2.7	0.5
10	0.0	-2.7	0.0

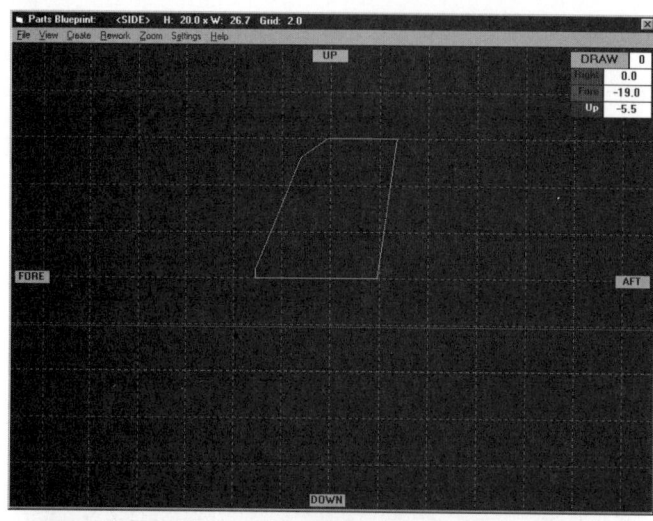

Elevator: T_ELEV.AFP

Point	Right	Fore	Up
1	0.0	-15.0	0.0
2	7.3	-18.0	0.0
3	7.6	-18.5	0.0
4	7.6	-20.7	0.0
5	0.0	-20.0	0.0

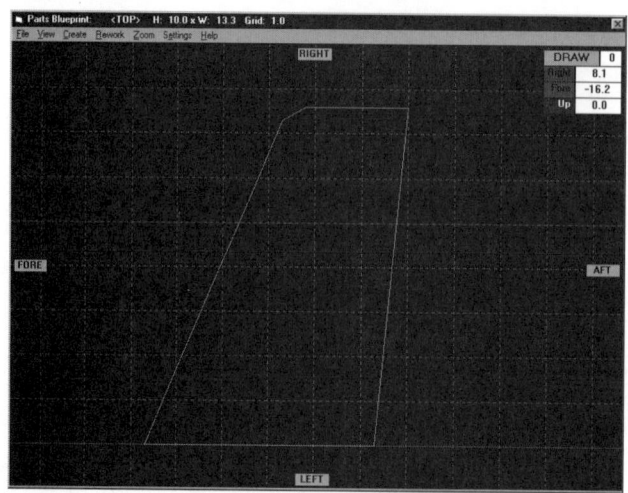

Side rudder: S_RUDD.APF			
Point	Right	Fore	Up
1	0.0	-15.0	2.5
2	0.0	-16.9	7.3
3	0.0	-18.0	8.1
4	0.0	-20.8	8.1
5	0.0	-20.0	2.1
6	0.0	-15.0	2.1

Once the body, wings and rudder are done, all of the important basic parts of the horned owl are constructed. For the wings and the two-part elevator, only the right-hand part has been drawn. The corresponding left-hand parts will be developed later simply using copying and mirroring.

Combining the parts into components and structures

Both views of the body have been stored as templates. These templates make it possible to use a selected cross-sectional structure to provide a three-dimensional volume to the body when it is assembled.

This cross-sectional shape is constructed in the Structure Shop of the Aircraft Factory Designer. The **Shuttle Bus to**... | **Structure Shop** will take us to the Structure Blueprint workplace.

The **File** menu loads both templates from the side and top views of the body: Load TOP Template and Load SIDE Template. Then we can select the appropriate parts T_BODY1.AFP and S_BODY1.AFP from the drop-down list. The importance of using a clear naming system for the files soon becomes apparent.

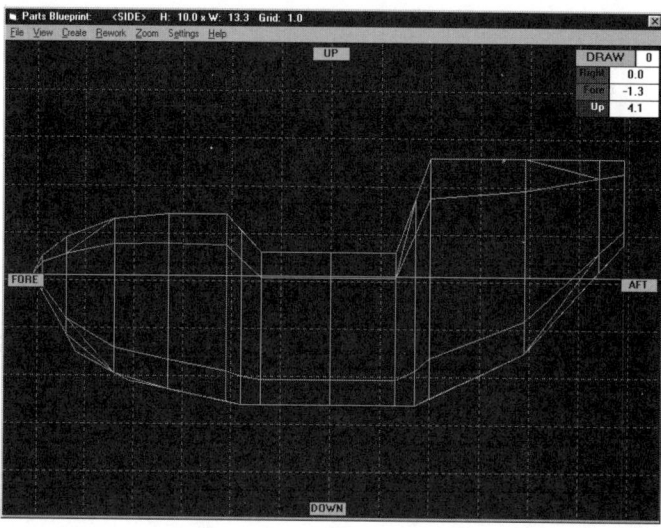

As soon as both views have been loaded and are displayed on the screen, the Bulkhead Tools dialog box appears. This is where you determine which cross-sectional shape you want to use for the body. The oval is a good selection for the owl, as it has a soft bevel at the edges and provides a somewhat more elegant shape.

The cross-section shape is attached to each corresponding corner point of the side and top views. The mouse pointer changes to a double arrow at these points. After all of the bulkheads have been set, you can build the structure.

The **Manufacture | Start** command takes both templates and the cross-section shape as the basis for calculating the body shape. Immediately after this, the representation of the three-dimensional body appears on the screen. The function keys F2, F3, F4 and Shift+F3 toggle among the different views.

Save the body structure we just created with a suitable file name and descriptive text: BODY1.AFS and Body Part 1.

Now construct the second body component in the same way. The new structure (from the parts S_BODY2.AFP and T_BODY2.AFP) generates the three-dimensional back part of the body: BODY2.AFS and Body Part 2.

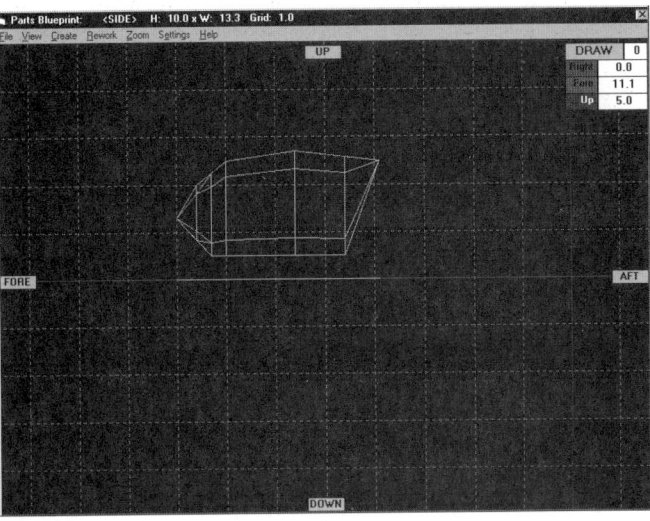

The third 3-D structure is the cockpit, formed from the two views S_CP.AFP and T_CP.AFP: COCKPIT.AFS and Cockpit.

With that, all of the parts and structures are completed and are ready for final assembly.

Finishing the aircraft

Click **Shuttle Bus to | Assembly Line** to go straight to the assembly line. The production department requires us to fill out some documents to describe the special dynamics of the aircraft. The **File** menu of the AFD Assembly Line opens a new blank form where we fill in this information and the file name of the project.

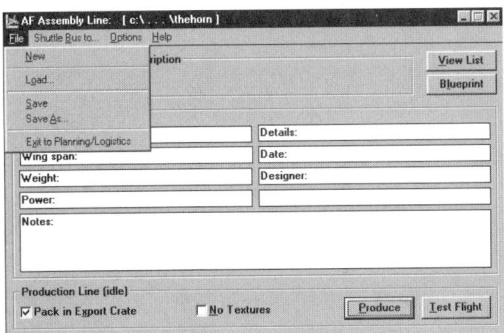

The flight dynamics of the model are established using the **Assign Flight Dynamics From Aircraft Library or From Template Library** in the **Options** menu. Select the appropriate file for the type of aircraft from the three samples provided (sailplane, propeller or turbine). For the horned owl, this is the file AF5GLIDE.ART, which represents the special properties of a sailplane.

The decisive steps in the entire construction take place in the Paint/Special Effects Shop. The spec sheet, which is empty at first, fills up in a hurry when we use the Add to Assembly to option load the parts and structures that we've previously constructed.

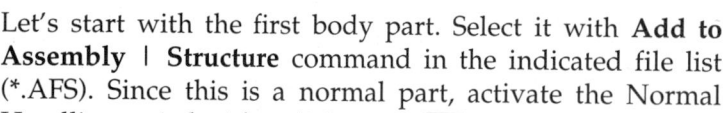
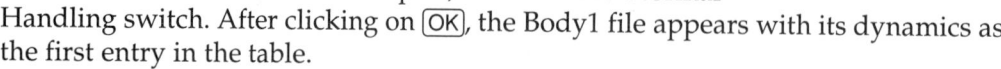

Horned Owl Objects	File	Assembly Group	Seq	Effects	Use as	Color	Technique
horned owl	owl2	Body, main	*** C	Always	Regular	[G]Gray, light	Regular
Body Part 1 Side	s_body1	Body, main	*** P	Always	Regular	[G]Gray, light	Regular
Body Part 2 Side	s_body2	Body, main	*** P	Always	Regular	[G]Gray, light	Regular
Cockpit Side	s_cp	Body, main	*** P	Always	Regular	[G]Gray, light	Regular
	s_rudd	Body, main	*** P	Always	Regular	[G]Gray, light	Regular
Body Part 1 top	t_body1	Body, main	*** P	Always	Regular	[G]Gray, light	Regular
Body Part 2 top	t_body2	Body, main	*** P	Always	Regular	[G]Gray, light	Regular
Cockpit top	t_cp	Body, main	*** P	Always	Regular	[G]Gray, light	Regular
Top Elevator1	t_elev	Body, main	*** P	Always	Regular	[G]Gray, light	Regular
Top Wing1	t_wing	Body, main	*** P	Always	Regular	[G]Gray, light	Regular
Body Part 1	body1	Body, main	*** S	Always	Regular	[G]Gray, light	Regular
Body Part 2	body2	Body, main	*** S	Always	Regular	[G]Gray, light	Regular
Cockpit	cockpit	Body, main	*** S	Always	Regular	[G]Gray, light	Regular

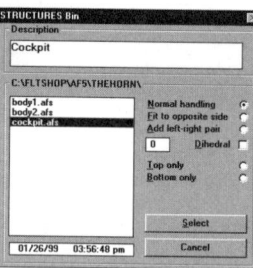

The individual elements are inserted into the production table based on their category—Part, Component or Structure. We know that we have constructed a total of three structures and three additional, individual parts. Now we will call up each of these, one after another, from the selection lists.

Let's start with the first body part. Select it with **Add to Assembly | Structure** command in the indicated file list (*.AFS). Since this is a normal part, activate the Normal Handling switch. After clicking on OK, the Body1 file appears with its dynamics as the first entry in the table.

The eight columns in the table contain the plain text description, the file name, the current subassembly, assembly number, the visibility effects, the assembly mode, the color/texture, and the assembly method for each integrated part.

Then we find the two other structures, Body Part 2 and Cockpit. We use the same options to insert them into the table one after another. Then we select the individual parts (wing, rudder and elevator) from the Parts list. The wing and elevator, both of which were built only for the right side, are entered into the table along with their mirrored counterpart with the *Add left-right pair* option. This type of assembly, which defines the correct side of the assembly, is noted in the last column of the table as Regular/Opposite Technique.

198

As a genuine, individual part, the side rudder is handled normally and appears as the last element in the table.

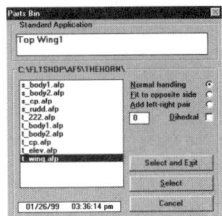

The individual parts of the body and cockpit construction are still in the parts list. We don't need them any more, because they are already contained in the structures with the same names, which have already been selected.

Now the table is finished. We just need to look at the construction drawing to admire the completed assembly. Use F5 or F8 to rapidly switch between the table and the drawing.

As always, you can change the view of the construction in the blueprint drawing with the keys F2 through F4 and Shift+F3. You can use the mouse to move a part that is highlighted in the table so you can move it into a different position.

All of the parts in the table are currently listed as the Body Main subassembly, so the elements are all on the same par. However, Flight Simulator has problems displaying the aircraft, because the special graphics routines don't know exactly which of these parts is in the background and which ones have to be drawn first. That's why some individual parts are included in subassemblies. The subassemblies define the display sequence in the viewing windows of Flight Simulator 98. The subassemblies can also be colored differently.

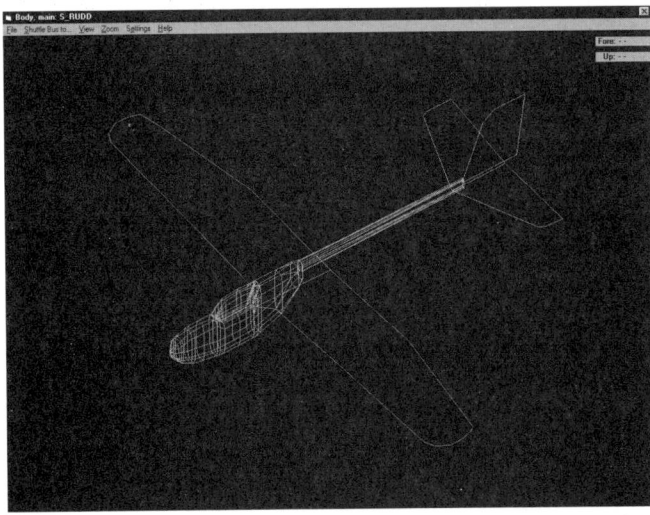

If you assign the wing to the correct subassembly right away (body, wing, canopy, tail, etc.), the subassemblies can be processed more rapidly.

The table shows several defaults for Body Part 1. You can accept them as is or change them using the part's Spec Sheet. The most important change will be the Application Type. The body construction using the Side and Top components hasn't closed the back end. Instead, an open area has developed. Flight Simulator would interpret this area as a transparent hole. Use the *Aft Bulkhead* option to close up this area.

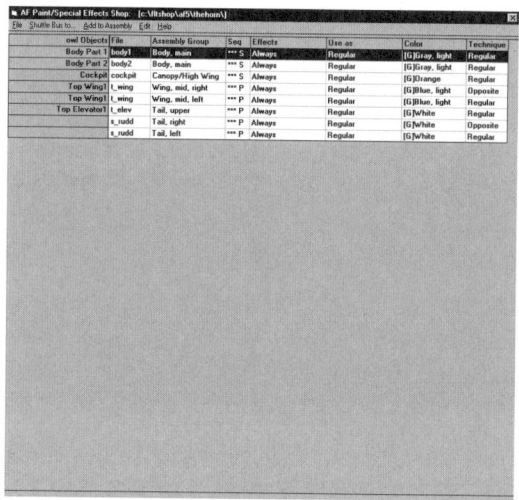

owl Objects	File	Assembly Group	Seq	Effects	Use as	Color	Technique
Body Part 1	body1	Body, main	*** S	Always	Regular	[G]Gray, light	Regular
Body Part 2	body2	Body, main	*** S	Always	Regular	[G]Gray, light	Regular
Cockpit	cockpit	Canopy/High Wing	*** S	Always	Regular	[G]Orange	Regular
Top Wing1	t_wing	Wing, mid, right	*** P	Always	Regular	[G]Blue, light	Opposite
Top Wing1	t_wing	Wing, mid, left	*** P	Always	Regular	[G]Blue, light	Regular
Top Elevator1	t_elev	Tail, upper	*** P	Always	Regular	[G]White	Regular
	s_rudd	Tail, right	*** P	Always	Regular	[G]White	Opposite
	s_rudd	Tail, left	*** P	Always	Regular	[G]White	Regular

Follow the same procedure with the second body part as well. Use the option on both ends to avoid having a hole in your fuselage.

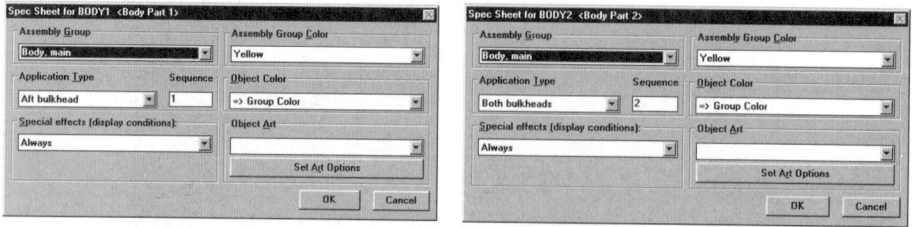

The subassembly's default light gray color can be changed to yellow or something else in the Spec Sheet.

The rest of the parts in the table are assigned to new subassemblies based on their position. The simplest solution for the horned owl might look something like this:

Object	Subassembly	Color
Body 1	Body, main	yellow
Body 2	Body, main	yellow
Cockpit	Canopy	blue light
Wing	Wing, mid, right	white
Wing	Wing, mid, left	white
Side rudder	Tail, upper	red
Elevator	Tail, right	red
Elevator	Tail, left	red

At this point, the aircraft model is complete enough to be manufactured as a prototype. Although it's still missing wheels, skids and some other parts, a test pilot can get by without those. He'll be amazed at the flight dynamics of the new model. Right now, however, we're interested in the aircraft's actual appearance. We'll complete the process using the following options in the Assembly Line:

Set Center of Rotation: Set the aircraft's center of balance in the blueprint. You can move the bright blue cross with the mouse. The best position for the center of gravity and center of rotation is about one-third of the way down the wing. This is where the torques of the front part of the body and the tail are somewhat balanced.

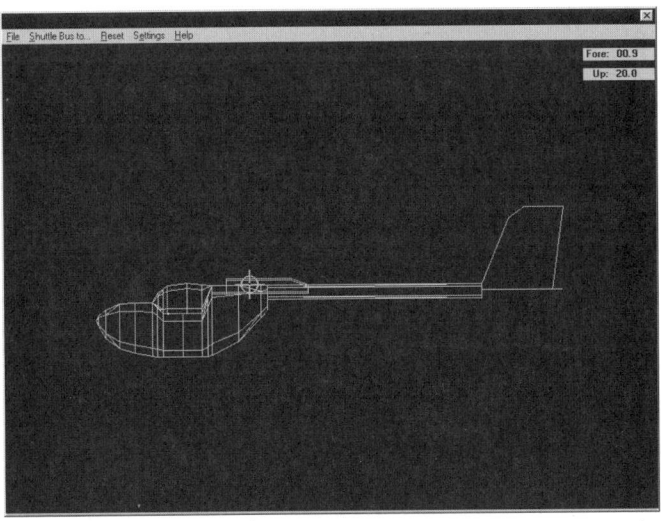

Set View Center: The view out of the cockpit is prepared by placing a marker. For the owl, that should be in the general area of the cockpit.

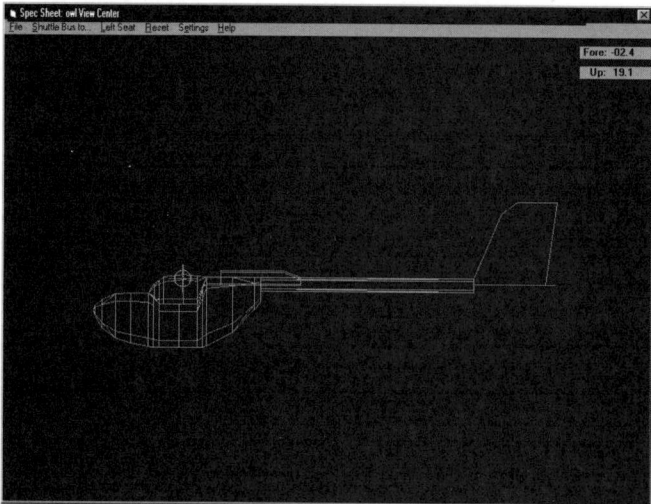

Assign Flight Dynamics: The actual flight dynamics and parameters of the glider are taken from a prepared file. This file, AF5GLIDE.ART in the Template Library, is a general parameter file for sailplanes. For example, in addition to the important data for lift coefficients and drag coefficients, it contains notes about the panel and instruments that should be installed.

Manufacturing the aircraft

The [Produce] button in the Assembly Line manufactures the aircraft based on the items listed in the parts table and produces the first version of the horned owl. The generated file OWL.AIR is automatically copied into the Pilots folder of Flight Simulator 5. The textures that are used are copied to the Textures folder.

Making aircraft compatible

Unfortunately, the [Test Flight] button doesn't really work with Flight Simulator 98 any more. As was indicated above, all aircraft that have been constructed using the Flight Shop Aircraft Factory Designer first have to be converted into a compatible form for Flight Simulator 98 using AAFCONV98. If this conversion can be successfully completed, a new folder is created in the Aircraft directory of Flight Simulator and it is filled with the files and subdirectories of the horned owl.

The brand new aircraft is brought from the FS98 hanger using the **Aircraft | Select Aircraft...** command. Since the owl is a sailplane without any motor, it's best if you start it from a good height. Using the **Go to... | Exact Position** menu command, we can quickly place the model at an elevation of 10,000 feet, so we can bring the glider back to earth.

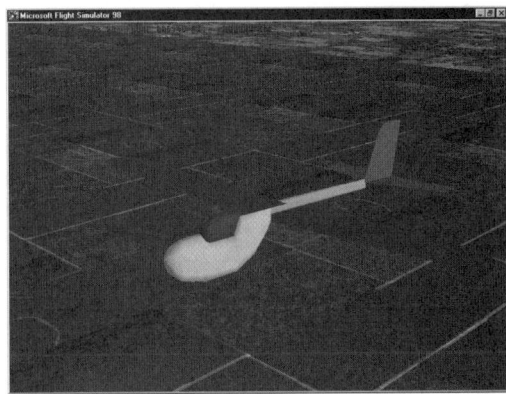

Textures

In contrast to the monotonous, basic color that a part or a subassembly has during the construction phase, textures can contain any colored pattern that you'd like. All kinds and sources of patterns can be used as textures: pictures created with a graphics program, scanned originals (such as photos or other flat objects), written descriptions, clip art from CD-ROM collections, etc.

Textures are projected on a part, a component or a structure. This projection is like showing a photographic slide on a screen. If there is an object between the slide projector and the screen, the image shows up on the object and, depending on the object's shape, the image is distorted or contorted.

At the same time, the projection only shines the picture on one side of the object; the side turned away from the light remains darkened. Therefore, for texture projection, we need at least three projectors from three different directions to illuminate the object correctly and completely.

Opposite sides of the object don't have to be displayed at the same time, because they block each other's view. So, although an object can be viewed from the side toward the front and above, it can't also be viewed from below and behind at the same time. For this reason, a texture for projection in Flight Simulator is always split into two halves, one half each for projection on the left or right side, on an upper or lower view, and on a front or back area.

Example 1: Side view with left and right (*Right/Left*)
Example 2: View above with top and bottom (*Top/Bottom*)

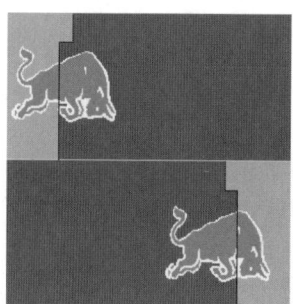 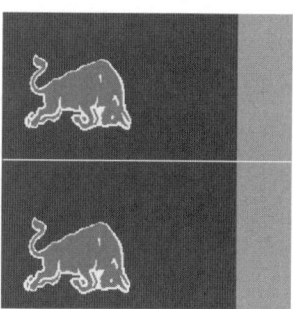

Example 3: Front view with fore and aft (*Aft/Fore*)

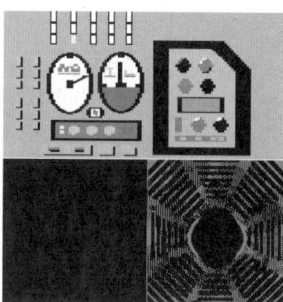

So the bitmap area depends on which part the texture is needed for. For wings, you'll always pick the texture that is specified for a vertical view, or the top/bottom combination, where the upper half of the texture image is for the top side of the wing and the lower half is for the bottom side.

How is a texture correctly positioned? Using the example of the slide projector, we can move the screen or the object back and forth in the projection path. Or we could follow a much easier plan and move the projector up, down and to the side until the part of the image that we want is projected onto the object.

The texture is always in the shape of a rectangle, i.e., the upper or lower half of the texture graphic is 256 pixels wide and 128 pixels high. The texture is oriented along its four outer edges relative to the corner points of the object.

Here is an example: We want to put a new paint job on the vertical tail subassembly of the T6. We'll exchange the old graphic (the bomb familiar to the Atari and Mac world) and the colors with the emblems from a new sponsor. (By the way, the idea for this conversion came from an article about the T6 written by the warbird pilot Walter Eichhorn in the German *Flieger* magazine, June 1997.)

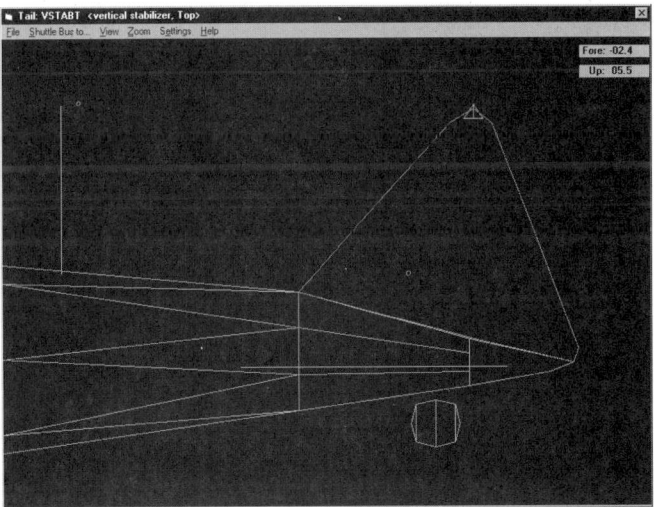

First, load the original texture T6_VSTAB.PCX that is stored in the Flight Shop folder of the T6 Texan into your favorite graphics program.

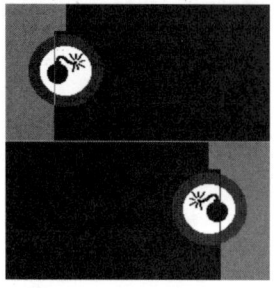
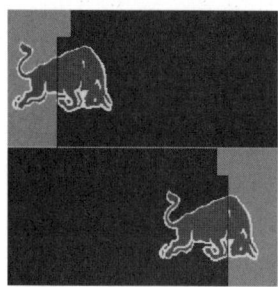

As mentioned above, the texture consists of two halves. In this case, we'll use the upper half as a projection on the right-side rudder surface and the lower half for the left-side rudder surface.

We eliminate the bomb graphic by painting over it with the background color, and we replace it with a scanned image of the sponsor logo found in the magazine article mentioned above. We've already adjusted the scan file to the appropriate size and resolution for the texture, and we can easily place it in both places in the texture using the Windows Clipboard, for example.

Now we determine the exact position of the texture relative to the area of the side rudder. Since we want the texture to be transferred without any distortion, we need to project it so that its image matches the side rudder area exactly.

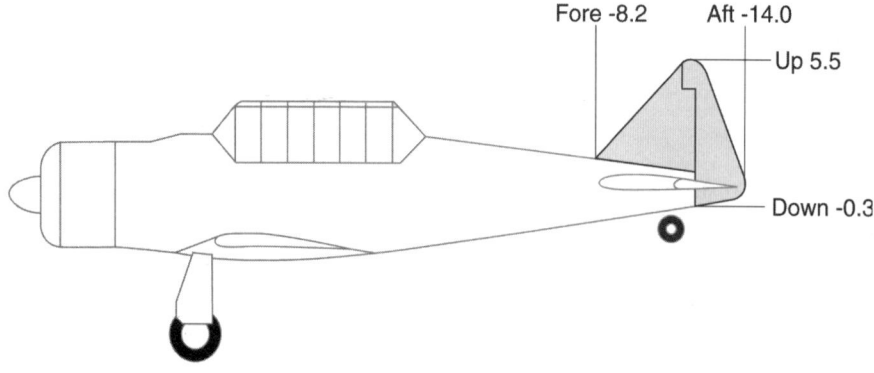

In the blueprint in the Assembly Line, the rudder area has the following corner points relative to the zero points:

Corner Points		
Up	5.5	(upper corner)
Down	-0.3	(lower corner)
Fore	-8.2	(front left corner)
Aft	-14.0	(back right corner)

We derive the height and breadth of the side rudder area from these simple calculations:

```
Width = Fore - Aft = (-8.2) - (-14.0) = 5.8 (ft)

Height = Up - Down = 5.5 - (-0.2) = 5.7 (ft)
```

For the texture, this means the following: The height of the .PCX graphic, 128 pixels, (either the upper or lower half) is projected onto the height of the side rudder area of 5.7 ft., and the width of the graphic (256 pixels) is projected onto twice the height, i.e., 2 x 5.7 ft = 11.4 ft.

If we lay the right edge of the .PCX file flush with the back-right corner (Aft = -14.0) of the side rudder, the left edge (Fore) of the projected texture will have these coordinates:

```
Fore = Aft + 2 * height = 14.0 + 2 * 5.7 = 14.0 + 11.4 = -2.6 (ft)
```

The positioning of the new side rudder graphic is done in the table in the Paint/Special Effect Shop:

North American T Objects	File	Assembly Group	Seq	Effects	Use as	Color	Technique
wing (right), trailing	w1124rt	Wing, mid, left	004 P	Always	Regular	Gray, light	Opposite
Flap Up Fill	wfuf	Wing, mid, left	004 P	Flaps, retracted	Regular	[G]Gray, light	Opposite
Wing Light, Left	winglite	Wing, mid, left	006 P	Lights, on	Fore, Left	[L] Red	Regular
flaps	flaps	Wing, low, left	001 P	Flaps, extended	Regular	Gray, light	Opposite
antenna	antenna	Tail	002 P	Always	Regular	Blue, light	Regular
Glue: antenna to body	g_a2b	Tail	003 G				Regular
body, rear	bodyd	Tail	004 S	Always	Aft bulkhead	[T][G]Gray, light	Regular
Glue Template for Tail	gluet1	Tail	005 G				Regular
Tail Tire [3D]	tailtire	Tail	006 S	Always	Regular	Black	Regular
Glue: body to vert stab	g_b2vf	Tail	007 G				Regular
vertical stabilizer, Top	vstabt	Tail	008 P	Always	Regular	[T]Gray, light	Regular
Glue: hor stab to body	g_hs2bl	Tail	009 G				Regular
Horizontal Stabilizer	hstab	Tail	010 C	Always	Collection	[T]Blue, light	Opposite
Glue: hor stab to body	g_hs2br	Tail	011 G				Regular
Horizontal Stabilizer	hstab	Tail	012 C	Always	Collection	[T]Blue, light	Regular
vertical stabilizer, bottom	vstabb	Tail	015 P	Always	Regular	[T]Red	Regular
Strobe Lamp	strobe	Tail, upper	001 C	Strobes, on	Regular	[L] Red	Regular
Wheel wells	wells	Gear, right	001 C	Gear, up	Below	Gray	Regular
Tire, 3D	tire	Gear, right	004 S	Gear, down	Regular	[T]Black	Regular
Glue: stuff to gear	g_s2g	Gear, right	007 G				Opposite
Lower gear strut	lowstrut	Gear, right	008 P	Gear, down	Regular	Gray	Opposite
gear door	gstrut	Gear, right	009 P	Gear, down	Regular	Gray, light	Regular
Glue strut to wheel	gs2w	Gear, right	010 G				Opposite
Gear strut	gstrut	Gear, right	011 S	Gear, down	Both bulkheads	[G]Gray	Opposite
Wheel wells	wells	Gear, left	001 C	Gear, up	Below	[G]Gray	Regular
Tire, 3D	tire	Gear, left	004 S	Gear, down	Regular	[T]Black	Regular
Glue: stuff to gear	g_s2g	Gear, left	007 G				Regular
Lower gear strut	lowstrut	Gear, left	008 P	Gear, down	Regular	Gray	Regular
Glue strut to wheel	gs2w	Gear, left	009 G				Regular
Gear strut	gstrut	Gear, left	010 S	Gear, down	Both bulkheads	[G]Gray	Regular

Double-clicking on the line for the side rudder (Vertical Stabilizer) opens the Spec Sheet, where we set up the new graphic:

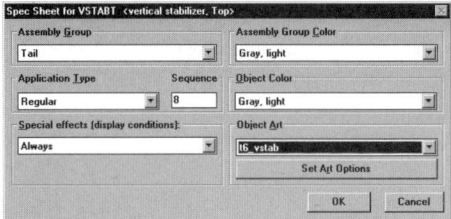

The [Set Art Options] button opens the dialog box for adjusting the planned texture. We type the calculated "corner values" of the projection into the four input fields:

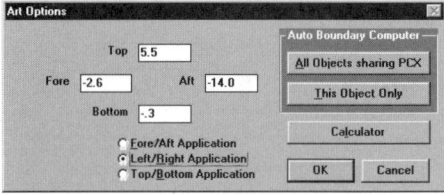

Here is a summary of these values:

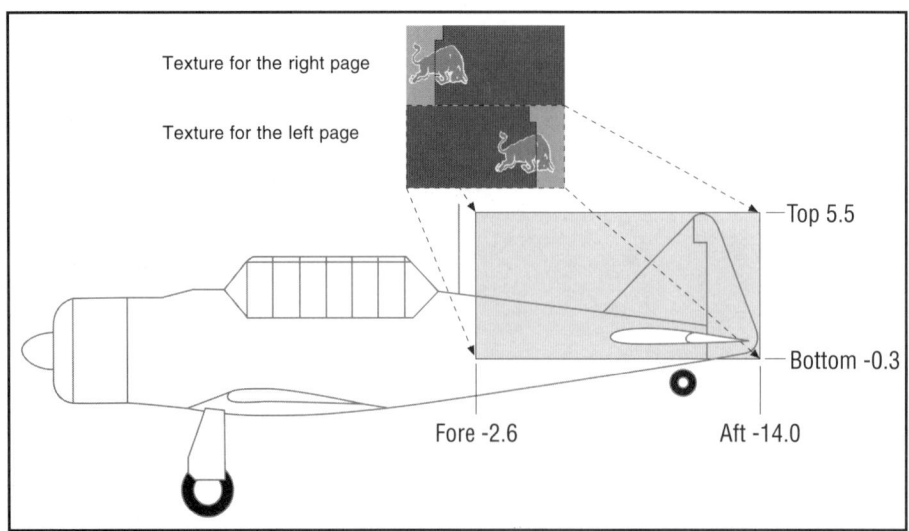

Corner values		
Top	=	5.5
Bottom	=	-0.3
Fore	=	-2.6 the new, calculated value
Aft	=	-14.0

It's very important that we activate the proper projection. In this situation, we select Left/Right Application, since the texture is supposed to be projected onto the left and right sides of the vertical rudder surface. Never initiate the automatic calculation of the limits of the edges using the [All Objects Sharing PCX] or [This Object Only] buttons. These calculate the selected texture file using the measurements of either the entire aircraft (All Objects) or of the current side rudder area (This Object), which isn't what the designer had in mind.

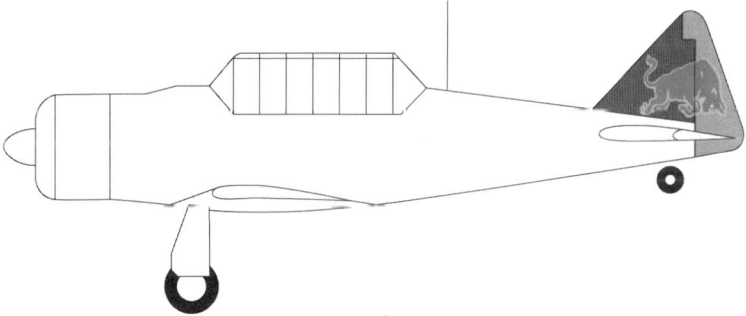

Multiple textures

In most cases, each part will have its own texture. However, picture elements for several small parts (like wheels) can be combined within a texture file. This way we can save storage space.

A multi-texture like this is used in the T6. The file T6_WHEEL.PCX contains not only the images for the wheels on the main landing gear, but also the displays for a very simple instrument panel and the front view of an eight-cylinder radial engine.

As usual, the texture's area of 256 x 256 pixels is divided into an upper and lower half, whereby the wheel images are situated diagonally across from each other. The rest of the area is occupied by the two other images we mentioned.

The wheel in the top half is projected onto the right wheel, listed in the table as part *Tire-3D, gear right*, and the wheel in the bottom half is projected onto part *Tire-3D, gear left*. As before, we need the absolute coordinates of the part. They can be quickly derived in the blueprint with the side view:

Absolute Coordinates		
Top (up)	=	-4.0
Bottom (down)	=	-6.0 Height = Top - Bottom = -4.0 - (-6.0) = 2 (ft)
Fore (left)	=	9.4
Aft (right)	=	7.4 Width = Fore - Aft = 9.4 - 7.4 = 2 (ft)

Again, you have to picture in your mind how the graphic will be projected onto the part: a height of 128 pixels is projected onto a height of two feet, and a width of 256 pixels is projected on a four foot width.

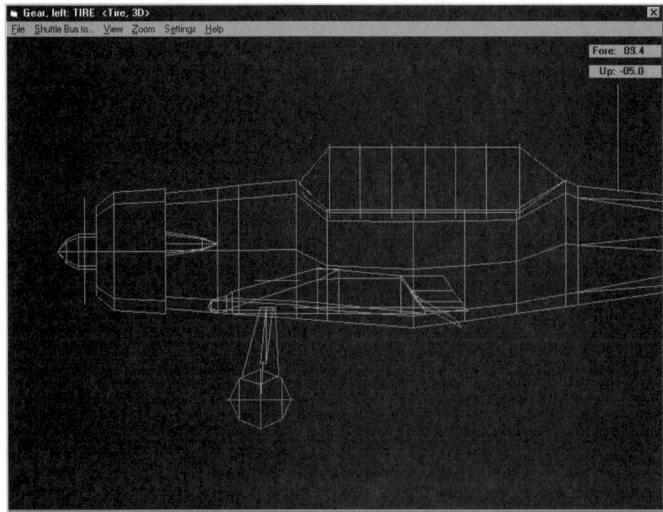

Since the same coordinates are valid for the wheel on the opposite side, the same ratios will be valid there as well, except they will apply to the top half of the texture.

In the Paint/Effect table, highlight the two parts *Tire-3D, gear left* and *Tire-3D, gear right* one at a time and call up the appropriate Spec Sheet by double-clicking. Keep the file T6_WHEEL.PCX as the graphical object. The (Set Art Options) button opens the dialog field for adjusting the texture coordinates. The Automatic Boundary Computer calculates the edge boundaries of the currently highlighted part using the

This Object Only button and confirms the data captured manually in the blueprint. However, the automatic calculation would compress each half of the texture in its width so much that the entire image wheel + panel or wheel + engine would be projected onto each wheel.

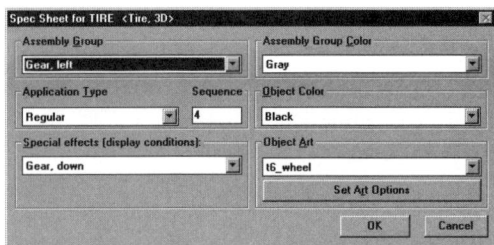

Therefore, we have to calculate the right-hand boundary. Use these calculations:

```
Wheel diameter = fore - aft = 9.4 - 7.4 = 2 ft
(also, see above)
```

```
Graphic aft = aft - wheel diameter = 7.4 - 2.0 = 5.4
```

The back calculation to check our figures is:

```
Graphic width = fore   graphic aft _ 9.4 - 5.4 = 4 ft or 256 pixels
```

This calculated new (right-hand) back edge at position 5.4 ft is entered into the Aft field of the object.

The "extra" 128 pixels from the width (the motor view) of the bottom half of the texture will be projected past the part on the left, and therefore they will remain invisible.

Duplicates are not always desired

A graphic for the texture always has to be at least large enough so that it can completely cover the intended part. If the area of a texture is set too small due to the edge boundaries (for example, via Set Art Options in the Spec Sheet), the texture will be copied and repeatedly placed side by side until the entire area of the part is filled.

So, you can't use a small national emblem on the side rudder by itself. Instead, you have to place it within an area of color that is projected completely onto the area of the side rudder.

Aerodynamics For The Virtual Pilot

When the aircraft is moved out of the Assembly Line in the Aircraft Factory Designer and it's taken over by the test pilot, the construction and the production of the model are largely complete, excepting a few later enhancements. However, the earliest problems show up in the first test flight, especially with the flight dynamics.

For the first production, the horned owl has been equipped with special dynamics that the Flight Dynamics for Aircraft (from the Template Library) prescribes. One of these dynamics templates is the Generic Glider Template, which contains the properties of a virtual sailplane. Actually, the airplane should be somewhat flyable just with this template. However, the constructor will be very surprised to find that the flight behavior is anything but normal.

We need another tool to make the flight dynamics of the little bird closer to normal: the Flight Dynamic Editor from the Flight Shop or the brand new Aircraft Dynamic Editor ADE98 version 1.4 from Ian J. Donohoe: http://www.flightsim.com/ade/.

However, before we can start working with the ADE98, we need to discuss a few theoretical considerations on the subject of flying.

An aircraft has forces and energy. The topic of the following paragraphs is how these physical properties can be utilized in flight (real and simulated).

Force and energy

What is force, and what is energy? If we gently tap a ball lying on a table with our hand, it moves and rolls a small distance. If we use the same movement to strike a large, heavy book on the table, nothing's going to move very much. We will, however, notice some pressure against our hand, which comes from the resistant book.

If the ball rolls over the edge of the table, it will continue its movement in a vertical direction downward, hit the floor, bounce back up, fall back down, and so on. If we push the book over the edge, it will also fall downward. However, after impact it will not bounce back up again, but it might possibly break apart or destroy another object.

These examples show different types of force and energy: The force of the hand (which placed an object in motion), the resisting force (exhibited by a heavy object) and the transformation of potential energy into kinetic energy and the different reactions.

Let's compare the thick book to Flight Simulator's 737-400 the when it's standing at the take-off position. To push the book, we need a certain force supplied by our hand. To start the 737 in motion means we have to generate several tons of thrust in the turbines. And again after the landing, large forces—reverse thrust and brakes—are necessary to bring the large airplane from the its landing speed of 140 knots down to zero.

And in fact, the 737 isn't that easy to move. But once it is in motion, it doesn't want to slow again very rapidly. It just wants to keep going at whatever its current speed is. To describe this, we say the airplane has inertia. The amount of inertia depends first on the mass of the object. The larger the mass, the larger the inertia of this mass.

The change of the speed of an object is defined as acceleration: If the speed increases through the application of force or the conversion of energy, we speak of positive acceleration. If the speed decreases, this is negative acceleration. A mathematical formula exists for both situations:

```
Force equals mass times acceleration, or: F = m * a.
```

The mass (m) is measured in kilograms (kg) and the acceleration is in meters per second squared (m/s^2). The product of kg * m/s^2 yields a unit of force called a *newton* (N).

Every body experiences a special type of acceleration at all times: the gravitational pull of the earth, or gravitational acceleration. Due to the constant attraction or acceleration that the earth exerts on every object due to the earth's mass, the object exhibits a particular force. This is the gravitational force, or simply stated, the weight of the body:

```
Weight equals mass times the acceleration due to gravity, or: Gravity =
m * g.
```

The acceleration due to gravity has a value of 9.81 m/s². Thus, a body with a mass of 1 kg has a weight of 9.81 kg * m/s 2 = 9.81 N.

Flight Simulator 98 Boeing 737 Specifications	
Length	36.45 m (119 ft 7 in)
Height	11.13 m (36 ft 6 in)
Wingspan	28.88 m (94 ft 9 in)
Wing surface	105.4 m² (1,135 sq ft)
Max. takeoff weight	62,830 kg (138.515 lbs)
Engines	2 CFM 56-3C-1 turbofans
with 104.5 kN of thrust each	23,500 lbs thrust
Cruising speed	0.74 Mach at 30,000 - 35,000 feet
Range	2,700 nautical miles (5,000 km)
V1	IAS 145 knots
Vr	IAS 151 knots
V2	IAS 160 knots
Stall speed (flaps and landing gear raised)	IAS 172 knots
Max speed (the lesser of the two)	IAS 340 knots or Mach 0.82

All these different units can create confusion. The takeoff weight is in kg and lb., the engine thrust is in kilonewtons (kN). But if everything is converted to the same unit base, we can introduce a couple small calculations to show the force at work. For example:

```
Weight = (mass) 62,830 kg * (acceleration due to gravity) 9.81 = 616,362
N
```

```
Engine takeoff power = 2 * 104,500 N = 209,000 N
```

```
Acceleration (a) = force / mass = 209,000 N / 62,830 kg = 3.33 m/s².
```

These figures mean that at the maximum start weight (full tank) and starting thrust, the speed of the 737 increases by about 3.33 meters per second. The conversion to knots yields an acceleration of 6.47 knots per second.

Now, if we use a take-off speed of 160 kts as a base, we can calculate the time from the roll-out time (T) to the point where the machine lifts off the runway:

```
T = 160 kts / 6.47 kts/s or T = 82.3 m/s / 3.33 m/s² = 24.7 s
```

According to these calculations, the 737 needs just under 25 seconds to reach the safe speed V2 of 160 kts. However, in the simulation, the 737 doesn't reach lift-off speed until about 32 seconds have passed. That would make us think that either the numbers from the technical specifications aren't accurate or the flight model of the simulated 737 isn't exact enough. Naturally, our calculations don't take into consideration a number of other unknown forces, such as the wind drag or the rolling drag of the wheels. As the speed increases, so does the air resistance, so that part of the thrust isn't available just for moving the mass. This lengthens the take-off run and the time until the aircraft can lift off.

Potential and kinetic energy

Let's pick the book up off the floor and put it back on the table. If the book has a mass of one kilogram (1 kg) and therefore a weight of 9.81 N, and the table top is one meter (1 m) above the floor, when we lift the book we are performing work equal to 1 Nm. We say we have done some work. The gravitational force of the book directed downward was moved the distance of one meter upwards. Therefore, we have performed work equal to exactly one newton meter (1 Nm).

As a result of performing this work, the book has been granted a particular property that it didn't have previously: potential energy. If the book is lying on the table again, it has a potential energy of 1 Nm. Thus, work and energy are of equal nature: We exert work to create energy.

If we let the book fall off the table a second time, the potential energy is converted into kinetic energy during the free fall. After exactly one meter, all the potential energy is converted into kinetic energy. The rate of fall has reached its highest value. The kinetic energy looks like this when expressed in a formula:

```
Ekin = ½ * m * v2
```

where Ekin is in newton meters (Nm) like the potential energy, mass is in kilograms (kg) again, and the speed is in meters per second (m/s). So, the kinetic energy is directly proportional to the mass and changes with the speed squared. (The mathematicians among you will have derived the kinetic energy as the integral of the theorem of momentum I = m * v).

Unfortunately, the free fall with the maximum possible speed ends after exactly one meter, because that's where it reaches the floor. Now the kinetic energy is suddenly converted into another form, because the book can't go any further. For example, in controlled environments you can generate thermal energy, which is beneficial. Depending on the binding, the book might be torn apart and destroyed when it lands. The heavier the book and the larger the kinetic energy, the larger the energy of destruction.

These findings lead to one of the most important laws of physics: In a closed system, the sum of the types of energy remains constant. In a physical sense, a closed system is a room in which no energy is conveyed from the outside and from which no energy gets lost to the outside.

The four forces on the aircraft

As soon as the aircraft is in the air after take-off, different forces impact it:

- ✈ Lift, directed upwards, is generated by the wings.

- ✈ Counteracting the lift is the weight of the aircraft, which consists of the weight of the aircraft and its load.

- ✈ The thrust generated by the engine and the propeller is directed toward the front.

- ✈ The corresponding drag force is directed toward the rear.

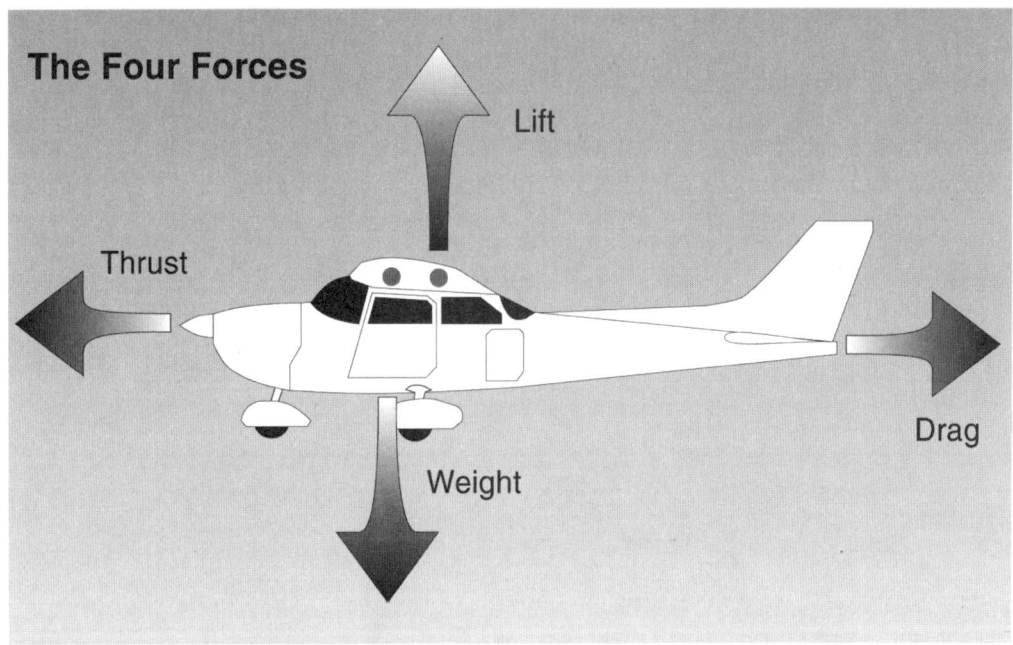

Lift

Lift is generated along the curved profile of the wings due to the on-coming air. At some time you have probably stuck your hand out the window while riding in a car and held your hand like a wing. When you did, you noticed that if your hand was tilted at a slight angle, it was pushed up and back. The air flow under your hand has generated a positive pressure, the lift upwards, and at the same time there is a resistant force directed behind you.

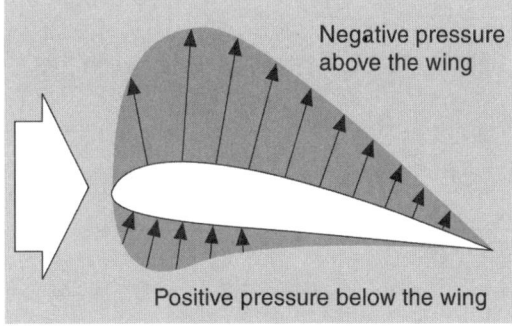

In addition to the positive pressure beneath the wing, an area of negative pressure is created along the upper surface of the wing due to the curvature of the wing (Bernoulli's principle). You can read more about fluid mechanics in technical literature or textbooks. A little experiment can provide a quick general overview here. Take a strip of heavy paper or cardstock, and roll up one end of it so that it can hang loosely on a pencil or other object held horizontally.

Put a slight upward curve in the strip of paper, and let it hang down from the pencil. Hold this construction in front of your mouth so that you can generate a flow of air across the top of it by blowing. And voila, (hopefully) to your amazement you will see that the paper rises upward. It is not pushed away downward, like one would think. In this experiment you used a flow of air to generate negative pressure on the upper side, which raises the strip of paper upwards because it is directed upwards.

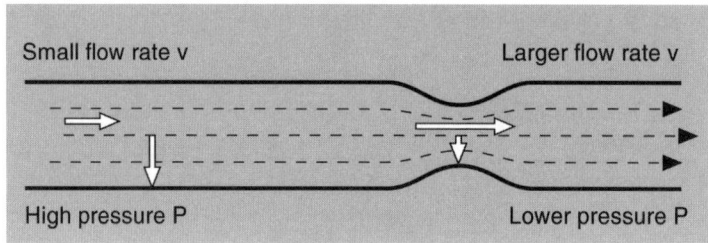

We have seen that the shape of a body in a current of air can generate a lifting force. An airplane designer uses this knowledge to give the wings of the airplane a special profile that can produce this lift when air flows across them. The angle between the direction of air flow and the profile of the wing is called the *angle of attack* or *incidence*. This angle is determined by the horizontal axis of the airplane and is a primary factor in generating the lifting force.

The aerodynamic force resulting from the lift and the drag are directly associated with the angle of attack between the wings and the flowing air. As the angle of attack increases, the aerodynamic force reaches a maximum with a high amount of lift and a large amount of induced drag. In a stall condition, only the drag increases; the lift suddenly collapses.

For a given specific wing profile, the lift that develops is proportional to the volume of flowing air, the area of the wing, and the speed squared. Bernoulli derived the complete lift formula:

$L = \frac{1}{2} * CL * r * A * v2$	
L	Lift (N)
CL	Lift coefficient (no units)
r	Air density (rho) (kg/m3)
A	Area (m²)
v	Velocity (m/s)

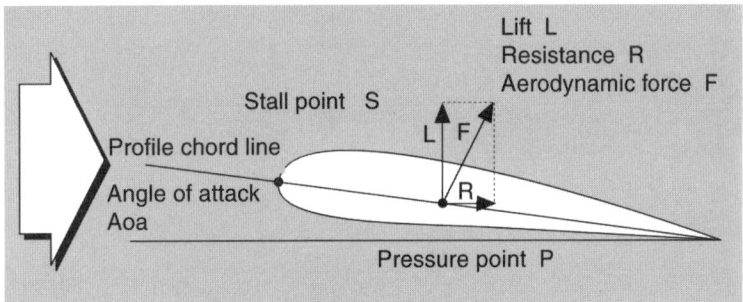

Lift L
Resistance R
Aerodynamic force F

Stall point S

Profile chord line

Angle of attack
Aoa

Pressure point P

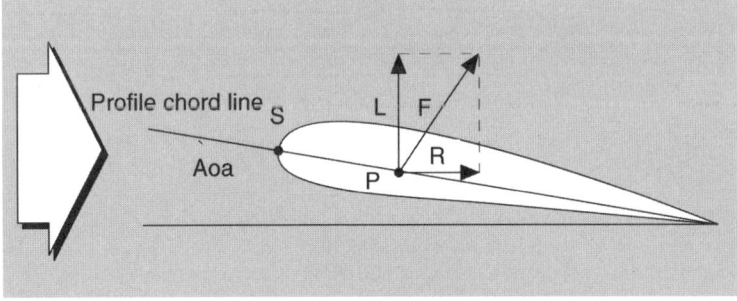

Profile chord line S

Aoa

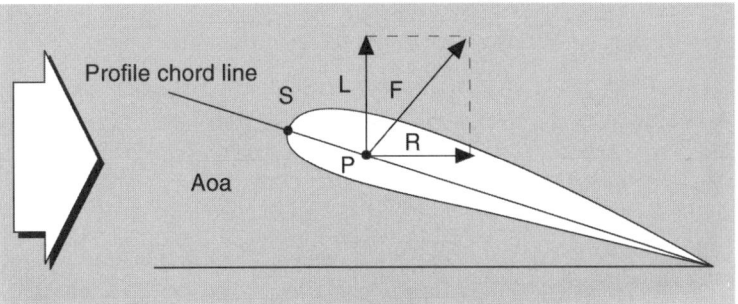

Profile chord line

S

Aoa

The denser air, larger wings, and faster speeds, mean more lift is produced by the profile. The air density ρ decreases as the elevation increases. At standard conditions (15°C temperature and 1013.26 hPa air pressure), air density is 1.29 kg/m³ at sea level, 0.92 kg/m³ at 10,000 feet and 0.34 kg/m³ at 30,000 feet.

The lift coefficient C_L is a scaling factor that can have positive as well as negative values. In most cases, C_L will be barely higher than 1; extreme values are at $C_L = 1.4$. The lift coefficient is influenced by things like special flaps in the wings, or by the profile's angle of attack: $C_L = 2 * \pi * Aoa$, where the angle of attack (Aoa) is given in radians.

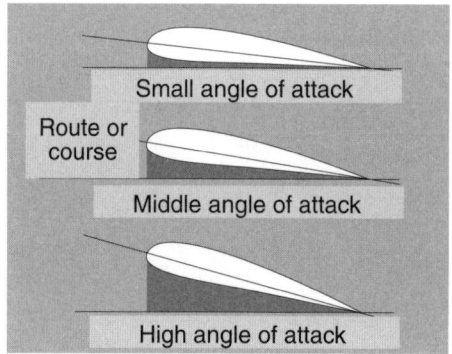

Now a lift coefficient C_L can be calculated for different situations. Let's look at the ratios for the B737 at 10,000 feet altitude at 300, 250 and 200 knots speed. C_L can be readily calculated using the formulas cited above. For an unaccelerated flight we get:

```
Lift = weight = ½ * C_L * r * A * v² = L

or C_L = 2 * L / (r * A * v²)

and Aoa = C_L / (2 * p) = C_L *180 / (2 * p²) = C_L * 90 / p² = 9,12 C_L
```

Let's say the current flying weight is 500,000 N. The lift force is equal to this. The wing surface of the 737 measures 105.4 m², the air density (ρ) at 10,000 feet is 0.92 kg/m³. Then we get the following values for C_L and Aoa:

```
at 300 kts = 154.3 m/s

    C_L = 2 * 500,000 / (0.92 * 105.4 * 154.3²) = 0.433

    Aoa = 9.12 * 0.433 = 3.9°
```

```
at 250 kts = 128.6 m/s
```

$$C_L = 2 * 500{,}000 / (0.92 * 105.4 * 128.6^2) = 0.624$$

$$Aoa = 9.12 * 0.624 = 5.7°$$

```
at 200 kts =102.9 m/s
```

$$C_L = 2 * 500{,}000 / (0.92 * 105.4 * 102.9^2) = 0.974$$

$$Aoa = 9.12 * 0.974 = 8.9°$$

At high speeds, the lift coefficient and the angle of attack are relatively small. There is no problem in that situation to generate sufficient lift. However, these values increase at lower speeds, because more lift must be produced via the angle of attack (by pulling on the elevator) to keep the altitude constant.

Drag

In our discussion about lift, you already learned a bit about resistance, or drag. Using the example of your hand held out of a window as a model of a wing, you saw that besides the force directed upwards, a force is also generated which is directed toward the back. This resistance is generated when the lift is created, so it is called *induced drag*.

However, far and away the largest portion of the total drag is produced as *form* drag and *frictional* drag. These two types of drag combined are sometimes called *parasitic* (or damaging) drag. The parasitic drag depends basically on the shape and size of the airplane and on the condition of its surface. English-language literature usually refers to this parasitic drag as *zero elevator* drag.

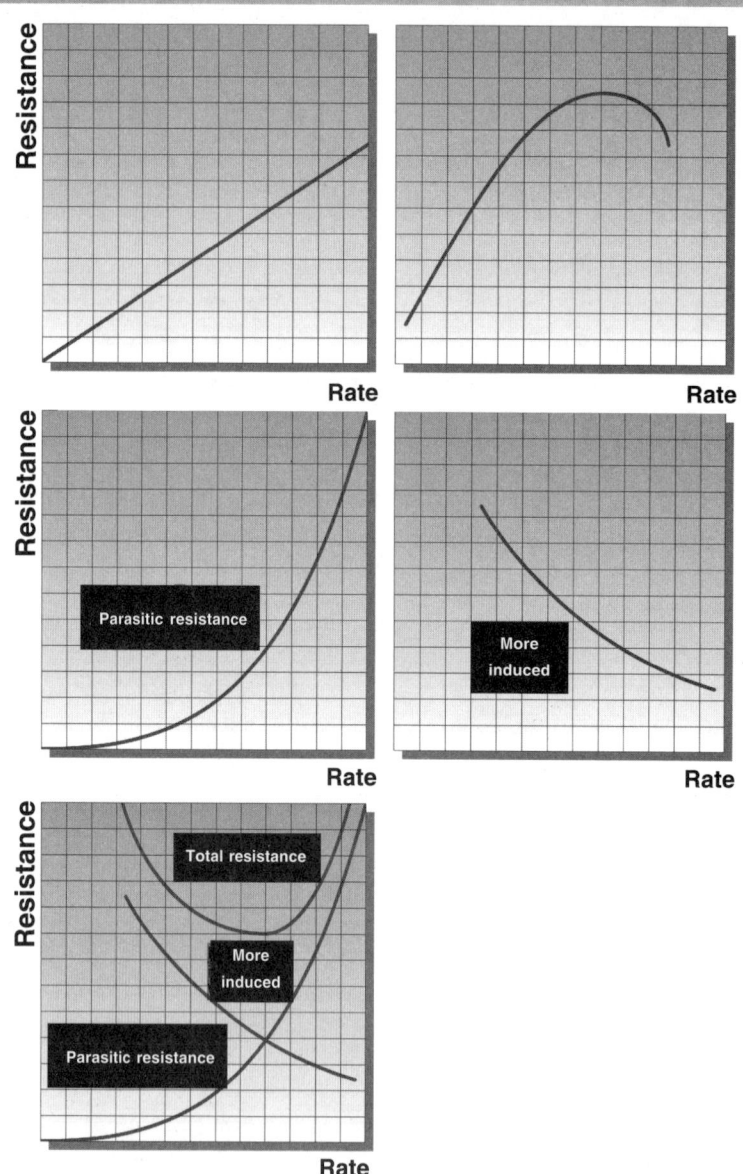

The figures make it very clear that a minimum of total drag is introduced at a certain speed. At any rate, changes in speed let the drag grow, regardless of whether the airplane flies faster or slower. Drag behaves similar to lift, and it can therefore be expressed in a formula that has the same construction:

$$\textbf{Drag} = \tfrac{1}{2} * C_D * \rho * A * v^2$$

Just as with lift, drag is also determined primarily by speed. The scalar value C_D is the drag coefficient, which appears not only during aircraft construction, but which is also known to be a characteristic of automobiles. As was mentioned above, drag is a composition of several different types, so more drag coefficients show up in the formulas:

C_{D0} Zero Lift Drag Coefficient

C_{Di} Induced Drag Coefficient

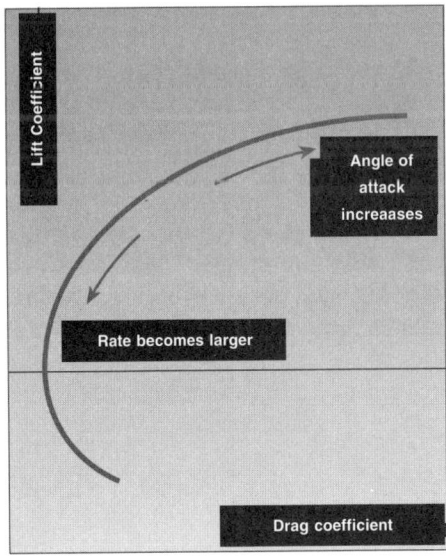

Comparing both the lift and drag coefficients in a graph yields a polar diagram. We determine the appropriate coefficients for the different angles of attack during flight. They yield a characteristic curve for the wing profile in the diagram.

In the figure, Curve A stands for a perfectly symmetrical profile, close to what is used by aerobatic aircraft so that they can achieve good lift values upwards even when flying upside down.

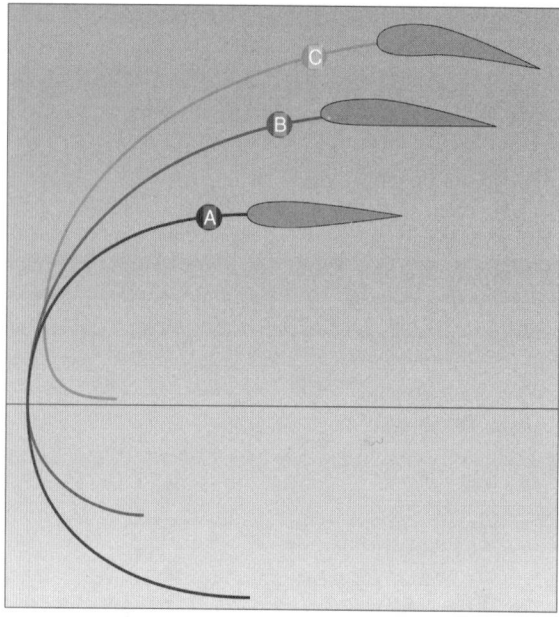

Curve B stands for a slightly asymmetrical profile, which also generates sufficient lift when flying upside down, but only at relatively high speed.

Curve C shows a strongly asymmetrical profile, which still produces a lot of lift at low speeds, but which is totally unsuitable for upside-down flight. The profiles of old airplanes were designed in this way, because in the early days of flying, the designers focused primarily on lift. Only later did they consider the induced drag by improving the profile.

Otto Lilienthal established the real connection between angle of attack, velocity, drag and lift towards the end of the 19th century. He drew the aerodynamic force resulting from drag and lift as polar tangents, and in this way he determined the theoretical best values for a certain profile. Before 1881, attempts to develop airplanes and gliders were occasional and sporadic but this changed with Lilienthal.

Before Lilienthal, designing and building a heavier-than-air craft was though to be the work of only dreamers and fools. However, Lilienthal's work and efforts made it seem possible to fly. His efforts mark the beginning of the experimental period of active research on heavier-than-air flight. Lilienthal developed eighteen models of his gliders over a five year period. His efforts were known worldwide and his successes encouraged others — including the Wright Brothers — to follow in his footsteps.

Fifteen of Lilienthal's gliders were monoplanes, three were biplanes. Each model was a hang glider, controlled by the pilot shifting his weight rather than through the use of any active control surfaces.

Two famous quotes can be attributed to Lilienthal on inventing airplanes. The first shows the discipline needed for an inventor: *"To invent an airplane is nothing. To build one is something. But to fly is everything."* The second quote is *"Sacrifices must be made."*

He died August 10, 1896 — two days after crashing in one of his hang gliders. For more information check out two other web sites. The Otto Lilienthal Museum Online (http://hawaii.cogsci.uiuc.edu/LilienthalMuseum/Lilmuseum.html) and the Otto Lilienthal Museum in Anklam, Germany (http://home.t-online.de/home/LilienthalMuseum/index.htm). Although the site is German, check out the photographs of Lilienthal replica gliders.

Thrust

Thrust, the forward movement of an airplane, is produced via the motor/propeller unit or via a turbine.

Spark-ignition engine

The conventional motor is an internal combustion engine based on the Otto type of construction (in addition to the somewhat rarer diesel motors). That means it works with carburetor technology or fuel injection. The propeller, which starts rotating via the crankshaft, then generates movement towards the front due to its special shape. The thrust can be seen as being directly connected to the power of the engine, or the number of horsepower it has.

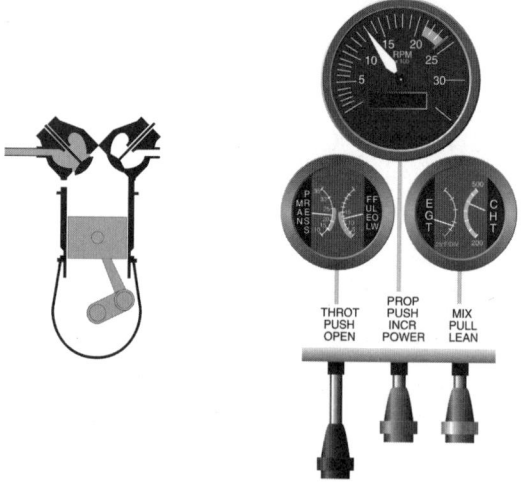

Similar to a wing, the blade of a propeller has a certain angle of incidence, but it continually increases from the outer tip up to the hub. Therefore, the propeller has its smallest slope at the tip and its greatest slope at the hub. This is necessary because it would be difficult to generate thrust if there were a constant slope over the entire propeller blade because of the different circumferential velocity at the middle of the propeller, while at the tip, the air current would stop flowing because the angle of incidence is too large.

A very special feature of all single-motor airplanes is the torque effect, the torque of the propeller, which affects the airplane in two different axes. This effect has its greatest consequence during the start-up stage, when the engine turns at its peak rotation, but the airplane itself isn't rolling very fast yet. The air stream generated by the propeller then flows around the body in a spiral fashion and meets at the left side of the rudder. In this way, torque is generated to the left around the vertical axis, and the airplane starts rolling toward the left on the runway. You have to counter this torque by pushing the side rudder to the right. The second appearance of this torque effect is felt immediately after leaving the ground: The airplane turns to the left about the vertical axis, the left wing slants downward, and a curve is started. This effect is also based on the rotation of the motor and the propeller, which generate an opposing torque.

The consequences of the torque effect are regulated by the level of reality set in Flight Simulator's **Aircraft | Aircraft settings**. If the degree of reality in the flight is set to less than 4, you'll be spared the rotation and yaw due to the torque effect. With anything above 4, you'll notice it more and more.

The gas turbine

The modern gas turbine engines from Learjet or Boeing work based on the principle of continuous combustion of an air/kerosene mixture. To convert this mixture into a forward motion, these engines use air compressors, combustion chambers and turbines.

The compressor inside the engine sucks in outside air, compresses it in a system of rotating and stationary blades, and heats it in the process. Air that has been compressed as a result of several of these compression stages is fed into combustion chambers made of a system of steel tubes. Prescribed amounts of kerosene spray into the combustion chambers filled with heated air, and the kerosene mixes with the heated air to form a combustible gas. Spark plugs in several locations ignite this mixture continuously when the engine is started, not just at certain piston positions and at a particular time, as in a piston engine. As would be expected, when the mixture is ignited and burned, the temperature and pressure increase dramatically. The excess pressure is pushed out toward the back through the propulsion nozzle with a high excess of air, and this creates the forward motion of the airplane.

The blades of the turbine are integrated between the combustion chamber and the outlet through the propulsion nozzle. These blades are set in motion by the exiting gas flow. On the one hand, the rotation of the turbine generates power like a normal generator, and on the other hand, it also drives the compressor by means of a common shaft. This is a closed energy cycle. It is only during start-up that suitable external starters have to be used to bring everything into motion so that the cycle can run on its own: intake air, compress it, heat it, mix with kerosene, ignite and exhaust.

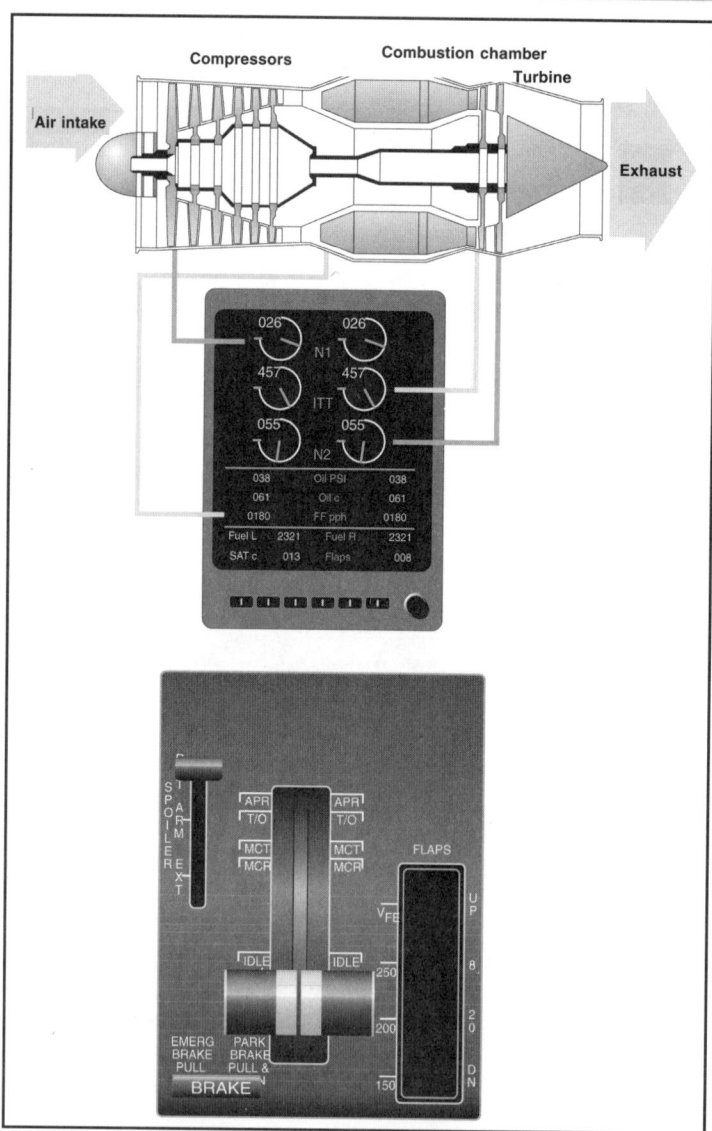

Basic principle of the turbine engine

The gas flow out the back provides the motion. This follows a physical law whereby a force in one direction invokes a counter-force in the opposite direction: for every action there is a reaction. The idea that you'll hear from some people that the gas flow "pushes off" of the surrounding air mass simply cannot be accepted. Otherwise, how could a rocket move forward in a vacuum in space? Perhaps an earthly example might make the idea even clearer. Let's say a man is standing quietly on roller blades or on a skateboard, without moving. Somebody throws him a ball, which he is holding in his hands now. When asked to throw it back, the man throws the ball away from his body using the full force of his arm. If he's not careful, he'll land directly on his nose, because the throwing motion and the resulting force have generated a rolling motion of the wheels under his feet in the opposite direction as a reaction, and the wheels move away from his upper body. It takes longer to write about it than it does for the reaction to occur, so try it out some time.

Regulating power

The six circular displays in the top part of the EICAS display in the Learjet cockpit indicate the condition of the engines: N1 shows the revolutions of the compressor, N2 shows that of the left and right turbine. ITT is the Inlet Turbine Temperature. With the Boeing 737, the exhaust gas temperature (EGT) is shown in this place. N1 and N2 are given as relative percent values of the maximum possible revolutions of the compressor/turbine. Absolute values can't be used here, because the efficiency and revolutions of a turbine change or adapt with increasing elevation.

N1: The top set of instruments shows the rpms of the compressor. The optimal operating range of the compressor's rotational speed lies between 50 and 100%. The rpms shown by N1 indicate the standard values for the settings for starting, increasing elevation, decreasing elevation, and for landing.

N2: The two lower pairs of instruments show the rpms of the turbine. The normal operating range of a turbine lies between 55 and 100%, although more than 100% is needed during take-off to accelerate the airplane enough on the runway. Right after take-off, you need to bring the rpms back to 100% or less to avoid overheating.

ITT or EGT: These two instruments indicate the current operating temperature of each of the two turbines in degrees Celsius. The normal range is between 230° and 920°.

Weight

In these calculations, the weight of the aircraft includes all of the weights: the empty weight of the aircraft, the weight of the load in the form of fuel and baggage, and the weight of the personnel and passengers. The weight has a direct effect on the dynamics because it works opposite to the lifting force. A larger weight requires greater lift, which can only be achieved by the increased application of thrust force. The Cessna has an empty weight of 1,783 lb. and can carry up to 1,329 lb. of payload, including pilot, passengers, baggage and fuel. The total weight amounts to 3,113 lb., whereby about 11 lb. of fuel are required to start the motor and to roll into starting position, so that the maximum start weight has to be 3,099 lb.

In the simulator, you can only calculate the total weight with the assumption that pilots, all passengers, and the corresponding baggage are on board. The only variable in the weight value is the usable amount of fuel, which is listed as 2 x 1499 gallons in the main tanks and 2 x 1156 gallons in the reserve tanks for the Boeing 737-400, for example. With a specific gravity of 0.791 kg/L for kerosene, this yields a total weight for fuel of a maximum of 5,310 gallons.

Forces at equilibrium

After take-off and the initial climb, the airplane is now at cruising altitude, say at flight level 330, or 33,000 feet MSL. The airplane flies stabilized at a constant speed, straight ahead and horizontal. Since the horizontal and vertical speeds remain unchanged, there is no acceleration. What is happening with the forces now?

The maximum weight force of the 737 of approximately 600,000 N directed downward is balanced by an upward directed force of the same size. This force directed upward is generated from the lift on the wings. So, two forces of the same magnitude act on the vertical axis of the machine, and the sum of the resulting force works out to be zero. The lift and the weight are in equilibrium.

Along the horizontal axis, the powerful turbines pull the airplane forward, but the drag which is generated by the air flowing along the outer shape of the airplane pulls back. Now, since there is no change in speed, the thrust and the drag are equal. They too are in equilibrium. So, a stabilized flight attitude can be expressed in very simple formulas:

```
Lift = Weight and Thrust = Drag
```

The pilot and passengers sense this equilibrium of the forces as a pleasant, calm flight. But if the pilot plays with the throttle or programs the autopilot with a different altitude, the horizontal and vertical acceleration change, the forces go into disequilibrium, and they have to be brought back into equilibrium by means of an attitude adjustment.

The angle of approach

The relationship between the horizontal forward speed and the vertical descending or ascending speed can, if we consider time, also be expressed as the ratio of the horizontal and vertical distance. With a sailplane, which has to fly without its own motorized thrust, the potential energy is the only possibility of getting over a certain stretch by converting the potential energy into kinetic energy.

The mathematical conversion of the profile diagram into a velocity diagram (which we won't bother to show here) is shown by the following figure:

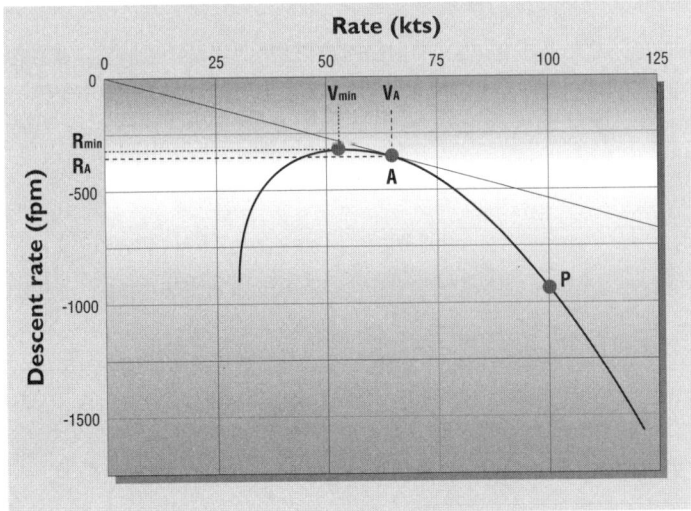

The curve shows for a given point P exactly a specific ratio of the current speed in knots and the rate of descent in feet per minute. The tangent, which extends from the zero point, intersects the curve at point A. This point represents the most favorable ratio of the two speeds. In other words, at velocity VA the rate of descent RA establishes itself, at which the sailplane can fly the furthest, i.e., the best angle of approach.

Although all speeds lower than VA provide smaller rates of descent, the distance covered during the time period is smaller. This is especially important for a sailplane which would like to stay in the air as long as possible (approximately a five hour flight). Where a horizontal tangent touches the curve, this is where the minimum velocity Vmin becomes established for the smallest rate of descent.

Using the ADE98

If you have made your first test flight with the horned owl (probably the best solution was to secretly bring yourself down using the parachute!), I'm sure you'll want to fill out the test report now and request that the designers make some serious changes in the flight dynamics immediately.

This is where the ADE98 comes into play. The editor allows you to directly view the data that describe the properties of an aircraft. Beyond that, immediate and targeted intervention into the dynamic behavior of the airframe and the engine parameters is possible—even during operation with Flight Simulator 98.

Besides the technical capabilities of the ADE98, its strengths lie in a complete summary of all data in the form of a table that can be saved at any time and can be printed if desired. By using a spreadsheet (like Excel), you can even place several worksheets of different aircraft models next to each other and directly compare their properties.

After you see the start-up screen and load an aircraft file via the Open File button, you see an extensive dialog window with six registration cards, which display the special properties of the aircraft. Here are the various modifications you can make to the aircraft data (*.AIR) with ADE98:

Description

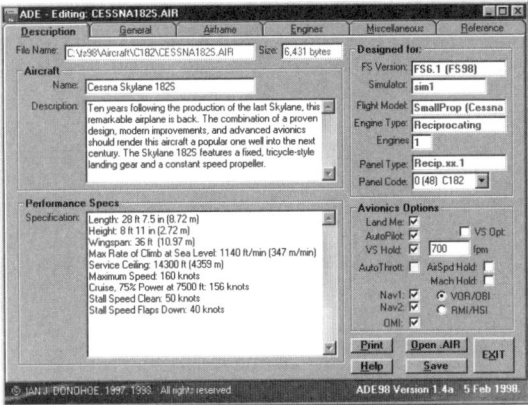

Change the descriptive information about an aircraft that is shown in the Flight Simulator 98 dialog box, for example, to uniformly label the aircraft by manufacturer and model or by airline. In addition, the specific technical data can be changed or enhanced in the text field.

General

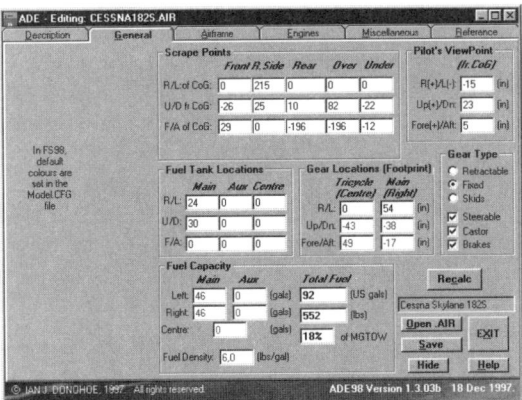

The equipment and configuration of an aircraft (landing gear, ground controls, flaps, fuel tanks, radio equipment, autopilot, etc.) can be modified almost to your heart's content. The location of the geometrical center of gravity, the pilot's viewpoint, the

233

touching points of the parts of the airplane with the ground (footprints and scrape points) and many other parts that could impact the flight dynamics can be changed after the fact.

Airframe

Set the properties of the airframe. Important data with potentially significant impact on the dynamics are weight, lift and drag coefficients, inertial mass, stalling speed, wing form, etc.

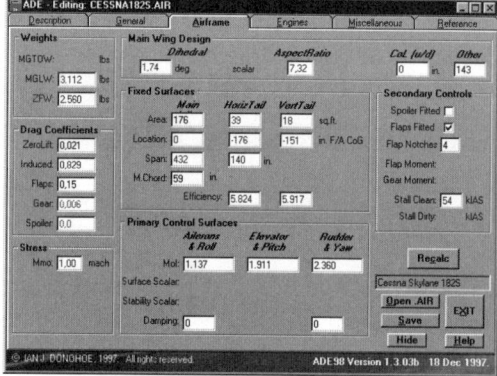

Engines

The propulsive thrust of the motors or turbines, propeller size, number of engines, maximum operational times, and fuel consumption can be adjusted or enhanced.

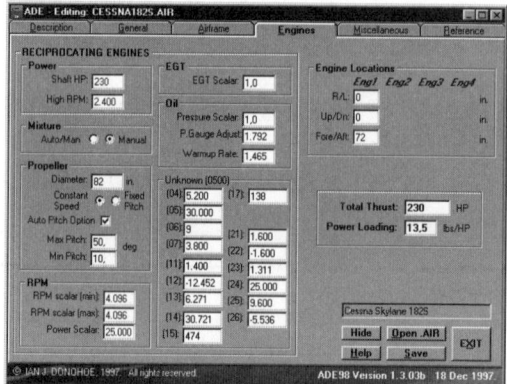

Miscellaneous

Here you may enter different base values, scaling factors and stabilization components.

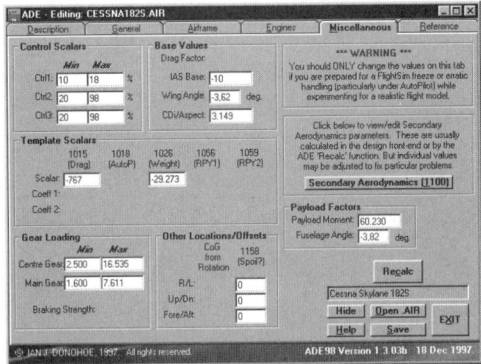

Reference

Adjust the files required or used to display the 3-D model of the aircraft, the instrument panel based on internal coding, and other as-yet undefined options that can be used in Flight Simulator 98.

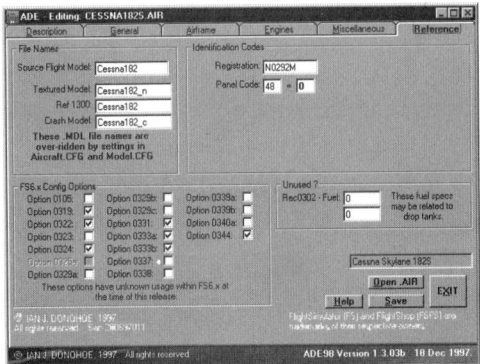

Almost every group of parameters and some of the individual data fields have help screens, which refer to specifics about the input options and often provide helpful tips. You can run the ADE98 along with Flight Simulator 98. However, if you have

ADE running in the foreground, you should minimize the Flight Simulator window to insure that ADE (with 32 MB of RAM) gets the full computational power of the computer.

As soon as changes have been made to the aircraft file with ADE, the file is saved. In Flight Simulator 98, you first have to use click **Aircraft | Select Aircraft** to switch to another aircraft, and that aircraft has to be loaded before you can select the aircraft you have modified. This is the only way you can force the simulator to load the aircraft file again. Unfortunately, it isn't enough to just switch between two models in FS98's **Aircraft | Select Aircraft** dialog box.

Comparing models

The easiest way to make a completely new aircraft like the horned owl really flight-ready is to compare it with a finished model. Since the horned owl is designed as a sailplane, it's only natural to use the same kind of aircraft: the Schweizer S2-32. This sailplane is part of the basic repertoire in Flight Simulator 98.

Use the ⌈Open File⌉ button on the start-up page of the ADE98 to load the file SCHWEIZER2_32.AIR. Immediately after that, load ADE98 a second time and this time load the aircraft file OWL.AIR. Now you can directly compare both files on the screen.

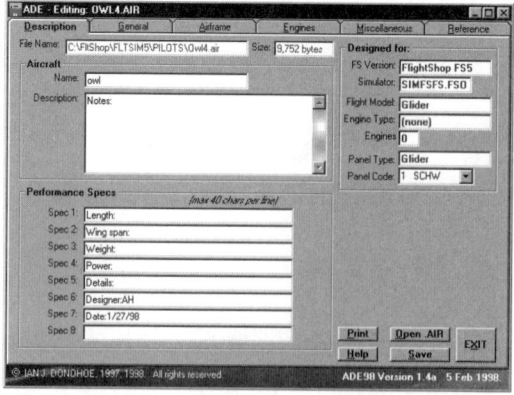

Since even the relatively simple sailplane models have a considerably large amount of data, the complete catalog of properties and performance of each model can be saved to a text file with the ⌈Print⌉ button on the Descriptions page. This text file can be read by a word processor that supports calculation or, even better, by a spreadsheet.

Printed by ADE98 Version 1.3.0c on Friday, 6 February 1998 at 11:51:33

(c)1997 Ian J. Donohoe

```
============================================================
```

Model File: SCHWEIZER2_32.AIR   OWL_1.AIR

FS Version: FS6.1 (FS98)   FS6.1 (FS98)Ground speed

Section 00 - Identification

   1   Aircraft Name: Schweizer 2-32

   2   Description:

   3   Specification: Notes:

Length: 8.15 m (26 ft, 9 in)

Height: 2.74 m (9 ft)

Wingspan: 17.37 m (57 ft)

Extension: 18.05

Flying weight: 608 kg (1340 lb.)

Standard empty weight: 377 kg (831 lb.)

Max. load: 222 kg (490 lb.)

Flying performance:

  Wing loading: 63.5 kg /m² (7.44 lb./sq. ft)

  Maximum speed: 276 km/h (172 mph)

  Stall speed: 74 km/h (46 mph)

  Maximum lift/drag ratio: 34/1 at 102 km/h (63.5 mph)

   4   Registration: N0425P   N0425P

Section 01 - Reference Files

   100   Simulator: sim1   sim1

   101   Complex Model: Schweizer2_32_n   Owl_1

   102   Simple Model: ---   ---

   103   Crash Model: ---   ---

   104   Source Name?:   Schweizer2_32   ---

   105   Rotary/Fixed: 0   ---

   1300   AirFileName?: ---

Since both text files contain the same entries except for the descriptive elements (Aircraft Name, Description, Performance Specifications), the values can even be combined into a single (Excel) worksheet. Highlight the column with the values for the second aircraft (always the fourth tab stop in the text file or in Column D in the spreadsheet) and use the Clipboard to paste it in an empty column in the first aircraft's spreadsheet. Since the descriptions and specifications have different lengths, you might have to slide the new column over starting at the line Section 01 – Reference Files until the data are all on a single line.

```
Section 03 - Configuration
0300a Control 1 Min:  16 0 X
0300b Control 1 Max:  35 0 X
0300c Control 2 Min:  16 0 X
0300d Control 2 Max:  35 0 X
0300e Control 3 Min:  16 0 X
0300f Control 3 Max:  35 0 X
0300g Aileron Sens:   — —
0300h Elevator Sens:  — —
0300i Rudder Sens:    — —
0301a Pilot Locn RL:  0 0
0301b Pilot Locn UD:  18 -2 X
0301c Pilot Locn FA:  27 53 X
0301d Payload Moment:  43.282 49.950 X
0301e Fuselage Angle:  4,65 0 X
0302a Center Fuel:  0 0
0302b L.Main Fuel:  0 0
0302c R.Main Fuel:  0 0
0302d L.Aux Fuel:   0 0
0302e R.Aux Fuel:   0 0
0302f Other Fuel1:  0 0
0302g Other Fuel2:  0 0

—
```

```
310 Engine Type:  2 2
 311 Engines:   0 0
 312 Fuel Density:  0 6,6 X
 313 Reverse Thrust:  0% -25% X
 314 Land Me:   0 0
 315 Flap Notches:  2 — X
 316 Mmo:    1 0,37 X
0317a Autopilot:   0 0
0317b AP VS Hold:   0 0
0317c AP Default ROC:  ROC ROC
0317d AP AutoThrottle: 0 0
 318 Flaps:    0 0
 319 ?:    1 1
 321 Auto Mixture: — —
 322 ?:    0 — X
 323 ?:    0 — X
 324 ?:    0 0
0325a ?:    0 0
0325b ?:    0 0
 327 Spoiler:   1 1
 328 Steering:   0 0
0329a ?:    0 0
0329b ?:    0 0
0329c ?:    0 0
 330 Auto Pitch:   0 0
 331 ?:    0 0
 332 Brakes:    1 1
0333a ?:    0 0
0333b ?:    0 0
 334 Nav OBI/RMI:  0 0
0335a Nav1 Radio:   0 0
0335b Nav2 Radio:   0 0
0335c OMI Radio:   0 0
```

Section 10 - Primary Aerodynamics
1001 Panel Code: 49 49
1002 CoG RL: — —
1003 CoG UD: — —
1004 CoG FA: — —
1005 Roll Mol: 2.400 1.200 X
1006 Roll Damper: 0 0
1007 Pitch Mol: 1.800 1.200 X
1008 Yaw Mol: 1.800 1.800
1009 CD ZeroLift: 0,044 0 X
1010 Drag Factor: — —
1011 CD Flaps: 0 0
1012 CD Gear: 0 0
1013 CD Induced: 1,004 1 X
1014 CD Spoiler: 0,084 0,098 X
1015 Drag Scalar: -364 -1.412 X
1016 Drag Coeff1:   — —
1017 Drag Coeff2:   — —
1018 AutoP Scalar: — —
1019 AutoP Coeff1:   — —
1020 AutoP Coeff2:   — —
1021 StallSpd Clean: 40 38 X
1022 StallSpd Dirty: — —
1023 MGLW: 1.340 1.020 X
1024 MGTOW: 1.340 1.020 X
1025 IAS Adjust: 0 0
1026 IAS Scalar: -32.768 -32.768
1027 IAS? Coeff1:   — —
1028 IAS? Coeff2:   — —
1029 ZFW: 1.340 1.020 X
1030 Retract Gear: 0 0
1031 Winglets: — —
1032 HorStab Area: 21 21
1033 HorStab Canard: — —
1034 HorStab Effic'y: 11.229 11.229
1035 HorStab Locn: -193 -193

```
—
1036 HorStab Span:  95 95
1037 VerTail Area:   17 17
1038 VerTail Effic'y: 5.927 5.927
1039 VerTail Locn:  - 177 -177
1040 Wing Locn UD:  0 0
1041 Wing Locn FA:  0 0
1042 Wing MChord:  38 38
1043 Wing Area:    180 181 X
1044 Wing Dihedral:  3,5 3,5
1045 Wing (other?):  596 0 X
1046 Wing Span:    684 684
1047 Wing Angle:    -2 -1 X
1048 Wing Cdi/Aspect: 1.550 1.545 X
1049 Crash Resist:   — —
1050 Wing Mmo (FS5):  — —
1051 Wing Max AoA:   — —
1052 Wing Vmo:     — —
1053 Aileron Scalar:  — —
1054 Elevator Scalar:  — —
1055 Rudder Scalar:  — —
1056 RPY1 Scalar:   — —
1057 RPY1 Coeff1:   — —
1058 RPY1 Coeff2:   — —
1059 RPY2 Scalar:   — —
1060 RPY2 Coeff1:   — —
1061 RPY2 Coeff2:   — —
```

Section 11 - Secondary Aerodynamics
1101 Stability 1:   — —
1102 Pitch Stab Mom 1: 0 4.718 X
1103 PitchStabComp(D):   — —
1104 Pitch Stab Mom 2: 0 -13.226 X
1105 PitchStabComp(AP): -512 -754 X
1106 HorStab Lift: 1.310 1.302 X
1107 Flaps Lift: — —
1108 Stability 2:   170 181 X
1109 ?:   — —
1110 DihedStabComp: 37 46 X
1111 Aileron Lift: -343 -367 X
1112 Yaw Stab Mom 1: 10 12 X
1113 ?:   — —
1114 Wing Lift: — —
1115 ?:   — —
1116 Roll Stab Mom 1: -819 -819
1117 ?:   — —
1118 ?:   — —
1119 Yaw Stab Mom 2: -184 -183 X
1120 ?:   — —
1121 Pitch Stab Mom 3: -110 12 X
1122 Pitch Stab Comp: — —
1123 Pitch Stab Mom 4: 8.250 23.962 X
1124 Pitch Stab Mom 5: -3.400 -3.833 X
1125 Pitch Stab Mom 6: 6.653 6.613 X
1126 Pitch Stab Mom 7: — —
1127 Pitch Stab Mom 8: -66.950 -73.891 X
1128 (FS6 only):   — —
1129 (FS6 only):   — —
1130 Flap Moment: — —
1131 Gear Moment: — —
1132 Yaw Stab Mom 3: 103 -7 X
1133 Yaw Stab Comp: -14 -23 X
1134 ?:   — —
1135 ?:   — —
1136 ?:   — —

```
1137 Yaw Stab Mom 4: — —
1138 (FS6 only):   — —
1139 (FS6 only):   — —
1140 ?:     — —
1141 ?:     — —
1142 Yaw Stab Mom 5:  62 63 X

—
1143 ?:     — —
1144 Yaw Stab Comp:  -200 -204 X
1145 ?:     — —
1146 (FS6 only):   0 0
1147 (FS6 only):   0 0
1148 Yaw Stab Comp(AP): -840 -417 X
1149 ?:     — —
1150 Yaw Stab Comp(D): -143 -182 X
1151 ?:     — —
1152 Yaw Stab Mom 6:  10 76 X
1153 Yaw Stab Mom 7:  290 286 X
1154 (FS6 only):   — —
1155 (FS6 only):   — —
...
...
1163a MGear Loc RL:  0 0
1163b MGear Loc UD:   - -20 X
1163c MGear Loc FA:  -9 -9
1164a CGear Loc RL:  0 0
1164b CGear Loc UD:  0 -30 X
1164c CGear Loc FA:  0 -9 X
1165 Bounce CG Max:  11.000 0 X
1166 Bounce CG Min:  3.000 0 X
1167 Bounce MG Max:  0 0
1168 Bounce MG Min:  0 0
1169 ?:     — —
```

243

```
1170a Tail Scrape RL:  0 0
1170b Tail Scrape UD:  -8 -23 X
1170c Tail Scrape FA:  - 87 X
1171a Nose Scrape RL:  0 0
1171b Nose Scrape UD:  - -8 X
1171c Nose Scrape FA:  87 -170 X
1172a RWing Scrape RL:  3 260 X
1172b RWing Scrape UD:  6 5 X
1172c RWing Scrape FA:  0 -8 X
1172d Upper Scrape RL:  0 0
1172e Upper Scrape UD:  0 0
1172f Upper Scrape FA:  0 0
1172g Lower Scrape RL:  0 0
1172h Lower Scrape UD:  0 0
1172i Lower Scrape FA:  0 0
1173 ? max:    5.148 5.148
1174 ? min:    -3.276 -3.276
1175 ? max:    5.148 5.148
1176 ? min:    -3.276 -3.276
```

And finally, you can make an entry in a free column to the right of the data sets as to whether or not a parameter is the same for both models. A formula in Excel format can check the contents of the cells and display an "X" if they don't match, leaving the cell blank if they do:

```
Formula in the sixth column: =IF(D#<>E#;"X";"")
```

where pound '#' is the corresponding row number in the table. If you copy the formula into each row, you get an immediate additional indication of which values differ.

The ADE worksheet itself consists of eight sections, which stand for the type of parameter:

Section 00	Identification
Section 01	Reference Files
Section 02	Colors
Section 03	Configuration
Section 04	Airframe Dynamics Template
Section 10	Primary Aerodynamics
Section 11	Secondary Aerodynamics
Section 14	TurboProp Dynamics
Section 12	Autopilot Dynamics

Some cells contain question marks '?'. In these places, either there were no values to evaluate or ADE98 didn't know how to formulate an unambiguous interpretation.

Things get really interesting starting with Section 03. This is where the relevant parameters of the aircraft start. For the S2-32, the first six values 0300a to 0300f (controls min/max) contain either 16 or 35, while the horned owl is full of zeroes. Comparisons with other .AIR files show that non-zero values are always used here. Therefore, it can't hurt to make our first modifications using these cells.

Unfortunately, making changes in an Excel table doesn't do much, because the changes have to be made in the ADE program. We find the corresponding input fields for control scales on the Miscellaneous page of the ADE.

The pilot's position (pilot locn right/left, up/down, fore/aft) starting with 0301 only differs because of the different size of the two aircraft, so it doesn't need to be changed. The Payload Moment and the tilt of the body on the ground shouldn't have any big effect on the flight dynamics either. Fuel Density and Reverse Thrust aren't meaningful for a glider, so we can set them to zero. The maximum Mach number (Mmo) of 0.37 means that the aircraft must not be flown faster than Mach 0.37 = 244 kts. The conversion from Mach to knots is done using the formula V (kts) = M * 38.9793 * the square root of (273.15°C + temperature°C).

Section 10 is where we get to the real meat of things. This is where the primary aerodynamic data are given, for example, the lift and drag factors we talked about in the theoretical part of this chapter. The drag coefficient Cd0 (CD Zero Lift) is perhaps the most important coefficient for determining the behavior when banking: The S2-32 shows a value of 0.044 here, while once again the Owl has a zero here. Likewise, the coefficients of the induced drag Cdi (CD Induced) and especially the scalar Drag

Factor differ for both aircraft. Change these values in the ADE on the Airframe page in the parameter group Drag Coefficients and on the Miscellaneous page for the parameter Template Scalars.

Section 11 for the Secondary Aerodynamics contains additional parameters with widely varying dimensions for the two aircraft. These are largely the components and resulting moments of the side rudder and elevator, which have affect the divergent flight dynamics of the two models. Make the changes to these values again on the Miscellaneous page, but this time using the [Secondary Aerodynamics 1100] button in the corresponding parameter fields.

Note: We can't provide any absolute values for a do-it-yourself aircraft model, since the FlightShop Aircraft Factory lets you build models that are totally one-of-a-kind. In that case, transfer comparable data and parameters from completed machines only one step at a time and in small doses. After every change you make in the aircraft file (.AIR) with the ADE98, regardless of how small it seems, conduct a test flight to evaluate the effect of modifying those parameters.

Many parameters result from combining (addition, multiplication, division, etc.) them with other variables. In certain situations, innocently changing a value to zero can cause Flight Simulator 98 to completely crash. So, if you make changes to too many parameters at a time, you lose track of the changes, and you have to start the whole thing from scratch with a new file.

Chapter 7
The FS Cockpit

C hapter 7 climbs into the cockpit to describe the instrument panel, the gauges and what makes them work.

Needles And Numbers

The previous chapter showed how to design a custom aircraft model. Individual components and structures (such as body, wings, tail unit, etc.) were combined to make a complete aircraft. The aircraft's weight, the location of the center of gravity and the torque determine the flight properties. The production and the test flights of the new or modified design concluded our successful project. The only thing we left out was designing and configuring the cockpit. Until now, we relied on one of the Flight Simulator default instrument panels that was the closest match to the new or modified aircraft type: the Cessna panel for single-motor, light aircraft, the Learjet panel for business class airplanes and the Boeing panel for large, turbine-driven aircraft.

As far back as the spring 1997, Microsoft wanted to stop further support for software development on the Flight Simulator. They wanted to leave this area to the enthusiasts and fans of the program. However, the appearance of Flight Simulator 98 heralded two important innovations: First, an improved panel system simplified creating and installing new instrument panels in old or new airplane models.

Second, Microsoft introduced the first Flight Simulator developer's kit, the panel SDK, for developing all kinds of individual instruments.

This makes it possible to install your own panels or ones you've gotten from other sources into the airplane with relatively little hassle, without overwriting the original version.

However, the SDK panel does require advanced knowledge of the programming language C++ or Visual C++, so to stay within the scope of this book, we won't look into the more intensive techniques with the SDK. If you'd like to learn more about the panel SDK, visit Microsoft's Web site (www.microsoft.com/games/fsim/downloads.htm).

What's Inside The .CFG File?

Let's take a quick look at the directory of a sample aircraft. Each airplane model has a separate folder inside the Aircraft folder, and each of these contains the airplane-specific data in sub-folders. Each of the aircraft directories always contains the following folders and files:

Name	Contents, using the T6 Texan as an example	
Model folder	MODEL.CFG, T6TEXAN.MDL	Contains the model configuration, which is described by the flight properties
Panel folder	PANEL.CFG, T6TEXAN.BMP	Contains the instrument panel configuration
Sound folder	SOUND.CFG	Contains references to aircraft-specific sounds
Texture folder	T6TEXAN.0AF...T6TEXAN.6AF	Contains the texture of the aircraft model
Aircraft configuration file	AIRCRAFT.CFG, T6TEXAN.AIR	Contains references to the different component folders
Checklist configuration file	T6TEXAN_CHECK	If this file is listed, it contains the text of the aircraft's checklists

If you want to modify a panel, you will need to understand the data in the Panel folder and in the aircraft configuration file.

AIRCRAFT.CFG

An aircraft configuration file (AIRCRAFT.CFG) exists for each aircraft model. It contains the aircraft's descriptive name (as listed in the Select Aircraft window), as well as the connections and references to the individual components. A given aircraft file will have these basic elements:

```
[fltsim.0]
title=T6D Texan;appears as descriptive text in the Select Aircraft dialog
sim=T6texan    ;references the file AIRCRAFT.AIR
model=   ;folder for the aircraft properties, default is its own folder
panel=         ;folder for panel information, default
sound=         ;folder for sound information, default
texture=       ;folder for textures, default
checklists=    ;name of the checklist configuration file (see Chapter 5)
```

If there are several different versions of an aircraft model, the aircraft configuration file will contain the corresponding references. The counting begins with the number zero ([fltsim.0] for the first model), and is continued for each subsequent model. For example, here is the AIRCRAFT.CFG for both Cessna 182 models:

```
[fltsim.0]
title=Cessna Skylane 182R RG
sim=Cessna182RRG
model=rg
panel=rg
sound=
texture=rg
checklists=Cessna182RRG_check

[fltsim.1]
title=Cessna Skylane 182S
sim=Cessna182S
model=
panel=
sound=
texture=
checklists=Cessna182S_check
```

The first model, [fltsim.0], is the Cessna with retractable gear (RG). The pointers to the folders with the .RG extension, such as model=rg, panel=rg and texture=rg, determine its properties. The second Cessna model, [fltsim.1], gets its properties from the default folder, which is not explicitly identified. Each aircraft configuration file can hold up to 64 different models ([fltsim.0 ... 63]), which can vary by one or more characteristics.

The Panel folder and PANEL.CFG

The Panel folder for each aircraft model contains the panel configuration file, PANEL.CFG, and at least one .BMP file, which displays the blank instrument panel. Additional .BMP files can display items like the magnetic compass, an overhead panel or the minicontrols for remote control of the aircraft.

If several models of an aircraft are to be equipped with different panels, you must create the corresponding number of panel folders. A panel's default folder is always named Panel. Additional panel folders are indicated by adding an identifying number, expanding the folder's name to Panel.xxx. The aircraft configuration file identifies the proper files by indicating the panel number.

If the user directs Flight Simulator 98 to load a model, the corresponding panel configuration is loaded. The following example of a PANEL.CFG shows the relatively simple instrumentation of the Schweizer 2-32 sailplane:

```
// Panel Configuration file
// Schweizer
[Window Titles]
window00=Schweizer
window01=Minicontrols
[Window00]
file=Schweizer2_32.bmp
size_mm=515
window_size_ratio=1.0
position=7
visible=1
ident=0
gauge00=Schweizer.Compass, 0, 165
gauge01=Schweizer.Com-Radio, 214, 161
gauge02=Schweizer.Master, 298, 35
gauge03=Schweizer.Altimeter, 17, 78
gauge04=Schweizer.Airspeed, 106, 31
gauge05=Schweizer.Vertical-Speed, 396, 85
[Window01]
file=Minicontrols.bmp
size_mm=100
```

```
position=0
visible=0
ident=100
gauge00=Minicontrols, 0, 0
[8 Bit Colors]
color00= 99, 107, 123 ... thru ... color31= 66,  49,  49
[Default View]
X=0
Y=0
SIZE_X=8191
SIZE_Y=4890
```

After the aircraft model is loaded, Flight Simulator 98 opens the primary instrument window and possibly other instrument windows, as indicated in Flight Simulator's **View | Instrument Panel** menu. All of these instrument windows can be switched off and on using the ⒮+Ⓘ keyboard shortcut. The panel system starts with the first window, window00 (usually the main instrument panel), and continues the display until window63 or until the list of windows ends. The list of the maximum 64 individual windows must be numbered consecutively from window00 to window63, without skipping any numbers. Otherwise, the display assembly will be broken by the "numerical hole."

For each windowXX, the panel system looks for a section of PANEL.CFG with the same name ([windowXX]), which defines the separate components of the instrument panel. The variable file points to a .BMP file, which draws the basic picture for the instrument window. In the example for the sailplane, we see the file SCHWEIZER2_32.BMP, which is saved in the Panel folder. This 256-color (8-bit) bitmap with can be opened with any suitable graphics program, and it can be customized and changed as long as the original color palette and depth are retained. The variable size_mm contains the original width of the image file, while the variable window_size_ratio stores the ratio of the width of the window selected by the user to the original size of the panel window. The default value of 1 displays the panel in its original proportion. The variable position retains the relative position of the panel window on the screen. The positioning is represented by a numerical value:

0	= Top left	1	= Top center	2	= Top right
3	= Middle left	4	= Middle center	5	= Middle right
6	= Bottom left	7	= Bottom center	8	= Bottom right

If the position is not explicitly indicated, the default value is 7, providing a normal placement of the instruments in the middle at the lower edge of the screen.

The variable visible specifies whether the panel window should be visibly displayed after it has been loaded (corresponds to the Flight Simulator menu **View** | **Instrument Panel**). The values are:

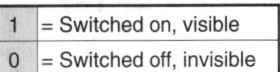

1	= Switched on, visible
0	= Switched off, invisible

If visible is not specified, 1=visible is the default value. However, if the aircraft model is loaded with a special situation file (chosen from Flight Simulator's **Flight** | **Select Flight** menu), the values stored in this file take precedence, and they overwrite the variable visible of the panel file. Some APIs of the panel system use a numerical value stored in the variable ident. Each separate panel of an aircraft is given an individually predetermined number, for example: 0 for the first panel, 50 for the second, and 100 for the third.

In the instrument panel of the Schweizer sailplane in the above example, six instruments have been built in, labeled using variables gauge00 to gauge05. The file PANEL.CFG gets the different instruments, such as the airspeed indicator or altimeter, from FS98's Gauges folder. This folder contains more than 100 finished instruments and devices that can be inserted into the different aircraft—everything from a chronometer to an artificial horizon to a complete radio console. Each instrument with the suffix .GAU is already calibrated and adjusted.

The gauge list in PANEL.CFG starts with gauge00 and counts up to a maximum of gauge63. It is essential that there be no break in the numbering, because the panel system stops accepting any additional instruments the first time a number is skipped. It's especially important to note this when adding a new instrument in the middle of a gauge list. Each of the subsequent gauge numbers has to be increased by one. If the device is added at the end of the list, it receives the next higher numerical value in the series.

After the equals sign, each of the gaugeXX variables is given the name of the .GAU file of the desired instrument (see the Gauges folder in the Flight Simulator directory). The name must exactly match the way it's written in the Gauges folder. Sometimes the instrument names can be very long, such as "Cessna_182.Manifold_Pressure_Fuel _Flow.1." In that case, it's helpful to just copy the name to the Clipboard and then paste the name into the panel file.

After the name, values (separated by commas) indicate the absolute position of the instrument in the panel window or panel bitmap. The values always indicate the upper-left corner of an instrument. With round or non-rectangular shapes, you need to imagine that they have a rectangular frame around them. An optional third number determines the proportional display size of the instrument and can be interpreted as a percentage. At any rate, you will need to do some experimenting if you want to place an instrument in an exact location in the instrument panel.

Special colors are defined in the 32 variables color00 to color31, which can be used in addition to the 256-color palette for displays within the instruments. However, it's not necessary in most cases for the user to change these default colors.

```
[8 Bit Colors]
color00= 99, 107, 123 ... thru ... color31= 66,  49,  49
```

Flight Simulator has already gone one step further than the current Windows 95 program. With a view to the next generation of Windows, the panel system is already prepared for the connection of multiple monitors to one computer. Multiple graphics boards and monitors can be managed with the image space of 8,191 x 4,890 pixels. You can use the **Undock Window** context (right-click) menu command to drag a window into any available monitor area, so if you have three monitors, you can quickly create a three-sided view out of the cockpit. This replaces awkwardly pressing different key combinations to change cockpit views with a realistic, if not particularly cheap, display.

```
[Default View]
X=0
Y=0
SIZE_X=8191
SIZE_Y=4890
```

The positioning of the panel file is given with X=0 and Y=0 by default for normal monitor operations.

Creating And Redesigning Instrument Panels

In the following sections, we will plan, design and install a new instrument panel for the North American T6D Texan built from the Flight Simulator Flight Shop. Sketches and technical drawings can serve as the basis for redesigning a cockpit. The best source is a detailed and sharp photo of an original cockpit, which you can scan into a graphics program to adjust its width to 800 pixels. If these kinds of documents aren't available, you can always design a new cockpit using a good graphics program, such as Photoshop, Paint Shop Pro or others. In any case, the final format must be a 256-color bitmap file (.BMP).

If the graphics program can handle picture elements in different layers (such as Adobe Photoshop—our favorite program!), the individual components of the basic panel can be constructed relatively easily, and they are especially easy to correct in the course of redesigning.

The .BMP Basic Graphic

Very simply, an instrument panel is a rectangle displayed in the lower half of the screen when the simulation is running. However, this geometry is very boring and does not represent reality. For example, on the Cessna's instrument panel we find a rounding on the left side, which mimics the construction of the cockpit in the area of the windshield. The Learjet's panel is similar. On the other hand, the trapeze form of the instrument panel in the single-seat aerobatic Extra 300 aircraft reflects very well how tight things are in the cockpit.

The 600 PS T6, which the Flight Shop provides as a finished model, is a two-seat training aircraft in which the pilot and the trainer or passenger sit behind one another in a very narrow canopy. The instrument panel is correspondingly narrow, but stretched vertically. It's always a little difficult for the pilot to have a good view outside the plane—the high instrument panel, the long engine cowling and the position of the airplane's tailwheel conspire to impede the pilot's forward view.

First, create the basic .BMP image in a graphics program (Paint Shop Pro v.5.0 is used in the following examples) as a new file measuring 800 x 600 pixels at 72 dpi (pixels per inch). An 800 x 600 pixels image will comfortably fit in FS's display window at most screen resolutions. Though we will reduce the color depth to 256 colors before using this image, select a higher color mode in order to use layers when building the panel in Paint Shop Pro.

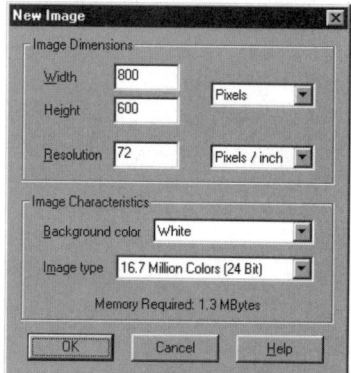

Create the general outline of the panel in the first layer. The height of the panel is set at about 180 pixels (measured from the top). Starting from the left edge of the screen, the corner points of the panel are set in the horizontal direction at pixel 220 and pixel 580. Use a line tool to draw the outline, then a freehand tool to round the top corners. This will form the panel's border. Create a new layer and fill the open area with a basic color, such as dark gray.

Making aircraft compatible

Don't use black when designing an instrument panel. Flight Simulator uses black to mask transparent areas of the bitmap, such as the airplane's windscreen. If you use black in your instrument panel, you will be able to see through these areas once the panel is installed in Flight Simulator.

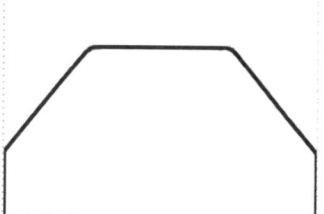

Now we have the basic form for our empty instrument panel. While we've made a good start, it doesn't yet look terribly impressive. To make it more realistic, use the filters and effects of your graphics program to create the illusions of light and depth. To do this in Paint Shop Pro, I'll use the retouch tool to lighten areas of the Panel layer. To further increase the realism, I've also textured the retouching tool.

Now select the layer of the panel's border to add highlights. I'm still using PSP's retouching tool, although I've selected a smaller brush size and a different, smaller, texture. This step may be easier with increased magnification.

For both components, lighten the upper left area, allowing the tone to darken toward the lower right. This creates an illusion of light coming from above and left.

The typical struts in the front cockpit area can be drawn in another layer, called Struts. These support the front windshield of the T6 towards the front and to the sides, and they form a prominent feature in the view out of the cockpit. Begin the left strut 40 pixels in from each edge, and bring it down to the corner of the instrument panel. Once drawn, use the **Copy** command to copy the strut to the clipboard. Then use the **Mirror** command to create the right strut. Now paste the left strut back into the upper left corner. Here, too, you can use the effects that we've already described to achieve a natural look, which can be further enhanced by adding rivets or screws.

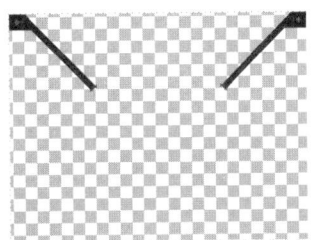

257

Now the instrument panel is almost ready. Be sure to save the image file to retain the color scheme and the individual layers. Next we will prepare it for use in Flight Simulator. We have to "flatten" the image to a single layer, convert it to a 256-color (8-bit) file, equip it with a mask for the front window view and save it as a .BMP file. Reduce the color depth in PSP's **Colors | Decrease Color Depth** menu. This also flattens the image's layers into a single layer. In this example, the file is named T6TEXAN2.BMP when we save it.

The mask

At 800 x 600 pixels, the finished rectangular image file of the panel .BMP covers the entire FS screen, including all viewing windows and map windows. To see through the aircraft's windows, the "glass" portions of the image in the panel file must be defined as transparent.

In Flight Simulator's panel system, transparency is defined by the color black. If a panel file contains the color black in any location, this location will appear transparent when the simulator runs, even if an instrument is supposed to be located at this position. So, these two rules apply:

1. Solid components in a panel must not contain the color black. To be safe, and to make sure that this doesn't occur, select the entire image and brighten it by a few percentage points. Or, you can specifically filter out the black locations and replace them with a slightly lighter color (like R=1, G=1, B=1).

2. Every portion of the panel image that is supposed to be transparent, such as the windshield or other view-ports, is masked using the color black and is thereby recognized as transparent.

In our example, three areas between and around the cockpit struts should be masked in black. These will be the transparent windows once the panel is installed in Flight Simulator. Use the Magic Wand and Fill Bucket tools to select the background areas and paint them solid black (R=0, G=0, B=0).

The actual composition of the panel and the "connection" of the instruments to the model in Flight Simulator take place in the previously mentioned panel configuration file. When you use AAFCONV98 to convert the T6texan2 Flight Shop file into an aircraft that is compatible with Flight Simulator, a directory is created that contains the previously mentioned folders and files. The Panel folder contains a PANEL.CFG file, which points to a default alias for a standard panel from the Flight Shop:

```
[fltsim]
alias=FSFSConv\panel.Recip.rg.1
```

This default setting equips the converted model with an instrument panel for piston-driven, single-motor aircraft with retractable landing gear. In our example, the familiar panel of the Cessna 182 RG is placed in the T6 cockpit. Naturally, that doesn't lend a realistic impression. Instead, let's install the panel we created.

Each panel file should start with at least one comment line—marked by double forward slashes at the beginning—to describe the contents. This allows you to sort things more easily if files get mixed up or exchanged with files from other aircraft models having the same filename. A kind of copyright notice with the date and version of the design complement the comments.

```
// Panel Configuration file
// for the T6 D Texan2 "Red Bull"
// Design Jan. 99
// Version 1.0.1
```

The first important position, [Window Titles], lists the individual windows that are to be displayed in the simulation with the Instruments option or with the keyboard shortcuts Shift+1 through Shift+3. Shift+1 displays the window titled window00, the instrument panel; (Shift)+(2) shows the window titled window01, the radio equipment; and (Shift)+(3) shows the window titled window02, with a scanned photo of your boyfriend or girlfriend.

```
[Window Titles]
window00=Instruments
window01=RadioStack
window02=Portrait
```

The window title [Window00] points to the .BMP image of the T6 panel and maintains its initial width and window size ratio. The panel is centered in the lower area of the screen and is visible after the aircraft has loaded. A zero is entered for the identification in the panel system.

```
[Window00]
file=T6texan2.bmp
size_mm=800
window_size_ratio=1.0
position=7
visible=1
ident=0
```

Now we still have to install the individual gauges. To do this, it is very helpful to prepare a screenshot of the still-empty panel in the simulation environment and print it out on paper. This screenshot should be printed as close as possible to its true size. For example, the printed image may be 160 mm wide. A ruler can then be used to determine the position coordinates of the gauges on the printout. A position with the coordinates x = 44 mm (from the left edge of the picture) and y = 56 mm (from the top edge of the picture) on the printout yields the monitor display coordinates of x = 220 and y = 280 pixels. You just need to divide the millimeter values by two and add a zero, which works because of the ratio of 160 mm to 800 pixels.

The two screen coordinates provide the position in the panel of the desired instrument. Unfortunately, the coordinates do not indicate the center point of the instrument, but the upper left corner. The width of the instrument to be displayed—if it differs from the default size—is established by a third numerical value. The width can also be used to derive the geometrical center of the gauge in the panel, using the simple equation:

```
X(midpoint) = x + width/2
```

For example, if you want to install the attitude indicator as the first gauge at the top in the center of the instrument panel, you derive the X component using the following equation:

x = X(midpoint) - width / 2	Where X(midpoint) = 400, or the middle of an image which is 800 pixels wide
x = 400 - 150 / 2	With 150 pixels for the width of the instrument
x = 325	

The upper edge, or the y-value of the coordinate, is simply measured with a ruler and converted. For example, if you measure out 42 mm, this results in a screen coordinate of 210 pixels, when calculated as above.

We want to install the same attitude indicator in the T6's cockpit that is used in the Cessna. We find this device in Flight Simulator's Gauge folder as a gauge file labeled cessna_182.attitude. All of the data that we have measured and calculated are now formulated into a syntax that is understood by Flight Simulator's panel system:

```
gauge00=cessna_182.attitude,325,210,150
```

In keeping with the classic arrangement of the instruments, below the attitude indicator we will insert a gyro compass, which is installed for both VOR and ILS navigation. The Bendix company makes a gauge like this called a Horizontal Situation Indicator, or HSI. The corresponding instrument file is found again in the Gauges folder: bendix_king.hsi. We can also get a suitable DME gauge from the same company, which we can install below the HSI in the panel.

```
gauge01=bendix_king.hsi,322,370,160
gauge02=bendix_king.dme,345,530,110
```

We can use the same methods for determining the coordinates for these last two gauges that we used before with the attitude indicator.

We can already test the successful installation of the partially equipped panel under simulation conditions by saving the PANEL.CFG file that we have so far in the corresponding Panel folder of the T6 model.

If you would rather work with a completed panel, then in addition to the first three instruments, which are installed beneath one another in the center, you may integrate all of the other instruments using the following listing. Add the airspeed indicator, the turn and bank indicator and the second VOR gauge just to the left of the center axis.

The Schweizer.Airspeed display is very interesting: it is not calibrated in knots (nautical miles per hour), but it displays the speed in land miles per hour. If the airplane flies at an indicated speed of 140 mph, that's only 122 knots. (The ratio of nautical miles NM to land miles LM is 1:0.87.) The speed in knots can always be called using the (Shift)+(Z) key combination, which also displays the coordinates and current altitude at the top edge of the screen.

The turn indicator from the Bell helicopter consists of the good old "paintbrush," which indicates the banking direction by leaning to the left or the right, and the ball-shaped spirit level is a measure of the curve grade.

```
gauge03=Schweizer.Airspeed,210,255,105
gauge04=bell_206b.turn_indicator,210,360,105
gauge05=bendix_king.vor2,210,470,105
```

The altimeter, variometer and the automatically added radio compass can be placed to the right of the center axis, one below the other. The altimeter from the Schweizer cockpit and the vertical speed indicator from the Bell helicopter are part of the standard instrumentation of every aircraft, whereas the "Slaved ADF"—again from

Bendix—can be considered one of the more modern devices. With it, you don't have to painstakingly recalculate the ADF bearing or determine it using the manually rotated course indicator disk.

```
gauge06=schweizer.altimeter,485,255,105
gauge07=bell_206b.vertical_speed,485,360,105
gauge08=Bendix_King.ADF.Slaved,485,470,105
```

All other instruments, levers and switches—tachometer and fuel gauge, landing gear lever and trim wheel, throttle lever and autopilot, etc.—are represented by the individual gauges in the variables gauge09 through gauge20. As you can see from the list, these devices are also made by different manufacturers and are normally used in totally different types of aircraft.

The clock from the B737 in gauge11 contains a stopwatch function as well as displays the simulation rate and the zoom factor of the view. This combined configuration is written permanently in the corresponding 737-400.clock-sim-rate gauge file, and can only be changed by modifying this file (more about that later).

If you are selecting a thrust lever from the Learjet instrument collection, note that there are installations for single-engine to four-engine aircraft. The lever that we need for the T6 comes from the file lear_45.thrust_levers.1, where the "1" stands for single-engine models. The parking brake is installed at the same time as the thrust lever.

The switches and rocker levers for engine start and navigation lights have their preset sizes and distances from one another in the corresponding gauge files and cannot be changed here.

```
gauge09=lear_45.elevator-trim, 240, 205, 21
gauge10=lear_45.control_surfaces, 267, 205, 40
gauge11=737-400.clock-sim-rate, 130, 320, 70
gauge12=lear_45.thrust_levers.1, 146, 470, 60
gauge13=737-400.engine-start, 30, 515, 85
gauge14=737-400.strob-nav-switch, 25, 540, 90
gauge15=cessna_182.omi, 40, 470, 70
gauge16=Cessna_182.Manifold_Pressure_Fuel_Flow.1,595,290,70
gauge17=Cessna_182.Oil.1,595,365,70
```

The highly versatile autopilot from Bendix, which is used in the Cessna, might not be all that common for a racing machine like the T6. However, since there's still room in the instrument panel and the T6 isn't all that easy to fly, why not make life easier?

263

```
gauge18=Bendix_King_Radio.AP,595,445,175
gauge19=lear_45.gear,600,500,100
gauge20=737-400.flaps,710,510,60
```

Since things are getting a little tight in the panel now, we'll put the radio stack, which should contain the COM, NAV and ADF receivers, in an additional window with the title "[Window01]=RadioStack." Here, too, we need to first identify a base bitmap and establish its size and position in the screen area. However, as an additional window, after the aircraft is loaded, the window should remain invisible and should only be displayed when it is needed. The single instrument gauge00 is represented by the radio stack from the B737, which is fixed to the position x = 0 and y = 0, or the upper left corner of the bitmap. In this case, this base bitmap can be a simple, single-color rectangular shape the same size as the gauge file.

```
[Window01]
file=RadioStack.bmp
size_mm=160
window_size_ratio=1.0
position=3
visible=0
ident=50
gauge00=737-400.Radio-Stack, 0, 0
```

A third small "instrument" window is meant more as a gag. Here you may place any desired photograph. This picture can be a special memento for the pilot (wife, girlfriend, boyfriend, dog, cat, mouse, etc.) or an external shot of the aircraft itself shortly before the first crash, or something like that.

```
[Window02]
file=portrait.bmp
size_mm=99
window_size_ratio=1.0
position=0
visible=0
ident=100
```

The final color table for 32 additional, 8-bit special colors contains the RGB color values (in each of the variables color00 through color31), which are to be used for particular displays if the general color palette can't provide them. In particular, the luminous colors red, yellow and green in the number displays and little lamps in the cockpit undergo a drastic adjustment in color due to this color table. Flight Simulator makes this adjustment whenever a new image file (scenery or panel file) is loaded. In so doing, the color palette of the new image is adapted as closely as possible to that of the existing image. This allows one or more colors to grow pale. We avoid that situation by using the special color table:

```
 [8 Bit Colors]
color00=106, 197, 213        ; percentage of red, green, blue
color01=185, 188, 199
color02=171, 177, 189
color03=184, 190, 202
color04=183, 189, 197
color05=192, 199, 211
color06=171, 184, 195
color07=183, 194, 211
color08= 42,  36,  24
color09= 40,  36,  25
color10= 39,  32,  24
color11=161,  66,  28
color12=106, 148, 148
color13=180, 139,  74
color14=172,   0,   0
color15=180,   0,   0
color16= 90, 123, 115
color17= 24, 106,  24
color18=213, 238,   0
color19=222,   0,   0
color20=255,   0,   0
color21=131, 106, 115
color21=131,  98,  98
color22=123, 106, 106
```

```
color23=189, 206, 214
color24=173, 173, 189
color25=115,  16,  16
color26=189, 180,  74
color27=181, 181, 255
color28=115, 115, 140
color29=198, 214, 255
color30= 66,  74,  90
color31= 82,  90,  99
```

When the panel configuration file PANEL.CFG is saved, the installation of all of the instruments into the base bitmap is as good as done. The user doesn't need to worry about how, whether, or why the instrument even works in the simulation. All of the internal functions of an instrument in Flight Simulator's Gauge folder are already fully "wired," and all of the necessary calibrations and adjustments have been made. The installation also completes all of the connections between the aircraft model and its properties or characteristics. The altimeter and airspeed indicator are connected correctly to the aircraft's air pressure system, and the gyroscopic instruments are kept in motion by an electrical or pneumatic pump. The navigational displays are connected to the radio receivers and they show the correct values when they are set to the proper frequency.

Working With .GAU And .BMP Graphics

Actually, the only other thing the user can do is to make one or more visual changes to an instrument. The individual instruments are adapted to Flight Simulator's operation down to the smallest detail using settings in the gauge file. The gauge file controls all of the necessary links (connections) in that it queries particular flight conditions using sensors (input) and it produces the appropriate display via conductors (output).

The VOR1 gauge—represented, for example, by the Bendix_king.vor1 file—uses its sensors to determine that the NAV1 receiver is receiving signals on a particular frequency. This receiver had already determined via its sensors that the user had set a particular frequency in a particular area of the screen using the mouse or the key combination N+1 and +−. So, the receiver determines the direction and perhaps distance using the aircraft's position data and the sending radio beacon's location coordinates. The conductors output these values and pass them on to the VOR1 device. The gauge file converts the input in the VOR1 into a value for the pointer position, which is then concluded with the output and display of the pointer needle after considering any other sensor data (user settings on the OBS switch).

As we mentioned, the complicated connections and the internal calculations of the gauge file aren't of any great interest to the basic user, since knowledge of C programming is required, but probably every user is interested in the graphical components of the instruments. Each gauge file contains one or more embedded bitmaps of its instrument the way it will appear on the screen in the instrument panel. To be able to get to the image data in these files, you need to have a program that can extract the data from a gauge. A popular freeware utility does exactly this: GAUBMP, by Chuck Dome (http://home.att.net/~chdome).

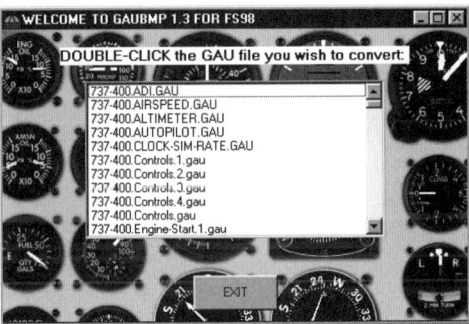

GAUBMP doesn't just convert the imbedded bitmaps from the gauge files into editable .BMP files; it also allows you to re-insert the manipulated image information into the gauge source file.

The newest version of GAUBMP is installed into the Gauge folder of Flight Simulator, so it has direct access to the files in that folder. After you start the little program, you see a "Welcome" page, complete with an alphabetically sorted list of the gauges contained in the folder.

To stay with our T6 panel example, we'll use GAUBMP to take a little closer look at the airspeed indicator from the Schweizer sailplane. Open the file named "Schweizer.airpseed.gau" by double-clicking it.

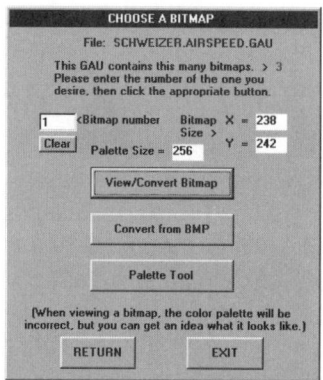

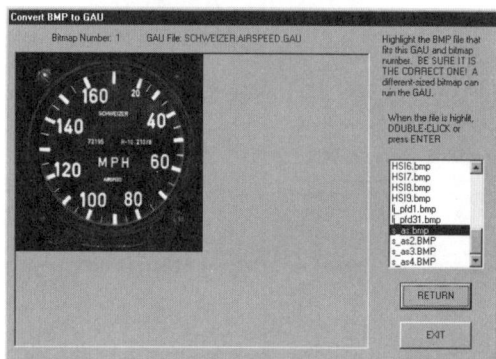

After a short wait, GAUBMP shows you the specifics about the selected file. In this case, it contains three separate bitmaps of different sizes: 238x242 pixels and 125x13 pixels, each with 256 colors. The top button, View/Convert Bitmap, displays the bitmaps in another window. Use the Next and Previous buttons to call up each of the images.

Bitmap #1 contains the airspeed indicator instrument as shown in the panel during the simulation, although it's missing the movable pointer.

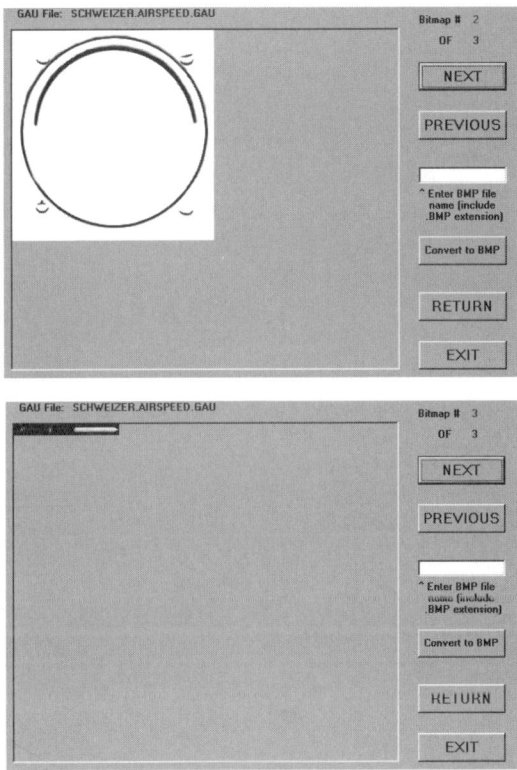

Bitmap #2 contains a mask or silhouette, which is used in the simulation to redraw the instrument and to temporarily fade out the pointer and the numerical values.

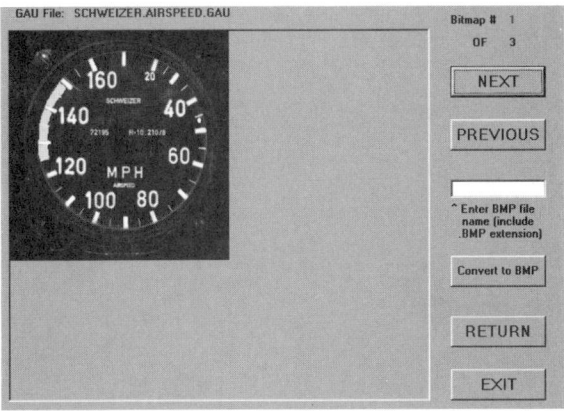

Bitmap #3 contains the airspeed indicator's pointer, which is surrounded by a narrow rectangle; since the rectangle is black (R=0, G=0, B=0), it is defined as transparent.

So, if we want to edit the airspeed indicator, we're probably interested in bitmap #1. The plain instrument doesn't have any coloration to indicate or delineate particular speeds. Usually, the region in which the landing flaps can be set is shown with a white band, while faster speeds at the end of the scale are indicated with a yellow band. The absolute highest speed of the aircraft model in straight flight and during calm weather conditions is defined with a warning red line.

To place these colored modifications into the scale on the gauge, we have to extract the bitmap, which is still embedded. To do so, let's unambiguously name the converted bitmap S_AS1.BMP ("S" for Schweizer, "AS1" for airspeed test 1) and use the [Convert to Bitmap] button to store the file on the hard drive in the same directory. You should now be able to modify this single image with any graphics editing program that works with Windows .BMP files. Unfortunately, not all programs follow the Windows standard, because some of the gauge bitmaps modified using Corel Photopaint or Photoshop couldn't be correctly re-converted in the end. In any case, in your first experiments avoid damaging the bitmap's color table by converting it to a high color or true color .RGB file, or distorting the bitmap using different screen resolutions. The gauge file doesn't like those kinds of modifications at all, and it will refuse to implement them when the simulation runs.

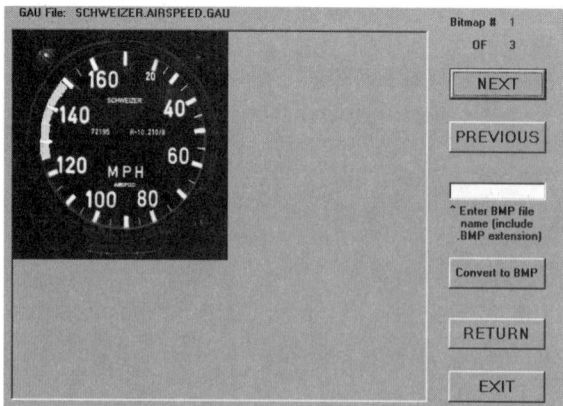

To be 100% certain that you don't accidentally ruin any of the original gauge files using GAUBMP, copy the entire Gauge folder to a safe directory before you make any changes. Then if one of the gauge files proves defective, you can rapidly restore it again.

Once you've made all the changes you want to the original airspeed indicator by adding colored areas, you can re-insert the new bitmap (saved as S_AS2.BMP) into the original gauge file using the [Convert from Bitmap] button. It is essential here that you make sure you've entered the correct bitmap number and that the image file that you really want to replace is the one that's highlighted in the selection list. And now this enhanced gauge is available to all of the instrument panels in which you might want to install the modified airspeed indicator.

The New T6 Texan Instrument Panel

The following figure and the panel configuration file show the new cockpit for the T6 Texan, and they indicate each instrument with key words:

```
// Panel Configuration file
// for the T6 D Texan 2
[Window Titles]
window00=Instruments
window01=Radio Stack
window02=Portrait
[Window00]
file=T6texan2.bmp
size_mm=800
window_size_ratio=1.0
position=7
visible=1
ident=0
gauge00=cessna_182.attitude,325,210,150    // 0
gauge01=bendix_king.hsi,322,370,160        // 1
gauge02=bendix_king.dme,345,530,110        // 2
gauge03=Schweizer.Airspeed,210,255,105     // 3
gauge04=bell_206b.turn_indicator,210,360,105    // 4
gauge05=bendix_king.vor2,210,470,105       // 5
gauge06=schweizer.altimeter,485,255,105    // 6
gauge07=bell_206b.vertical_speed,485,360,105    // 7
gauge08=Bendix_King.ADF.Slaved,485,470,105      // 8
```

```
gauge09=lear_45.elevator-trim,240,205,21  // 9
gauge10=lear_45.control_surfaces,267,205,40      // 10
gauge11=737-400.clock-sim-rate,130,320,70 // 11
gauge12=lear_45.thrust_levers.1,146,470,60       // 12
gauge13=737-400.engine-start,30,515,100   // 13
gauge14=737-400.strob-nav-switch,25,540,95       // 14
gauge15=cessna_182.omi,40,470,70   // 15
gauge16=Cessna_182.Manifold_Pressure_Fuel_Flow.1,595,290,70   // 16
gauge17=Cessna_182.Oil.1,595,365,70        // 17
gauge18=Bendix_King_Radio.AP,595,445,175 // 18
gauge19=lear_45.gear,600,500,100   // 19
gauge20=737-400.flaps,710,510,60   // 20
[Window01]
file=RadioStack.bmp
size_mm=120
position=3
visible=0
ident=50
gauge00=737-400.Radio-Stack, 0, 0,120
[Window02]
file=portrait.bmp
size_mm=99
window_size_ratio=1.0
position=0
visible=0
ident=100
```

The numbers in the text, inserted as comments after the double forward slashes, correspond to the gaugeXX instruments and refer to the numbers shown in the figure.

Chapter 8
Creating Scenery

Chapter 8 introduces you to the workings of scenery design. We'll explain the process of creating new FS environments using the commercial program Airport & Scenery Designer (ASD), as well as the shareware program SCASM. We'll explain how to modify, expand, and correct existing scenery and how to insert new scenery into areas of the FS landscape that were previously blank. We'll build a new airport (Bremen) and modify the landscape in Europe 1. The examples in this chapter will use the visual tool ASD to build a scenery step by step, which will then be compiled into an FS-compatible .BGL file.

Introduction

In this section we'll examine the basics of creating Flight Simulator scenery. This isn't intended to be a complete reference manual. Instead, it's an overview to answer most of the skilled user's questions. Although creating landscapes is perhaps more of an art, there are also technical issues to consider. These landscapes are, after all, computer-generated. For instance, in creating FS scenery you'll be facing hexadecimal numbers as well as other cryptic characters—but that shouldn't scare you. It's easier than it may at first appear.

Scenery Construction And Storage

The Flight Simulator world, as seen by the pilot, consists of many individual scenes. Each of these scenes may contain visible objects, including surfaces, mountains, bodies of water, towns, cities and airports. They may also contain objects that aren't directly visible, such as navigational devices, ATIS messages or local magnetic variations. The Flight Simulator user cannot directly affect any of these scenery objects since they're embedded into predetermined files. Unlike these basic elements, the pilot's airplane—or airplanes, in case of a multiplayer game—isn't part of the static scenery. It is in the hands of the pilot, who can cause drastic changes, such as turning the aircraft upside down.

However, the user has been able to change the basic elements of a static scenery starting with Flight Simulator version 5. It's possible to create new sceneries that may be a single, tiny runway or an entire continent with all of its landscape details. The previously tiny world consisting of seven standard regions (Seattle, San Francisco, Los Angeles, Chicago, Paris and Munich) has finally expanded in FS98 to a comprehensive collection of almost all US airports, as well as a large collection of airports in other countries around the globe.

All Flight Simulator scenes consist of the scenery data contained in the .BGL files. These files are located in different subfolders of the Scenery directory. The term "BGL" is generally believed to represent "Bruce Artwick Graphic Language," referring to the man who first invented Flight Simulator and its virtual world. These .BGL files contain most of the basic information for any given scenery, and one scene may consist of several .BGL files. In that case, the individual files will contain different types of information. For example, the first might contain only airports, the second contains the landscape details and the third might contain the navigational beacons. Using separate files lets you make little scenery changes much more quickly than if all the data was contained in one large file. The different contents of a .BGL file are separated into sections.

The following summarizes the different sections used in .BGL files.

Synthetic scenery

Synthetic scenery consists of one to six different size tiles. These tiles cover the surface of the entire landscape—somewhat like the little segments of mirror that make up a disco ball. The Flight Simulator world is divided into 8,192 x 4,096 such tiles, arranged by longitude and latitude. A tile can represent a land surface, water or a segment of coastline.

Latitude, starting at the equator, is measured in degrees to both the north and south. Flight Simulator calculates the distance between the equator (latitude 0°) and the poles (latitude 90°) as a linear distance, using a unit of two meters (defined as latUnit). The average global circumference is assumed to be 40,007 km. The distance from the equator to the north pole, then, is one-quarter of this distance, or 10,001.75 km (10,001,750 m). With a linear unit of two meters, this results in the following ratios:

90° lateral separation	=	5,000,875 latUnits
1° lateral separation	=	55,565.277 latUnits
1' lateral separation	=	926.08795 latUnits
1" lateral separation	=	15.434799 latUnits

in other words:

1 latUnit	=	2 m = 0.0647886"

Geographic longitude is measured in degrees starting at the Greenwich meridian (0° longitude). The linear unit of measure used for longitude is longUnit, which is defined as 360°=1,000,000 hex. This means one longitudinal degree can be represented with exactly 24 bits, i.e., three bytes.

90° longitude	=	4,194,304.0 longUnits
1° longitude	=	46,603.377 longUnits
1' longitude	=	776.72296 longUnits
1" longitude	=	12.945382 longUnits

which means:

1 longUnit	=	0.0772476"

Easterly longitudes are positive and values to 7FFFFFhex. Westerly longitudes are negative and can have values to 800000hex.

The elevation of a tile, sometimes incorrectly called altitude, is given in meters above mean sea level (MSL).

A scenery's synthetic tiles cannot contain specific, detailed information, such as houses, streets or rivers. Instead, they permit large areas to be rendered quickly and easily, forming the basis to which smaller elements can then be added. The most visible disadvantages of the tile system are the bland appearance and, particularly with "city tiles," some annoying flickering. Their most significant advantage, however, is they require relatively little memory and can be processed very quickly.

Procedural sceneries

Procedural sceneries contain landscape details. Unlike the tile bitmaps, these sceneries consist of predetermined program code that tells Flight Simulator what to display and when to display it. This program code contains a series of rather simple commands (for instance, for drawing a polygon), as well as several relatively complex instructions, such as ones that determine whether an object is visible from different vantage points. Points, lines and polygons are all created using simple commands. Flight Simulator is able to construct most larger objects using these basic elements, and may then continue to use them in the form of macros.

Flight Simulator also has to check for other simulation events within these procedural sceneries, for instance, detecting a crash or collision with a scenery object. It's actually not all that simple to tell in the program code when an aircraft makes contact with a mountain, a building or some other object. Another function checks the characteristics of the terrestrial surface—it might be smooth, rough or watery—or whether it might create an updraft zone for sailplanes.

Dynamic scenery

Dynamic scenery is used to define moving objects within the static scenery. These might be cars, boats or other planes (airborne or taxiing). However, dynamic scenery is somewhat limited. It also often creates problems with static scenery (such as the incompatibility encountered in the BAO Europe-1 scenery when dynamic scenery is activated).

Section 16

Section 16 is a special type of scenery. It contains the outer, middle and inner approach markers, as well as the runway information for use by FS's Land-Me function. This section may also be used to record slightly raised surfaces, which usually aren't specified within the synthetic scenery. You might encounter such a raised surface within a water tile, in the form of an aircraft carrier deck that is located at a certain height above sea level.

Scenery Management

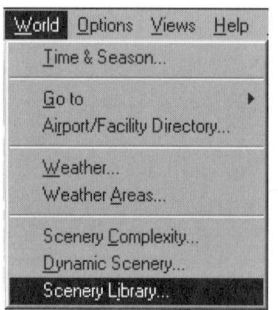

The Scenery Library manages the various sceneries and their attributes. It handles the new landscapes of Flight Simulator 98, the older ones from versions 6.0 (95) and 5 as well as third-party sceneries from commercial or shareware sources.

You'll find the library of available landscapes by selecting the **World | Scenery Library** command. All currently installed and loaded "global worlds" appear in the selection list. This is simply "FS98 World" in the Flight Simulator 98 standard version. It contains all the data required for rendering topographical objects (mountains, bodies of water, cities, streets and airports) as well as the navigational beacons.

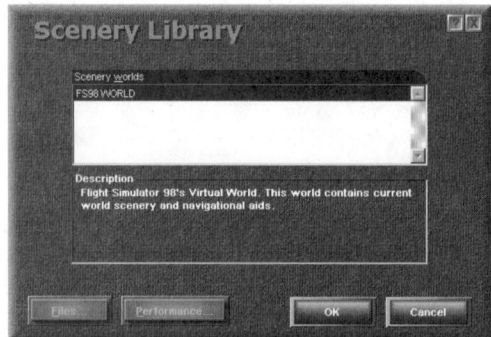

To better understand the scenery concept, let's look at how Flight Simulator constructs scenery. After all, before you examine the library and perhaps even make changes to it, you'll want to understand the underlying basics. An incorrect setting, deleting a CD-ROM booster or reorganizing the sceneries may require you to completely reinstall Flight Simulator (although that is a worst-case scenario).

The Scenery Library contains the arrangement and sequence of all the loaded scenery data. It also stores the paths to the CD-ROM and acceleration files that are used for reloading sceneries.

Flight Simulator 98 uses the Scenery Library to select only the sceneries that are currently needed in the simulation. When the aircraft moves—either when it's flying or in slew mode—the scenery directories and the .BGL files in them must be constantly checked to see if they are required for the current scenery. For this purpose, each scenery file includes a header that specifies the geographic boundaries of that scenery. These boundaries are defined using the smallest and largest latitude as well as the smallest and largest longitude covered by that scenery.

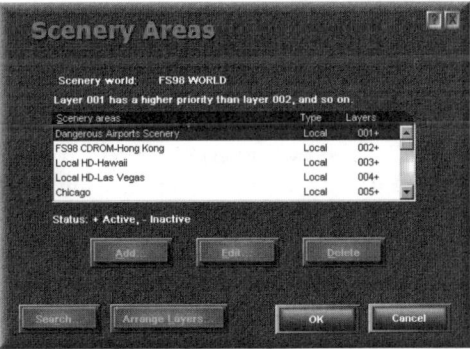

The simulator only loads and opens a scenery when the aircraft moves over such a boundary. Only then does the simulator check for the presence and visibility of the scenery file's contents. These include landscape details, airports, buildings, etc. So, after the aircraft has flown over a scenery boundary and has left a scenery, no objects from that scenery will be displayed. This is true even if they're still within the range of normal visibility. Therefore, the boundaries of .BGL files are set so no objects are located near them that would suddenly appear as the aircraft approached and disappear without warning as it left the area.

Three levels of scenery

Flight Simulator constructs its sceneries on three levels (beginning with the lowest):

Global

Global regions are the basic units that make up the Flight Simulator world. These include the continents and oceans as well as their textures and patterns. Within Flight Simulator, the entire planet is comprised of a great number of square ground or water surfaces. These cover the globe with small tiles, the way in which disco balls are covered with little mirrored squares. Each of these tiles is assigned a certain height that represents the elevation of that particular part of the globe. Only one global world can be active in Flight Simulator at any one time. This is the "FS98 WORLD" in the most recent version. It has the lowest priority in Flight Simulator's scenery level system.

Regional

The next level up is the regional scenery. It contains data that adds additional detail to the global landscape. These are, most importantly, airport objects with their runways, glide path indicators and the navigation stations (ILS, VOR, NDB, Markers, etc.). Regional sceneries can cover larger areas, extending beyond the boundaries of the basic global scenery areas. Their boundaries are specified by separate coordinates. Because there is so much of this data, it is stored almost exclusively on CD-ROM, and only loaded into memory when Flight Simulator needs it. CD boosters are used to create a cache for the CD-ROM data on the hard drive. From there, Flight Simulator can read them just like any of its data on the hard drive. When the aircraft leaves the current scenery, the cache is cleared again to make room for new scenery data.

Local

The top scenery layer consists of the local areas. These generally contain the data for landscape details (mountains, rivers, buildings and roads) and many other object details. These complete the Flight Simulator scenery as seen from the air. Local areas, like regional ones, may be contained on the CD-ROM (from where Flight Simulator will load them at run-time) or directly on the hard drive (from where they can be loaded directly into RAM on demand).

Although these local regions are valuable items, they're fairly easy to find. One likely source is through Flight Simulator forums. You can even write one because the necessary tools and utilities can be found both commercially and as shareware. The most widely used scenery tools are probably the Schiratti Commander (by Lago), Apollo's Scenery & Object Designer (by Apollo), FS5DesignerTools (by Aerosoft) and the Airport & Scenery Designer (by Abacus).

Exclude

Exclude files are a special type of scenery that tell Flight Simulator to ignore all visual and navigational objects in the lower scenery levels. An exclude scenery can define its own geographic boundary or use those of its .BGL file. Excludes are used to avoid conflicts with sceneries that have been defined for the same geographic region and contain similar objects, but ones that shouldn't be displayed. Depending on the settings used, Excludes can affect the display of visual scenery, navigational devices and ATIS messages, but not the synthetic or dynamic scenery or the section 16 data structures of any lower level.

To make new sceneries—as well old ones from FS5 or FS95—usable in Flight Simulator 98, you'll need to register them in the Scenery Library. If these files are stored on the hard drive in uncompressed format (presumably on drive C:), you can start the registration by clicking **World | Scenery Library**.

Browsing and entering new scenery files

Click the (Files...) button to browse for and enter the new scenery files. The Scenery Areas dialog box will help you locate the desired scenery. Once you've found it and know the correct path, use the (Add), (Edit) and (Delete) buttons to perform the desired operation. If you don't know the correct path, click (Search).

Searching for scenery files

Click the (Search...) button to open the Scenery Area Search dialog box. Click (Search Drive) to select the drive on which the files are located (in this case, C:). Flight Simulator will search for scenery files with the .BGL filename extension.

283

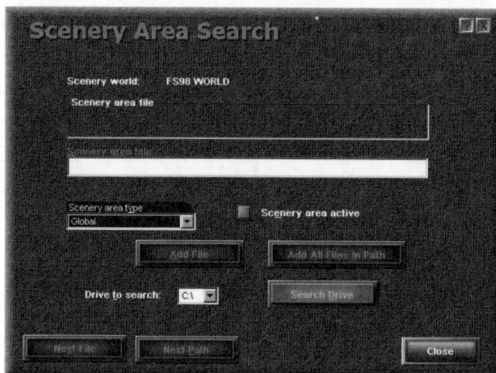

Then after completing the search, it shows the first file under *Scenery Area File* with its complete path. For example:

```
C:\...\Cache\namecach\Scenery\F532487.bgl
```

In this example, the \...\ represents the path of Flight Simulator 98 on your hard drive.

Advancing the Scenery Area file

Click the Next Path button to advance the scenery area file until you see the folder with the file for which you're looking. Click the Add All Files In Path button to add all the .BGL files in the selected scenery to your library. Now you can enter a scenery name in the Scenery area title box. Click the button next to "Scenery area active" to activate the new scenery.

Editing the scenery area file

This button opens the Edit Scenery Area dialog box. Notice the most recently added scenery path appears in the dialog box. You can enter a more descriptive title for the scenery below it. Usually you'll assign *local* from the Scenery area type list and click the Scenery area active button. Finally, click OK to close the dialog box and fully activate the new scenery in the library. Now you'll notice that the new scenery is visible at the very top in level 1, in the Scenery Area dialog box.

Installing Additional Scenery

Installing third-party scenery to your Flight Simulator can be intimidating. However, it's very simple once you understand a few basics of how Flight Simulator organizes and handles its scenery files. We will use the African Safari Scenery add-on from Abacus as our example. This package provides 23 airports and more than 10,000 square miles of African scenery, including many wildlife preserves and natural and man-made monuments, such as Egypt's famed pyramids.

African Safari Scenery provides an installation program that places all the scenery files into the proper Flight Simulator folders:

```
[Flight Simulator]\Scenery\ASafari\Scenery and [Flight Simulator]\Texture
```

(Other files are also installed, such as those for an aircraft, but we're only concerned with the scenery and texture files right now.) The scenery files (*.BGL) contain the features of the scenery, such as rivers, mountains, roads, buildings, etc. The texture files (*.R8, *.*AF, *.ASS and others) define the appearance of these scenery objects, such as making the river greenish-blue with whitecaps or a mountain forested with rocky outcroppings.

To install the African Safari Scenery, place the CD-ROM into your computer's CD-ROM drive and run MENU.EXE. Following the installation wizard's prompts, locate your Flight Simulator directory, and continue following the prompts. When the wizard finishes, the scenery has been installed onto your computer, but Flight Simulator still doesn't recognize it.

For Flight Simulator to use a scenery, the scenery must be installed onto the computer AND identified to Flight Simulator via the Scenery Library. African Safari Scenery includes a program that will do this for you, though most third-party sceneries require you to manually enter the scenery into the Scenery Library. To identify the scenery to Flight Simulator automatically, run the African Safari Setup program (ASSSETUP.EXE) from your Flight Simulator directory and select your Flight Simulator version (95 or 98). When the program completes, you will be able to select the new scenery from the FS **World** menu.

To manually register the new scenery in the Scenery Library, load Flight Simulator and click **World | Scenery Library...** Click OK to get past the warning message. Then click the Files... button and the Add... button. In the "Scenery area path" field, enter the folder path to the new scenery: [Flight Simulator]\Scenery\Asafari\Scenery*.bgl. This tells Flight Simulator to read all the .BGL files in the scenery's folder. Enter a name in the *Scenery area title* field, such as "African Safari." Next select a *Scenery area type* (usually this will be "Local"), and make the scenery active by clicking the *Scenery area active* button. Click OK three times to close the Scenery Library. Your new scenery is now available in Flight Simulator's **World | Go to | Airport...** menu.

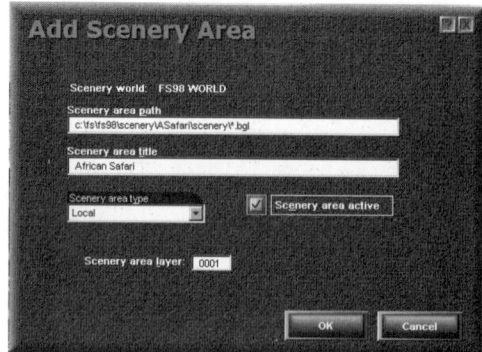

The Scenery Library is contained in the WORLD.VIS file, in Flight Simulator's main Scenery folder. This file is updated everytime you register a new scenery in the Scenery Library. It associates the names of the airports in the Go to Airport dialog with the proper *.BGL files. You can view the contents of WORLD.VIS by opening the file in a text editor, such as WordPad.

Displaying Scenery In Flight Simulator

Flight Simulator 98 creates the illusion of traveling through space by continually displaying individual still pictures of the scenery over which the aircraft is traveling. These stills are calculated using the scenery data, the aircraft's current position and the viewing direction from the cockpit. The speed of this calculation depends on the number of objects that need to be displayed and the computer's performance. The number of frames per second that can be displayed may vary quite widely. A fast Pentium compatible should display sceneries with only synthetic tiles at 30 frames per second (fps) or more. A slow 486 PC will top out at three or four fps with a complex visual scene (such as the Chicago skyline). A slow frame rate like this will result in very incremental, jerky movement.

To create the most fluid video display possible, Flight Simulator 98 creates two video pages in the graphic adapter. While the first page is being displayed, the application calculates and draws the contents of the second one in the background. Once the second one is complete, the two are swapped so the second page is displayed. The first page is then redrawn for the next frame.

The image in the current video page is not cleared until the next one has been completely drawn. This ensures that you'll always see a complete picture in the Flight Simulator window. When a scenery is created, it's a requirement that a complete picture, which may consist of sky, clouds, ground and many different objects, can be constructed at any geographic position. Flight Simulator 98 includes a "standard world" that can be used at any time for views in any direction.

When Flight Simulator begins to construct a new image, it starts with the blue sky. Next come all of the clouds above the pilot's vantage point. This means, for instance, that it won't be possible to hide mountain tops that may actually lie above the cloud ceiling, since the mountains are rendered after the clouds, and will therefore cover them.

After the clouds, Flight Simulator draws the synthetic scenery. Although each tile can have its own altitude, each of the tiles in the current scenery is drawn on a flat plane. The view from the cockpit confirms this. The relative altitude of the aircraft above the surface is calculated using the vertical distance to the surface and its absolute height above the mean sea level. In mathematical terms, this means:

```
Aircraft altitude = Elevation + Height AGL
```

Only once the aircraft crosses a tile boundary is the relative altitude, the distance between the aircraft and the ground, simulated: the ground seems to rise up or fall off, depending on what the height difference is to the neighboring tile.

Flight Simulator 98 differentiates between the aircraft's height above ground level (Height AGL) and its altitude above mean sea level (Altitude MSL), as well as the elevation of any point on the surface above mean sea level (Elevation MSL). The elevation above MSL, for instance, is used for objects such as runways. This is because their altitude relative to the aircraft is much more critical than buildings—at least in the opinion of most pilots, who are more concerned with runways than office buildings. Objects such as hotair balloons or blimps that aren't drawn directly on the ground but "float" in the air, also have an elevation above MSL. All other ground-based objects, such as buildings, bridges or mountains, are drawn at a height relative to the tile on which they're located. This way their relationship to the ground doesn't change when the tile is brought to the correct elevation as the aircraft flies over it.

Once the sky and the basic synthetic elements have been drawn, Flight Simulator calculates the visual objects such as roads, rivers, colored polygons with and without textures, runways and buildings for the still picture. The visual scenery differentiates between 2-D, "preferred" 2-D and 3-D objects. Flight Simulator 98 uses special routines for calculating each of these three categories. First, it renders all simple two-dimensional objects within the scenery. Only then does it draw the preferred 2-D and finally the 3-D objects.

Flight Simulator draws the 2-D objects onto the synthetic ground-tile in the exact sequence in which they're stored in the .BGL file. Most of the 2-D objects are roads, rivers, runways, polygons, etc. This also means that you can control how the 2-D scenery is arranged and displayed, thanks to the scenery-level system used in the scenery library.

Preferred 2-D objects have a level-parameter that determines the sequence in which they are drawn. Objects with a parameter for level one are drawn first, followed by those with level two, and so on. The sequence in which these objects are drawn can therefore not directly be changed by the user, for instance, to cover certain objects by changing the sequence of levels in the scenery library. The runways found in Flight Simulator 98's standard sceneries are among the preferred 2-D objects, as are most add-ons. The Europe 1 scenery also uses preferred 2-D objects for all its ground-textures, making it virtually impossible to layer simple 2-D polygons over them.

Flight Simulator 98 always calculates and draws 3-D objects so more distant objects are covered by closer ones. To make this possible, each object has a reference point. The distance of this reference point to the viewer is used to determine the order in which the object is drawn. This makes it possible to draw even large cityscapes with buildings of different heights very quickly. However, Flight Simulator has a much harder time drawing similarly sized objects that are the same distance from the viewer. A 3-D landscape of hills, such as Beverly Hills with its homes and buildings, is just impossible for the simulator's graphics routines.

Once all ground-based objects have been added to the still image, Flight Simulator begins drawing all of the cloud layers below the aircraft. Here again, the drawing sequence makes it impossible for any mountains or other tall objects to project above the clouds. Only objects that appear above the horizon line aren't covered by lower clouds, thus remaining visible on the horizon.

The computing power that would be necessary to display all possible objects in any given Flight Simulator scenery would be astronomical. This is why Flight Simulator uses individual sceneries with their own smaller boundaries to reduce the amount of data that has to be processed. Furthermore, each object is assigned a visibility range, beyond which the object does not need to be calculated and drawn.

Textures And Colors

Flight Simulator uses texture files in .R8 format to render all of the surfaces within the scenery. These textures are used with .BGL files as well as .AIR files. If, for example, a texture for the wall of a building is needed at a certain time, Flight Simulator will read the special texture from the assigned directory and then apply it to the object.

Flight Simulator caches the required texture files in RAM to avoid repeatedly accessing the hard drive, which would be much slower. Flight Simulator prepares one or more cache directories for each scenery area in which it can store the texture data.

Each texture contains a data field of 256x256 pixels. So that larger surfaces can be filled with these textures, the surfaces are divided up and filled with the assigned textures. Let's use the Meigs airport in Chicago as an example: the airport grounds are divided into two areas, and each of these is filled with the appropriate assigned texture; one area represents the northern part, the other the southern part of the airport.

Each pixel of this 256x256 matrix contains an 8-bit color value, corresponding to an index in a color table. This table may contain up to 256 RGB colors (2^8). Each of these colors consist of certain amounts of red, green and blue, which the graphics card then turns into a colored pixel.

Flight Simulator uses certain portions of the 256-color table for certain things. Here's the Flight Simulator color index:

Color index	Uses
0 ... 113	Used for scenery. Flight Simulator uses different color intensities (lighter or darker) to simulate day and night conditions.
114 ... 127	Scenery (specifically for special effects like lighting, billboards, etc.), a few special uses on the instrument panel, user dialog boxes.
128 ... 159	Instrument panel. The intensity is varied for day and night effects. The colors receive an additional orange component to simulate cockpit lighting during night-flight.
160 ... 191	Sky, clouds, and storms. The color intensity depends on the time of day. The colors receive an additional red/blue component to simulate dawn and dusk.
192 ... 255	Scenery. Unlike the previous colors, these can be re-defined by the .BGL file to achieve a realistic color rendering for the particular scenery.

Flight Simulator saves these colors in different palette files (*.PAL). Although each palette contains up to 256 colors, Flight Simulator always calculates a current color palette. This is done to ensure the colors in all view and instrument windows correspond to one another. The Flight Simulator 98 default color palette file, FS5.PAL, is stored in the Texture folder. Flight Simulator uses colors 0 to 115 from this palette, and in case the current scenery doesn't specify its own palette colors, colors 192 through 255 as well.

Since FS5.1, Flight Simulator has been able to simulate fog and haze much more realistically, which correspondingly reduces the visibility from the cockpit. It uses special haze color files (*.HAZ) to add a gray component to the color palette. Such a haze file contains 16x256 pixel values, in other words, 16 possible modifications for each color. When Flight Simulator draws scenery objects, colors with different amounts of gray from the haze file replace the original colors, in direct relationship to the distance between the objects and the aircraft.

Most of the surface polygons that are filled with textures simulate the haze effect quite realistically: Flight Simulator checks the distance of each pixel in the texture to the viewer. The greater this distance, the more gray is added to the pixel color and thus the hazier it seems. The stronger the preset haze-effect in the "Visibility" option of the **World | Weather...** menu, the smaller the distance at which pixels in the scenery texture begin to be grayed.

In Flight Simulator's distance calculation, each simple 2-D object in the landscape—roads, rivers and such—is only represented by its reference point. Therefore, it's only possible to add an equal amount of gray to the object as a whole to simulate the effect of haze. This means that as the aircraft approaches such an unobscured 2-D object, it will seem to penetrate the haze that lies over the surrounding textures. Therefore, it's best if a road, for example, consists of individual short segments instead of one continuous line.

Flight Simulator also has another tool for displaying textures called *image smoothing*. This technique effectively increases the resolution of the texture by adding an interpolated pixel between two neighboring pixels with different colors. The colors of these two pixels are simply mixed together and defined as a new color. Although this creates a softer transition between the pixels, the image ends up seeming a bit less sharp.

You can control the soft-rendering of textures by selecting the **Options | Preferences...** Then click the Display tab and the (Display Options) button. Finally, click the Scenery tab. To enable image smoothing, the scenery file must contain a command that permits the soft-rendering of its textures.

Colors In Flight Simulator

While some textures contain very detailed images (see CITY.R8 or FARM.R8, for examples), all line-elements and many simple surfaces in Flight Simulator are simply displayed in one solid color. However, that color may change, depending on the lighting conditions and the time of day—for instance from a bright, shining color at noon to pitch-black at night.

Since 256 colors isn't enough to achieve such a great range of intensities, Flight Simulator uses a 16-bit color algorithm internally. The lower 8 bits determine the base color; the upper 8 bits represent a value on an internal color table containing all of the possible intensities. This allows Flight Simulator to achieve a number of important effects.

The pixels representing the runway lights retain the same intensity throughout the course of the day and night, unlike other objects that dim with the fading daylight.

Although shadows cast by objects are black, they also have to be slightly transparent since you don't want them to completely hide the objects they're shading. Flight Simulator therefore uses a 50% grid for its shadows.

Flight Simulator uses an odd property here. Although objects may cast hard shadows (you'll notice this particularly through your map window early in the morning or in the evening), you never see the sun itself. It's an invisible virtual light-source despite changing its position relative to the scenery throughout the day to create realistic shadows. On the other hand, the moon is always visible at dusk toward the west (if the sky is clear), although it neither moves nor casts shadows.

The internal color table is quite complex, and as mentioned, is used to vary the intensity of specific surface colors. The luminosity of most of these surface colors varies according their locations in virtual space and the position of the sun. This creates a realistic simulation of direct sunlight. Once it has calculated the angle of incidence (the angle at which the light hits a surface), Flight Simulator assigns each surface a specific color index. Using this index Flight Simulator then obtains a color from the color table.

This method, by its nature, only applies to flat surfaces and not to curved or round surfaces. To illuminate a round tower naturally, it has to consist of more flat surfaces. Flight Simulator can then calculate the illumination of each of these separately. However, usually the transitions between each of these smaller surfaces are clearly visible.

You can overcome this problem by using shaded polygons. These are shaded with a continuous gradation from light to dark (according to the lighting conditions) instead of being filled with a single color. This way Flight Simulator can lend round objects like columns or towers a nearly life-like lighting effect.

Problems With 3-D Objects

Unlike 2-D objects that are simply drawn in the sequence in which they're stored in the .BGL file, 3-D objects have to be sorted before Flight Simulator can draw them. They're sorted according to their distance from the viewer. Flight Simulator checks which objects will be in the scene before it calculates and finally draws them. It starts with the farthest and works to the nearest object.

Flight Simulator has internal routines that perform these functions. These generally ensure that all the objects in the scenery are drawn correctly. This is true regardless of the pilot's direction of view or vantage point (aircraft, tower or map).

The only graphical elements that Flight Simulator supports directly are points, lines and polygons. They're also subject to the visibility criteria mentioned above. All other 3-D objects consist of these basic elements. Flight Simulator then draws these composite 3-D objects in the viewing window. However, what happens to the backsides of these objects? After all, you don't want to be able to see the rear wall of a building when you're looking at the front of it.

Flight Simulator uses a simple method to determine which elements are visible and which are hidden: each polygon is only visible from one side. So, for example, the exterior sides of a building (specifically those in the direction of the viewer)would be visible. Since the exterior of building's rear wall faces away from the viewer, it's not considered visible.

How does Flight Simulator actually determine which side of the polygon is visible? Each polygon is a surface defined by its vertices (and the lines connecting them). The scenery designer defines these vertices clockwise around the polygon, and Flight Simulator, or the scenery tool being used, then calculates a vector that is perpendicular to this surface, incorporating latitude, longitude and elevation. This vector defines the polygon's visible (exterior) side.

With this relatively simple method, Flight Simulator is unable to render the walls of a house, for example, if you enter it. After all, according to the definition above, the wall's interior sides are not visible (you'd be looking at the vertices of these polygons in a counterclockwise order). The same holds true for rendering mountains in Flight Simulator sceneries.

The only way to render more complex objects is to arrange their elements in such an order that the more inner (rearward) ones are covered up by the more outer (forward) elements. While Flight Simulator solves all these problems automatically with real 3-D objects, these types of composite 3-D objects have to be resolved within the program code of the scenery itself.

Creating Scenery With ASD

One of the many applications for creating sceneries for Flight Simulator 98 is Airport & Scenery Designer by Abacus. It lets you add new airports and landscape objects, such as rivers, lakes, shorelines and mountains, as well as roads and railroads. Although the Flight Simulator 98 world contains almost all navigational stations, a few changes and corrections will always be necessary to bring the sceneries completely up to date.

ASD allows you to add your own scenery to Flight Simulator's Go to Airport dialog. It also automatically adds a copyright notice to the .BGL file.

Map view and airport view

ASD operates on two viewing levels. The first level is the *map view* of the selected region; it contains the geographical and topological reference points. Here you can use special tools to place polygons for cities and lakes, as well as lines for roads and rivers. The second viewing level is the *airport or diagram view*. It's reserved specifically for the airport that is currently being edited. This level permits a more detailed view of the scenery than the map view. Its tools allow you to create complex runway systems, taxi-ways, airport properties, various kinds of lighting and other attributes.

Please note: the items discussed below are based on ASD Version 1.1. Registered users can download this free update to ASD Version 1 from the Abacus web site (http://www.abacuspub.com).

The sceneries created with ASD generate program code that must be translated into Flight Simulator's .BGL format using special compilers. The best known of these compilers are SCASM and FSASM. SCASM (Scenery Assembler) is already integrated into the ASD package.

Because you must use one of these two compilers to compile the scenery files, ASD makes certain stipulations to make certain the .BGL compilation will work correctly. For example, ASD stipulates the units used for heights and distances. These units of measure correspond exactly with those used by the compilers and by Flight Simulator 98. Therefore, it's impossible to switch between US measurements and the metric system when working with ASD. This means you'll have to enter airport elevations, for instance, in meters, even if you have that information in feet. Another example is when you know the length of a certain runway in meters, but have to convert this length into feet before you can enter it in ASD.

Settings in ASD

Once you've installed ASD (it's a standard Windows 95 program installation), you need to specify certain settings. The standard installation will create a program folder called ASD that contains these subfolders:

ASDesign
> Contains the ASDESIGN.EXE main application program and folders for textures and images. You'll also find completed .BGL files in this folder.

Florida
> Contains the Florida bonus scenery with map, scenery and texture folders.

Maps
> Contains maps for Florida, Illinois, New York and Europe. There is also a map installer program to install the maps of the U.S. (all 50 states) and various countries.

SCASM

Contains the SCASM compiler and several macros used to display simple or also complex objects, such as trees, cranes or windmills.

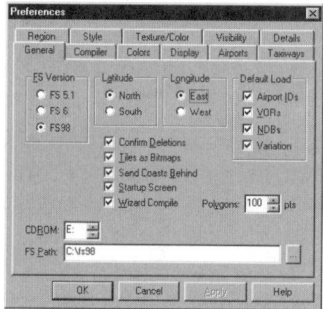

Click **File** I **Preferences** to set the Preference options in ASD. One of the most important of these is the Flight Simulator version number that you're using (FS5.1, FS95 or FS98).

In this section we'll discuss using ASD in a specific example. We'll assume that you're using the FS98 default scenery for Europe (without the Europe 1 add-on from BAO). In our example, we'd like to add the Bremen airport to this still relatively empty region of the Flight Simulator world.

Setting the airport coordinates

The quickest way to create our new airport is to use the ASD Wizard. This tool allows you to create basic elements almost instantly.

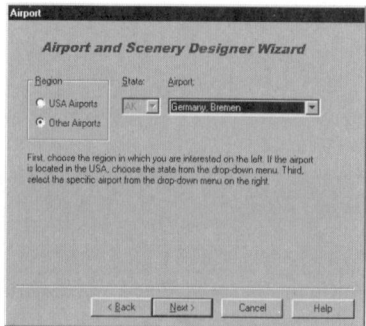

ASD includes a long list of new locations that may be selected as the starting point for your addition to the Flight Simulator environment.

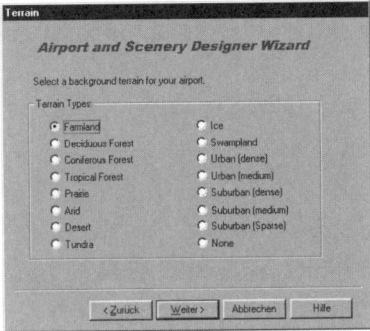

The first question asked by the Wizard is in which region you'd like to create the new airport. ASD gives you two choices: "USA" and "Other Airports". Selecting airports outside the U.S. encompasses the entire world from Argentina (Buenos Aires) to Venezuela (Caracas). You'll find Bremen under Germany. Select it with a mouse click.

Next you'll need to select the base-texture for this region. The available choices range from farmland to prairie, from desert to densely populated areas.

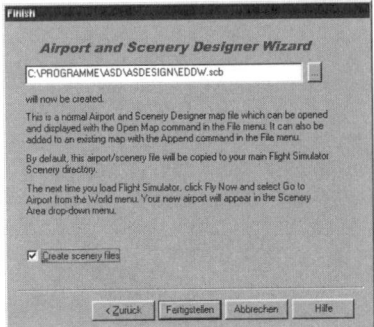

You can complete this simple scenery with the next click. It will save the new base-map containing the Bremen airport in the ASD directory. This means you can compile the .BGL file that will automatically be copied into the Flight Simulator 98 Scenery folder. Now you can access the new airport by selecting **World | Go To | Airport**, where you should see Bremen included in the list of available airports.

You'll also find your Bremen base-map in a file called EDDW.SCB for further editing. The international abbreviation for Bremen is Eddw and .SCB is the extension for scenery base-map. Before giving in to our curiosity for what the new airport looks like in Flight Simulator 98, let's take a look at what the ASD Wizard has drawn into the base-map.

You can open the eddw base-map by selecting the file in ASD in **File | Open Map**. ASD will display the map in its editing window. At first all you'll see is this very simple map with its boundaries and a tiny line approximately in the middle. You can use the magnifier in the toolbar to zoom in to locate needles in the haystack.

The Wizard always creates the base-map around a new airport as a rectangle, 60 nautical miles north to south (equivalent to exactly one degree of latitude) and one longitudinal degree east to west (this distance varies depending on the latitude). The airport will be centered within this rectangle. In the Bremen airport example, the base-map has the following measurements:

```
Latitude of N 52° 32' 52" to N 53° 32' 52" = 60 NM
```

```
Longitude of E 008° 16' 31" to E 009° 16' 31" = 60 * cos(mLat) = 36 NM
```

where mLat=53° is the latitude in the middle of the rectangle, and cos(53°)=0.6018.

You can view the contents and properties of the map under **Edit | Map Properties**.

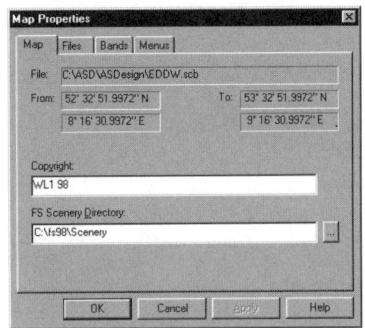

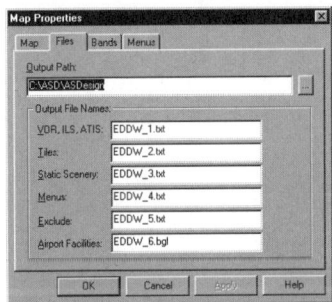

The current map scale is visible in ASD's status bar at the bottom of the window. It also indicates the current geographic position of the mouse pointer within the map, as well as the map's orientation relative to the geographic north. The *Row R=...* and *Column C=...* values indicate the Flight Simulator 98 block-coordinates for the mouse pointer.

As explained above, a block is a rectangular tile representing the portion of the globe at that position. The block's absolute dimensions vary according to the latitude. The largest blocks are located along the equator, the smallest are found at the poles. Flight Simulator differentiates between six different block sizes. Block size 1 measures exactly 1/256 of the earth's circumference in its east-west dimension:

```
Block 1 = Earth circumference in degrees / 256
= 360° / 256
= 1° 24' 32" = 1,40625°
```

The other five block sizes are obtained by cutting the block's east-west dimension in half (see tables below).

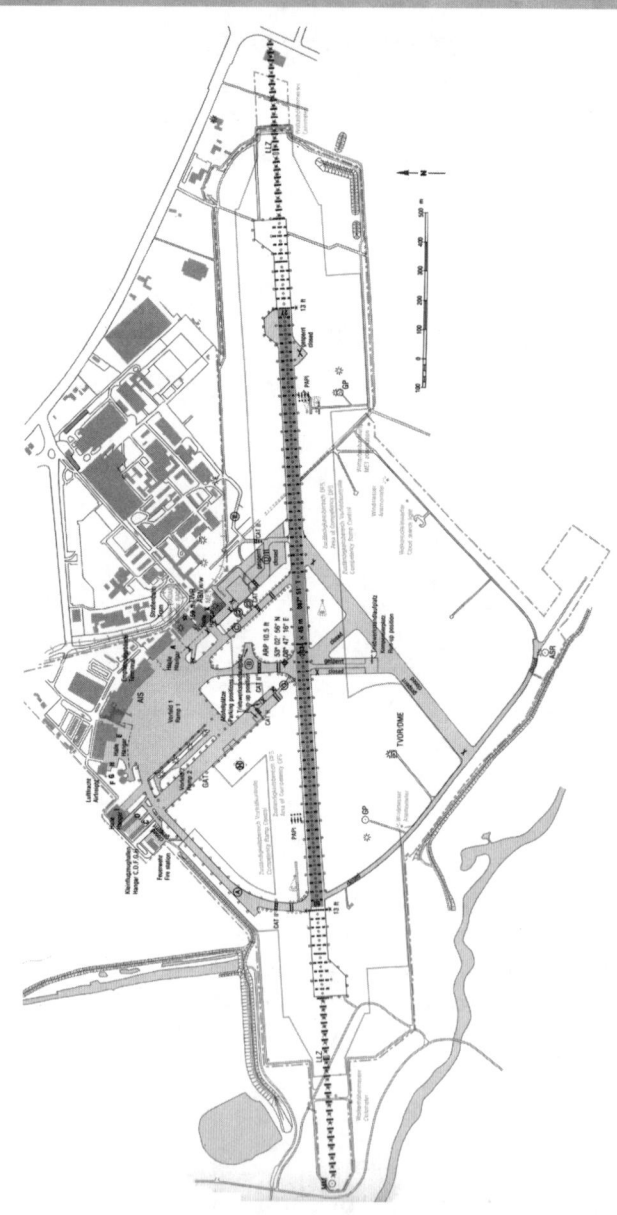

Converting absolute coordinates into block coordinates

The relationship between the latitude component of block coordinates and their corresponding absolute latitude is non-linear. That means no simple formula exists to convert an absolute coordinate into a block coordinate. The following table lists the equivalent absolute latitude for each block-coordinate latitude for block type 1 (lowest resolution, largest block).

Block value	Latitude (rounded to nearest minute)	Block value	Latitude (rounded to nearest minute)
0	00° 00'	15	20° 43'
1	01° 25'	16	22° 02'
2	02° 49'	17	23° 20'
3	04° 13'	18	24° 38'
4	05° 38'	19	25° 54'
5	07° 02'	20	27° 10'
6	08° 26'	21	28° 26'
7	09° 49'	22	29° 41'
8	11° 13'	23	30° 53'
9	12° 36'	24	32° 06'
10	13° 58'	25	33° 17'
11	15° 20'	26	34° 28'
12	16° 42'	27	35° 37'
13	18° 02'	28	36° 46'
14	19° 23'	29	37° 54'
15	20° 43'	30	39° 00'
16	22° 02'	31	40° 06'

Block value	Latitude (rounded to nearest minute)		Block value	Latitude (rounded to nearest minute)	
32	41°	11'	49	56°	51'
33	42°	15'	50	57°	37'
34	43°	17'	51	58°	22'
35	44°	18'	52	59°	07'
36	45°	19'	53	59°	50'
37	46°	18'	54	61°	00'
38	47°	17'	55	61°	14'
39	48°	14'	56	61°	55'
40	49°	10'	57	62°	35'
41	50°	06'	58	63°	13'
42	50°	33'	59	63°	52'
43	51°	53'	60	64°	29'
44	52°	45'	61	65°	05'
45	53°	36'	62	65°	40'
46	54°	27'	63	66°	15'
47	55°	15'	64	66°	49'
48	56°	04'	65	67°	23'

The longitude components of block coordinates, on the other hand, can easily be calculated from their absolute longitudes. These two values *do* have a linear relationship:

Type	Block size						
1	1°	24'	22.5"	=	1.40625°	=	5062.5"
2		42'	11.25"	=	0.703125°	=	2531.25"
3		21'	5.625"	=	0.3515625°	=	1265.625"
4		10'	32.8125"	=	0.17578125°	=	632.8125"
5		5'	16.40625"	=	0.087890625°	=	316.40625"
6		2'	38.203125"	=	0.0439453125°	=	158.203125"

Double-click the thin horizontal line to open the Airport Properties dialog box. Notice it includes five tabbed pages. The properties include the airport's name, its international ID, its geographic position in latitude, longitude and elevation. It also has entries for country, state and city that are needed for the Airport list in Flight Simulator 98.

EDDW

The default values that the ASD Wizard has assigned for the geographic position of the airport deviate slightly from its actual position (at least according to the data we have). According to this data, these are the correct coordinates:

Airport coordinates	
Latitude	N 53° 02' 56"
Longitude	E 008° 47' 16"
Elevation	13 feet = 3,96 meters

If you're a stickler for detail, you may want to make your very first correction right here.

On the second tab, **ATIS**, you can make the settings for the automatic terminal information service for Bremen. During flight simulation, you'll be able to receive the message on a specific, reserved COM frequency.

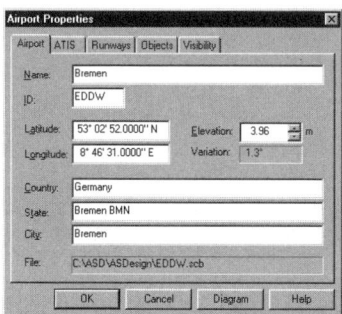 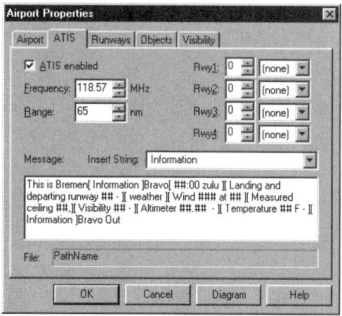

The next two tabs are Runways and Objects. They list the different elements contained in the scenery. The still rather bare Bremen airport currently only contains runway 9/27, the airport polygon with four vertices, and the grass texture.

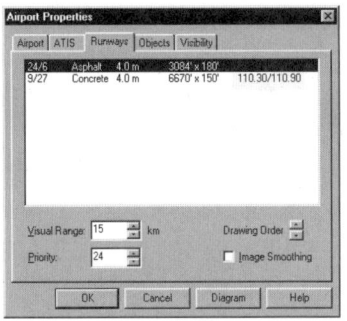
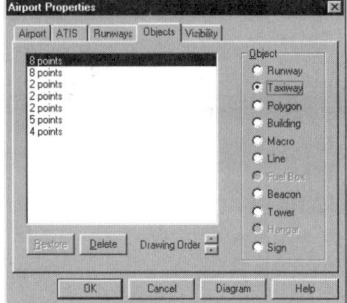

The last tab is Visibility. It contains the scenery's visibility criteria and the reference point that is needed for the further additions of points, lines and polygons.

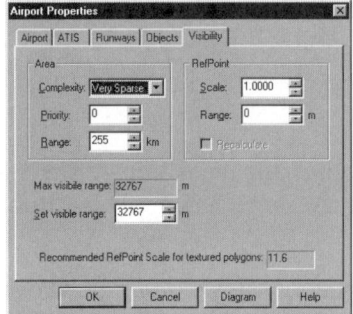

Accept the changes you've made in Airport Properties by clicking OK or lose any changes by clicking Cancel. Click Diagram to switch to the more detailed viewing level for editing the airport more precisely. The Bremen airport, as created by the ASD Wizard, is on the sparse side as you saw in its Airport Properties. It includes only the airport reference point in the middle, the ARP, the green airport polygon and the gray runway 09/27.

You can also select and move (carefully) the polygon and the runway with your mouse. By double-clicking an object, you can open its properties dialog box, where you can make further changes.

Editing runways

The **Runway Properties** are divided into five tabbed pages. The ASD Wizard will already have entered the geographic coordinates, the dimensions and the heading of the runway. The other pages contain the runway and approach lights, the runway's features and the menu entry for FS98.

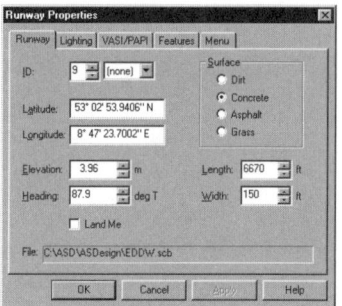 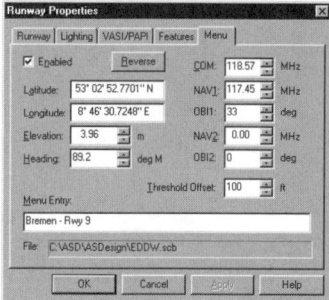

All runway properties that are to be integrated into Flight Simulator 98 should come from official data sources. This helps ensure the scenery corresponds to reality as much as possible. Such data is made available either directly by the airport or by the authorities as well as commercial providers. They're available in graphic and written format, as an airport card, and for US airports you should be able to find the necessary data on the Internet for free. At the end of this chapter you'll see such a data source for the Boston airport.

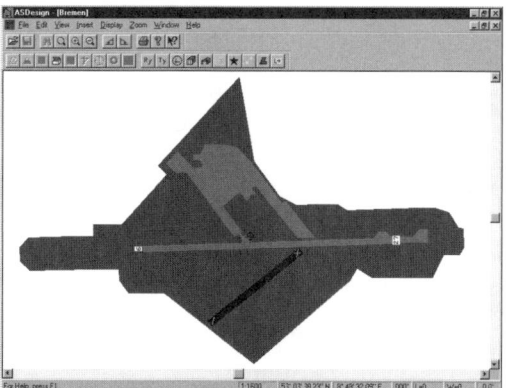

305

Back to the runway in Bremen. Generally the center of a main runway will coincide with the ARP (airport reference point). However, in Bremen the runway centerpoint is approximately 60 meters south and 270 meters east of the ARP, which makes it a bit trickier to position it in the map window.

These are the runway's properties in the first tab-page after making the corrections:

Latitude	53° 02' 53.9406" N
Longitude	008° 47' 23.7002" E
Elevation	3.96 ft = 13 m
Heading	87.9° true
Length	6670 ft = 2034 m
Width	150 ft = 50 m
Surface	Concrete

If you wish, you could also delete the runway from your map entirely and completely reconstruct it. Delete it by first highlighting it, then selecting **Edit I Delete** from the menu or by pressing Ctrl+D (or simply press Del). Then select **Insert I Runway** or click the Airport icon to insert a new runway.

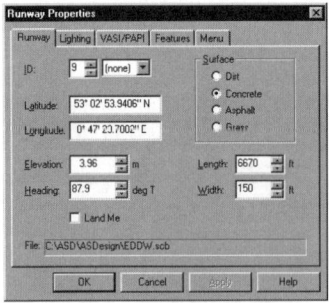

To insert a new runway, position the cross-hairs at the centerpoint of the new runway (you'll see the mouse pointer's coordinates in the status bar), hold the mouse button down and drag the pointer in the approximate heading of the runway. The total runway length and specified width are also visible in the status bar. Once you've placed the basic runway shape, you can make corrections by dragging one of its four corners or its center point. You can also modify its location, heading and proportions by right-clicking and selecting **Runway I Properties**.

Enter the heading in the properties dialog box as a *true heading* (the heading referenced off of geographical north). Note you must consider the local magnetic variation when determining magnetic north. ASD obtains the magnetic variation data from the magdac file, which is part of Flight Simulator. The current magnetic deviation for Bremen amounts to 1.3° west. You can obtain the local variation from the base-map: position the mouse pointer in the area of the airport and click the right mouse button. The pop-up menu contains the local magnetic variation.

The properties for the runway lights are specified on the second tab page. Flight Simulator 98 and ASD make it possible to simulate runway lighting systems very realistically. These systems include:

Medium Intensity Runway Lights	MIRL	Approach Light System	ALS
		- flashlights, CAT I	ALSF-I
		- flashlights, CAT II	ALSF-II
		- medium	MALS
		- medium, flashlight	MALSF
		- omni direction	ODALS
		- simplified short, flash	SSALF
		- simplified short, rwy align	SSALR
		- according to ICAO standards	ICAO III
High Intensity Runway Lights	HIRL	Strobes	
Runway Centerline Light System	RCLS		
Threshold Lights			
Runway End Identifier Lights	REIL		

According to the official data, runway 09/27 is equipped with the following: HIRL, RCLS, ALSF-II and REIL. To install approach lighting, you need to at least activate the threshold lights. These are the first link in a complete approach lighting system, whether a simplified short SSALS or a fully equipped CAT III system for instrument approaches.

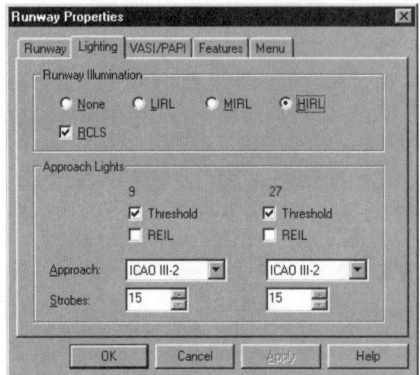

The VASI/PAPI tab completes the list of runway lighting systems. This page contains the properties for the Visual Approach Slope Indicators (VASI) and the Precision Approach Path Indicators (PAPI). Both of these light systems allow the pilot to maintain the correct glide path on final approach.

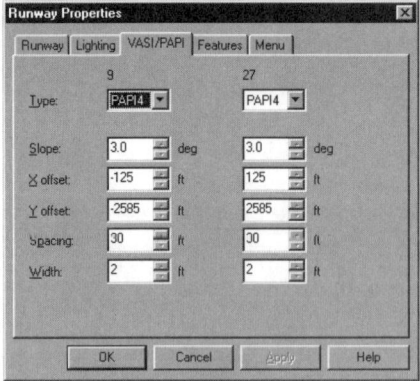

VASI consists of two or three colored, horizontal rows of lights, that are usually mounted on the left side of the runway (the pilot's side). These lights indicate the glide path and ideal touchdown point. Each of these rows contain covered red and white lights that are only visible to the pilot if the aircraft is more or less on the glide-path. The aircraft is on the optimal glide path if white light is visible in the front row and red light in the back row. If both rows appear white, the plane is too high. The plane is too low if both are red.

The two-row VASI is set up for a 3° glide path. The three-row system is usually installed if the runway is going to be used by predominantly large aircraft, including jumbo jets. The pilot in these large aircraft sits many meters above the ground, which changes the perspective, or angle of view relative to the glide-path lights. The third row of lights is set approximately ¼° higher to correct for this change in perspective.

The PAPI system works similar to the VASI but it has only one row of lights with two or four lights. The aircraft is on the correct glide path if the inner light is red and the outer is white. If both (or all four) are white, the plane is too high and if both (or all four) are red, the plane is too low.

The approach lighting system type is specified separately for each runway. The proper slope ranges between 2.5 degrees and 3.5 degrees but is generally 3 degrees. This corresponds to the normal ILS glide path. Topographic conditions may also require a steeper approach slope. Airports with such conditions include Innsbruck in Austria and London City. Innsbruck requires an approach slope of 4° to runway 26 and London City requires a glide path of 5.5° to ILS runways 10 and 28.

X and Y offset are the values for the distance from the centerline, or rather centerpoint, of the runway. In our example, the PAPI lights are located 125 feet left (negative value) of the runway centerline and 2,585 feet from the runway's center point. Given a total runway length of 6,670 feet (3,335 feet for each half), the lights are located 750 feet (3,335 - 2,582) behind the runway's threshold. However, according to our data, they're at a distance of 320 meters (1,050 feet), which means the Y offset ought to be 2,285 feet. The Spacing and Width values determine the distance between the individual lights or light rows and the width of the individual lights, respectively. The suggested values should be close to reality.

Features

The runways at any larger airport will also have additional markings that further help to orient the pilot. These markings include the colored runway edge lines and thresholds, the centerline, the runway number, the touchdown zone, as well as the distance lines.

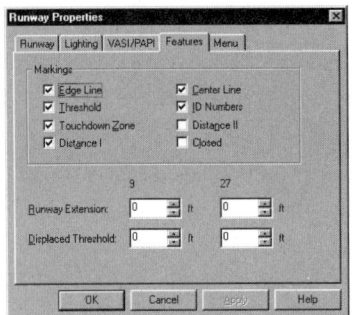

One special runway characteristic is the special runway extensions. These extensions aren't regularly used for take-offs and landings, since they don't meet the same load limitations as the main runway. The Bremen airport has runway extensions of 984 feet on both ends of the runway to allow the Supper Guppy transport to ferry Airbus aircraft components between Bremen and Toulouse. This transport plane requires the extra runway distance. The displaced threshold is used if it's not entirely safe to use the full runway length (for instance, due to obstacles in the approach path).

Menu

The last tab page controls the airport's integration into Flight Simulator's **World | Go To Airport** menu. The options on this page place the aircraft at a certain location. ASD generally provides the coordinates, altitude and heading that place the aircraft on a runway. However, you can also specify other values, for instance, to place the aircraft at an airport terminal.

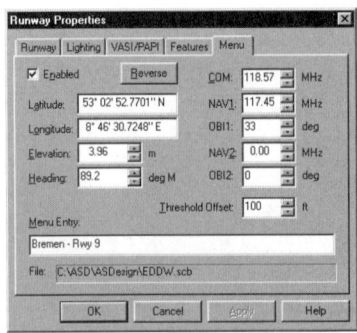

You can also specify frequencies and headings for the COM and NAV equipment. A COM frequency of 118.5 would allow the aircraft to receive the ATIS message when it's placed into the new Bremen scenery using **World I Go To I Airport** command.

Setting up the ILS

The Instrument Landing System (ILS) is probably the most interesting option in Flight Simulator. In compliance with ICAO standards, CAT I landing systems (the lowest category) are always equipped with an LOC or LLZ transmitter (localizer) as well as a GP or GS transmitter (glide path or glide slope). This system can be enhanced with additional radio approach markers in the approach path (outer marker, middle marker and inner marker).

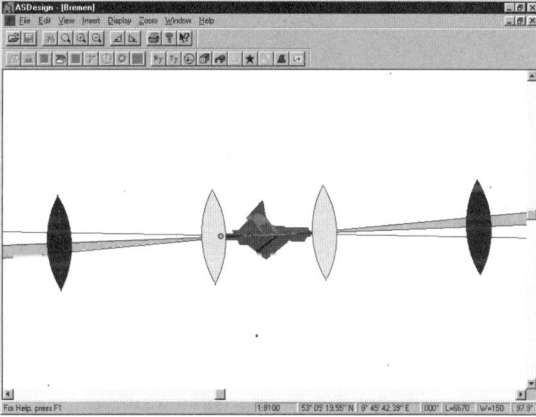

You can insert an ILS using **Insert I ILS** or by using the **ILS** tool in the toolbar. In the ILS dialog box, you'll find a list of the airport's runways that can be fitted with an ILS. For Bremen, these are the two approach directions for runway 09/27.

The values for GS (glide slope) and TCH (threshold crossing height) determine the ILS slope and the optimum height at which the runway threshold should be crossed. ASD uses these two values to calculate all the remaining data required for setting up the ILS (coordinates, heading, heights).

By selecting the [IM], [MM] and [OM] options, you can place the approach markers at the predetermined positions. ASD uses the ILS data it has calculated together with the Airport Properties settings to position these markers. These settings call for a height of 200 feet over the inner marker, a distance of 0.6 nautical miles between the middle marker and the threshold, and a height of 1,500 feet AGL for the outer marker. You can also change these values, either in the airport map or using the menu option, to conform to specific conditions.

When you close the ILS dialog box, you'll see that the runway already bears the visual ILS markings in both approach directions:

1. The typical, narrow approach heading arrows in white and yellow.

2. The elliptical shapes of the OM approach marker in dark blue and the MM in yellow.

3. A red dot showing the position of the LOC approach heading transmitter.

4. A light-blue dot showing the position of the glide path transmitter (GS).

Now you can change the values for the two instrument landing systems to conform to those at the Bremen airport. To do so, it's easiest to double-click the red dot representing the glide-path transmitter. This opens the ILS Properties dialog box, with four tabbed pages containing the system's properties.

On the first page, **General**, general properties such as the name and ID of the ILS are specified. The ILS for runway 27 (westerly approach) should carry the ID "DLR," the name "Bremen ILS 27," and a transmission frequency of 110.9 MHz. You may want to reduce its transmission range to a more realistic 16 NM, from the 25 NM suggested by ASD.

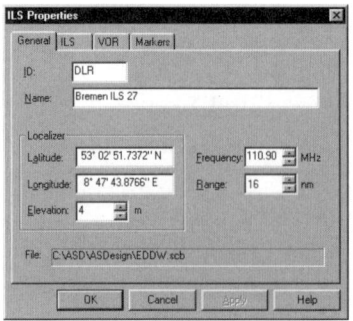

The localizer's coordinates and height are still set to the values calculated by ASD. Notice the height has been rounded to the nearest meter. You can simply drag the light-blue localizer dot with your mouse to change its position (also indicated by its Lat. and Long. values). The point automatically remains oriented in the proper approach heading, so you can't misplace it. Normally, the antennas for the approach heading transmitter are located about 1,000 feet behind the opposite end of the runway, so that the directional signal they transmit can still be received by an aircraft that has already landed.

The second page deals mostly with the glide-path properties. ASD has already calculated its geographic position and altitude, but you may want to reduce the suggested threshold crossing height (TCH) from 55 feet to a more realistic 51 feet.

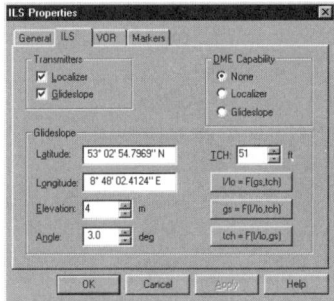

Three buttons can be used to recalculate the other values after you've changed one (Lat, Long, GS or TCH). If, for instance, you've changed the TCH to 51 feet, you'd use the upper button, [L/LO=F(GS,TCH)], to calculate the new latitude (L) and longitude (LO), given a glide-slope of 3° and a TCH of 51 feet.

Be sure not to change the L/LO coordinates in the dialog box, since this can cause considerable confusion in the localizer.

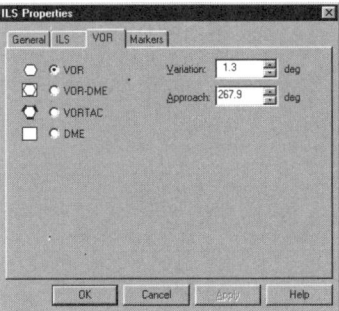

The third page, VOR, contains the localizer's transmission specifications. The system will be designated as one of four types [VOR], [VOR /DME], [VORTAC] or [DME] depending on the DME setting on the ILS page.

You'll also see the local magnetic variation for Bremen on this page, Var=1.3°, as well as the true approach heading: App=267.9°. By adding these values, you'll get the magnetic heading that'll be used by the pilot:

```
Magnetic Heading MH = True Course TC + Variation Var
= 267.9° + 1.3° = 269.2°
```

The last page is Markers and is where you'll find the geographical data for the three available approach markers. According to the official information, Bremen does not have an inner marker. The middle marker is located 0.6 nautical miles in front of the runway threshold, the outer marker is at 3.8 NM, exactly at the position of the Bremen NDB locator (346.5 BMN).

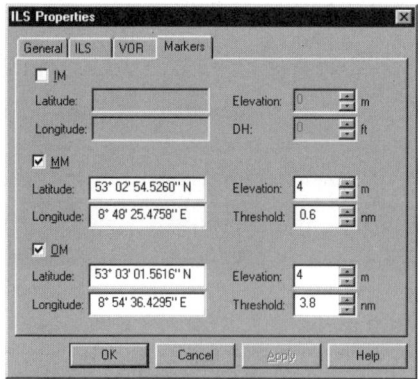

Given a constant slope, the slightly shorter distance between the OM and the threshold will result in a lower threshold crossing height. The new TCH will be around 1,260 ft, instead of the 1,500 ft determined by ASD.

All the important features supported by Flight Simulator and ASD for runway 27 in Bremen are now installed and operable. Here's a list of the steps and technical information it took to get here:

1. The Bremen airport is created using the ASD Wizard.

2. The resulting scenery map, EDDW.SCB, is loaded and its dimensions and positions are corrected.

3. The airport map for the selected airport, EDDW, is opened by double-clicking the airport and selecting [Diagram] or by using the shortcut menu opened by the right mouse button.

4. Double-clicking objects in the airport map opens their Properties dialog box.

5. The Runway Properties dialog box contains all of the settings required to set up and display a runway. Most of the values suggested by the ASD can be retained, though some should be corrected if they're going to correspond to reality.

6. **Insert | ILS** is used to add the two instrument landing systems to runway 09/27.

7. The properties are then set to correspond to the real systems in Bremen on the ILS Properties tab page:

	Rwy 09	Rwy 27
General		
ID	IBMN	DLR
Name	Bremen ILS 09	Bremen ILS 27
Latitude	53° 02' 55.0138" N	53° 02' 52.1607" N
Longitude	8° 48' 24.9078" E	008° 46' 15.7503" E
Elevation	4 m	4 m
Frequency	110.3 MHz	110.9 MHz
Range	16 nm	16 nm
ILS		
Transmitter	LOC GS no DME	LOC GS no DME
Latitude	53° 02' 52.7057" N	53° 02' 54.4704" N
Longitude	8° 46' 40.4694" E	008° 48' 00.2629" E
Elevation	4 m	4 m
Angle	3.0°	3.0°
TCH	50 ft	51 ft
VOR		
Type	VOR	VOR
Variation	1.3°W	1.3°W
Approach	087.9°	267.9°

(continued)	Rwy 09	Rwy 27
Markers		
MM Latitude	53° 02' 51.0413" N	53° 02' 56.0932" N
MM Longitude	008° 45' 25.1085" E	008° 49' 13.7352" E
MM Elevation	4 m	4 m
MM Threshold	0.5 nm	0.6 nm
OM Latitude	53° 02' 44.0057" N	53° 03' 03.1288" N
OM Longitude	008° 40' 06.7192" E	00 8° 54' 32.1494" E
OM Elevation	4 m	4 m
OM Threshold	3.8 nm	3.8 nm

Positioning multiple runways

Bremen has no second active runway. However, a short 052°/232° runway was used in the past. It measures approximately 940 meters (3,084 ft) long by 50 meters (164 ft) wide. The runway has been closed for several years and isn't even used as a backup. A large, white X at each end marks its surface as unusable.

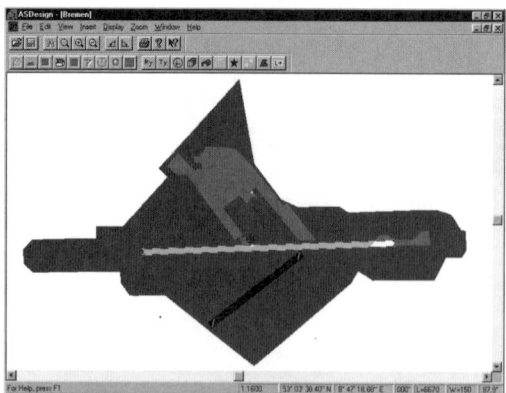

ASD can also add abandoned runways like the one in Bremen to your sceneries. Simply use **Insert | Runway** or the [Ry] button in the toolbar to draw a runway of the desired proportions with the mouse. Then use the Runway Properties to give the virtual runway the same characteristics as the physical one:

Runway	
ID	5 or 23
Lat.	53° 02' 43.4400" N
Long.	008° 47' 16.3346" E
Elevation	3.96 m
Heading	052° / 232°
Length	3,084 ft
Width	164 ft
Surface	Asphalt
Features	
Markings	Closed

By selecting the "X" markings, you're essentially shutting down the other Runway Properties; settings for other markings, lighting and VASI/PAPI are no longer available. After all, an unusable runway doesn't need to be equipped with expensive lighting systems.

The new runway has one problem, even though it's unusable. Since it was added to the Bremen scenery after the active 09/27 runway and is therefore drawn as the second, its north-east end will appear to cover the main runway. You can solve this problem by changing the drawing sequence in the Airport Properties. You can access these from the base-map window by either double-clicking on the airport or right-clicking on it with the mouse.

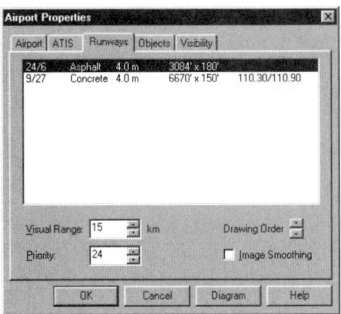

The **Runways** page in the Airport Properties dialog box lists all of the runways that the airport currently has. The most recently drawn runway will be last in the list. You can move the runway up in the list or switch it with the second runway in the list using the [Drawing Order Up] and [Drawing Order Down] buttons. If the abandoned runway is first in the list, it'll be drawn first, and thus covered by the other runway.

Adding the ATIS frequency and message

In this same dialog box in which you've just set the runway drawing order, you can also specify an automatic terminal information message (ATIS). Click [ATIS Enabled] on the ATIS tab page to enable this option. The transmission has a range of about 65 to 80 nm. The frequency of Bremen's ATIS is actually set to 117.45 MHz, and is therefore modeled on the signal of the terminal VOR. However, Flight Simulator only supports ATIS on the COM frequencies between 118.000 to 136.975 MHz.

Although ASD won't give you an error message if you specify a frequency of 117.45 MHz, opening the dialog box the next time will show that the application did not accept the entry. Instead, you'll find that the value defaulted to 118.000 MHz. You'll have to compromise and choose a COM frequency that lies in the range reserved for the Bremen area, for instance the second tower frequency of 118.575 MHz. However, opening the dialog box again after entering this value will reveal that ASD isn't quite happy with this frequency, either. It rounded the frequency to 118.58 MHz. You'll have to live with this or set the frequency to 118.57 MHz.

The ATIS transmission specifies the current take-off and landing runway headings depending on the current wind conditions on the ground. The runway headings for each wind-quadrant are entered under Rwy1 to Rwy4. For instance:

Rwy1	09	with north-easterly winds from 360°/000° to 089°
Rwy2	09	with south-easterly winds from 090° to 179°.
Rwy3	27	with south-westerly winds from 180° to 269°
Rwy4	27	with north-westerly winds from 270° to 359°

The ATIS message is entered under *Message*. A standard message will contain the name of the transmitting station, the message ID letter, the UTC (Zulu) time, the runway in use, the most important weather data and any other significant information.

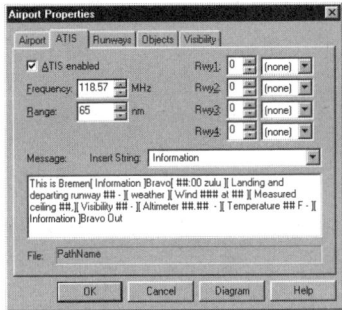

The *Message* text box may only contain characters in the ASCII range of 32 to 127, so no special characters are permitted. Characters between ASCII 128 and 148 are converted into strings, according to the table below. However, it's easiest to insert such a string into the ATIS text using the [Insert String] selection box. Here are some examples for the use of such strings, which are always inserted at the current position of the cursor:

| [Wind ### at ##] | Flight Simulator will replace ### with the current wind-direction and ## with the current wind-speed. For instance. Wind 280° at 12 knots. |
| [Altimeter ##.## -] | Flight Simulator will replace ##.## with the current barometric pressure in inches of mercury. For instance: Altimeter 29.91" Hg |

Please note the spaces and dashes in the strings; the brackets are only present for clarity and won't appear in the message.

A complete ATIS text might look something like this:

> This is Bremen[Information]Bravo[##:00 zulu][Landing and departing runway ## -][weather][Wind ### at ##][Measured ceiling ##,][Visibility ## -][Altimeter ##.## -][Temperature ## F -][Information]Bravo Out

The ATIS message may not exceed 255 characters in length.

Adding aprons and taxiways

Let's return to the map of the Bremen airport. By now we've fleshed out the rapid installation of the airport carried out with the ASD Wizard with a few important object properties. The main runway has received its final markings, and ILSes now permit instrument landings in both runway directions.

However, the infrastructure of an airport also includes a few other objects that make airports easier to use: buildings and aprons. ASD and Flight Simulator draw aprons using polygons that receive the characteristic apron colors. However, all we have up to now is the very simple, dark-green rectangle that the Wizard has drawn around runway 09/27.

Here again, you can double-click the polygon to modify its properties. The Polygon Properties dialog box contains four tab pages: **Style**, **Texture/Color**, **Visibility** and **Menu**.

When drawing polygons (as well as taxiways), it's best to draw vertical and horizontal lines whenever possible, since they're easier to draw. ASD has [Rotate CW] and [Rotate CCW] buttons in its airport map toolbar, which can rotate the map so that the runway is oriented vertically or horizontally in your window—naturally this doesn't change the actual heading of the runway. Now it's much easier to draw lines or polygons parallel to the runway.

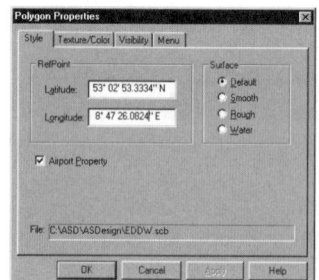 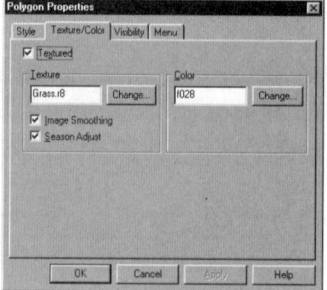 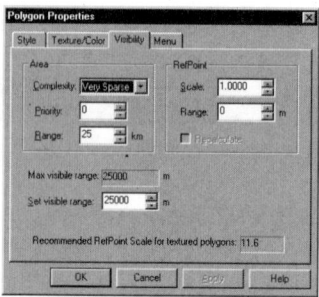

Unfortunately, ASD won't allow you to scan in a bitmap image of an airport map, which you could then redraw using the application's drawing tools. Instead, you'll have to use the physical measurements available to you and your own sense of proportion and scale to position the objects as realistically as possible. You may find guidelines very helpful in this process.

It's easiest to place such guidelines using your Runway tool, since it's very easy to edit the runway's length and heading, either directly with the mouse or in the Runway Properties. After you're done with the guideline, simply delete it or move it aside if you're going to use it later.

Our example would benefit from the use of at least four guidelines. The first one will be about 720 meters (2,360 ft) long, with a heading of 178°/358°. The centerpoint of this "guideline-runway" will be located close to the ARP—an excellent place to start. The second line will be approximately 950 meters (3,120 ft) long with a heading of 112°/332°. This places it vertically on the old, closed runway, crossing the main one. The third guideline will be parallel to the second, starting at the intersection of the closed runway and the main runway. The fourth, and for now the last, guideline will mark the south-western boundary of the airport; it is nearly parallel to the second and third guideline and has no specific length. However, it connects the thresholds of the active 09 runway and the closed 05. With that, we've nearly completed the basic and rather unusual layout of the Bremen airport.

Now we can modify the base polygon created by the ASD Wizard by adding new points, so that it will encompass the new airport grounds as defined by our guidelines.

To add a new point to the outline of an existing polygon, press I and click one of the existing points. The new point will be added between the selected point and the next one over in the counter-clockwise direction. You can delete a point by holding down D and clicking on the point you want to delete.

You can move the whole polygon by drawing the polygon; simply place the mouse pointer within the polygon's area, hold the mouse button down and drag it to the desired location. You can also use the mouse to move individual points. You can also rotate the polygon about its center by holding down Shift while dragging a selected point on the polygon.

To draw the aprons, rotate the airport map so that the guidelines can be used to determine the lengths and headings of these polygons. Aprons 1 and 2 as well as the terminal aprons can be drawn in this way.

Use the Polygon tool or select **Insert | Polygon** to draw a new polygon. Each mouse click will set a new point, and you can finish the polygon with a double-click. ASD then automatically connects the last point with the first and fills the polygon's surface with color. The fill color depends on the **File | Preferences** settings, or you can change it in the Polygon Properties.

ASD has standard textures for concrete runways and aprons. The Change button on the **Texture/Color** tab page allows you to select from a list of colors and textures. The texture list opens the Texture directory of Flight Simulator 98. Among these texture files (which usually have the .R8 file name extension, although you can select others, like .TXR), you'll find a bitmap for concrete (CONCRETE.R8). The color palette has a selection of 56 colors for the apron surface, the first 48 of which have variable intensities to simulate the effects of changing light conditions. Medium gray, with the internal number f002, is only used if no texture is specified, and is usually only used for the ASD screen. You can select this color by clicking its color patch or entering the appropriate value.

Building taxiways

What good is the most posh airport if, after a picture-perfect, gentle touchdown, you've got to taxi to the terminal on a bumpy, grassy field? Taxiways make the connection between the terminal aprons and the airport's runways.

Here again, it's a lot easier to draw the taxiways using guidelines that outline their basic layout and proportions.

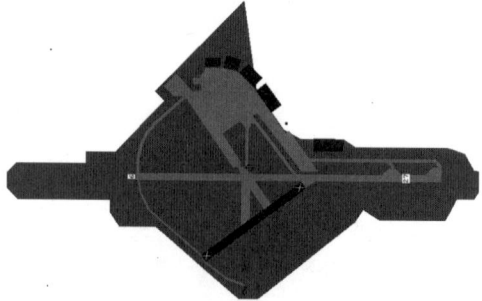

Let's start with taxiway A. It starts at the threshold of runway 09 and then curves slightly toward the northeast. From there, it runs to the end of guideline 2, in a straight line. This curve is approximate with several points, since Flight Simulator doesn't support true, radiused curves. Taxiway B is located starting at the main runway and leading all the way to apron 1. Taxiway C starts at this spot, ending at the main runway.

Let's take some liberties with taxiway D. For years now pilots and others have been requesting a more direct path to the take-off position on runway 27. Currently, the only way to get there is to taxi down the runway itself and then turn the aircraft 180°. So, we'd like to propose taxiway D, which would run parallel to the runway toward the east, connecting to the runway at the turnaround position.

You can make the connections between the taxiways and the runways or aprons quite realistic by using smaller polygons, with the necessary shapes and proportions.

The taxiway properties are specified in the Taxiway Properties dialog box. The points of greatest interest are their width, texture and/or color, as well as the [Lighted] option. The technical aspects here that concern Flight Simulator 98 are the reference point and the visibility criteria.

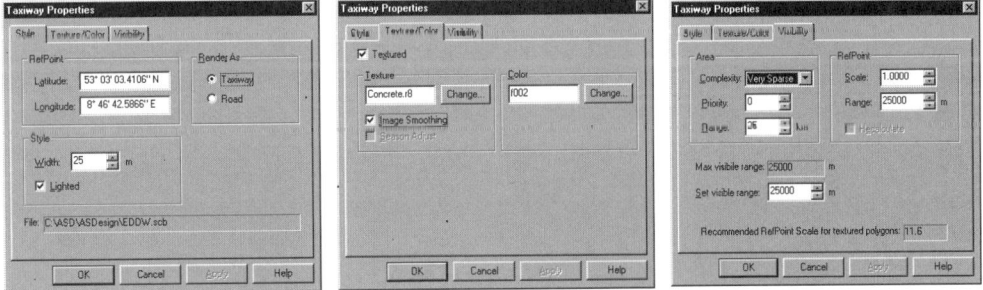

Adding the tower, terminals and hangars

The flat, Northern-German scenery around Bremen receives its three-dimensionality through the addition of the first true buildings, including the tower, the terminals and the hangars. With ASD, it's quite easy to create these elements and integrate them into our existing scenery. ASD is equipped with a number of tools that allow you to create buildings with different characteristics:

Building Tool	general buildings
Hangar Tool	hangars
Tower Tool	control tower
Macro Tool	user-programmed objects

Using the [Building] button in your airport map toolbar or the **Insert | Building** command, you can insert a building into your scenery. Hold down the left mouse button and drag open a rectangle with your mouse—you'll notice that the pointer is a building symbol—that is approximately the size of the building's outline.

Then double-click the area within the building's outline to open the Building Properties dialog box. On the four tabbed pages you can specify the geographical location of the reference point and the measurements and characteristics of the building's walls and roof. On the second page, you can specify the building type, which ASD simulates by applying different building textures. On the **Preview** tab, you can see what the building is going to look like—whether you've chosen one of the eight facades ASD allows you to chose from, or whether you've made your own.

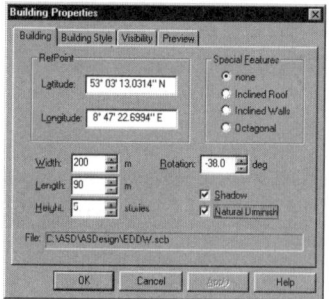 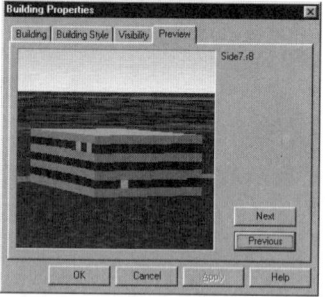

Using the mouse, you can establish the building footprint, its proportions in elevation (the horizontal view), as well as any desired rotation, in the same way in which you draw polygons. Then using the building's properties settings, you can specify the number of walls as well as other effects, like [Shadow] or [Natural Diminish], which prevents buildings from looking like poles when viewed from a distance.

Using **Insert | Tower**, you can add a control tower at any desired location in your airport map. You can specify the precise location in the tower's properties dialog box. On the properties tab pages you can also determine its footprint, height and appearance (you can choose from four basic shapes). Using **Preview**, you can get an impression of what the tower will look like in the simulation.

324

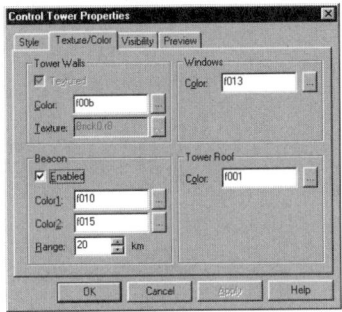 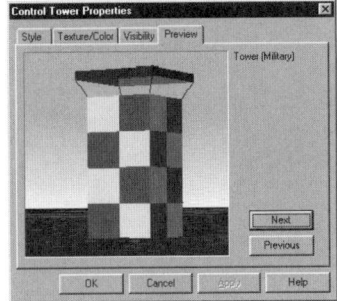

You can construct the airport's hangars using the [Hangar] tool. A special characteristic of ASD hangars is the large hangar doors, through which you can roll the aircraft into the hangar for storage. When you're creating the hangar, the side with the doors is indicated by a little arrow on the building's footprint. This way you can make sure that the doors will face in the right direction.

To change the hangar's size and to rotate its footprint, you can use the usual mouse and keyboard operations. As with the other building types, its characteristics are specified in the Hangar Properties dialog box.

To determine the outward appearance of the building, you can choose from four basic types: [Rectangular w/ Flat Roof], [Rectangular w/ Peaked Roof], [Cylindrical and Cylindrical w/ Side Walls].

Shading and interior illumination of hangars are special effects supported by ASD. The walls, roofs and hangar doors can be covered with textures of your choice. Hangar doors can be open, closed or even set to open automatically as they are approached.

Setting the airport lighting

Lights lend a special touch to flight simulations at dawn, dusk and night. ASD uses special palette colors for these lights, which do not vary with different daylight conditions, so that they retain the same luminosity. ASD permits light sources of different kinds to be added to the scenery.

Taxiway tool

All taxiways are equipped with curb lights that are lit from dusk to dawn.

Beacon tool

Most of these pre-programmed transmission and light-towers have a certain type of light-beacon at the very top.

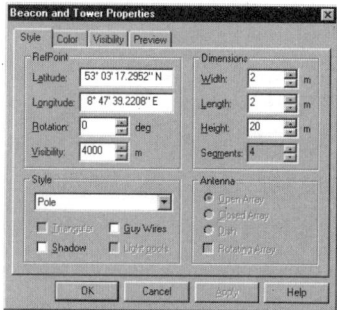
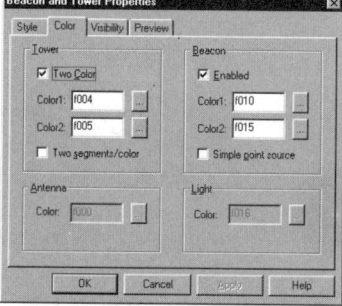
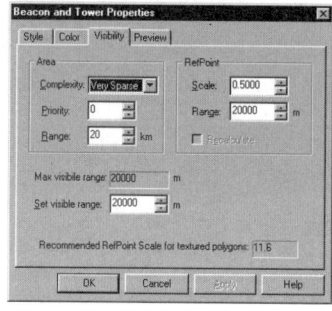
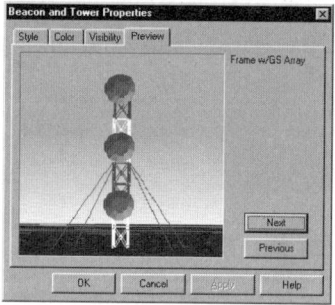

Line tool

You can create strings of lights with the line tool. Their characteristics are determined by settings in the Line Properties dialog box.

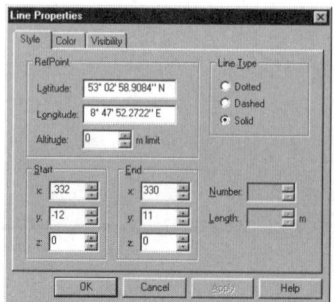
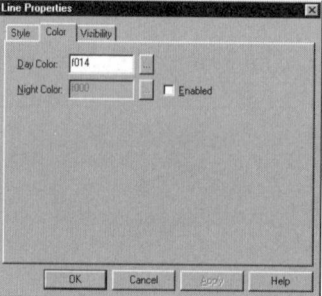
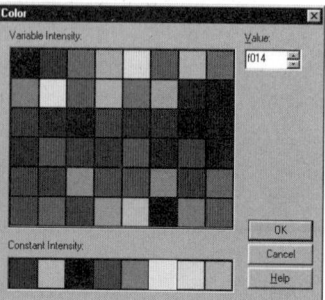

The line properties allow you to choose from [Solid] lines, [Dotted] lines and [Dashed] lines. The dotted-line tool is ideal for adding yellow center-line lights to the runway for night use or to outline specific polygon shapes with a string of red lights. The distance between the light points is determined by the length of the line and the number of lights you specify.

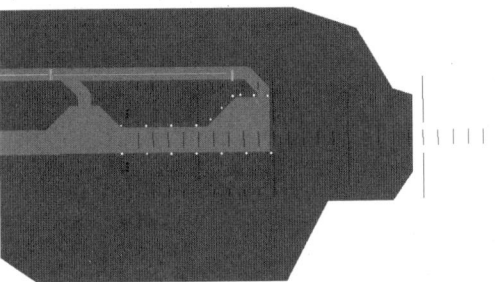

ASD 1.1 supports 13 basic transmission and light-tower types. You can modify these with a large number of choices in the Beacon and Tower Properties dialog box. Using the [Beacon] tool, you can insert such towers at any location on the airport grounds. You might choose a simple steel tower with guy-wires, a solid, reinforced concrete column or a trussed structure with a rotating antenna.

Signs

Large airports often have a hair-raising number of runways and taxiways. Just look at Chicago's O'Hare. To be able to follow an instruction from the tower (uhm, so how do I get to the runway?), you'll either have to know the airport inside and out, have an airport map directly in front of you or be able to understand the taxiway signs.

The view from the Flight Simulator cockpit while taxiing isn't exactly overwhelming; this perspective makes it quite difficult to gauge the distances of two-dimensional objects. this can make it quite tricky to find your way to the runway even at small and simple airports.

It's easy to add international standard signs to guide pilots through those airport runway and taxiway mazes with ASD. The [Sign] tool inserts lit or unlit signs into your scenery. They comply with FAA standards, and there are four different types:

Type	Description
L-858Y	Direction and destination: black type on yellow background
L-858R	Mandatory Instruction : white type on red background
L-858L	Taxi and Runway Location: yellow type on black background
L-858B	Runway Distance Remaining: white type on dark-blue or black background

Mandatory Instruction signs are easily identified by their red and white colors. You'll always find them at the holding position just before the runway and at intersections of taxiways and/or runways. They're generally located on the left side, the pilot side, and they designate the runway heading. If your aircraft is positioned at the start of runway A in Bremen, you'll see a signs reading "09." If you're on runway B, coming from the apron—which puts you in the middle of the runway—you'll see a sign reading "27-09." This means that the threshold of runway 27 is to your left, and that of runway 09 is to your right.

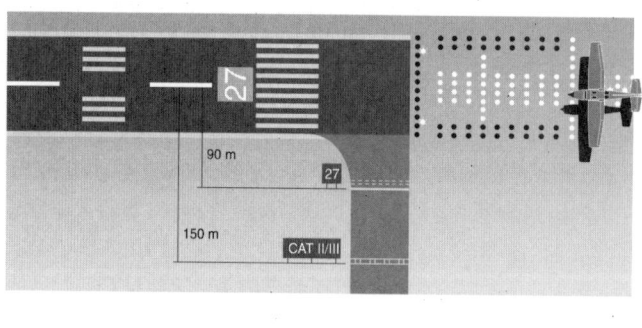

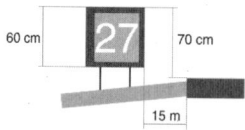

The red and white warning signs are positioned at least 90 meters from the center of the runway. In poor weather conditions, an ILS standard, CAT II or CAT III, will most likely be in effect. These more stringent standards require aircraft to stop farther from the center of the runway, at a distance of at least 150 meters. This position will be marked with a sign reading "CAT II/III," and when these standards are in effect, aircraft most stop at this sign instead.

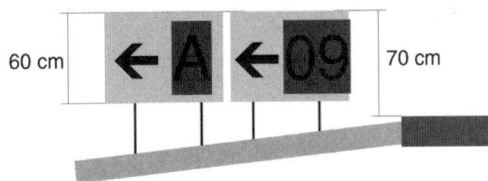

There are two types of signs for general orientation: *direction and destination* signs, with heading arrows and black type on a yellow background, and *taxi and runway location* signs, with yellow type on a black background.

Direction and destination signs have an arrow that points in the direction of the specified runway or taxiway. Left to taxiway A, and right to runway 09, for instance. The combined information on a *direction and destination* sign tells you where you are and how to get where you're going at the same time:

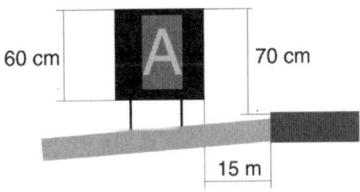

Taxi and runway location signs simply tell you on what taxiway you currently are. On long taxiways or at junctions with other taxiways, this information can often be quite useful.

The [Sign] tool places the sign at the current mouse pointer position. The contents of the sign are entered in the Signs Properties dialog box. You'll need to select the sign type and size, as well as any special characteristics (illumination, shading, and sign-posts).

On the **Message** tab page, you can enter the text that you want to appear on the sign. Enter the desired text in the text box, for instance "HOLD," "CARGO" or "GAT" for direct instructions to identify the cargo buildings or the general air terminal.

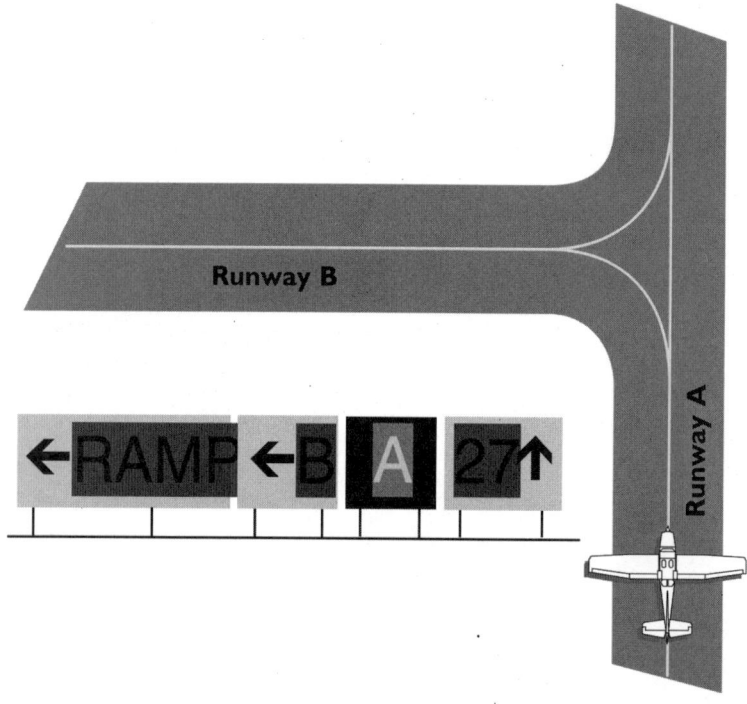

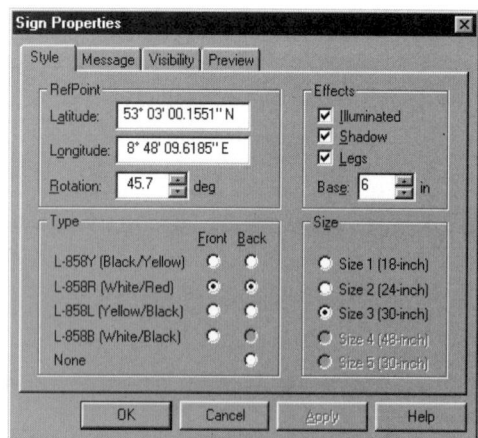

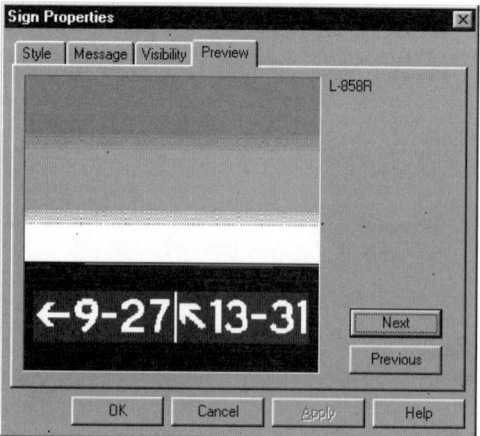

Destination signs always include an arrow. The arrow orientation is selected using the [Direction Arrow] buttons. You'll notice that once you select one of these, a slash and a number indicating the direction (like the arrows on the cursor keys on your numeric keypad) appear in the text box. The dash identifies the number as a heading parameter, so that it's not included in the text of the sign. Such text might consist of the letter "A," pointing the way to taxiway A.

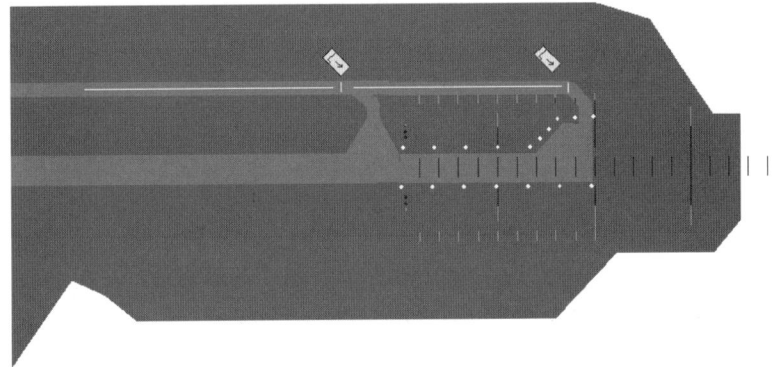

Code	Arrow pointing
\8	up
\6	right
\4	left
\2	down
\7	left & up
\9	right & up
\1	left & down
\3	right & down
\5	end

Most location signs consists of only one letter; after all, you're either on taxiway A or B, but not both. The text for this type of sign will therefore be very simple:

A

To get a combined destination and location sign, simply add a slash in the text box followed by the appropriate parameter:

Letter	
\Y	Destination
\L	Location
\R	Warning
\B	remaining runway length

You can also enter the desired parameter by simply clicking the sign type that you want to use.

The entry for a combined destination and location sign might look like this:

```
\Y \8 A \8 09 \L C \Y \6 RAMP
```

Here the first parameter selects a yellow destination sign, the next one a black arrow pointing up, followed by the letter "A" for taxiway A, another up-arrow, followed by the number "09" for runway 09. The next parameter switches to a location sign with the letter C. Finally, we switch back to a destination sign with a right-arrow pointing to the "RAMP." We've printed the entered text in bold, to make the entry easier to read.

The terminal VOR

In addition to the ILS and the NDB locators, the Bremen airport is equipped with a terminal VOR with DME. This system is primarily used to locate the airport during instrument flight.

Unlike its predecessors, Flight Simulator 98 distinguishes between the different classes of VOR stations. These are defined by the stations' transmission power, and therefore the transmission range. The strength of the VOR signal that is picked up by the NAV receiver in the aircraft also depends on the plane's altitude, since the VOR signal is an ultra-shortwave signal. Such a high-frequency signal only travels in a straight line and does not follow the earth's curvature (the way that the mid- and long-wave signals of NDB transmitters do). Furthermore, these high-frequency signals can be deflected or even blocked by obstacles (buildings, hills, mountains, etc.).

So, VOR signals will only be received if there is a straight-line between the transmitter and the receiver and the signal is strong enough to bridge the distance. In practice, these conditions may be met by different transmitters at different times:

1. The aircraft is positioned on the apron at the Bremen airport. The NAV receivers are set to VOR frequencies, for example, NAV1 to Weser VORTAC (112.9 WSR) and NAV2 to Bremen TVOR/DME (117.45 BMN). Although the Weser VORTAC uses a powerful transmitter and is only 19 nautical miles distant, the VOR1 receiver in the cockpit shows no reading because there's no straight-line connection between the transmitter and the receiver. The VOR2 receiver is locked onto the Bremen VOR, since there is a straight-line connection between the aircraft and the transmitter, despite the relative weakness of the Terminal VOR signal.

2. The aircraft is at 1,500 feet ASL, approximately 30 NM south of Bremen (position N52°32' E008°50'). VOR1 is locked on, indicating about 49 DME and a course of 002° to the Weser VOR. The altitude, the signal strength and the straight line between the two allow the signal to be received. However, the VOR2 receiver is not receiving a signal. Although there is a straight line to the transmitter, the transmission power is too low, so that the Bremen TVOR is out of range at this position.

VOR transmitters are generally divided into three classes, according to their use and range. Here's a table with the classification criteria:

Class	Altitude in ft	Max. range in NM
Terminal Class	up to 12,000	25 ... 40
Low Class	1,000 ... 18,000	40
High Class	1,000 ... 14,000	40
	14,000 ... 18,000	100
	18,000 ... 45,000	130

In Germany, the VOR stations are listed individually in the airtravel handbook, and all special data pertaining to the stations is recorded in the COM register. Using ASD you can install VOR stations in your base map. Using the [VOR Tool], position the mouse pointer at the desired location and click the left mouse button. As usual, you'll see the current geographic coordinates in the status bar. You can set the exact coordinates of the station in the VOR Properties dialog box by double-clicking the station once you've placed it. Flight Simulator and ASD only distinguish between the different VOR classes in the station's indicated range. For the VOR in Bremen, we'd like to use the following data:

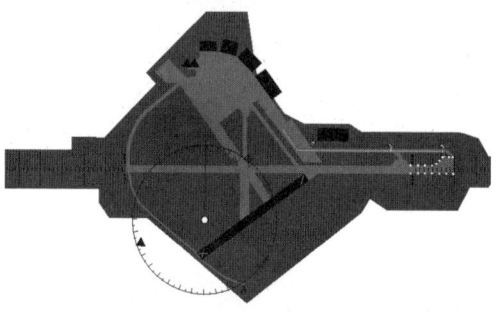

Kennung	BMN
Name	Bremen TVOR/DME
Latitude	N 53° 02' 42"
Longitude	E 008° 47' 00"
Elevation	4 m
Frequency	117.45 MHz
Range	25 NM
VOR Type	VOR-DME
Variation	+1.3°
Approach	— (only with ILS)

You'll see that the VOR symbol is now visible both in the airport map and the basemap. Using the map's options, you can choose not to display this rather large symbol.

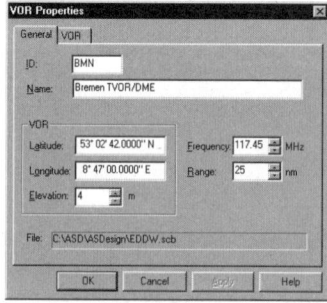
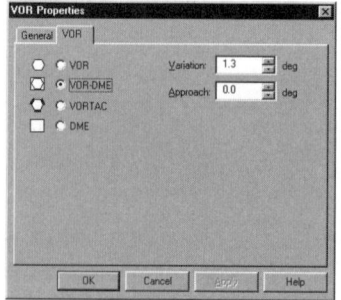

Replacing or excluding original scenery

Often your own scenery will enhance an existing Flight Simulator scenery area, and sometimes you'll want to replace it entirely. For instance, if you're not happy with the airport in Hamburg, northern Germany, in the shape and form that Microsoft has given it, you can replace it with your very own version.

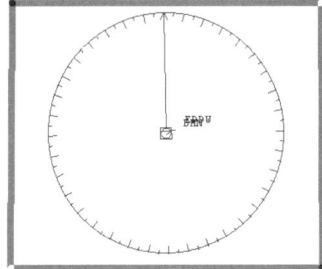

However, it's not all that easy to remove a standard Flight Simulator scenery with 3-D objects and runways from the landscape. That is, unless you turn the scenery off in your scenery library. However, this will remove all of central Europe from the Flight Simulator 98 world, even if all you want to do is exclude the standard scenery for Hamburg.

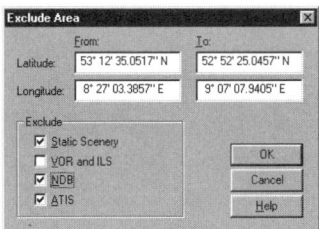

You can use a special scenery type to get rid of a specific area with all of its objects: the Exclude Area. The exclude area is defined as a surface between two longitudes and two latitudes.

On one hand you can specify this area by viewing the scenery in Flight Simulator 98's *slew* mode by clicking **Aircraft | Slew Control** and then getting the coordinates for the corners of a sufficiently large area. However, you can view the scenery just as easily with ASD. Simply load the .BGL file and view the basemap of the scenery in question. In our example, this might be the Europe 1 scenery.

You can use **Edit | Find** to locate the Hamburg airport (or any other place) more quickly. Enter "Hamburg" or "ham" to search the long Europe scenery list for the matching location (airport or navaid). The found location will be centered in the map window.

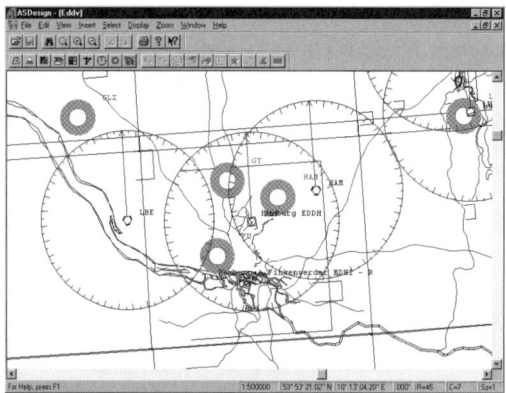

Now you can use the [Exclude Tool] to drag open a rectangle on the map—on which both your own scenery and the loaded .BGL file are visible—that defines the area to be excluded. Start in the upper-left corner and drag to the lower right.

As usual, you can specify the special characteristics for the exclude area in the Exclude Area dialog box. In addition to the area's exact latitudinal and longitudinal boundaries, you can specify which types of objects should be excluded from the (standard) .BGL files.

Exclude	
Static Scenery	all 2-D and 3-D objects
VOR and ILS	all high-frequency navigational transmitters
NDB	all medium-frequency transmitters
ATIS	all COM transmissions

This makes it possible to correct a positional error of an NDB transmitter in the Bremen area: the western NDB locator for runway 09 (frequency 276.5 BW) is located much too far to the south in the original scenery. Using the [Exclude Tool], which allows you to specifically exclude NDB transmitters, you can reposition the transmitter correctly right at the western outer ILS marker.

However, you can't exclude synthetic scenery objects, since they represent good old Mother Earth. After all, you wouldn't want to just blow some huge, gaping crater in the Flight Simulator planet.

Translating your scenery into textcode and compiling it

Your scenery consists almost entirely of graphic information, with the exception of a little bit of data that you've entered in a few dialog boxes. This scenery now has to be converted into a pure textcode before it can be compiled into machine language.

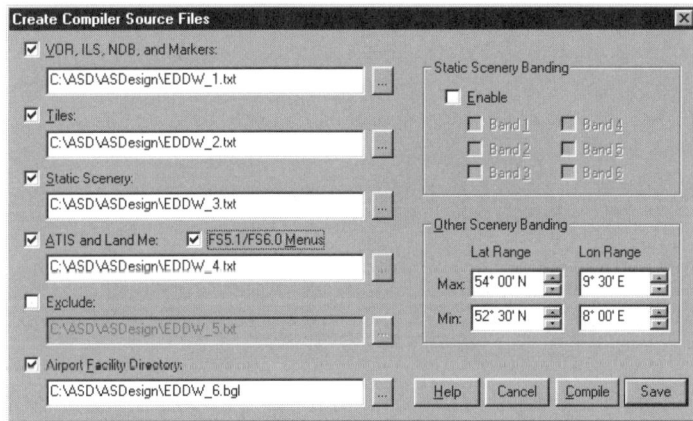

In the airport map window, select **File | Create Scenery Files** to initiate this process. First the objects within the new scenery are put into text-form, according to their property settings. In the Create Compiler Source Files dialog box, you'll see that all the objects within the scenery (VOR, Tiles, Static Scenery, etc.) that have been selected in the current airport map have been activated. Each of these objects has a text field where you can specify a path. The paths that ASD has assigned to these objects come from the filenames in the **Edit | Map Properties** section.

Select the appropriate options if you wish to compile and save other or all of your scenery's object groups. If a group, perhaps [Exclude] or [Tiles], can't be activated, then that object isn't contained in the current scenery. Click [Save] to save the selected scenery objects from your airport map in SCASM source-code text-files with the specified names. Clicking [Compile] will first save the source code and then translate it directly into .BGL files using the SCASM compiler. If you've activated [Copy

Compiled Files To Scenery Directory] in **Files | Preferences**, the compiled .BGL file will automatically be copied to Flight Simulator 98's or any other specified Scenery folder.

Testing

The new Bremen scenery is now ready for a fly-over. After starting Flight Simulator, select **World | Go To | Airport** and choose Bremen. Be sure that the option *Scenery of Version 6.0 and lower* is activated. The position at which the aircraft will be placed depends on the property settings for the runways or polygons. On the **Menu** tab, you'll find entries for the Flight Simulator airport list. For instance, you could place the aircraft near the tower when **World | Go To | Airport**: *Bremen* is selected by entering the following data on the Menu page for the apron polygon:

Latitude	53° 03' 10.0000" N
Longitude	008° 47' 06.0000" E
Elevation	3.96 m
Heading	358°

The other settings in this dialog box specify the most important COM and NAV frequencies for Bremen, so that they're immediately available:

COM	118.57	ATIS
NAV1	110.9	ILS 27
OBS1	268°	
NAV2	117.45	BMN TVOR/DME
OBS	360°	

Under Menu Entry, you'll want to enter the name of the airport with a precise aircraft position, for instance:

```
Bremen Ramp 1 Pos 10
```

The ramp position 10 at Bremen is officially reserved for aircraft of the type Boeing 727, Fokker 50 or ATP, and its documented coordinates can be used to calibrate the aircraft's GPS and INS systems.

Source Code Files

When you select **Files | Create Scenery Files** with the appropriate compiler and file settings in the dialog box, ASD creates the actual source code from the objects contained in the scenery basemap (EDDW.SCB). This source code text is the basis for the BGL binary code used by Flight Simulator 98. ASD creates up to five different text files, each of which describes a specific object group (Nav, Tile, Static Scenery, ATIS and Exclude) from the map you've created.

Let's take a closer look at such a source code. You can open the text with any text editor or word processor, such as Write, NotePad or WordPad. You'll find the text files in the ASD directory. The filenames will be the base map name followed by an ID number for the object group, *i.e.*, EDDW_1.TXT for the navigation source code file.

```
; ScBuild output for SCASM
Header( 3 53:30:00.0000 53:00:00.0000 9:00:00.0000 8:30:00.0000 )
CopyRight( WL 1.98 )

LatRange( 53:00:00.0000 53:30:00.0000 )

VOR( 117.45 25 01 1.30 BMN Bremen_TVOR/DME 53:02:42.0000 8:47:00.0000
4 0.0 )
ILS( 110.30 16 C0 1.30 IBMN Bremen_ILS_09 53:02:55.8029 8:48:46.7135 4
87.90 53:02:53.0931 8:46:44.0513 4 3.0 )
```

```
ILS( 110.90 16 C0 1.30 DLR Bremen_ILS_27 53:02:51.7628 8:45:43.7058 4
267.90 53:02:54.8225 8:48:02.2416 4 3.0 )

MM( 53:02:51.4403 8:45:29.2174 4 )
OM( 53:02:44.4047 8:40:10.8279 4 )
MM( 53:02:56.4922 8:49:17.8442 4 )
OM( 53:03:03.5278 8:54:36.2586 4 )
```

Each ASD source code begins with the remark *ScBuild output for SCASM*, followed by a header. The header is always the first instruction in a scenery source code file. It generates the .BGL file header, which will be responsible for the visual output in Flight Simulator. The header's parameters specify the object type and scenery boundaries. The general format for such a header is this:

```
Header( Type maxLat minLat maxLong minLong)
```

The object type is defined by a number between one and four, which also indicates the object type's priority level in Flight Simulator. The lower the type number, the more important the object type is, and the more often Flight Simulator updates the object during the simulation.

Type = 1	Visual scenery objects for section 9 and synthetic blocks for section 6
Type = 2	Former Crop Duster World—don't use!
Type = 3	VOR, NDB and ILS navigation systems and markers
Type = 4	ATIS, airport menu options

You can see that the visible scenery objects are ranked higher than other information.

The next parameters specify the scenery's geographic boundaries in latitude and longitude. The numeric format for these values is always DDD:MM:SS.SSSS—note that ASD drops any leading zeroes in the number.

The *Copyright* line is only added to the source text if the corresponding option has been activated in the **Edit | Map Properties** section.

LatRange is used in block calculations and in determining the block size. As discussed earlier, the block size varies with latitude.

The data for the VOR and ILS systems is next; remember that in the header the file was already defined as a navigation systems source code file (type=3).

The general text code format for VOR stations and ILS systems is:

340

```
VOR(Freq Range Flag Var Ident Name Lat Lon Elev Hdg)
ILS(Freq  Range  Flag  Var  Ident  Name  LOCLat  LOCLon  Elev  Hdg
 GSLat GSLon Elev Slope)
```

You may remember these parameters from the VOR and ILS Properties dialog boxes.
Here's a list:

```
VOR     (
        Freq    Frequency MHz (from 108.00 to 117.95)
        Range   Transmission range in nautical miles (whole numbers)
        Flag    Installation signal (two-digit hexadecimal value):
                80      LOC active
                40      GS active
                20      LOC with DME
                10      GS with DME
                01      equipped with DME
                02      not known!
                08      DME inactive
                09      DME without VOR
        Var     Local magnetic variation (in degrees)
                Westerly variation is positive (i.e. +1.3)
                Easterly variation is negative (i.e. -2.5)
        Ident   Station ID, up to five letters
        Name    Station name, up to 24 characters
        Lat     Latitude DD:MM:SS.SSSS
        Lon     Longitude DDD:MM:SS.SSSS
        Elev    Elevation above MSL in meters
        Hdg     Always zero for VOR
        )

ILS     (
        Freq    Frequency in MHz (from 108.00 to 111.95)
        Range   Transmission range in nautical miles (whole numbers)
        Flag    Installation signal (two digits, hexadecimal):
                80      LOC active
                40      GS active
                20      LOC with DME
                10      GS with DME
                01      Equipped with DME
                02      not known!
                08      DME inactive
                09      DME without VOR
        Var     Local magnetic variation in degrees
                Westerly variation is positive (i.e. +1.3)
```

```
         Easterly variation is negative (i.e. -2.5)
Ident  Station ID, up to five letters
Name   Station name, up to 24 characters
LOCLat Latitude of approach heading transmitter
LOCLon Longitude of approach heading transmitter
Elev   Elevation above MSL in meters
Hdg    Approach heading
GSLat  Latitude of glide slope transmitter
GSLon  Longitude of glide slope transmitter
Slope  Glide slope in degrees
)
```

The final lines of the source code file are dedicated to the approach markers: *IM* for inner marker, *MM* for middle marker, and *OM* for outer marker. For ASD they're an integral part of every ILS system, and the application records their location using their geographic coordinates (latitude and longitude, with the usual DD:MM:SS.SSSS format) and their elevation above the mean sea level in meters:

```
IM(Lat Lon Elev)
MM(Lat Lon Elev)
OM(Lat Lon Elev)
```

You can also create such a source-code text to add missing VOR and NDB stations to existing scenery or to replace mispositioned ones very quickly and easily—even without the graphical interface of ASD. All you need to do is create the source-code file using a text editor and the correct commands, and then compile it into a .BGL file using the SCASM compiler.

The compiler is started from an MS-DOS command specifying the source-code file, the .BGL target file and an optional parameter for additional output:

```
scasm <Source file> <Target file> [<parameter>]
```

If we wanted to compile the source code from above, this would be the command line:

```
scasm eddw_1.txt eddw_1.bgl -L
```

The compiler will take the text in EDDW_1.TXT and transform it into machine code in a .BGL file for Flight Simulator 98. The parameter *L* tells the compiler to create a protocol file called *SCAERROR*, in which any errors that might be contained in the source code or occur during the compilation are recorded.

The second ASD source-code file contains the scenery's synthetic objects, which represent Mother Earth for all of the other visual 2-D and 3-D objects. Followed by the usual header containing the object type and coordinate boundaries, the tile that is to make up this particular piece of Mother Earth with its surface and texture is identified.

```
; ScBuild output for SCASM

Header(1 53:36:46.5611 52:45:37.7913 9:50:37.5000 8:26:15.0000 )

CopyRight( WL 1.98 )

synth  1 44
block  6 04 00 1111 3.960000
```

The coordinates in the header correspond to the calculated block size (see above) for this particular latitude and longitude, on which the numeric identification for the tile is based:

```
synth  Section Row
```

The *Section* is what actually determines the tile's size (one through six), which will be used in the subsequent block calculation. The *Row* identifies the tile's row in the north-south direction (in other words, its latitude). The southern edge of this size-one tile is located at a minLat of 52:45:37.7913 extending to a maxLat of 53:36:46.5611, and it is the 44th tile north of the equator. Both of these numeric values have already been defined in the header.

```
block  Column Selector1 Selector2 Object Elev
```

Block specifies the column, *i.e.*, the longitude, for the left edge of the tile. A size-one tile spans 1/256th of the earth's circumference, therefore $360°/256° = 1.4063° = 1° 24'$ 22.5″. For the area around Bremen we'll need a tile that includes the ARP, which is at E008° 47' = +8,7883°. When you divide this coordinate by a tile's east-west size, the resulting whole number gives you the tile's column:

$$8,7883° : 1,4063° = 6,2449...$$

The tile containing this point is therefore the sixth tile east of the Greenwich meridian.

Selector1 contains a two-digit hexadecimal number, indicating which ground texture is to be used for the tile. Here's a list of the different ground textures:

Selector 1		Texture
hex	dec	
00	0	ocean
01	1	green-brown landscape
02	2	different green-brown landscape
03	3	brown and green landscape
04	4	green landscape with hedges
05	5	light green hills
06	6	brown with a little green
07	7	brown
08	8	white
09	9	bright white
0A	10	green-brown landscape with lakes
0B	11	parceled landscape
0C	12	like 0B, but darker
80	128	field
81	129	high-density urban area
82	130	low-density urban area
83	131	town
84	132	rural countryside
85	133	other rural countryside
86	134	other rural countryside
87	135	pastures
88	136	green hills
89	137	brown hills
8A	138	concrete landscape
8B	139	other concrete landscape
8C	140	green-gray mixture
8D	141	swamplands
8E	142	concrete landscape with high-rises
8F	143	other concrete landscape

Selector2 is currently an unused function, and should be set to zero. *Object* contains a four-digit hexadecimal value specifying the Flight Simulator landscape type:

Object	Type
1111	Flat countryside
2222	Mountains, type 1
3333	Coast, type 1
4444	Coast, type 2
1222	Mountains, type 2
F011	Flat countryside, soft rendering

Elev contains the tile's elevation in meters above MSL. All of the other two- and three-dimensional scenery objects (except for runways and nav objects) are placed directly at this elevation. Runways have their own elevation parameter, which will generally be the same as that of the tile. However, in some cases, for instance, if it is located on a mesa or perhaps an aircraft carrier, the runway elevation can be higher.

Simple objects of the airport scenery

We won't discuss the following listings in great detail—the large number of commands and functions supported by Flight Simulator and SCASM make it impossible to cover every aspect of the code here.

All of the scenery's visual objects are classified as *type one*. The header of the EDDW_3.TXT object file contains this type parameter and also defines a geographic region of sufficient size in which to place these objects:

```
; ScBuild output for SCASM

Header( 1 54:00:00.0000 52:30:00.0000 9:30:00.0000 8:00:00.0000 )
CopyRight( WL 1.98 )
LatRange( 52:30:00.0000 54:00:00.0000 )

; Bremen
Area( B 53:02:56.0000 8:47:16.0000 36 )
```

The name "Bremen" in the remark line comes for the Map Properties. The *Area* statement defines the scenery boundaries for the visual objects. The individual elements or objects of the visual scene can be defined after this:

```
Area    (
        Type   An object's range of visibility is specified using a
hexadecimal value:
                5        visible from 0 to 22 km
                8        visible from 40 to 130 km
                B        visible from 0 to 255 km
        Lat    latitude
        Lon    longitude
        Range  range of visibility in kilometers, seems to function as a
scenery buffer
        )
```

The visual scenery is ended using *EndA* at the end of the source code file.

```
RefPoint( 7 :L00001 1.000000 53:02:54.1332 8:47:26.0824 V1= 25000 V2= 2907
)
```

Each visual object (for instance, lines, taxiways or polygons) requires a reference point:

```
RefPoint(
        Type   2 = absolute reference point, above MSL
                        this object will be placed at the elevation defined
by "E=" regardless
of the scenery tile's elevation
                7 = relative reference point, at ground level
                        this object will be placed at the same elevation as
the scenery tile
                3 = reference point with no scale

        :Label label for marking points within the code
                ASD numbers all labels serially, starting at :L00001
        Scale  the scale at which the object will be drawn, usually 1
        Lat    latitude of the reference point
        Lon    longitude of the reference point
        E=###  height of the point in meters, only for type 2
        V1= #####    general visibility range of the scenery
        V2= #####
        )
```

The first requirement for the creation of a simple 2-D or 3-D object is the definition of its reference point. Such an object might be the airport polygon on which an airport is placed, with a uniform color or texture to identify the airport grounds.

```
Points(
      num0   the first vertex of the polygon, usually this is the
RefPoint, which was just defined
      x1 z1 y1    table for the relative distances in meters
      to     from RefPoint, to the first point, and on through the
last point:
      xn zn yn    x=horizontal, y=vertical, z=height
      )
```

The individual vertices of the polygon are listed and drawn by the *Points* command:

```
Points( 0
 -1453   0   65
 -1456   0  156
 -1227   0  158
 -863    0  550
 -937    0  621
 -278    0 1327
 -152    0  655
  60     0  377
  196    0  312
  527    0  322
  607    0  273
 1313    0  296
 1441    0  258
 1517    0  141
 1558    0  129
 1563    0  -22
 1525    0  -81
 1393    0  -85
 1309    0 -263
  813    0 -268
  690    0 -189
  634    0 -287
 -156    0 -948
 -887    0 -388
 -1169   0 -395
 -1248   0 -291
 -1251   0 -201
 -1969   0 -216
 -2050   0 -140
 -2054   0  -26
 -1984   0   47
  )
```

When you look at a list of polygon points like this, you realize how much easier it is to create a polygon using a graphical tool like the Airport & Scenery Designer. In any event, once the polygon has been defined, it's very easy to fill it with a color or texture:

```
Smoothing( 1 )
SurfaceColor( 28 F0 )
```

With *Smoothing*, the polygon is drawn with increased resolution to give a smoother, more muted appearance. *SurfaceColor* fills the polygon with the specified color:

```
SurfaceColor(
        num     color ID (hex)
        attr    color attribute
                F0 = normal color, with varying
                intensity depending on daylight
                69 = direct color palette
        )
```

Flight Simulator controls the use of colored textures by taking the visibility criteria and several other variables into account. *If...* statements are used to deal with different conditions:

```
IfVarAnd( :L00002 340 FFFF )
IfVarRange( :L00005 6F8 0 2 )
IfVarRange( :L00004 6F8 0 1 )
IfVarRange( :L00003 6F8 0 0 )
```

The two most important *If* statements check the values of internal Flight Simulator variables.

```
IfVarAnd(
        :Label jump to
        Variable     the contents of the Flight Simulator variables
(hex) are AND-linked with the value of Mask. If the statement is TRUE,
the command immediately following is executed. Otherwise, Flight
Simulator jumps to the specified label

        Mask   bitmask, every possible 16 bit value (hex)
        )
IFVarRange(
        :Label jump to
```

```
      Variable     the contents of the Flight Simulator variables
(hex) are being tested: if the values are within the Min and Max
limits, the command immediately following is executed, otherwise
Flight Simulator jumps to the specified label
      Min    minimum limit, decimal or 0x. hexadecimal
      Max    maximum limit, decimal or 0x. hexadecimal
      )
```

In the source code, destination labels are differentiated from other text by a colon. The next command line applies the bitmap texture to the previously drawn airport polygon:

```
:L00006
Bitmap( Grassw.r8 0 128 0 128 )
Jump( :L00007 )
:L00005
Bitmap( Grassf.r8 0 128 0 128 )
Jump( :L00007 )
:L00004
Bitmap( Grasss.r8 0 128 0 128 )
Jump( :L00007 )
:L00003
Bitmap( Grass.r8 0 128 0 128 )
:L00007
:L00002
```

Bitmap loads the specified texture from the active texture directory on the hard drive. Depending on the scenery you're flying over, this may be Flight Simulator 98's main Texture directory or the scenery's own Texture subdirectory.

```
Bitmap(
      Name.xxx     standard textures use the .R8 filename extension.
However, many add-on textures use filename extensions specific to
their scenery, such as .EU1 or .EU2.
      x      undefined value, most often 0, 1 or 8
      dx     east shift in RefPoint units
      dz     elevation shift
      dy     north shift
      )
```

Flight Simulator texture bitmaps are 256x256 pixels, with 8 color bits for each pixel, giving a palette of 256 different colors. The system for identifying the individual pixels is this:

Corner	Pixel coordinates	
Upper left	x=0	y=0
Upper right	x=255	y=0
Lower left	x=0	y=255
Lower right	x=255	y=255

RunwayData creates the runways in the Bremen scenery. Its large number of parameters reflects the many options in ASD's Runway Properties. Runways are not simple objects—they have their own *Area* field with special parameters.

Here again, *Area* is used to determine the visibility range for the runway using the type parameter. With a value of five, the runway will be visible at a maximum of 22 kilometers. The last parameter, 15, after Lat/Lon, defines the actual visibility limit.

```
; Bremen Runways
Area( 5 53:02:56.0000 8:47:16.0000 15 )
```

Flight Simulator actually starts constructing the runway with *LayerCall*, which includes a destination label and a level number (the default is often 24) which ensures that the runway is always drawn as the last, and thus the topmost, object. Once the RunwayData parameters have been entered in the scenery, Flight Simulator jumps back to the next command; in our example this is a jump forward to the *:Label*, which is usually the end of the runway routine.

```
LayerCall( :L00086 24 )
Jump( :L00087 )
:L00086
```

The RunwayData structure contains all of the parameters that are included in the ASD Runway Properties. The first two parameters must contain the geographic coordinates, while the subsequent values have to be identified by a keyword. The keyword and its data value must be separated by at least one space. The key-letters N and F stand for **n**ear runway end and **f**ar runway end.

```
RunwayData( 53:02:53.9662 8:47:23.5298
 altitude   4.0 heading   87.9
 id    9
 length   6670 width   150
 surface   1 markers   3F
 lights    7
```

```
ThrLightsN  1 ThrLightsF  1
AprLN    10 AprLF    10
ThrOffN   0 ThrOffF   0
ExtN    0 ExtF     0
StrobesN  15 StrobesF  15
VasiBarsN  0 VasiBarsF  0
VasiSlopeN 0.0 VasiSlopeF 0.0
VasiSideN  0 VasiSideF  0
VasiDistN  0 VasiDistF  0
VasiSpaceN  0 VasiSpaceF  0
)
```

The individual RunwayData parameters are:

```
RunwayData(
      Lat    latitude of runway center
      Lon    longitude
      ALTitude     height of runway in meters above MSL (floating
point)
      HEADing     heading in degrees (floating point)
      ID    heading ID; usually a whole number, rounded up (Heading/
10),
            with L, R, or C for multiple parallel runways (Left,
Right, Center)
      LENgth runway length in feet (whole number)
      WIDth  runway width in feet (whole number)
      SURFace     runway surface
            0 = bare ground
            1 = concrete
            2 = asphalt
            3 = grass
      Markers     runway markers, two-digit hex value, individual
marker values are added up
            01 = white edges
            02 = threshold marker
            04 = touchdown zone
            08 = distance markings after 300 meters
            10 = white center line
            20 = ID number
            40 = distance markings every 150 meters
            80 = unknown
      Lights
            00 = turned off
            01 = low intensity
            02 = high intensity
```

```
                  04 = illuminated centerline
        ThrLights    threshold lights (for N and F respectively)
                  01 = green/red threshold lights
                  04 = white strobes as additional REIL
        AprL   approach lights (only active when threshold lights are
on)
                  0 = no lights
                  1 = row of synchronized strobes
                  2 = MALSF
                  3 = MALSR
                  6 = ALSF-1
                  7 = ALSF-2
                  8 = running line of strobes
                  10 = ICAO III
        Strobes       number of strobe lights (whole decimal number)
        VasiBars      number of VASI light bars
                  0 = no VASI
                  1 = two bars
                  2 = three bars
        VasiSlope     VASI glide slope in degrees (floating point
decimal)
        VasiSide      VASI distance from runway centerline in feet
                  normally on the left side of the runway
                  L120 = 120 ft left of the runway
                  R150 = 150 ft right of the runway
        VasiDist      distance from center of the two or three VASI bars
to the runway center in feet. Should correspond to touchdown and ILS
GS.
        VasiSpace     distance between VASI lights
        )
```

Your Own Scenery Objects

Flight Simulator and its scenery programming language, BGL, support a building function that renders geometrically simple buildings. The building outline is always rectangular, and the walls, with the exception of a few special effects, are always vertical. Flight Simulator's Texture folder contains different .R8 texture files for texturing the walls, with brightness levels that adapt to simulate changing daylight conditions.

With ASD you can easily and quickly view these textures, without the aid of a special R8 converter. Simply open the **Polygon Properties** for any polygon in the current scenery, and select the **Texture/Color** tab. Under [Change] you'll find a list of the textures in the Texture directory, complete with a preview of the selected texture.

This list contains the standard textures for side-walls (SIDE.R8 through SIDE8.R8) as well as the more detailed facades of various Chicago buildings (CHBLD1.R8 through CHBLD6.R8) and even special textures for billboards and similar things.

As mentioned above, the *LayerCall* function is used to draw simple 2-D objects and runways. 3-D objects, on the other hand, are drawn using *PerspectiveCall*. This command initiates Flight Simulator's 3-D rendering routines:

```
PerspectiveCall ( :MyHouse )

:MyHouse
Perspective
RefPoint ( 7 :EndHouse 1 latitude longitude )
```

The *Perspective* command always starts the drawing routine. It is followed by the relative reference point for the building, with its geographic coordinates. The drawing subroutine concludes with the jump to *:EndHouse* at the end of *Area*). A typical command sequence for a 3-D object would look something like this:

```
;
Area( ... )
PerspectiveCall( :MyHouse )
Jump( :Label)
:MyHouse
Perspective
RefPoint ( 7 :EndHouse 1 latitude longitude )
SurfaceColor ( ... )
Poly ( ... )

:EndHouse
        Return

EndA
;
```

Not all objects in this world are aligned on the north-south axis; some lie at an angle to it. Here's the command to rotate a 3-D object about its centerpoint:

```
RotatedCall( :House 0 0 25)
Return
```

This would rotate the house clockwise 25° from geographic north. *Return* concludes the subroutine. Flight Simulator begins actually drawing the building at the *:House* label, first with the definition of its corners:

```
Points( 0
      x1 z1 y1 ; first corner with east, Alt, north
      x2 z2 y2 ; second corner, and so on….
      . . .
      xn zn yn ; to the last corner
      )
```

It's easiest to determine the corner coordinates by doing a sketch on graph paper. This way you immediately have a usable scale, and you can simply read off the corner coordinates.

Since a building consists of at least five separate components (four walls and a roof), it's important that Flight Simulator draws these elements in the correct order. Depending on the viewing direction, the farthest walls are drawn first, followed by the nearer ones. The viewing direction—or rather the vector to the wall surface—therefore determines the drawing sequence. *VectorJump()* causes Flight Simulator to calculate these vectors before it selects the appropriate subprocedures.

```
VectorJump( :W 32767 0 0 0 )
VectorJump( :SE 0 0 32767 0)
:NE
Call( :DrawSW)
Call( :DrawNW)
Call( :DrawSE)
Call( :DrawNE)
Return
:SE
Call( :DrawSW)
Call( :DrawNW)
Call( :DrawSE)
Call( :DrawNE)
Return
:W
VectorJump( :SW 0 0 32767 0 )
:NW
Call( :DrawSW)
```

```
Call( :DrawNW)
Call( :DrawSE)
Call( :DrawNE)
Return
:SW
Call( :DrawSW)
Call( :DrawNW)
Call( :DrawSE)
Call( :DrawNE)
Return
```

This segment of code draws a house that can be viewed from all four directions: north-east, south-east, north-west and south-west.

The surfaces of 3-D objects are drawn using one of the many different polygon functions. Which one of these is used determines the effects that are needed. Whether a polygon will be visible is determined by the visibility range.

The most simple polygon function is *Poly*. It draws a surface with the specified dimensions and color:

```
:DrawW
SurfaceColor( B F0 )
Poly( a p1 p2 p3 ... pn )
...
...
Return
```

The south-west side of the house is assigned the color beige (hex B = dec 11) and is drawn using vertices from the *Points()* list.

The following code demonstrates the method described just now by drawing a simple, red, square object 32 meters high and 16 meters wide:

```
;
Area( B latitude longitude 255 )
PerspectiveCall( :MyHouse )
Jump( :End)

:MyHouse
        Perspective
        RefPoint( 7 :EndHouse latitude longitude )
        RotatedCall( :DrawHouse 0 0 30)
        Return
```

```
:DrawHouse
      Points( 0
   -8  0  8 ; 1=upper left
   -8 32  8 ; 2
    8  0  8 ; 3=upper right
    8 32  8 ;
    8  0 -8 ; 4=lower right
    8 32 -8 ; 5
   -8  0 -8 ; 6=lower left
   -8 32 -8 ; 7

      SurfaceColor( 05 F0 )
      Poly( a 1 3 5 7 ) ; roof
      Poly( a 0 1 3 2 ) ; north side
      Poly( a 2 3 5 4 ) ; east side
      Poly( a 4 5 7 6 ) ; south side
      Poly( a 6 7 1 0 ) ; west side

:EndHouse
Return

:End
EndA
```

If you want to turn this red box into something that looks more like a house, you might use some of Flight Simulator's building textures. These have windows that are illuminated at light, as well as color gradations that respond to changing daylight conditions. The files with the name SIDE*.R8 are each divided into eight, vertical stripes with different brightnesses. They provide a very simple exterior facade with windows.

We'll use special *Texture* functions to apply these bitmaps to the polygon surfaces:

```
:DrawHouse
      Bitmap( side.r8 0 0 0 0 )
      Inst_7D
      TexPolyShading( 0 0 32767)
      TexPoly( a p1 bx1 by1 p2 bx2 by2 ... pn bxn byn )
Return
```

Bitmap loads the SIDE.R8 file, consisting of a beige surface with vertical stripes and windows. The file has to be located either in Flight Simulator 98's Texture folder or in the appropriate subdirectory of the scenery. You cannot specify a drive or path for the file in *Bitmap*.

Inst_7D starts the application of the texture each time the subprocedure is called. *TexPolyShading* is used specifically for lighting effects; it utilizes the texture's eight brightness levels. The parameters in parentheses specify a vector that determines the position of the sun (32767 = infinity) and thus the position and shape of the object's shadow.

TexPoly draws the structured polygon surface, similar to the *Poly* function. It uses the strip with the appropriate brightness level from the loaded texture file. The texture itself consists of 256x256 pixels, each of the eight strips being 32 pixels wide. The texture can be stretched as required, so that it can be used to create a whole number of different facades. The standard buildings used by Flight Simulator 98 utilize a ration of one texture pixel to four meters of building length. The individual parameters for *TexPoly* are:

```
TexPoly(
        a         automatically calculates the vector on the polygon
exterior
        p1        point 1 of the polygon
        bx1       X-coordinate of the bitmap pixel
        by1       Y-coordinate of the bitmap pixel
        ...
        pn        last point of the polygon
        bxn
        byn
        )
```

Here's how we can redecorate our red box:

```
SurfaceColor( 05 F0 )
Poly( a 1 3 5 7)     ; roof stays the same
Inst_7D
TexPolyShading( 0 0 32767 )
TexPoly( a 0 0 0 1 0 8 3 4 8 2 4 0 ); north side
Inst_7D
TexPolyShading( 32767 0 0 )
TexPoly( a 2 0 0 3 0 8 5 4 8 4 4 0 ); east side
Inst_7D
TexPolyShading( 0 0 -32767 )
```

```
TexPoly( a 4 0 0 5 0 8 7 4 8 6 4 0 ); south side
Inst_7D
TexPolyShading( 32767 0 0 )
TexPoly( a 6 0 0 7 0 8 1 4 8 0 4 0 ); west side
```

In addition to rectangular block shapes, Flight Simulator's graphics functions also support other forms, such as cylindrical silos or towers, or arched structures, such as bridges. The radiused surfaces are approximated using multiple flat polygons that create facets around the desired form. To create a cylinder, you'll need at least eight individual surfaces, but the cylinder will look a lot smoother if you use 16.

In an eight-sided cylinder, the individual surfaces are at 45° to each other (360°/ 8=45°); in a 16-sided cylinder, this angle is reduced to 22.5°. The vertices of the individual cylinder surfaces are calculated from their distance to the center axis of the cylinder and the angle of the surface. You can assemble the *VecPoints()* more quickly using a programmable calculator or a matrix calculation. The X and Y coordinates of each vertex are obtained with the following formulas:

```
x = radius * cos(angle)
y = radius * sin(angle)
```

An eight-sided cylinder with a diameter of 50 meters would have a radius of 25 meters. So the first surface, which is at an angle of 0°, the coordinates are quite simple, since cos(0°) = 1 and sin(0°) = 0. Here we've used a simple Excel table to calculate all of the points:

Calculation of the points of cylindrical objects:

Diameter		Height	Number of Polygons
50	100	16	

Radius	Angle
25	22,5

Vertex	angle	xn	zn	yn
0	0.0	25	0	0
1		25	100	0
2	22.5	23	0	10
3		23	100	10
4	45.0	18	0	18
5		18	100	18

358

```
6      67.5   10     0      23
7             10     100    23
8      90.0   0      0      25
9             0      100    25
```

The first quarter of the cylinder, starting at an angle of 0°, includes five pairs of points, each pair having one point at the ground and one at the top of the cylinder. The other three quarters of the cylinder, from 90° to 360°, are obtained by simply rotating the quarter-form, in other words, by simply swapping the X and Y coordinates with opposite signs. The following table shows the point list for the ground-points. The corresponding points at the top of the cylinder are identical, except they have a vertical (z) component of 100:

```
Pt    Angle   xn     zn    yn
5     112.5   -10    0     23
6     135.0   -18    0     18
7     157.5   -23    0     10
8     180.0   -25    0     0
9     202.5   -23    0     -10
10    235.0   -18    0     -18
11    257.5   -10    0     -23
12    270.0   0      0     -25
13    292.5   10     0     -23
14    315.0   18     0     -18
15    337.5   23     0     -10
```

The whole-number points that have been calculated are not transferred to *VecPoints*, in nearly the same format as that of the Excel table:

```
VecPoints( a 0
          25     0      0      ; 0    0.0 grad
          25     100    0      ; 1
          23     0      10     ; 2    22.5
          23     100    10     ; 3
          18     0      18     ; 4    45.0
          18     100    18     ; 5
          10     0      23     ; 6    67.5
          10     100    23     ; 7
          0      0      25     ; 8    90.0
          0      100    25     ; 9
          . . .
          . . .
          )
```

Now that we have the point list, we can use *ShadedTexPoly* to begin drawing the polygons. This function also uses bitmap pointers that specify which strip of the texture file is to be used:

```
Bitmap( SIDE.R8 )
Inst_7D
ShadedTexPoly( a      p1 bx1 by1
        p2 bx2 by2
        p3 bx3 by3
        p4 bx4 by4 )
```

The Y coordinate in the bitmap is easy to calculate—all you need to do is divide the cylinder's height by four, and $100/4 = 25$.

The X coordinate in the texture bitmap depends on the position of the polygon surface on the cylinder's circumference.

circumference = 2 x radius x pwhere p = 3.14159...

circumference = 2 x 25 x 3.14159 = 157.08 meters

Given this total cylinder circumference, each of the individual sixteen polygons has the following width:

Polygon width = circumference / 16 = 157.08 / 16 = 9.81 meters or approximately 10 meters.

Here you could calculate the X value with 5, which results in the following parameters for *ShadedTexPoly*:

```
ShadedTexPoly( a     0 0 0
        1 0 25
        3 5 25
        2 5 0 )
```

What to draw first

We've neglected one thing so far in the process of drawing our Flight Simulator scenery: the visibility of objects and the order in which they need to be drawn. At the start of the chapter we briefly touched on these issues; here we'd like to use a short example to cover them in detail. If two objects are located next to or in front of each other, a drawing order must be established using jumps in the program source code. The subprocedures that are jumped to, in turn, must take the object's position and that of the viewer into account.

Let's assume two viewers at different positions are looking at two buildings placed between them. The first viewer sees the right house behind the left, so the left ought to be drawn last. The second viewer sees the right house in front of the left, so the right house should be drawn last.

Depending on the viewer's position, *VectorJump* goes to the appropriate drawing procedures. It determines which procedures to use by calculating the vectors perpendicular to the object polygons and comparing them with the parameters:

```
VectorJump( :Label p Angle Heading Length )
Here's a general example of the drawing sequence in the source code:
VectorJump( :Left 32767 0 0 0 )
:Right
Call( :LeftObject)
Call( :RightObject)
Return

:Left
Call( :RightObject)
Call( :LeftObject)
Return
```

Homemade textures

Flight Simulator texture files are simple bitmaps, with a square format of 256x256 pixels and a palette of 256 different colors. These colors are stored in a special palette file called FS.PAL that contains the RGB values for each of the 256 colors.

You can draw a texture bitmap with any drawing or painting program that supports 256-color mode (indexed colors). The program must also be able to load an existing color palette and, if necessary, edit it. The program must not convert the image into a higher color resolution (HighColor or TrueColor) or alter the existing palette.

Flight Simulator's default palette, FS5.PAL, is in binary code, so unfortunately you can't load it directly into a painting program. Instead, you'll need palettes in ASCII format. A very simple, if not very precise, method of obtaining a usable palette is to get a screenshot of your viewing window. To get as close a copy of the standard palette, you'll have to select summer as the time of year, 12 noon as the time of day, and a cloudless sky with no haze. You'll get the purest colors under these conditions. This screenshot, either in .PCX or .BMP format, is then loaded with the painting application, where you can get a palette from the image. Make sure you choose a name for the palette file that clearly distinguishes it from FS5.PAL.

After these preparations, you can draw a new texture in the required 256x256 pixel format. If you're using a scanned image as your texture bitmap, perhaps an aerial image or a photograph of a building facade, load the file and apply the palette. You'll also want to make any other modifications that will improve the bitmap as a texture.

Once you've completed the texture and saved it in .PCX or .BMP format, you'll still have to convert it into Flight Simulator's texture format. Several tools are available as shareware or freeware (as well as commercial programs) that will do this, for example R8paint, R8manip or Texture from the Shiratti Commander. These programs generally also have a few demo images and textures that use the FS5.PAL palette. This makes them great for obtaining the color palettes for your own textures.

The easiest way to implement a new texture is using ASD or directly in the source code.

```
Area ( ... )
RefPoint ( 7 :L00069 1.000000
53:03:02.6214 8:47:49.5109
V1= 0 V2= 226 )
SurfaceColor ( B F0 )
Bitmap ( newTex.r8 0 0 0 0 )
Building ( 0 0 0 2 226 92 8000 1F )
...
EndA
```

The user-defined texture NEWTEX.R8 is loaded using Bitmap and then drawn by Building. In ASD you can achieve the same thing using the **Building Style** tab from the Building Properties dialog box; simply specify the NEWTEX.R8 texture from the [User Bitmap] selection.

Basemaps For ASD

Every scenery that is created with ASD is entered in a basemap. The ASD Wizard also lays out the mini-scene with a basemap whose boundaries are derived from the airport's geographic coordinates. The resulting boundary values can then be found in the scenery's Map Properties by clicking **Edit | Map Properties**.

The ASD Wizard only has a limit set of base-data with which to create the airport. If you want to build a special airport that is not in the Wizard's list, you'll need to generate your own basemap.

The basemap is saved in a text file (*.TXT). The first piece of information in this file is always the R2 file ID, which tells ASD that this is a revision two map and that it may contain scenery data. The file header needs to contain the following information:

```
R2
"Name of Region" Points Definition Scale

lat1 lon1
lat2 lon2
lat3 lon3
...
lat lon

#define RGN_NONE     0        ; black line
#define RGN_RIVER    1        ; blue line
#define RGN_LAKE     2        ; blue surface
#define RGN_ROAD     3        ; gray line
#define RGN_CITY     4        ; yellow surface
#define RGN_HIGHWAY  5        ; magenta line
#define RGN_LIMITED  6        ; red line
#define RGN_ISLAND   7        ; white surface
#define RGN_COAST    8        ; blue surface
#define RGN_RAILWAY  9        ; black line
#define RGN_MOUNTAIN    10    ; gray-green mountains
```

The R2 ID is followed by the description of the region. The first part of this description is the region's name as cleartext within quotation marks. The *Points* parameters contains the number of coordinate pairs (lat/lon) used to describe the region. For the most simple region, there will be four coordinate pairs that define a rectangle covering a specific portion of the globe. A region outlining the shape of an island, on the other hand, will require many more coordinate pairs. The map may use up to 16,000 coordinate pairs.

The actual coordinate pairs are stored as decimal numbers with up to six digits to the right of the decimal point. Northerly and easterly coordinates are positive, southerly and westerly ones are negative numbers.

The number of coordinate pairs is followed by the *Definition* parameter, which specifies the number of object-definitions in the region (its scenery objects and their palettes). For a simple, rectangular map with no other elements such as rivers, roads or mountains, only the black boundary outline will be defined. A detailed map, on the other hand, will contain numerous definitions.

The third parameter, *Scale*, specifies the map's scale and at what point an object's symbol will become visible on the map. A typical value for this parameter is 50, which means that an object will appear on the map at a scale of at least 1:50,000,000.

The simplest possible map would be a rectangular segment outlining a specific geographic region, with no further details. However, such a bare basemap might then be the basis for an entirely new scenery. BAO's Europe 1 scenery currently still has several blank regions in the east of the German Republic. For example two newer German airports, the one at Laage near Rostock and at Neubrandenburg, are not included in the Euro-scenery—an ideal opportunity to put in your own two cents.

The basemap for the north-east German area is easily defined using a simple text editor:

```
R2
"Germany northeast" 5 0 10
54.200000  012.000000
54.200000  014.000000
53.300000  014.000000
53.300000  012.000000
54.200000  012.000000
```

The outline of the rectangular map segment consists of four corner points; however, you absolutely have to define five coordinate pairs in the *Points* parameter: The first point is also the last point in the sequence. We've defined the points in the clockwise direction, starting in the north-east corner (N 54.2° E 012.0°), although you can start at any point and go in either direction. Since no other objects are defined for this basemap, *Definition* contains the value 0. With a value of 10 for *Scale*, objects will appear on the map at a scale of 1:10,000,000.

The file is then saved using a self-explanatory name, such as *D_NORTHEAST.TXT* in ASD's Maps folder. This way ASD will be able to access the file directly. Select **File | Import Map** to display the map on your screen.

The two missing German airports can be inserted immediately using the Airport Tool. Their exact reference coordinates (ARP) and other geographical data are defined in the Airport Properties dialog box:

Position of Rostock (EDOR)		
Latitude	53° 55' 11.0000" N	53° 36' 09.0000" N
Longitude	12° 16' 51.0000" E	13° 18' 28.0000" E
Elevation	42.1 m (= 138 ft)	69.5 m (= 228 ft)
Variation	-0.8°	-1.2°
ATIS	124.00 MHz	119.17 MHz

All the remaining steps, right up to the airports' opening ceremonies are identical to the ones that we took with the Bremen airport. The runways are created directly on the ARPs in the respective Airport Properties dialog boxes. Here are their positions and attributes:

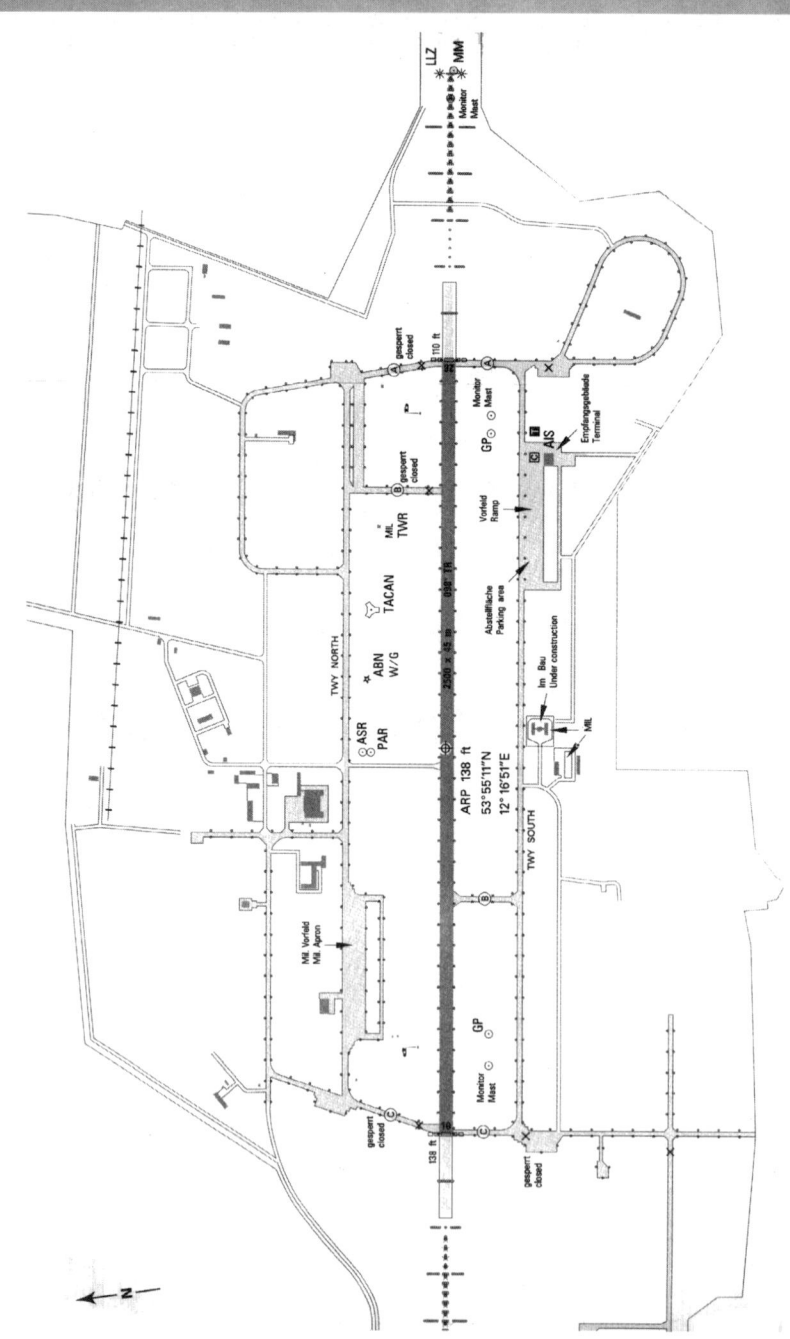

Position of Rostock (EDOR)		
Latitude	53° 55' 11.0000" N	53° 36' 09.0000" N
Longitude	12° 16' 51.0000" E	13° 18' 28.0000" E
Elevation	42.1 m	69.5 m
Heading	098°/ 278°	088°/268°
Length	8202 ft	7523 ft
Width	148 ft	148 ft
Lights	LIRL	LIRL
	Threshold	Threshold
	REIL	-
	ICAO-III-1	-
Markings	Edge	Edge
	Centerline	Centerline
	Touchdown	-
	Threshold	Threshold
	ID	ID
Rwy Ext	820 ft each	-

Laage is equipped with ILS systems, and both airports have NDB/DME or TACAN systems. The following table contains the most important data:

	Position of Rostock (EDOR)	Neubrandenburg (EDBN)
ILS 10	108.3 - ILAE	-
OM	3.5 nm	
MM	0.5 nm	
ILS 28	108.3 - ILAW	-
OM	4.0 nm	
MM	0.6 nm	
TACAN	114.25 (only DME)	108.05 (only DME)
Lat	53° 55' 12.0000" N	53° 36' 18.0000" N
Lon	12° 16' 52.0000" E	13° 18' 36.0000" E
NDB	383 LAG	357 NRG
Lat	53° 54' 42.0000" N	53° 36' 18.0000" N
Lon	12° 21' 40.0000" E	13° 23' 30.0000" E

This should be enough data to permit flawless instrument landings, so you're ready to flesh out the rest of the airport sceneries using polygons, aprons, taxiways and buildings.

Downloading US Airport Data

For US airspace in particular, there is a wealth of information available from both commercial and private sources. There are even some free sources for geographical data, maps and aerial images. Almost every major US airport has its own Web site or a similar service with which to promote its services.

Here we'd like to use the Logan International airport in Boston as an example. The data it makes available pertains both to the airport itself and its navigational systems. Much of the data can be entered directly in Flight Simulator or ASD.

```
BOS - GENERAL EDWARD LAWRENCE LOGAN INTL AIRPORT
BOSTON, MA
AIRPORT INFORMATION CURRENT AS OF 06 NOVEMBER 1997
Location Lat/Long: 42-21-51.651N / 071-00-18.645W
(42.3643475 / 71.0051792)
```

```
(estimated)
Elevation: 20 ft / 6.1 m (surveyed)
Variation: 16°W (1995)
From city: 1 mile E of BOSTON, MA
County: SUFFOLK
Airport Operations
Facility use: Open to the public
Sectional chart: NEW YORK
Control tower: yes
ARTCC: BOSTON CENTER
FSS: BRIDGEPORT FLIGHT SERVICE STATION [1-800-WX-BRIEF]
NOTAMs facility: BOS (NOTAM-D service available)
Attendance: CONTINUOUS
Segmented circle: no
Lights: Dusk-Dawn
Beacon: white-green (lighted land airport)
Landing fee: yes
Fire and rescue: ARFF index E
Airline operations: Full FAR Part 139 certification, currently
receiving scheduled air carrier service
Int'l operations: customs landing rights airport

Airport Communications
UNICOM: 122.95
ATIS: 135.0 (617-567-0160)
Boston Ground: 121.9
Boston Tower: 119.1 128.8 128.8 121.75 (Helicopters) 257.8
Boston Approach: 118.25 (north) 120.6 (south) 127.2 (west) 126.5 263.1
382.0
Boston Departure: 133.0 343.6
Clearance Delivery: 121.65 257.8
Pre-Taxi Clearance: 121.65
(ARR/DEP RYS 04R/22L 09/27): 128.8
(ARR/DEP RYS 4L/22R 15R/33L 15L/33R): 128.8
(ARR/DEP RYS 4R/22L 9/27): 119.1
Class B: 124.1 (091°-269°) 124.4 (270°-090°) 279.6 (270°-090°) 343.6
(091°-269°)
Emerg: 121.5 243.0
Gate Ctl: 134.05
IC: 120.6 (south) 263.1

Radio aids to navigate to the Airport

VOR Name      Freq   Ident  morse I.D.    Var
Boston VORTAC 112.70 BOS    -.. — ...     at field    16°W
```

```
Lawrence VOR/DME     112.50 LWM     .-.. .— —     R185/22.9     15°W
Manchester VOR/DME   114.40 MHT     — .... -      R167/34.3     15°W
```

```
NDB Name          Freq   Ident morse I.D.    Var
Lyndy 382         LQ     .-.. —.-      215°/5.6      16°W
Shaker Hill       251    SKR    ... -.- .-.   142°/9.4      16°W
Topsfield         269    TOF    - — ..-.      204°/15.4     16°W
Marshfield        368    IMR    .. — .-.      333°/21.7     16°W
Mansfield         220    IHM    .. .... —     037°/23.3     16°W
Taunton           227    TAN    - .- -.       017°/29.3     16°W
Central           241    SFZ    ... ..-. —..  054°/34.3     15°W
Derry 338         DRY    -.. .-. -.—   166°/34.9     16°W
Fitchburg         365    FIT    ..-. .. -     124°/35.1     15°W
Provincetown 389  PVC    .—. ...- -.-.313°/39.0     16°W
```

Airport Services
Fuel available: A 100LL
Airframe service: MAJOR
Powerplant service: MAJOR
Bottled oxygen: HIGH/LOW
Bulk oxygen: HIGH/LOW

Runway Information
Helipad H1

Dimensions: 150 x 150 ft / 46 x 46 m
Surface: asphalt, in good condition
Runway edge lights: high intensity
Operational restrictions: INGRESS/EGRESS 35 DEGS THRU 215 DEGS.
Traffic pattern: left
Displaced threshold: no
Touchdown point: no
Obstructions: NONE

Runway 04L/22R
Dimensions   7860 x 150 ft / 2396 x 46 m
Surface   asphalt/grooved, in good condition
Weight limitations PCN 61/F/B/W/U
Runway edge lights high intensity

	Rwy 04L	**Rwy 22R**
Traffic pattern	left	left
Runway heading	036° magnetic, 020° true	216° magnetic, 200° true
Markings	precision instrument	precision instrument
Markings condition	good	good

```
Latitude       42-21-28.764N 42-22-41.852N
Longitude      071-00-51.617W     071-00-16.274W
Elevation      15.1 ft          16.1 ft
Threshold crossing height 50 ft AGL     55 ft AGL
Visual glide path angle    3.00° 3.00°
Visual slope indicator     4-light PAPI on left       4-box VASI on left
Rwy end identifier lights yes    no
Displaced Threshold no     yes
DT distance              815 ft
DT latitude              42-22-34.270N
DT longitude             071-00-19.941W
DT elevation             16.3 ft
Touchdown point     yes    yes
TD elevation 15.2 ft          16.3 ft
Obstructions BOAT    BOAT
Height 161 ft 44 ft
Slope to clear       18:1   10:1
Distance from threshold    3250 ft          670 ft
Additional obstruction remarks: APCH RATIO 33:1 FROM DSPLCD THR; 50:1
TO THR WHEN CHANNEL IS CLEAR.


Runway 04R/22L
Dimensions     10005 x 150 ft / 3050 x 46 m
Surface        asphalt/grooved, in good condition
Weight limitations PCN 61/F/B/W/U
Runway edge lights high intensity


         Rwy 04R        Rwy 22L
Traffic pattern        left   left
Runway heading         036° magnetic, 020° true  216° magnetic, 200° true
Markings       precision instrument       precision instrument
Markings condition good    good
Latitude       42-21-03.813N 42-22-36.841N
Longitude      071-00-42.462W     070-59-57.449W
Elevation      19.5 ft          15.7 ft
Threshold crossing height 51 ft AGL
Visual glide path angle    3.00°
Visual slope indicator     4-light PAPI on left
RVR equipment touchdown, midfield,        touchdown, midfield,
        rollout        rollout
Approach lights     ALSF2 standard 2400 ft     MALSF: 1400 ft
        high intensity        medium intensity
        approach lighting     approach lighting
        system with centerline     system with sequenced
        sequenced flashers  flashers
```

```
        (category II or III)
Rwy end identifier lights no      no
Centerline lights  yes    yes
Displaced Threshold yes   yes
DT distance   1155 ft      1199 ft
DT latitude   42-21-14.550N42-22-25.695N
DT longitude 071-00-37.270W     071-00-02.844W
DT elevation 18.4 ft     16.7 ft
Touchdown Point    yes    yes
TD elevation 18.4 ft     16.7 ft
TD lights    yes    no
Obstructions NONE   NONE
```

```
Runway 09/27
Dimensions   7000 x 150 ft / 2134 x 46 m
Surface      asphalt/grooved, in good condition
Weight limitations  PCN 61/F/B/W/U
Runway edge lights  high intensity
```

```
        Rwy 09 Rwy 27
Traffic pattern     left   left
Runway heading      093° magnetic, 077° true   273° magnetic, 257° true
Markings      precision instrument       precision instrument
Markings condition  good   good
Latitude      42-21-20.718N42-21-36.781N
Longitude     071-00-46.415°W     070-59-15.738W
Elevation     17.7 ft       15.2 ft
Threshold crossing height  71 ft AGL
Visual glide path angle         3.00°
Visual slope indicator     none   4-light PAPI on left
RVR equipmenttouchdown, rollout  touchdown, rollout
Rwy end identifier lights no    yes
Centerline lights  yes    yes
Displaced threshold no     no
Touchdown Point     yes    yes
TD elevation 17.7 ft       17.3 ft
TD lights    no     no
Obstructions NONE   NONE
```

```
Runway 15L/33R
Dimensions   2557 x 100 ft / 779 x 30 m
Surface      asphalt, in good condition
Weight limitations  PCN 61/F/B/W/U
Runway edge lights  medium intensity
```

```
        Rwy 15L      Rwy 33R
Traffic pattern      left    left
Runway heading       151° magnetic, 135° true   331° magnetic, 315° true
Markings      basic  basic
Markings condition good    good
Latitude      42-22-24.889N42-22-06.966N
Longitude     071-00-32.860W      071-00-08.850W
Elevation     15.8 ft       15.7 ft
Visual slope indicator      none    none
Rwy end identifier lights no      no
Displaced threshold no      no
Touchdown point      no      no
Obstructions NONE    NONE


Runway 15R/33L
Dimensions    10081 x 150 ft / 3073 x 46 m
Surface       asphalt/grooved, in good condition
Weight limitations PCN 61/F/B/W/U
Runway edge lights  high intensity


        Rwy 15R      Rwy 33L
Traffic pattern      left    left
Runway heading       151° magnetic, 135° true   331° magnetic, 315° true
Markings      precision instrument      precision instrument
Markings condition good    good
Latitude      42-22-27.367N42-21-16.744N
Longitude     071-01-04.393W      070-59-29.715W
Elevation     19.8 ft       16.0 ft
Threshold crossing height 58 ft AGL    59 ft AGL
Visual glide path angle    3.00 degrees 3.00 degrees
Visual slope indicator     4-box VASI on left 4-box VASI on right
RVR equipmenttouchdown, midfield,      touchdown, midfield,
      rollout        rollout
Approach lights      MALSR: 1400 ft      MALSR: 1400 ft
      medium intensity   medium intensity
      approach lighting  approach lighting
      system with runway system with runway
      alignment indicator alignment indicator
      lights lights
Rwy end identifier lights no      no
Centerline lights   yes     yes
Displaced Threshold yes     no
DT distance   880 ft
DT latitude   42-22-21.203N
DT longitude 071-00-56.125W
```

```
DT elevation 18.3 ft
Touchdown Point: yes       yes
TD elevation: 18.3 ft      16.8 ft
TD lights: yes       yes
Obstructions Trees  Boat
Height 62 ft  160 ft
Slope to clear        45:1   30:1
Distance from threshold    3040 ft        5075 ft
Distance from centerline   140 ft
Additional obstruction remarks: +2 FT FENCE 180 FT FROM THLD 480 FT
RIGHT

Fuel Prices
Stand 26 Feb 1997
FBOBrand        100LL  AA1+
$2.62  $2.20  $2.23
```

Here are other Web sites with information on the Boston airport.

Boston Airport Information Http://www.massport.com/logan/logan.html Http://www.thetrip.com/airport/BOS/ Http://www.quickaid.com/airports/bos/ http://www.airwise.com/airports/us/BOS/BOS_01.html http://www.bit-net.com/~tjotoole/logan.htm

ASD And SCASM Colors

Several Color commands use default colors that are identified by hexadecimal values. These color codes are quite different from the colors in a bitmap texture. Here's a table listing the F0 colors for the Color functions:

Colors with variable intensity		
Number		Color
hex	dec	
00	0	black
01	1	dark gray
02	2	middle gray
03	3	light gray
04	4	white
05	5	red
06	6	green
07	7	blue
08	8	orange
09	9	yellow
0A	10	brown
0B	11	beige
0C	12	orange-brown
0D	13	gray-green
0E	14	marine-blue

Colors with fixed intensity		
number		
hex	dec	
0F	15	red
10	16	green
11	17	blue
12	18	dark green
13	19	orange
14	20	yellow
15	21	bright white
16	22	white

Flight Simulator variables

Flight Simulator uses a large number of internal variables that can be accessed and changed from within scenery files. Here are all of the Flight Simulator variables known to us:

Number		Variable	Notes
hex	dec		
	632	Aircraft altitude	in meters
282	642	ticker	4-byte value in which only 1 bit is set at any time—it runs from right to left every six seconds. Used for strobe lights
284	644	crash Flag	2 = mountain crash 4 = normal crash 8 = splash 14 = building crash 16 = aircraft crash
288	648	fuel tanks	1 = tanks full
28A	650	FS Version	BCD coded
28C	652	time of day	1 = day 2 = dusk/dawn 4 = night
33B		distance	shortest distance to reference point
340	832	ground texture	0 – no ground textures otherwise = ground textures
342	834	building texture	
346	838	scenery density	0 = very sparse 1 = sparse 2 = normal 3 = dense 4 = very dense
37E	894	X coordinate (east)	in meters, relative to reference point
382	898	Z coordinate (height)	in meters, relative to reference point
386	902	Y coordinate (north)	in meters, relative to reference point
38A	906	Day	numbered from 1 to 365
390	908	year	e.g., 1998
	1784	time of year (for the northern hemisphere)	0 = winter 1 = spring 2 = summer 3 = fall

Index

Symbols

A

PC catalog

Order Toll Free 1-800-451-4319
Books and Software

www.abacuspub.com

To order direct call Toll Free 1-800-451-4319

In US and Canada add $5.00 shipping and handling. Foreign orders add $13.00 per item.
Michigan residents add 6% sales tax.

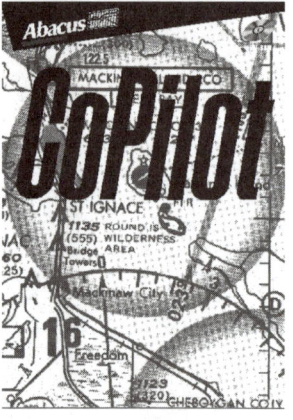